The Jewish Lights Spirituality Handbook

Contributors

Isa Aron
Miriam Carey Berkowitz
Ellen Bernstein
Sylvia Boorstein
Eugene B. Borowitz
Anne Brener
Norman J. Cohen
David A. Cooper
Avram Davis
Wayne Dosick
Edward Feld
Nancy Flam
Tamar Frankiel
Nan Fink Gefen
Neil Gillman
Elyse Goldstein
Arthur Green
Judy Greenfeld
David Hartman
Mark Hass
Lee Meyerhoff Hendler
Lawrence A. Hoffman
Karyn D. Kedar
Lawrence Kushner
Jane Rachel Litman
Stuart M. Matlins

Daniel C. Matt
Levi Meier
James L. Mirel
Rebbe Nachman of Breslov
Kerry M. Olitzky
Jonathan Omer-Man
Debra Orenstein
Daniel F. Polish
Jack Riemer
Debra Judith Robbins
Jeffrey K. Salkin
Sandy Eisenberg Sasso
Zalman M. Schachter-Shalomi
Dannel I. Schwartz
Sharon L. Sobel
Rifat Sonsino
Elie Kaplan Spitz
Nathaniel Stampfer
Ira F. Stone
Leora Tanenbaum
Arthur Waskow
Karen Bonnell Werth
Ron Wolfson
David Zeller
Sheldon Zimmerman

The Jewish Lights Spirituality Handbook

A Guide to Understanding, Exploring & Living a Spiritual Life

Edited by
Stuart M. Matlins,
Editor-in-Chief, Jewish Lights Publishing

JEWISH LIGHTS Publishing
Woodstock, Vermont

The Jewish Lights Spirituality Handbook:
A Guide to Understanding, Exploring & Living a Spiritual Life

© 2001 by Jewish Lights Publishing

Library of Congress Cataloging-in-Publication Data
The Jewish lights spirituality handbook : a guide to understanding, exploring & living a spiritual life / edited by Stuart M. Matlins.
p. cm.
Includes index.
ISBN 1-58023-093-8 (Paperback) — ISBN 1-58023-100-4 (Hardcover)
1. Spiritual life—Judaism. 2. Jewish way of life. I. Matlins, Stuart M.
BM723 .J478 2001
296.7—dc21
2001001858

10 9 8 7 6 5 4 3 2 1
Manufactured in the United States of America

Published by Jewish Lights Publishing
A Division of LongHill Partners, Inc.
Sunset Farm Offices, Route 4, P.O. Box 237
Woodstock, VT 05091
Tel: (802) 457-4000 Fax: (802) 457-4004
www.jewishlights.com

For the authors and readers of Jewish Lights books
who have brought us to this place.

Yose ben Yoezer said,
"Let your house be a meeting place for the wise;
sit humbly at their feet;
and, with thirst, drink in their words."

Joshua ben Perachyah said,
"Get yourself a teacher,
find someone to study with,
and judge everyone favorably."
—*Pirke Avot*

Contents

Part III

THE TIMES AND SEASONS OF YOUR LIFE:
WHEN DOES SPIRITUALITY ENTER?

Part V

SO WHAT DO YOU DO WITH IT?
WHY SPIRITUALITY SHOULD BE PART OF YOUR LIFE

On the Spiritual Journey

Rebbe Nachman said that, often, even just his daily religious obligations felt like a crushing burden. But the Rebbe found a way to bear the weight of his devotions by each morning saying to himself, "I will ignore tomorrow and all future tomorrows—today is all there is!"

The Rebbe understood that what wears us down most on our spiritual journey is the feeling that there is too much to accomplish. Instead, he advised focusing only on the task at hand. By doing so, we can overcome even the most daunting obstacles.

. . . .

Spiritual awakening begins with
inspiration coming from Without.
Then, once you are already on the
road, the real work begins.
Keep at it and inspiration will
come from within.

— from *The Empty Chair: Finding Hope and Joy—
Timeless Wisdom from a Hasidic Master,
Rebbe Nachman of Breslov*
Adapted by Moshe Mykoff and the Breslov Research Institute

Introduction

STUART M. MATLINS

Why are you reading this? Is it just a random event that has caused you to pick up this book, or is it part of a larger plan? Is it just a way to pass some time, or will it affect your life? Are you just mildly curious, or are you intently searching for greater personal meaning on your life's journey? Do you yearn for a sense of a closer personal relationship with God? Whatever your reason, this handbook offers a way to enter the world of Jewish spirituality.

Personally, I believe there are too many places I have been taken on my own Jewish journey for it all to be merely coincidence. In those places—from Jerusalem to Los Angeles, from Toronto to Rio de Janeiro, and lots of stops in between—I have been fortunate enough to meet and learn from some of the great spiritual teachers in the Jewish world today: rabbis, cantors, educators from *all* movements. A significant part of their teaching has become the books published by Jewish Lights. The purpose of this book is to share their wisdom with you.

The central question to address as a Jew, Rabbi Sheldon Zimmerman told me twenty years ago, is "What does God want you to do with your life?" It has not been fashionable for very long for people like me to admit openly that they are on a spiritual search, particularly not in the Jewish world. For me—totally career involved—religion had its separate place, within limits of time and style. Coming from a very traditional Orthodox background, and attending Orthodox yeshiva as a child, did not provide me with a religious life model with which I was comfortable as an adult.

But, at the same time, for reasons I have never understood, since childhood I have always felt a very personal connection to God. In times of personal crisis, I never felt alone. It is not something that I talked about openly or often, and still don't very much. In fact, writing this makes me feel uncomfortable, personally exposed and vulnerable. Perhaps you feel the same way as you deal with these matters in your own life. Every once in a while I would meet someone who shared similar feelings of strong spiritual connection; but, interestingly, almost all of them were Christians. Jewish people I knew didn't seem to talk about such things. We would talk tentatively about a vague sense of something beyond ourselves, of trying to integrate the seemingly incompatible worlds of religion, social and work life, of trying to figure it out. But I was groping in the dark. While secularly well educated, I had no understanding of the rich Jewish resources—ancient and modern—available to me, waiting for me to engage them, to put them to use in my search.

The teachers I found came into my life seemingly by chance and radically affected my life and the life of my wife, Antoinette. I did not set out consciously on a bold expedition to discover life's meaning. There is a Jewish saying: "People plan and God laughs." I was very busy planning my life. But, when we learned about the resources that were waiting to be found, waiting to be used, it also was clear that there were so many people like us whose lives would benefit from exposure to teachers who could speak to them in a voice that they could hear. My wife and I started Jewish Lights to extend the reach of our teachers' voices, to attract, engage, educate, and spiritually inspire other people just like us. Perhaps you are one of them.

Ten years ago, when we began Jewish Lights, *spirituality* was not a word said readily or heard comfortably in most of the Jewish world. As we initially talked to people about our plans to develop an inspirational literature, a spiritually inspiring body of work based on the Jewish wisdom tradition, we often were greeted with suspicion: amateurs in the world of book publishing; suspects in the world of organized Judaism. Few people provided any encouragement. Skepticism and condescension were the typical reactions when we shared our dreams. But not everywhere. At each stage in the development of Jewish Lights, people appeared to teach us how to make the dreams into a reality.

What is this spirituality thing? Where is God and where is "religion" in all of this? What is Jewish about it? What does it have to say that has meaning for your life? Where do you find it? How do you do it? How can it help you on your journey as a Jewish person, or as a person whose spiritual life can be enriched by the wisdom of Judaism? How can you bring about greater harmony between your spiritual life and the rest of your life? How can you find or create a spiritual community that you want to be part of, that will nurture your soul and help you grow? In your personal search for God, finding God and losing God over and over again throughout life, how can these teachers help you?

In this extraordinary time of religious renewal in America, an exciting time for people of all faiths, what are the things that you need to know to help you on your journey, to find the path that is right for you? How does all of this relate to your doing God's work in the world, to changing and repairing the world?

This is not a book that you have to sit down and read from start to finish, nor is it intended to be comprehensive. It is a beginning. Like a great reception, it is designed to let you wander around and meet lots of interesting people who will stimulate your thinking and offer you the ideas that you can use to meet your unique needs. You may not find all of the offerings exactly to your liking, but you can learn even from those that make you uncomfortable.

Come and meet our teachers and make them your own.

I

Awakening the Possibilities: What Is Jewish Spirituality?

In the early stages of your
spiritual journey, it may seem that
Heaven is rejecting you and
spurning all your efforts.
Stay on course. Don't give up.
In time, all barriers will disappear.

• • • •

Growing spiritually can be like
a roller coaster ride. Take comfort
in the knowledge that
the way down is only
preparation for the way up.

— from *The Empty Chair: Finding Hope and Joy—*
Timeless Wisdom from a Hasidic Master,
Rebbe Nachman of Breslov

Dr. Arthur Green, rabbi, is Lown Professor of Jewish Thought at Brandeis University and former president of the Reconstructionist Rabbinical College in Philadelphia. He is a student of Jewish theology and mysticism who has combined scholarly career and personal commitment. In *These Are the Words: A Vocabulary of Jewish Spiritual Life,* Rabbi Green teaches us about the meaning of *Ruḥaniyyut,* which is "spirituality" in Hebrew.

Ruḥaniyyut   רוחניות

ARTHUR GREEN

Ruḥaniyyut is "spirituality" in Hebrew. It derives from the word *ruaḥ,* which means both "wind" and "spirit," and was seen by the ancients as a mysterious, Godly wind that blows through the world. The word *ruaḥ* goes back as far as Genesis 1:2: "a wind from God" or "the spirit of God hovered over the face of the waters."

But abstractions like *ruḥaniyyut* are not part of the biblical way of thinking, and it is no surprise that this word does not appear in Hebrew until the Middle Ages. Part of the Hebrew language's complex history lies in the work of medieval translators. In the 11th and 12th centuries, the great works of Greek and Islamic philosophy, as well as many books of science, were translated into Hebrew, mostly from Arabic. Spanish and North African Jews had read these books in Arabic. But the Jews of Europe now became anxious for this education, and Hebrew, though not spoken, was the only language they read. The problem was that Hebrew, an ancient Semitic tongue, tended toward the concrete and pictorial. It did not have terms for the sorts of abstract concepts that filled the philosophical tracts. The translators remedied this by expanding the Hebrew language, taking ancient roots and finding new ways to create words out of them. *Ruḥaniyyut* (along with its companion *gashmiyyut* or "corporeality") is such a word. It refers to that which contains the presence of God.

The term is most widely used in Hasidism; here it finds its way into Yiddish speech as well. There it is mostly a value statement: A person should devote his or her life to *ruḥaniyyut* (pronounced *rukhniyes* in Yiddish). This refers to such spiritual things as study, prayer, and good deeds, as opposed to *gashmiyyut,* which would mean acquisition of wealth, bodily pleasures, and other "worldly" concerns. While it is true that Judaism is somewhat less other-worldly than this division seems to indicate (note that "good deeds," expressed very concretely, are part of *ruḥaniyyut*), the terms are to be found.

Hasidism struggled mightily with the question of whether true spirituality requires abstinence from the pleasures of this world. On the one hand it may be said that Hasidism was born when the Ba'al Shem Tov (Rabbi Israel ben Eliezer, 1700–1760, the first central figure of Hasidism) rejected asceticism. He realized that God is to be found everywhere, including the ordinary and the physical. Hasidism is characterized by a certain acceptance of worldliness. Yet Hasidism's most profound teachers called for simple living, for finding God's presence in such "ordinary" events as dawn and dusk and in the miracle of life's renewal each day. They viewed "excess" as dangerous to the spiritual life, even in times that could not have conceived the wealth and excess that surround us today.

Dr. **Arthur Green**, rabbi, is Lown Professor of Jewish Thought at Brandeis University and former president of the Reconstructionist Rabbinical College in Philadelphia. He is a student of Jewish theology and mysticism who has combined scholarly career and personal commitment. In *These Are the Words: A Vocabulary of Jewish Spiritual Life,* Rabbi Green teaches us about the meaning of *Neshamah,* the truest self.

Neshamah נשמה

ARTHUR GREEN

Neshamah is the usual word for "soul" in Jewish speech. It refers to the essence of the person, the truest self. In Yiddish *"a gute neshomeh"* is "a good-hearted person"; *"a teyere neshomeh"* is "a precious soul," a person of unusual sensitivity or extraordinary devotion.

There is no clear concept of soul (as distinguished from body) in the Bible. The word *neshamah* actually means "breath," the noun form of נ-ש-ם / n-sh-m, "to breathe." It is first used in Genesis 2:7, when God "blew the breath of life *[nishmat ḥayyim]*" into Adam's nostrils. It thus comes to mean "life-force" or "animating spirit" in various biblical contexts.

In the rabbinic period, partially under Hellenistic influence, Judaism developed a full-fledged notion of soul. Here the *neshamah,* a daily restored gift from "above," is sent by God to dwell in the body, whose origin is worldly. A daily recited prayer asserts the purity of each soul as it was given and acknowledges that God will one day take it back and thus end life. But that same prayer also affirms that the soul will be restored when the dead are resurrected at the end of time. The rabbis believe that each soul is both unique and eternal *('olam ha-ba).* Between death and resurrection (after a one-year period of purgation, if required by sin) the soul dwells in "the Garden of Eden," where God visits nightly "to take delight in the souls of the righteous."

Neshamah alternates in the early sources with two other terms for soul: *nefesh,* which means "self," and *ruaḥ,* or "spirit." Eventually *nefesh, ruaḥ,* and *neshamah* (which are collectively sometimes abbreviated as *NaRaN* in the literature) came to be viewed as three parts or "levels" of the soul. In the Middle Ages, these came to be linked with various neo-Platonic or Aristotelian theories of the tripartite soul, with *nefesh* as the lowest, followed by *ruaḥ,* and finally *neshamah.*

The Kabbalists *(Kabbalah)* view the soul as an actual "part of God above"; that which God blows into Adam is the presence of God's own Self. Nothing humans can do will eradicate this Divine Presence from the deepest recesses of each person's heart. Some sources try to limit possession of *neshamah* or divine soul to Jews, but this is inconsistent with the belief in universal descent from Adam and Eve and thus contradicts the most essential teachings of Judaism *(tselem elohim).*

The concluding verse of the Psalter (Psalm 150:6) also refers to *neshamah,* and may be translated "May every breath praise God," or "Let each soul praise God. Halleluyah!"

Rabbi Lawrence Kushner is Rabbi-in-Residence at Hebrew Union College–Jewish Institute of Religion. He teaches and lectures widely to audiences of all ages, faiths and backgrounds, and has been a frequent commentator on National Public Radio's *All Things Considered*. In *The Book of Words: Talking Spiritual Life, Living Spiritual Talk,* Rabbi Kushner teaches us about the primary words we use to describe the spiritual dimension of life and how rethinking what they mean can add power and focus to the lives we live every day.

Self   נשמה

LAWRENCE KUSHNER

You are (like everyone else who is not crazy) a barely coherent hodgepodge of contradictory thoughts, feelings, and deeds. What keeps you "together" is an imaginary center called a "self." The parts may not organize themselves gracefully, but their totality is literally "you." Without a "self" you would literally disintegrate.

We speak about our self as if it were real even though it possesses neither substance nor location. It is precisely the same way with God. God is the self of the universe. To

> *And God blew into his nostrils the soul of life.*
>
> GENESIS 2:7

say, "There is a God," is to say that creation has some inner coherence and integrity that can make sense. For this reason, our innermost self and God are related. In the same way, our alienation is self-estrangement and estrangement from God.

The old joke about the madman who thought he was God and explained his delusion by observing that whenever he prayed to God he always wound up talking to himself is more than a joke. Our "self" is the "part" of us we share with God and every other human being, just as it may be what remains of our soul.

(n´•shäh•mäh´)   **Soul**

TALMUD

The phrase, "Bless the Lord, O' my soul," is used five times in the Book of Psalms. To whom did David refer in these verses? He was alluding only to the Holy One of Being and to the soul. Just as the Holy One of Being fills the whole world, so the soul fills the body. Just as the Holy One of Being sees, but is not seen, so the soul sees but is not itself seen. Just as the Holy One of Being feeds the whole world, so the soul feeds the whole body. Just as the Holy One of Being is pure, so the soul is pure. Just as the Holy One of Being abides in the innermost precincts, so the soul abides in the innermost precincts. Let that which has these five qualities come and praise the One who has these five qualities.

LIVING SPIRITUAL TALK—*KAVANAH*

Listen to the sound of your own breathing. Gently hold the tips of the fingers on the inside of your wrist until you can feel your own pulse. Become aware of the blinking of your eyes. This life in you is not your own creation. Through it you are given permission to become aware of the interconnectedness of all being. Now look at another human being. The breathing, the heartbeat, the blinking. They are in the other also.

Rabbi Rifat Sonsino, Ph.D, is spiritual leader of Temple Beth Shalom in Needham, Massachusetts. He holds a degree in law and a Ph.D. in Bible and ancient Near Eastern studies. In *Six Jewish Spiritual Paths: A Rationalist Looks at Spirituality*, Rabbi Sonsino teaches about finding our own ways to spirituality within Judaism.

Jewish Definitions of Spirituality

RIFAT SONSINO

Though spirituality is popularly discussed in many sources, there is no clear definition of this term. It has become like a buzzword, dealing in general with liturgy, ritual, study, meditation, community, social justice, and certainly God. Rabbi Jeffrey J. Weisblatt *(z"l)* of Temple Ohev Shalom in Harrisburg, Pennsylvania, put it succinctly: "There is no one definition for it."[1]

Although not all Jewish thinkers agree on a definition of spirituality, several have been proposed. Here are a few examples:

- "Spirituality may inclusively be regarded as the sum of the efforts of the human psyche, individually and collectively, to attune to the impulses and rhythms of the universe, whether internal to the individual or external in nature."[2] (Dr. Martin A. Cohen, Hebrew Union College–Jewish Institute of Religion)

- "Man's spiritual life can easily be thought of in three divisions: his pursuit of truth, of beauty, and of moral goodness."[3] (Rabbi Roland B. Gittelsohn [1910–1995], Temple Israel, Boston)

- "Spirituality, as I understand it, is noticing the wonder, noticing that what seems disparate and confusing to us is actually whole."[4] (Rabbi Nancy Fuchs-Kreimer, Reconstructionist Rabbinical College, Philadelphia)

- "The striving for life in the presence of God and the fashioning of a life of holiness appropriate to such striving."[5] (Rabbi Arthur Green, Brandeis University, Boston)

- "The cognitive and/or behavioral activities designed to help individual and community to reconnect to God."[6] (Deanne H. Shapiro and Johanna Shapiro, psychologists at the University of California, Irvine)

- "The immediacy of God's presence."[7] (Rabbi Lawrence Kushner, Rabbi-in-Residence, Hebrew Union College–Jewish Institute of Religion)

- "Spirituality is essentially a way of responding to God, becoming conscious of God."[8] (Rabbi Jeffrey J. Weisblatt [d. 1995], Temple Ohev Shalom, Harrisburg, Pennsylvania)

- "Spirituality is the process through which the individual strives to meet God."[9] (Rabbi Kerry M. Olitzky, Jewish Outreach Institute, New York)

- "A highly personal outlook about what is sacred about us; it is the expression of our most deeply held values, and it is that sense of higher purpose that guides our daily lives."[10] (Dr. David S. Ariel, Cleveland College of Jewish Studies)

We can see that these definitions are not that different from one another and that they share connections. My personal preference is to define spirituality as broadly as possible, seeing in it an overarching experience involving our search for meaning and purpose in life.[11]

Spirituality is an act of will as well as a process. But primarily it is a state of mind. It can—and should—lead to action and often does, but basically it elevates our spirit and makes us more aware of ourselves and the place we occupy in life. Ultimately, it brings us closer to God as the source of our existence. Living a spiritual life enables us to reach a comprehensive and integrative sense of our purpose and role in life—in effect, mindfully placing ourselves in God's universe suffused with God's wonders. I define spirituality as simply "the awareness of standing before God," no matter how the term *God* is defined within the larger Jewish tradition, and whether or not God can be "met," "experienced," or "felt." In this definition I hear an echo of the text on top of many synagogue Torah arks: "Know before whom you stand" (Berakhot 28b). When we really "know"—in the sense of reaching an intimate inner transformation, as in the Hebrew term *da'at* ("knowledge")—that we are standing before the Ultimate Source of Reality, we are filled with awe and wonder, and we consequently respond to the divine and to the reality that surrounds us with an open heart and total commitment.

TERMINOLOGY

In modern Hebrew, the term spirituality is usually rendered as *ruhaniyut*. This word is based on the Hebrew word *ruah,* which is frequently combined or used with two other Hebrew words: *nefesh* and *neshamah*. Over the course of time, these words have become almost synonymous, meaning "spirit" or "soul." In the past, however, these terms had more restricted meanings. To gain a better understanding of spirituality in Judaism today, it is appropriate to survey the development of these words in the Jewish sacred texts over the centuries.

Ruah

The root meaning of *ruah* is "wind" or "a movement of air." For example, when Moses in one of his confrontations with the Pharaoh held out his rod over the land of Egypt, the Bible tells us that God drove an "east wind" *(ruah kadim)* over the land all day and all night (Exodus 10:13).[12] Similarly, according to the Book of Proverbs, "A north wind *[ruah tzafon]* produces rain" (25:23). It is also in this sense that we read, at the beginning of creation, that "a wind from God" *(ruah Elohim)* swept over the water (Genesis 1:2).

The word *ruah*, by extension, also means "breath." Thus, God tells Noah, "I am about to bring the Flood…to destroy all flesh under the sky in which there is the breath of life" *(ruah hayyim)* (Genesis

6:17). In the Book of Job, one of Job's companions, Eliphaz, says that the wicked person shall "pass away by the breath of His mouth" *(ruah piv)* (15:30). Job himself complains that "My odor [literally, 'my breath,' *ruhi*] is offensive to my wife" (19:17).

The word *ruah* also refers to "prophetic spirit." For instance, when the disciples of Elisha saw him crossing the Jordan, they shouted, "The spirit of Elijah *[ruah Eliyahu]* has settled on Elisha" (II Kings 2:15). When Joseph was able to interpret the Pharaoh's dreams to the king's satisfaction, the Pharaoh asked his courtiers, "Could we find another like him [namely, Joseph], a man in whom is the spirit of God *[ruah Elohim]*?" (Genesis 41:38).

The word *ruah* frequently means "spirit" in the sense of disposition, vigor, temper, courage. Thus, for example, during the days of Joshua, when the local kings heard what God had done on behalf of the Israelites, "they lost heart, and no spirit *(ruah)* was left in them" (Joshua 5:10). The Book of Proverbs praises the one who has "self-control" *(moshel ruho)* (16:32). After Pharaoh's second dream, the Bible tells us, he woke up because "his spirit *(ruho)* was agitated" (Genesis 41:8).

In the rabbinic period, the sages expanded the definition of *ruah* to include demons as well. Thus, for example, we find in the Talmud the following statement: "R. Jeremiah b. Eleazar stated: In all those years [after his expulsion from the Garden of Eden] during which Adam was under the ban, he begot ghosts *(ruhin)* and male and female demons" (Erub. 18b). Centuries later, in Spain, the medieval Jewish philosopher Moses Maimonides (1125–1204) used the term to mean "intellect," "purpose," or will."[13] In modern Hebrew, *ruah* combines most of these meanings and refers to "wind," "spirit," or "mind."

Nefesh

Another Hebrew term connoting "spirit" is *nefesh,* a word related to the Akkadian *napishtu* or Ugaritic *npsh,* meaning "throat."

(A trace of this original definition can be found in Psalms 105:28: "an iron collar was put on his neck" [*nafsho*].)

In time, by extension, the term came to mean "a living being," "the person himself/herself." Thus, for instance, in Job 12:10, we read: "In His hand is every living soul [literally, 'being,' *nefesh kol hai*]." Similarly, when God blew into Adam's nostrils the breath of life, he became a "living being" *(nefesh hayyah)* (Genesis 2:7). Speaking about his sons Simeon and Levi, Jacob prayed, "Let not my person *(nafshi)* be included in their assembly" (Genesis 49:6). In the Book of Leviticus, many laws begin with the words "If a person..." *(nefesh ki...)* (Leviticus 5:1, 2, 4, 15, 17, 20, etc.). The word *nefesh* can sometimes best be translated as "life." For example, when someone murders another, the penalty is "life for life" *(nefesh tahat nefesh)* (Exodus 21:23).

In certain contexts, the word *nefesh* also refers to human feelings, as, for example, in Exodus 23:9, where the law tells us not to oppress the stranger, "for you know the feelings [*nefesh*] of the stranger." When paired with a qualifying adjective, *nefesh* is used at times to express the fulfillment of basic human needs, such as "For He has satisfied the thirsty [*nefesh shokekah*], filled the hungry [*venefesh r'evah*] with all good things" (Psalms 107:9).

In rabbinic literature, *nefesh* took on the additional meaning of "soul," "desire," "will," and even "a resting place," "a cemetery monument." Many medieval Jewish philosophers used it in the sense of "rational soul." In modern Hebrew, *nefesh* is a general term for "soul," "spirit," "person," "self," "mind," "will," "tomb," and so on.

Neshamah

In the Bible the basic meaning of *neshamah* is "breath," very much like *ruah*.

Thus, in the Book of Isaiah, we read, "Oh, cease to glorify man, who has only a breath [*neshamah*] in his nostrils" (2:22). Very often, this word is used synonymously with *nefesh*, as in Joshua 11:11,

"They proscribed and put to the sword every person [*nefesh*] in it. Not a soul [literally, 'a person,' *neshamah*] survived." At times, it appears in combination with the word *ruah,* as in Genesis 7:22, where we are told that during the Flood the devastation was so great that "All in whose nostrils was the merest breath of life [*nishmat ruah*] died."

The word *neshamah* also refers to the divine vital principle that makes an individual a person. Thus, for example, when God created Adam, God blew into his nostrils "the breath of life" *(nishmat hayyim),* and he became a human being (Genesis 2:7). Similarly, according to the Book of Proverbs, "the life breath of man [*nishmat adam*] is the lamp of the Lord" (20:27). In rabbinic literature, the word means "a person" but also an independent "soul." In modern Hebrew, *neshamah* refers to "soul," "spirit," or "life" and often has the connotation of "a good person."

Nefesh, Ruah, and *Neshamah* as Levels of the Soul

For some Jewish thinkers, each of these three terms for spirit or soul plays a special role in the development of a human being. According to the *Zohar, nefesh, ruah,* and *neshamah,* collectively called NaRaN, form a sequence from lower to higher: *nefesh* enters at the time of birth and is the source of vitality; *ruah* is postnatal and is aroused when a person is able to surmount purely physical desires; and *neshamah,* the highest of the three, is developed when a person engages in Torah and its commandments and "opens his higher power of apprehension, especially his ability to mystically apprehend the Godhead and the secrets of the Universe."[14] And according to this hierarchy, "At death, the *nefesh* remains in the grave, lamenting over the death of the body. The *ruah* ascends to whatever level of celestial paradise it has earned by the merits it has accrued, and the neshamah goes directly back to the fullness of God."[15]

For Rabbi Wayne Dosick—teacher and author, and spiritual guide of the Elijah Minyan in San Diego—the soul has not three but five different levels, radiating from the innermost to the outermost level, which is the level of union with God. *Nefesh* represents the physical being, *ruah* stands for the qualities of our uniqueness, and *neshamah,* separating us from animals, reflects our ability to think, reason, and remember. Here Rabbi Dosick adds two more levels: *hayyah* is our life force, and *yehidah* is our intuition, "where the singular, unique oneness of each soul crosses the abyss and knows that there is no distance to *Yachid,* the Infinite Oneness of God."[16]

The shades of meaning of these three Hebrew words—*ruah, nefesh*, and *neshamah*—point to the emphasis in Jewish thought and tradition that a human being is more than a physical entity. There is in him or her an invisible element described by the Jewish mystics as a divine spark that enables every individual to aspire for something greater than the self. This assertion is the basis of any kind of spirituality.

THE JEWISH PATHS TO SPIRITUALITY

"The impulse behind the new spirituality," writes Rabbi Neil Gillman, Professor of Jewish Philosophy at The Jewish Theological Seminary in New York, "is the primacy of feeling."[17] Obviously, the experience of spirituality is a highly personal matter. What appeals to one individual does not always appeal to another. Two people who experience the same event may respond in opposite ways: one considers it as highly spiritual, whereas the other feels it as inconsequential. There cannot be one type of spirituality that is valid for everybody. Life experiences show us that there are various types of spirituality, just as there are different kinds of people.

Authentic Jewish spiritual expression takes different forms. Whether one chooses to explore it through acts of transcendence, study, prayer, meditation, or relationships and good deeds, each alternative expression, practiced separately or with the others, must be considered an authentic expression of Jewish commitment.[18]

Furthermore, these paths of spirituality are not mutually exclusive. In other words, a person who expresses his or her spirituality primarily through Torah study can also, on other occasions and under different circumstances, experience a spiritual high through a good deed or during a meditation session. An insight obtained during prayer may lead an individual to carry out a *mitzvah* for another human being. A religious ritual may at times elevate one's soul to great spiritual heights. As spiritual experiences these special moments are like roads that intersect at some points and then separate from one another. They may be practiced one after the other. One person may prefer to combine two or three together. They are like pentimento, wherein one image in a painting overlies an earlier image but does not obliterate it. They are like fabrics in which one shade of color is interwoven with another. We are not dealing here with parallel lines of spirituality but with paths that often meet in an upward movement toward a Light that uplifts the spirit and makes one whole.

It is said that Rabbi Menahem Mendel of Kotzk once asked his students, "Where does God dwell?" Thinking the answer obvious, one of them said, "God dwells everywhere!" "No," said the Rabbi, "God dwells wherever we let God in." Each person must do this according to his or her own personal needs and disposition.

The challenge for the modern Jew is to understand these paths, to assimilate them, and then to choose, out of the plethora of Jewish ideas, the approach to spirituality that best expresses a sense of personal transcendence.

Dr. **Wayne Dosick**, rabbi, is spiritual guide of the Elijah Minyan in San Diego, California, and an adjunct professor of Jewish studies at the University of San Diego. Author of many books on spirituality and living Jewishly, in *Soul Judaism: Dancing with God into a New Era*, Rabbi Dosick teaches us how we can add a rich spiritual dimension to our lives.

The State of the Faith

WAYNE DOSICK

For most of us, the world of the mind has become the highest order and the highest good. The world of God is distant; the world of the spirit is little more than bedtime *bubbe meises*, "old grandmothers' tales," and flights of fancy.

Many of us are unfamiliar with the transcendent world of the spirit.

We hardly know God.

We don't know *about* God; we seem embarrassed to talk *of* God; we seem uncomfortable trying to talk *to* God.

When, in our gladness or our pain, we are somehow moved to speak to God, we barely have the words. When, in our desire or need, we are moved to find God, we don't know where to look.

WHAT HAPPENED?

After World War II, we built and maintained our new suburban synagogues and Jewish communal institutions to reflect our highly rational, intellectual worldview.

Contemporary Judaism became, and remains, more communal and cultural than spiritual, let alone mystical.

We Jews became very successful at creating community, doing acts of social justice, saving oppressed Jewry, supporting the State of

Israel, raising money for "good causes," building Jewish institutions, defending against discrimination, and, with a few notable and most lamentable exceptions, fulfilling Judaism's ethical mandates. We are an accepted and respected part of the fabric of America. And we have contributed mightily to the ongoing growth and development of our society in virtually every aspect of human endeavor.

But the one thing Judaism is supposed to do best, it rarely does at all anymore.

Judaism is supposed to help each person find the way to create a personal, intimate relationship with God; a life of cosmic meaning and purpose; a life of soul-satisfaction, true inner happiness, and deep-felt joy and fulfillment.

There are, of course, sincere and serious contemporary Jews of every denomination of modern Jewry who feel a personal closeness to God found through faith, piety, and devotion to study, ritual, and worship.

But for most Jews, Judaism—the way it is practiced and conveyed in contemporary America—his failed to respond to our deepest yearnings and most profound needs.

While Judaism got caught up in modernity's reverence for rational, scientific, intellectual discourse and in the myth that building communal institutions and grand buildings meant the same thing as building Jewish hearts and souls, most Jews began to feel the ache of spiritual emptiness.

When Jews came to Judaism seeking God, most often all we found were sign-up sheets for the Hebrew school carpool and pledge cards for the building fund.

The synagogues, schools, and the community organizations and we the rabbis, teachers, and Jewish leaders failed our Jews. We failed to convey the greatness and the grandeur—indeed, the very existence—of the world of the Jewish spirit.

That is why, despite all of Judaism's outward manifestations of success in America, the vast majority of Jews are "voting with their feet," staying far away from Judaism, from the synagogue, from Jewish life and lifestyle.

The contemporary Judaism we have created does not speak sufficiently to searching Jewish hearts and does not sufficiently nourish hungering Jewish souls; it has become, for too many, stale, hollow, and irrelevant.

We Jews rarely, if ever, hear the word or see the vision of God anymore.

We hear no still small voice calling out to us.

We do not know how to find the voice or even where to search.

So we respond in silence.

The *pintele Yid,* the ever-enduring spark of Judaism, still burns, but the *Yiddishe neshamah,* the Jewish soul, the hearts and souls of individual Jews, are empty and forlorn.

HUNGERING FOR THE SACRED

Yet, there is an inherent human hunger, a continual human yearning, for the sacred, for the spiritual, for the transcendent, for the eternal.

We all want to be in touch with our creation and our Creator; we want answers to the mysteries of existence—to understand and somehow to tame the mighty forces of the universe; to define our place and our purpose in being.

We want to find meaning and value in life; to celebrate joy and triumph; to understand pain, suffering, and evil; and, ultimately, to confront death and the vast unknown.

No less than did our ancient forebears, we contemporary Jews want the explanations, the answers, the assurances that religion brings.

We want all that Judaism is supposed to offer: a spiritual pathway from and to God; intellectually honest and emotionally fulfilling answers to the questions of existence; life made holy by ethical commands that ennoble the human spirit; rituals and observances that give rhythm and purpose to the everyday; a community, linked by history and faith, deeply committed to the common good and to the dignity and sanctity of each human being.

We long for the deepest understanding, the timeless, the holy. We want, as the modern prayer so profoundly puts it, "purpose to our work, meaning to our struggle, direction to our striving." We hunger for God and for the world of the spirit, but, sadly, we rarely find it in institutional Judaism.

And so, many Jews, young and older alike, turn to other places seeking connection to God and the universe, seeking spiritual satisfaction and fulfillment.

Our Jews wind up in the meditation centers, the ashrams, the spiritual retreats, the communes, the self-improvement seminars, the twelve-step programs, the support groups, the yoga classes, the self-help bookshelves, est, Esalen, and the cults.

Three stories—of the thousands that could be recounted—tell the tale.

Not long ago, a sincere and serious young man phoned my call-in radio show to report that he, a Jew, attends Friday evening services every week but feels very little spiritual connection or uplift. His wife, also a Jew, meditates at the Self-Realization Fellowship and feels a great sense of cosmic connection and inner peace.

Recently a young woman told me, almost sheepishly and then with increasing passion and a face filled with light, that only a few months ago, when she was feeling deeply depressed, she went on a seven-day Buddhist retreat of silence where she found self-awareness, spiritual inspiration, and life guidance. She reported that sixty of the one hundred participants and three of the four leaders in this Buddhist retreat were Jews.

In the mid-1990s, a book called *The Jew in the Lotus,* by Rodger Kamenetz, chronicled the journey of several rabbis and Jewish leaders who met with the Dalai Lama to discuss the similarities between two seemingly disparate religious traditions. The book became an instant "cult classic" among Jews who were already integrating and balancing Eastern and Western spiritual traditions in their lives, and among Jews who were just learning that there is more to the Jewish spiritual journey than was ever taught in a suburban synagogue.

THE LONGEST JOURNEY BEGINS AND ENDS AT THE SAME PLACE

We all know people—we all are people—who jog *religiously,* who exercise, sail, cook gourmet meals, perform in community theater, collect stamps, read, or play trumpet *religiously.*

We do things we love, we love the things we do, because doing them makes us feel better, happier, more fulfilled; doing them brings us satisfaction and joy and makes our lives richer and fuller. Without them something important is missing; there is a gap, an emptiness, in our very existence.

If Judaism made us feel more satisfied, more fulfilled, made us happier and better human beings, we would practice it *religiously;* we would embrace it with the same joy, enthusiasm, and intensity that joggers and stamp collectors bring to their passions, for it would touch us at the core of our beings, at that deep place where happiness and fulfillment reside.

Jews! Listen!

Though no one ever told us, though no one ever showed us, everything we want, everything we need, everything we have been searching for, everything that will satisfy our souls, everything that will bring us to God is not far from home. It need not be sought in another place or another culture, another heritage or tradition. It lies in what is familiar, what is comfortable, what is us.

All that we are seeking is right in Judaism.

It is in Judaism's beginnings and its forever, in Judaism's sources and texts, in Judaism's words and prayers, in Judaism's rituals and practices, in Judaism's music and movement, in Judaism's "sounds of silence."

And all that we are seeking is right in us.

It is in our Jewish history and destiny, it is in our vocabulary and language, our poetry, our idiom, our metaphor. It is in our consciousness and in our deepest, hidden places; it is in our source, our roots, our rhythms, our genes, our DNA.

Within Judaism are the sacred pathways for our spiritual journey guiding each one of us to a personal, intimate relationship with God; bathing our souls in God's guidance and love; helping us struggle with and prevail over life's most perplexing questions and mysteries; leading us toward a rich, noble, fulfilling existence; bringing us wholeness and holiness at the very core of our beings.

Judaism's deeply spiritual pathways, which began with God's direct and personal conversations with our long-ago ancestors, are still indelibly carved into the collective Jewish memory and experience. They are the channel into God's presence; they are the guideposts for the transformation of Jewish hearts and souls.

Judaism's rituals and practices, which have become, for so many, empty and sterile rote, can still hold the deep spiritual secrets, the viscerally felt life-cadence rhythms that bring harmony to body and soul, that provide the pathway to the holy, to God.

These pathways have been hidden and sent underground, where they were shrouded in the shadows of Jewish life. But they are there, waiting to be joyously reclaimed and renewed by this generation of Jewish seekers.

TRADITION AND CHANGE

During its first two thousand years, Judaism was characterized by direct revelation enhanced by God-given law. In this period—which we now call Biblical Judaism—each person could hope for and expect personal communication and a personal relationship with God.

Born with Abraham (ca. 1800 B.C.E.) and affirmed by Moses at Sinai, Biblical Judaism continued through the period of the judges, the kings, and the prophets.

During all this time, our ancestors worshiped God by means of animal and agricultural sacrifices brought, eventually, to a centralized altar at the Holy Temple in Jerusalem. There, priests officiated over the sacrifices, hoping that God would be pleased by the "sweet smells" that wafted up to the heavens.

But then the world changed radically.

In quick succession, Jews experienced exile and return, religious reformation, religious repression, political persecution, the birth of a powerful new religion, destruction, and, once again, exile.

Any one of these traumas and challenges—and, surely, all of them together—might have been enough to decimate the Jewish people. When prophecy was silenced, they could have claimed to no longer hear God. When the Temple was destroyed, they could have claimed to no longer be able to worship God. When their land was ripped away from them, they could have claimed to have no place to be with God.

Instead, the Jews rose up to meet the challenges, totally revamped the Judaism they knew, developed a new Judaism, and reconstituted themselves as a new and stronger faith community.

The Holy Temple was replaced by the synagogue, the cultic priest was replaced by the scholar-rabbi, and animal sacrifice was replaced by prayer.

Most significantly, direct Divine revelation—personal prophecy—was replaced by the advent of Oral Law, the extension of Torah Law that was given at Sinai.

The rabbis and sages who introduced the Oral Law contended that God's word and will would no longer be given directly to individuals but would come through this new law, which would be articulated only by the sages themselves. Continuing revelation, they claimed, came through them alone.

This new Judaism came to be called Rabbinic Judaism. It is the Judaism that we have lived and practiced for these past two thousand years.

Born and sustained out of flexibility and adaptability, it was committed to maintaining the core of tradition while at the same time being ever ready to interpret, modify, and change in order to meet new circumstances and challenges.

Transcendent beyond the limitations of time and space, Rabbinic Judaism saved Judaism from possible ruination and oblivion.

* * * *

Yet Rabbinic Judaism's unwavering commitment to the world of the law stifled and frustrated proponents of the world of the spirit, those who still sought direct revelation from God and direct communication with God.

To be certain that the people would not enter realms where they no longer belonged, the sages tell this story in the Talmud.

Four went into paradise, into the dwelling place of God. They went seeking the deepest meaning of God's word, and so, metaphorically, they entered into the glory of God's heavenly kingdom.

One was so overcome by what he saw that he died; another went mad; the third became an apostate. Only one could look upon God's holy place and delve into the deepest meaning of God's holy word and survive unscathed. And that one was Rabbi Akiba, the greatest scholar of them all.

The message from the sages was clear: unless you are as great and learned a scholar as Rabbi Akiba—and none of you is—then don't even think of entering the realm of personal prophecy, of continuing revelation, of the mystical interpretation of God's word. For if you do, you will cease to believe, you will go mad, or you will die.

Then, just as the primacy of Jewish law was being deeply ingrained into the collective Jewish psyche, another messenger came into the world.

● ● ● ●

Jesus taught that in the relationship between God and humankind, the world of the law is far less important than the world of the spirit.

Jesus contended that belief, faith, and love, which Judaism assumes and sometimes takes for granted, are really the core of the relationship between God and His children and thus should be the central spiritual quest of humankind.

While Judaism rightly rejected the basic *forms* of Christianity—for they contained theological assertions that we simply could not accept—Judaism also ignored the *substance* that we would have done well to reaffirm: that God and humankind are connected through deep faith and love, that God can truly be a personal God, deeply involved in the life of each human being.

* * * *

All the while, human consciousness was evolving and growing. The universe was revealing more of its secrets; people were wiser, more attuned. Simple answers that had satisfied desert-dwelling ancestors were no longer enough.

The parameters imposed by the sages constrained the human spirit.

So twice in these ensuing two thousand years of Rabbinic Judaism, movements within Judaism—most notably the Kabbalists, beginning in the thirteenth century, and the Chasidim of the early eighteenth century—have tried to bring Jews back to finding the spiritual, to celebrating faith.

But their attempts were most often smothered and rejected by the rationalists and the legalists.

The world of the spirit was, at best, sent to the far edges of Jewish life and, at worst, was hidden away and practiced by only a few mystics and their followers.

In these last 250 years, since the Enlightenment and the Emancipation, attempts to bring Judaism back to the world of the spirit have been eschewed by the so-called rationalists and intellectuals as but fanciful conjecture, folk fantasy, overworked imagination, or mere superstition.

THE COMING NEW ERA

In the past 250 years, there have been massive and radical changes in the Jewish and in the secular world: the Enlightenment with its emphasis on scientific scholarship; the Emancipation with its territorial and political freedoms; global warfare with its threat of mass destruction; the rise and growth of the highly creative American Jewish community; the devastation wrought by the Holocaust; the rise and growth of political Zionism and the establishment of the modern State of Israel;

the quantum leaps of science and technology that are making the vast world into a "global village"; the deep ecumenism that is bringing diverse people ever closer together; the serious concern about ecology and the preservation of the planet.

At the same time, human consciousness is expanding to ever-greater awareness.

There has been a dramatic awakening to the knowledge that the universe is so much more than what we can see, feel, hear, or experience at this moment in time. There has been ever-growing recognition that we are continually developing the capacity to perceive and receive that which has been there all along but is still to be revealed.

The universe continues to unfold bit by bit, revealing its mysteries, divulging its secrets. The veil is lifting. The distinction—and the distance—between this side and the other side is ever fading.

Some call it the world of intuition or perception, some call it the world of the psychic or the mystical, some call it the world of the spirit. We call it the world of God.

Dr. Daniel C. Matt is currently composing an annotated English translation of the *Zohar*. He was formerly a professor of Jewish spirituality at the Graduate Theological Union in Berkeley, California. In *God & the Big Bang: Discovering Harmony Between Science & Spirituality*, Dr. Matt teaches us about the sense of wonder and oneness that connects us with the universe and with God.

The Personal God—and Beyond

DANIEL C. MATT

The God of the Jewish Bible is treated almost as a person. Only rarely described as feminine, God often appears as a heavenly patriarch, compassionate yet irascible. Called by such names as *Shaddai, El, Elohim, YHVH,* this God is so personal that He is in love with the people of Israel and jealous of any other gods trying to lure away His beloved. Conceiving God as person implies a relationship, but also implies a gap, since the divine personality is assumed to be separate from us and from all nature. God did not emanate and become the world; God majestically spoke the world into being. As Saint Augustine formulated the view, "The works of creation were made from nothing by You, not of You." Intimacy with God forms the core of spiritual life: loving God with heart, soul and force. But our relationship depends on the separateness of divine and human identities. Though I am created in the image of God, we relate to each other *as other.*

Without a personal God, there is no possibility of relationship with the divine. How can I relate to the boundless? The boundless includes and subsumes me, along with everything else. Nothing is separate from infinity.

The God of the Jewish mystics is both personal and impersonal. In the personal mode, God becomes even more anthropomorphic than in the Bible. Yet the roots of divine personality are embedded in nothingness and infinity. The personal God is born out of *Ayin.*

THE TEN *SEFIROT:* THE COSMIC TREE OF LIFE

The mystics are reticent about *Ein Sof,* which is fitting when speaking of the infinite, but they indulge in describing the ten *sefirot:* the various stages of God's inner life and the dynamics of divine personality. The *sefirot* depict God more graphically than we find anywhere in the Bible or the Talmud. Not only does God feel, respond and act through the *sefirot,* but they constitute an androgynous divine body, complete with arms, legs and sexual organs. Here, God is both He and She, and the union of the divine couple bestows blessing on the world.

We have already encountered the first *sefirah: Ayin.* The nothingness of *Ayin* is undifferentiated oneness, roughly the same as infinity. In fact, some kabbalists treat *Ein Sof* and *Ayin* as one and the same. From here, the other nine *sefirot* emerge.

More commonly, the first *sefirah* is called *Keter,* "Crown." It is the crown on the head of *Adam Qadmon,* primordial Adam.

According to the opening chapter of Genesis, the human being is created in the image of God. The *sefirot* are the divine original of that image, the mythical paragon of the human being, our archetypal nature. The *sefirot* are also pictured as a cosmic tree, growing downward from its roots above, from *Keter,* the highest *sefirah,* "the root of roots."

From the depths of Nothingness shines the next *sefirah:* the primordial point of *Hokhmah,* "Wisdom." This point, called "Beginning," marks the beginning of creation, or rather, emanation: the flow of divine being. From here, the sefirotic tree branches out and eventually yields all existence. From this point, space and time unfold, just as the singularity of the big bang signals the beginning of spacetime. From the singularity, the universe expands; from the primordial point, a circle expands: the next *sefirah, Binah,* "Understanding." *Binah* is the womb, the divine mother. Surrounding the primordial point, the cosmic seed of *Hokhmah,* She conceives the rest of the *sefirot,* which emerge from Her. Within *Binah,* the "personality" of God begins to take shape; here, infinity

The Ten *Sefirot*

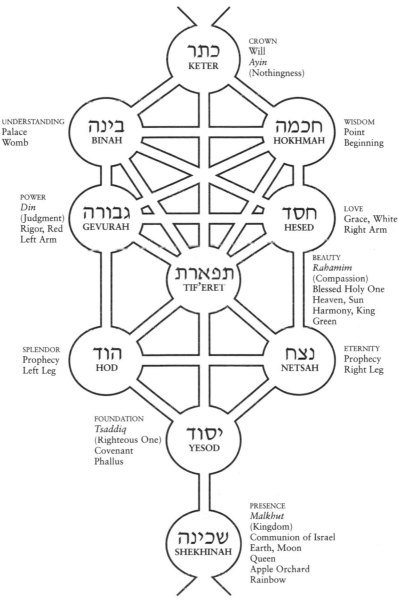

CROWN
Will
Ayin
(Nothingness)

כתר
KETER

UNDERSTANDING
Palace
Womb

בינה
BINAH

חכמה
HOKHMAH

WISDOM
Point
Beginning

POWER
Din
(Judgment)
Rigor, Red
Left Arm

גבורה
GEVURAH

חסד
HESED

LOVE
Grace, White
Right Arm

תפארת
TIF'ERET

BEAUTY
Rahamim
(Compassion)
Blessed Holy One
Heaven, Sun
Harmony, King
Green

SPLENDOR
Prophecy
Left Leg

הוד
HOD

נצח
NETSAH

ETERNITY
Prophecy
Right Leg

FOUNDATION
Tsaddiq
(Righteous One)
Covenant
Phallus

יסוד
YESOD

PRESENCE
Malkhut
(Kingdom)
Communion of Israel
Earth, Moon
Queen
Apple Orchard
Rainbow

שכינה
SHEKHINAH

turns into God. As the *Zohar* reads the opening words of Genesis, "With Beginning, through Wisdom, the Infinite created God."

The three highest *sefirot (Keter, Hokhmah* and *Binah)* represent the head of the divine body and are considered more hidden than the offspring of *Binah*. She gives birth first to *Hesed* (Love) and *Din* (Judgment), often referred to as *Gevurah* (Power). This pair constitutes the right and left arms of God, two poles of the divine personality: free-flowing love and strict judgment, grace and limitation. For proper functioning of the world, both are essential and, ideally, a balance is achieved, which is symbolized by the central *sefirah, Tif'eret* (Beauty), also called *Rahamim* (Compassion). If judgment is not softened by love, then it lashes out and threatens to destroy life. Here lies the origin of evil, which is called *Sitra Ahra,* "the other side." The demonic is rooted in the divine.

Tif'eret is the masculine trunk of the sefirotic body. He is called "Heaven," "Sun," "King," and "the Holy One, blessed be He," the standard rabbinic name for God. The next two *sefirot* are *Netsah* (Eternity) and *Hod* (Splendor). They form the right and left legs of the divine body. Relatively little is said about them, except that they are the source of prophecy. *Yesod* (Foundation) is the ninth *sefirah* and represents the phallus, the procreative life force of the universe. *Yesod* is the *axis mundi,* the cosmic pillar. The light and power of the preceding *sefirot* are channeled through *Yesod* to the tenth *sefirah, Malkhut* (Kingdom), or *Shekhinah* (Presence).

THE RETURN OF THE GODDESS

Shekhinah is the name for God's immanence in the Talmud and Midrash. But in the Kabbalah, *Shekhinah* becomes a full-fledged She: the feminine side of God, daughter of *Binah,* bride of *Tif'eret. Shekhinah* is "the secret of the possible," receiving emanation from above and engendering varieties of life below. She complements Her masculine partner, the Holy One, blessed be He, mollifying His occasional outbursts. The joining of *Shekhinah* and *Tif'eret*—the feminine and masculine halves of God—becomes the focus of spiritual life.

Human beings stimulate the divine union by acting ethically and religiously, thereby assuring an abundant flow of blessing to the world. Human marriage symbolizes and actualizes divine marriage, while the evening of Sabbath turns into a weekly celebration of the cosmic wedding—and the ideal time for human lovers to unite.

Shekhinah represents a partial, yet significant corrective to patriarchal religion. God's maleness was no Jewish invention. The transition from Goddess to God, from dominant female deities to dominant male deities, occurred long before the composition of the earliest books of the Bible. To the ancient Hindus, Indra, the warrior god, reigned supreme; to the Greeks, it was Zeus; to the Germanic tribes, Thor. The Bible gradually elevates a tribal warrior god, *YHVH*, to the status of the transcendent monotheistic deity of the universe. The prophets rail against *YHVH*'s rivals among the Canaanite fertility gods and goddesses, which proves that the Israelites engaged in such forbidden worship. The Goddess may have been expunged from the official religion of biblical and rabbinic Judaism, but She reemerges as *Shekhinah* in Kabbalah.

This new flowering is a testament to the Goddess's enduring hold on religious consciousness. Mythical depictions of the divine had been attacked for centuries and pronounced dead by medieval philosophy, but now myth had its revenge. Portrayed boldly in the Kabbalah, the feminine *Shekhinah* became immensely popular among the Jewish masses over the course of several hundred years. Clearly, She answered a deep religious and psychological need: Her intimacy and accessibility balanced the august demeanor of the patriarchal God.

The kabbalists were not proto-feminists. *Shekhinah*, relegated to the last rung of the sefirotic ladder, is subservient to the Holy One, blessed be He. *Shekhinah* is generally passive and receptive; She transmits the flow of divine emanation, but is said to have "nothing at all of Her own." Contemporary feminists are suspicious of this domesticated Goddess: Some prefer a God beyond gender; others are more attracted to *Shekhinah*'s independent and demonic shadow, Lilith, who was a proto-feminist.

As Adam's first wife, she refused to lie beneath him while making love and fled, causing mischief ever since. Clearly, the kabbalistic image of *Shekhinah* is a masculine product, fashioned by men for men. Yet, She is a leading character in the masterpiece of Kabbalah, the *Zohar*, which devotes more space to Her than to any other *sefirah*. She fascinated the *Zohar*'s male composer, Moses ben Shem Tov de León, who realized something radically obvious: God cannot be adequately described in solely masculine terms. Today, seven hundred years later, de León's theological critique is still widely unheeded.

Rabbi Ira F. Stone, spiritual leader at Temple Beth Zion-Beth Israel in Philadelphia, began his spiritual odyssey as a para-professional social worker and street worker with drug abusing youth in New York City. He is a Visiting Lecturer in the Department of Jewish Philosophy at The Jewish Theological Seminary of America. In *Seeking the Path to Life: Theological Meditations on God and the Nature of People, Love, Life and Death,* Rabbi Stone teaches us about our inner struggles that define our relationship with God.

God

IRA F. STONE

God is where I come from and where I'm going. At any point along this continuum, He alone can know me fully. Knowing me fully He is able to love me.

What I know of God is that I am created in His image. That is the most profound religious statement I've ever encountered. Not for what it tells me about me, but for what it tells me about God. Since I create the world I live in through language, so must God. Since I can love and nurture, so must God. Since I am easily hurt or destructively angry so, too, God.

But God's characteristics are not bound by death and, therefore, are fundamentally different from those characteristics in me. There are moments when the qualities we identify as being feminine are essential to my sense of self. Then, God is She, comfortably and lovingly for me.

My nature is often contradictory. I can be frustrated, vindictive, sometimes nihilistic, often afraid. I believe this applies to God as well, but He can always be available in love behind these states even as I can be, too. I believe that God fails me only when His being is constrained by His immortality. I, on the other hand, must ultimately be human, which means I must die. And death is the only place where I am alone.

Rabbi Karyn D. Kedar is the regional director of the Great Lakes Region of the Union of American Hebrew Congregations. She was the first woman rabbi to serve in Jerusalem and lived and worked in Israel for ten years. In *The Women's Torah Commentary: New Insights from Women Rabbis on the 54 Weekly Torah Portions,* Rabbi Kedar teaches us about the many names of God.

Va-era: ואדא
The Many Names of God

KARYN D. KEDAR

> God spoke to Moses saying, "I am YHVH. I appeared to Abraham, Isaac, and Jacob as El Shaddai, but I did not make Myself known to them as YHVH."
>
> *(Exodus 6:2–3)*

The names of God are manifold. Each name bears a different image, nuance, reality. The names contradict, mix metaphors and often confuse. In the opening verses of *Va-era,* God admits to a confusion by design: "I am called YHVH but I was called El Shaddai, but I didn't tell them that I am also YHVH, but you should know I am that same God." We are beckoned amid the confusion to know the many names of God; if we could only say It, then perhaps we could understand It.

For so many years I searched for the different expressions of God. Yet, one name remained dominant: the King. I tried to erase the man with the white beard from behind the lids of my eyes and find a reasonable substitute—one that defies a male authority pulling at my life as the "King of the Universe." I longed to utter God's name and see wind or waves of purple light. I found myself on a treasure hunt, searching for more buried images and concepts that were undeniably female.

Suddenly I saw the word *shaddai* sparkling like gold from the mezuzah on the doorpost of my house. *Shaddai,* used in a biblical name for God, translates as "breast," and evokes the images of mountains and breasts, much like the mountain range the Grand Tetons. Dare we say in English what our ancestors understood in their native Hebrew? El Shaddai—the God of Breasts.

In the verses that open *Va-era,* the name El Shaddai is juxtaposed with the name YHVH. YHVH is a curious word. It seems to come from the word "to be." It is never pronounced as it is written. In fact, the true pronunciation was uttered once a year on Yom Kippur, in the second century in the great Temple of Jerusalem, by the high priest in the seclusion of the Holy of Holies, where no one else could hear. When the Temple was destroyed, the high priest lost his moment and we lost the sound of YHVH. As a proper noun, grammatically it ends in the feminine form, but we read it as "Adonai," a masculine name that is translated as "Lord." Is the feminine rendition of God's name the reason we lost the pronunciation? We are dangerously close to the goddesses of the pagan world when we evoke female images to describe the Deity. Is there conceptual room in a monotheistic system for conflicting, even competing, images of God, sometimes male, other times female? In the name of monotheism and in defiance of paganism, we became blind to the rich variety of ways we describe God.

Consider the opening verses of Genesis: In the beginning God created heaven and earth—the earth being unformed and void, with darkness over the surface of the deep and the spirit of God sweeping over the water—and God said, "Let there be light," and there was light.

Look closely and we reveal a description of the womb. The deep, unformed darkness is the womb, ripe with potential. The water is the amniotic waters that protect the fragility of life. There is the spirit of God within, windlike and soul-like all at once. God is the Mother, the force that makes sense out of the chaos. And then there is light: God births the world into being. It was quite common in the ancient polytheistic world to describe creation as the result of the consorting of male and female gods. The Mesopotamian myth *Enuma Elish* is particularly interesting to us for its similarities to Genesis. The goddess Tiamat is slain and cut in half by the god Marduk. He forms the world from her corpse: her upper half becomes the heavens and her lower half becomes the earth, which is similar to the biblical creation, where the waters above are separated from the waters below. It seems that the Hebrew word for waters, *yam,* may share the same Semitic root as the name Tiamat. Is the Genesis story a distant relative to the Mesopotamian myth? Do they share the Mother? If they do, the two stories differ in tone and content: The Mesopotamian story creates the world in violence and death, while the Genesis story births the world gently and with goodness.

It was when I found the Mother that I understood the King. We mistake the metaphor for the literal. The King of the Universe is singular in his name and one in his essence. But it's not that God is the king; rather, God is merely *called* king. What God *is* is beyond description. What we mean is that God is *like* the King of the Universe, that there is a ruling principle that guides our spiritual life just as there is a ruling principle that governs the physical world. Every time I say, "King," I think, "Ruling Principle."

Maimonides has noted that "the Torah is written in the language of human beings." What he is teaching us is that we use words to describe truth, not to ultimately define truth. God defies definition. So when we use King of the Universe, we are not describing God in any literal sense, but rather, metaphorically.

The truth is, when we speak of God with male terminology, we tolerate contradiction. Consider *Avinu Malkeinu,* "Our Father, Our King." The Father conjures the image of a loving parent, a caring, intimate, accessible figure. Juxtapose that to the King, a distant, ruling, powerful, inaccessible figure. When Father and King are said together in one breath, the metaphor is mixed, as if to remind us not to take these words literally but figuratively. God is not a father and not a king, but if I were to describe my experience of God, I could say that at times God seems like a little of both.

Freeing God from the literal frees us all from narrow and, often, dangerous concepts. On one level, the Mother of Genesis liberates the female of our world. God is not only in the experience of men; she is now within the experience of women. Yet she has always been there, hiding.

We say and we pray to *Av HaRachamim. Rachamim* is derived from the Hebrew root that means "womb." The word is often translated as "mercy" or "compassion." I prefer to render it as "compassion," meaning "with passion." God loves us and envelops us with the same passion as that of a mother protecting her creation in her womb. Contrast this to the English words "hysterical" or "hysterectomy," which originate from the Greek *hystera*, "womb." In the Jewish culture, which values women, the essence of the female, her passion and great love, is a word assigned to God. In the Greek world, that emotion comes to us as excessive and negative.

What I like most about the feminine imagery of God is the mixing of the metaphors. The etymology of *Av HaRachamim* evokes the image of the Father of the Womb. When you mix metaphors—father and mother, for example—you realize the truth is that God is neither. The truth is that only in recent memory have we forgotten female imagery to describe God. The mystics and kabbalists used a variety of images: When we pray and say, "...the Great God," God clothes himself with greatness. When we say, "the Mighty," God clothes himself in might. When we say, "the Fearsome," God clothes himself in fearsomeness. The attribute through which God clothes himself through our prayers is called "Mother."

In more recent times, Reform Judaism has recalled the feminine imagery of the kabbalists and took a courageous step in *Gates of Forgiveness*, published by the Central Conference of American Rabbis. In their prayerbook they juxtapose "Our Father, Our King" with a feminine image by introducing a prayer that evokes the Shechinah and translates it as "Mothering Presence."[1] Years later, the Israel Movement for Progressive Judaism took a similar step when they published the following prayer in their Hebrew *Machzor*, the High Holiday prayerbook:

Shechinah, the source of our life—hear our prayer and have compassion for us.

Shechinah, the source of our life—remember that we are Your sons and daughters.

Shechinah, the source of our life—teach us to recognize our limitations.

Shechinah, the source of our life—guide us in the ways of pleasantness.

Shechinah, the source of our life—teach us compassion and tzedakah.

Shechinah, the source of our life—be with us for the sake of those who struggle for peace and justice.

Shechinah, the source of our life—turn our mourning to joy and our sadness to happiness.

Shechinah, the source of our life—bless our land and the work of our hands.

Shechinah, the source of our life—gather Your children from the four corners of the earth.

Shechinah, the source of our life—complete the building of Jerusalem Your holy city.[2]

What is so compelling in the Hebrew is that since Shechinah is a feminine noun, all of the verbs that follow are in the feminine grammatical form. The impact is breathtaking. The Mother has reentered our prayers during the most holy of days of the year, Rosh Hashanah and Yom Kippur.

Va-era seems to tell us that once God was known to Abraham by the concrete image El Shaddai, the Great Mother, but now will be known to Moses as YHVH, the God who sustains all being.

Apparently, our ancestors understood that the vastness of God can be understood only if we use words that include as much of the human experience as possible. God is like a judge, like a birthing woman, like a compassionate mother, like a warrior, like a ruler, like a friend. When seen clearly, God is not seen at all, at least not as we see our mother or father. Rather God is, as Moses was told, a great beingness that sustains the universe with grace and goodness. We are challenged to find the combination of words that will help us sense and experience the reality of YHVH.

Rabbi Lawrence Kushner is Rabbi-in-Residence at Hebrew Union College–Jewish Institute of Religion. He teaches and lectures widely to audiences of all ages, faiths and backgrounds, and has been a frequent commentator on National Public Radio's *All Things Considered*. In *The Book of Words: Talking Spiritual Life, Living Spiritual Talk,* Rabbi Kushner teaches us about the primary words we use to describe the spiritual dimension of life and how rethinking what they mean can add power and focus to the lives we live every day.

Breathing   השם

LAWRENCE KUSHNER

And lo, the Lord passed by. There was a great and mighty wind; splitting mountains and shattering rocks by the power of the Lord; but the Lord was not in the wind.

After the wind, an earthquake, but the Lord was not in the earthquake. After the earthquake, fire; but the Lord was not in the fire. And after the fire, the soft barely audible sound of almost breathing.

(I Kings 19:11–12)

Moses said to God, "When I come to the Israelites and say to them, 'The God of your parents has sent me to you,' and they ask me, 'What is God's name?' What shall I say to them?" And God said to Moses, "Ehyeh-asher-ehyeh."

EXODUS 3:13–14

The letters of the name of God in Hebrew are *yod, hay, vav,* and *hay.* They are frequently mispronounced *Yahveh.* But in truth they are unutterable. Not because of the holiness they evoke, but because they are all vowels and you cannot pronounce all the vowels at once without risking respiratory injury.

God spoke to Moses and said to him, "I am the Lord. I appeared to Abraham, Isaac, and Jacob as El Shaddai, but I did not make myself known to them by my Name Yod Hay Vav Hay."

EXODUS 6:2

(*hä•shem´*)   The Name of God

39

This word is the sound of breathing. The holiest Name in the world, the Name of the Creator, is the sound of your own breathing.

That these letters are unpronounceable is no accident. Just as it is no accident that they are also the root letters of the Hebrew verb "to be." Scholars have suggested that a reasonable translation of the four-letter Name of God might be: *The One Who Brings Into Being All That Is.* So God's Name is the Name of Being itself. And, since God is holy, then so is all creation.

At the burning bush Moses asks God for God's Name, but God only replies with *Ehyeh-asher-ehyeh,* often incorrectly rendered by the static English, "I am who I am." But in truth the Hebrew future is unequivocal: *"I will be who I will be."* Here is a Name (and a God) who is neither completed nor finished. This God is literally *not yet.*

MISHNA

On the Day of Atonement, in the Temple in Jerusalem, the High Priest would say, "I pray, O God, your people, the House of Israel, have done wrong, they have transgressed, they have sinned before you. I pray, by Your Name, pardon, I pray, the iniquities, the transgressions, and the sins which Your people the House of Israel, have wrongly committed, and which they have transgressed, and which they have sinned before You, as it is written in the Torah of Moses, Your servant, 'For on this day shall atonement be made for you to cleanse you from all your sins, before God shall you be clean.' And the priests and the people who were standing in the forecourt, when they heard the Ineffable Name come forth from the mouth of the High Priest, used to kneel and prostrate themselves and fall down on their faces and say, 'Blessed is God's Name, the glory of God's Universe is for ever and ever.'"

LIVING SPIRITUAL TALK—KAVANAH

If God's Name is the Name of Being, then perhaps breathing itself is the sound of the unpronounceable Name. Find a place and a time that are quiet enough to hear the sound of your own breathing. Simply listen to that barely audible noise and intend that with each inhalation and exhalation you sound the Name of Being. It may be no accident that this exercise is universally acknowledged as an easy and effective method for focusing and relaxation.

Dr. **Arthur Green,** rabbi, is Lown Professor of Jewish Thought at Brandeis University and former president of the Reconstructionist Rabbinical College in Philadelphia. He is a student of Jewish theology and mysticism who has combined scholarly career and personal commitment. In *These Are the Words: A Vocabulary of Jewish Spiritual Life,* Rabbi Green teaches us about the meaning of *Y-H-W-H,* the hidden, mysterious name of God.

Y-H-W-H

י-ה-ו-ה

ARTHUR GREEN

The Torah calls *Y-H-W-H* the name of God. When the Lord appears to Moses at the burning bush to send him on his mission (Exodus 3:15), this name is revealed to him. He is told that this is God's name "forever," though that word is written in a way that also could mean "secret" or "hidden." The commentaries take it to mean that י-ה-ו-ה / *Y-H-W-H* is the hidden, mysterious name of God.

What is its mystery? First, it has no vowels. Without vowels, which usually appear as dots beneath or alongside the letters, it is impossible to pronounce a word. But *Y-H-W-H* also has no real consonants! Y, H, and W really are blowing sounds, rushings of air through the mouth. There is nothing hard or concrete about them, no "B" or "K" sound that requires a definite action of the lips, teeth, or throat. The point is one of elusiveness or abstraction. The name of God is so subtle it could slip away from you. *Y-H-W-H* is not a God you can grab hold of and be sure you've got firmly in your mental "grasp."

Y-H-W-H, like most Hebrew words, appears to be derived from a three-letter root. H-W-H is the root for "being" or "existence." The Y at the beginning of *Y-H-W-H* could indicate the imperfect tense, so that we could translate the name to mean "that which is" or "that which will be." But *Y-H-W-H* is more likely to be an awkward

41

conflation of all the tenses, and it is really best to translate it as "Is-Was-Will Be." In fact, the Hebrew word for "being" is HaWaYaH, which is simply a switching around of the letters in *Y-H-W-H*. The commanding verb of Genesis 1, *yehi* or "Let there be," is closely related to it. *Y-H-W-H*, in fact, is not really a noun at all, but a verb caught in motion, artificially frozen by our simple minds into noun form, a movement conceived as though it were a "thing." This occurs in the same way a still camera might frame an action shot, giving you the impression of having "captured" something motionless.

Not only can we not properly pronounce this word; we are not permitted even to try. This "explicit" name of God was to be pronounced only once a year by the high priest in the Holy of Holies on Yom Kippur. No lesser setting was considered adequate for its utterance. After the Second Temple was destroyed (in 70 C.E., by the Romans) its pronunciation was forbidden altogether and various other terms, beginning with *adonai,* were substituted for it.

Dr. Arthur Green, rabbi, is Lown Professor of Jewish Thought at Brandeis University and former president of the Reconstructionist Rabbinical College in Philadelphia. He is a student of Jewish theology and mysticism who has combined scholarly career and personal commitment. In *These Are the Words: A Vocabulary of Jewish Spiritual Life*, Rabbi Green teaches us about the meaning of *Adonai*, the name of God in our prayers.

Adonai אֲדֹנָי

ARTHUR GREEN

Literally "My Lord," a word by which to address one's superior, like "m' lord" in old English usage. Since very early times this term has been used to replace *Y-H-W-H*, which may not be pronounced. When the Hebrew Bible was first translated into Greek (around 200 B.C.E.), it was the word *adonai* that the Greek translators rendered as *kyrios* or Lord.

Midrashic tradition offers an illuminating explanation for the origin of this term as a substitute for the name of God. When God created Adam, it is told, the angels were filled with jealous wrath. "A mere earthling!" they said, denying that Adam had any special worth. But God loved Adam and wanted him to display his wisdom. So God brought forth the animals, one after another, and asked the angels what they were to be called. Having no experience of the animal world, the angels did not know. Then God called Adam and asked him to name the animals. Adam did so in short order. "And now," said God," what should you be called?" Adam answered, "I should be called Adam, for I was taken from *adamah* ('earth')." "And what should I be called?" asked God. "You," Adam replied immediately, "should be called *adonai*, for You are Lord over all Your works."

A twofold lesson can be learned from this midrash. One part is that being Lord over us is not God's most essential Self. The divine essence is better expressed by the name *Y-H-W-H,* for God's presence permeates all of being. It is we humans who ascribe lordship to God, out of our need for submission. Lordship is a projection from human society onto the mysterious, unknowable, divine Being. Even though that is true, however, we call God *adonai* even in our most intimate prayers. We use this word as though it really were a name, and those prayers are acceptable. This is the second part of the lesson. Saying "Lord" puts us into *relationship* with *Y-H-W-H.* This desire for relationship, even with so abstract a being as *Y-H-W-H,* is a sign of our love. God responds to our love and chooses to be called by this name we made up for God in our infancy, rather than by the Explicit Name itself, *Y-H-W-H.*

Dr. Arthur Green, rabbi, is Lown Professor of Jewish Thought at Brandeis University and former president of the Reconstructionist Rabbinical College in Philadelphia. He is a student of Jewish theology and mysticism who has combined scholarly career and personal commitment. In *These Are the Words: A Vocabulary of Jewish Spiritual Life,* Rabbi Green teaches us about the meaning of *Elohim,* the name of God in our prayers.

Elohim אלהים

ARTHUR GREEN

Elohim is the generic Hebrew term for "god." The Bible uses it when referring both to the "God" of Israel and to the "gods" of other nations. The word is also occasionally used in the sense of "great one," referring to a respected human authority.

The most interesting thing about *Elohim* is the fact that it is a plural form. The Bible acknowledges that fact by using it when speaking of "other gods." Then plural verbs or adjectives are used with it, as required by the rules of proper grammar. But when the same plural word is used to refer to the God of Israel, those rules are intentionally violated and *Elohim* is treated as though it were singular. Thus the Bible's opening words, *Bereshit bara' elohim* ("In the beginning God created..."), are something of a grammatical abomination! Every time the Torah says *va-yomer 'elohim* ("God said") the rules of grammar are broken.

This is, of course, no accident. The point is that *Elohim* in this context is used as a *collective.* All the powers that once belonged to all the deities of the pantheon—such as love, power, wisdom, war, fruitfulness—are now concentrated in this single Being Who contains them all. The blessings needed for every aspect of human life are now all seen to come from a single source. This is the essence of the monotheistic revolution, embodied in the language each time you use this common Hebrew word for "God."

The *Zohar,* the great compendium of Kabbalah, opens with a profound interpretation of the word *Elohim.* It reads the word as composed of two shorter Hebrew terms: אלה / *eleh* and מי / *mi. Eleh* means "these," referring to all the images and attributes of God available to us through the *sefirot. Mi* means "who?" always in the interrogative form. Despite all our thinking and imagining, the *Zohar* teaches, God remains a mystery. If you think you understand God, you lose the "Who?" Then you become an idolater, worshipping your own images, just like those who made the golden calf and said: "*These* are your gods, O Israel!" (Exodus 32:4).

Rabbi Elyse Goldstein is the Director of Kolel, The Adult Center for Liberal Jewish Learning, a full-time progressive adult Jewish learning center, and is widely recognized as an innovative and thought-provoking teacher of Torah. In *ReVisions: Seeing Torah through a Feminist Lens,* Rabbi Goldstein offers us a modern, feminist perspective of the texts, practices and beliefs central to Jewish tradition.

God-Language

ELYSE GOLDSTEIN

The Jewish feminist task is one of symbiosis. It involves merging the old goddess imagery, the new ways of thinking about God, and the Kabbalistic notions of the Shekhinah with a rejection of stereotypical femininity; together with a staunch monotheism, an engagement with Rabbinic theologies and images of the Divine, and a respect for the ways in which all our early ancestors related to God. If our common Jewish notions of the One God can finally include feminine attributes, female pronouns, depictions of God as Mother and/or Father, descriptions of God as indwelling as well as being outside of us, if we can be bold, multifaceted and broad in our views, then the One God can yet be a symbol of the "newfound beauty, strength, and power of women."

We spoke of the goddess aspect inherent in the One God, and of the Shekhinah having aspects which are attractive to the feminine soul. Now we close by asking about why, and how, we can speak of the One God in a more feminist manner.

When I was a little girl growing up in Queens, New York, my family would go to the Reform temple every Friday night. I would sit proudly in the front row. I loved the still serenity, the solemnity of the cantor's old European-style singing, and the sonorous tones of the rabbi's sermon. As I looked up at the *bima* (and from a little girl's vantage point, the *bima* looked very high up indeed), I thought surely God must be paying attention to all those deep and serious voices. When the rabbi invoked what he called the "final benediction," standing right in the middle of the *bima* with his arms spread out majestically, my father would put his hand on mine protectively and give it a little squeeze, his own silent blessing. I felt safe and secure with God the Father, the rabbi and my own father mysteriously intertwined.

Then I grew up. I found out that the rabbi was human, my father was flawed and God could not take care of everything. God as "He" does help re-create that safe and protective father of little boys and girls, but it lacks spiritual maturity.

God-language is not an academic discussion; nor is it a trivial matter, as some have suggested. Language can of course be poetic, esoteric, or symbolic in nature, but it is not arbitrary; language both *describes* and *creates* reality. While people rightly protest that symbols are not reality but only symbols, through centuries of familiarity, symbols lose their transparency and come to be seen as descriptive of, and not merely metaphors for, reality.

Language is not arbitrary. When we say table, we mean table, not chair. "Animal" is the generic term for certain creatures, but "cow" is specific. No one would argue that "cow" can also mean "chicken." How can we still argue then that He can also mean She? "God" is generic for that Being we try and describe, but "He" and "King" and "Father" are not.

Christian minister Sharon Neufer Emswiler once told of her experience in church, after years of singing hymns of the fatherhood of God and the brotherhood of men. She asked simply, "Why am I going away feeling less human than when I came?" If God is Father, and the Children of Israel are his "firstborn sons," then women are perpetually another class, wives and mothers of those fathers and sons.

The representation of God in the Torah is predominantly male, expressed not only through the male pronoun, but through many male characteristics, such as God as a "man of war" (Exodus 15). Judith Plaskow writes,

God's maleness is so deeply and firmly established as part of the Jewish conception of God that it is almost difficult to document: It is simply part of the lenses through which God is seen. Maleness is not a distinct attribute, separable from God's anger or mercy or justice. Rather, it is expressed through the total picture of God in Jewish texts and liturgy.[1]

It is true that later Jewish philosophers, such as Maimonides, did champion an invisible, incorporeal God and rejected the anthropomorphism of the Torah as a projection of human need, noting that "the Torah speaks in a human language." But intertwined with that human, male language are issues of male dominance and male authority. If to be God-like is to be a Father and a King, a warrior and "Lord of hosts," and if to be God-like is the Jewish task of Imitatio Dei, then how can women ever be God-like? It is no accident that women do not experience themselves as equals within a society that encourages a masculine image for its highest divinity. And it is no accident that the highest source of our values, the ultimate model of holiness, the pinnacle of our search for meaning, is imagined in such male terms.

Plaskow further notes,

If the feminist objections to Jewish God language were confined to the issues of gender, the manipulation of pronouns and creation of female imagery would fairly easily resolve the difficulties described...while feminist criticisms of traditional language begin with gender, they come to focus on the deeper issue of images of God's power as dominance.[2]

God's relationship to us is based on hierarchical opposites: father/son; king/servant; God is majestic, distant, exalted. This God is a Being utterly outside us, above, insisting on obedience and authority, punishing the wicked and rewarding the faithful. Seen in this context, human male dominance makes sense, and is supported by the theological system as well as the legal system.

Language that envisions God as male or female correlates to the emergence of gender as a defining concern. What we say about God colors what we say about ourselves on a personal level. On a communal level, a religious society uses its theology to justify what women can/cannot and should/should not do within its social system. Thus God's maleness, a male priesthood, and the chosenness of "first-born sons" all connect to a preoccupation with the rules, roles and rights of women. Feminism questions root assumptions and root beliefs about God and the resulting hierarchical nature of religion. It confronts root conceptions, and the root comfort, of God as Father.

If we are frightened to replace God the Father, it may be because we cannot imagine ritual, prayer, tradition and belief system with God the Partner. A male clergy will no longer be able to claim ultimate authority from a male God. Halacha, with all its assumptions about what women are and what women want, and what women can or cannot do, will have to deal with a new category.

There are several ways to approach this new area of "God-talk" in an attempt to move away from a mostly male religious lexicon. We can change the language to include "She." The use of "She" helps point out the anthropomorphism and ultimate blasphemy of centuries of using He. If we never *really* meant that God was a "He," we should have no problem whatsoever using the term "She." However, use of the term "She" provokes the old cries of paganism, although "He" never has. I have yet to hear that "He" is reminiscent of the old gods.

Or we can use neutral language. We can speak of God as "God" instead of either He or She. King becomes Ruler, Father becomes Parent. Such neutralization works only when the listeners divest themselves of all male stereotypes and archetypes so that the word "Parent" does not automatically conjure up a father. Neutral language only works when it doesn't let us hide our still-male imagery behind masks of neutrality. When we say Ruler, we still think King. Neutralizing the words does not always neutralize the effect of centuries of predominant images.

English, being a non-gendered language, is easy to change. We have to be more creative about Hebrew, which, like French and other romance languages, is gendered. Marcia Falk has done groundbreaking work in her *Book of Blessings,* offering a new Hebrew, which speaks not only in a non-gendered way but also in a non-hierarchical way. No longer does she use the "Blessed Art Thou, Lord Our God, King of the Universe" formula; instead she suggests: "We bless the Source of Life." (The word "we" in Hebrew takes neither the male nor the female form, but is a truly "neutral" pronoun.) Rather than God remaining the distant King or becoming a Queen, God becomes the Core of Life, the Fountain of Life, and other more immanent (inner) rather than transcendent (outer) idioms. Her use of language moves the enterprise not only away from gender, but also away from traditional formulations of God as over us, reigning supreme, and demanding our praise.[3]

But neutral language has limitations, because we learn that we are created in God's image, and we ourselves are gendered beings. By degendering God we minimize our own human male and femaleness. We see humanity clearly in God's image when that imagery is both male and female, since we exist as male and female.

And we can add the little bit of female imagery that already exists. For example, God is called the Rock who gives birth (Deuteronomy 32), and in the same chapter the Rock is portrayed as an object of suckling. The prophet Isaiah speaks of God as a mother (Isaiah 42, 49 and 66). Job speaks of God's womb (Job 38).

Do we have to go outside the Torah to find the integration of maleness and femaleness in our description of God, or is there something, either obvious or hidden, in the Torah itself that can lead us in that direction? I find a starting point in the very oldest layers of Judaism and pre-biblical religion. I have to "re-vision" what the Torah had in mind when it shunned the goddess. I want to understand the fear of paganism and yet, in uncovering the layers of symbolism familiar to our ancestors, I try to "remythologize"[4] and create a new Jewish mythos, which includes the feminine aspects along with the masculine aspects of the One God.

II

The Worlds of Your Life:
Where Is Spirituality Found?

Thirsting for God
is our task
in this world.

Quenching that thirst
will be our reward
in the World to Come.

— from *The Empty Chair: Finding Hope and Joy—*
Timeless Wisdom from a Hasidic Master,
Rebbe Nachman of Breslov

Dr. Wayne Dosick, rabbi, is spiritual guide of the Elijah Minyan in San Diego, California, and an adjunct professor of Jewish studies at the University of San Diego. Author of many books on spirituality and living Jewishly, in *Soul Judaism: Dancing with God into a New Era,* Rabbi Dosick teaches us about the God within.

God Within

WAYNE DOSICK

For most of us, the god we met in childhood is "up there" in heaven, while we live "down here" on earth.

Bible stories tell of an all-powerful God looking down from on high. Many prayers, especially in the High Holiday liturgy, create the poetic metaphor of an almighty God sitting on His heavenly throne, meting out Divine reward or punishment to His children who follow or transgress His commands.

For many children, the image of God is of an all-knowing, all-wise old man whose grandfatherly love and compassion hardly mitigates His awesome strength, His untouchable grandeur, and His stern sense of justice.

While God may be addressed through prayer, for most, He seems distant and remote—too far away to ever be close or intimate, too splendiferous to ever be truly approachable.

We grow in education, wisdom, and emotion; we become experienced and worldly wise, sophisticated, and cultured, but many of us never outgrow our childhood notion of God. We still envision old man God "up there" grandly overseeing the universe.

Of course, as it should, our rational intellect soundly rejects this naive, simplistic conception of God. But rather than struggling to redefine God, rather than doing the work to form a realistic, mature, adult relationship with God, many find it easier to just ignore—or reject—God.

But without God we sense something is missing; there is an emptiness, a void in our lives.

We want to know God; we want to be sure that God knows us. We want an ongoing, personal, intimate relationship with God. We want the certitude, the assurance, the inner peace that knowing God brings.

* * * *

The Kabbalists taught that there are ways to lessen the distance between the infinite God and finite human beings. If God is indeed "up there" and we are "down here," then at least we can bridge the gap.

The Kabbalists taught that there are ten emanations or steps—which they called *sefirot*—between God and humankind. Through prayer, contemplation, and meditation, the steps can be climbed in both directions, up from us to God and down from God to us, so that "holy sparks" of God's fiery light and the glint of the Divine within us can touch, and we can meet God in intimate dialogue.

Here is one way to meet God, to bring God into our lives with immediacy, with ever-evolving place and purpose.

Life begins with a cry or perhaps a whimper, the very first breath of earthly existence.

Life ends with a whimper or perhaps a cry, the final breath of earthly being.

From where does that first breath come? To where does that final breath go? And what of all the breaths in between—more than twenty-three thousand every single day?

A modern prayer affirms an eternal truth:

"You send forth Your breath, O God, and we are created. You take away our breath, and we die and return to the dust. We are ever in Your merciful power."

From God. To God.

Breath is the life force, the life energy. Without it, we human beings are no more than a lump of clay, a collection of chemicals worth no more than a few dollars.

But with breath, we are living human beings, precious children of the universe, created in the image of God, just a little lower than the angels.

Every moment, we are just one breath away from the end of our earthly sojourn. Yet how often do we appreciate—how often do we even notice—the life-gift of breath that flows within us?

* * * *

Snorkelers and scuba divers report a greatly heightened awareness of life when hearing their own breathing. Old yoga techniques and modern rebirthing therapies teach concentration on the very act of breathing. Buddhists speak of "mindful" or "conscious" breathing as the most basic practice for touching peace.

Focus on breath is focus on being—on creation and on existence.

The Hebrew word for breath is *ruach,* which is the very same word for spirit.

And to whom does original breath, original spirit, belong? What is the source of breath, of spirit, of life itself?

In its opening sentences, the Bible reports that in the beginning the earth was "unformed and void, with darkness upon the deep; and *ruach Elohim*"—the spirit, the breath of God—"hovered over the water." And then God began to create.

What, then, is the source of creation? *Ruach Elohim,* the spirit, the life-breath of God.

Later on, in the second version of the creation of man, the Bible says, "The Lord God formed man from the dust of the earth, and He blew into his nostrils the breath of life, and man became a living soul" (Genesis 2:7).

Aha! There it is!

The breath of God is the breath, the life force, of human beings.

We exist, we live, we are, because our breath is the breath of God.

Every day we can feel God's intimate presence and can affirm our inseparable intertwined oneness with God.

Every day we can merge our breath with God's, with the life force of the universe. And we can feel God's breath, God's spirit, fill us with life, with energy, with love.

Dr. Neil Gillman, rabbi, is Professor of Jewish Philosophy at The Jewish Theological Seminary in New York, where he has also served as Chair of the Department of Jewish Philosophy and Dean of the Rabbinical School. In *The Way Into Encountering God in Judaism,* Rabbi Gillman teaches us about the sometimes conflicting ways of relating to God.

Seeing the Invisible

NEIL GILLMAN

The notion that all of our talk of God is composed of metaphors created by human beings leads inevitably to the charge that human beings "invent" God. The only appropriate response to this charge is that no, human beings discover God and then invent metaphors to characterize the God they experience. Sometimes the metaphors come first; they make it possible for us to feel God's presence in our lives in certain distinctive ways. However, these metaphors also originate in an act of discovery, a genuine experience of a reality that infinitely transcends us.

How do we know that these experiences are genuine? How do we respond to the charge that these experiences of a God who is "out there" are simply wishes, projections, or illusions? This question touches upon the central issue in the philosophy of religion, an issue that has agitated philosophers for centuries and that is clearly beyond the scope of this inquiry. It must be addressed here in a preliminary way, however.

One way of addressing it is to show that religion is not the only instance in which we speak at great length about realities that are not clearly visible, and that we do so in ways that remain quite indispensable and meaningful. For example, suppose I am sitting next to a clinical psychologist who is observing the behavior of a child through a one-way mirror. Suddenly the psychologist turns to me and exclaims, "Neil, look at this child's ego!"

I look. What do I literally see? A child playing with dolls, blocks, and a tricycle. The psychologist sees all this but also something more—the child's ego, which he clearly admires. Yet, where is this ego? In some sense, it is "in" the child—not as an object like the child's heart or brain, but still very much "within" the child, more as a pattern that suffuses the child and her behavior, the way she plays with her dolls and her tricycle. The child's ego is then both invisible and visible—invisible because it is not explicitly seen, but very much visible to someone who is trained to observe and evaluate human behavior and, most important, to someone who believes that human beings have egos in the first place. Were this psychologist to work with a theory of human behavior that does not include the ego, he would not be looking for an ego and would never see one.

The ego functions within a complex theory that seeks to explain human behavior. Psychologists who accept this theory believe that in order to explain what they do explicitly see—the way human beings behave—they need to construct an inner world that they don't explicitly see but that has to be there. However, no psychologist who works within this theory would deny that there is an "out-thereness" to the ego. None would claim that the ego is a pure fabrication or fiction. Two assumptions are required for seeing the ego: a belief that there is an ego out there to be seen, and that one has been sufficiently well trained in the observation of human behavior to know what to look for when looking for the ego.

Believers in God are like psychologists: they too want to explain what they do explicitly see—in this case the ultimate canvas, the entire complex of nature, history, and human experience viewed as one integrated whole. To explain all this, believers have to posit that beyond what they do see, there is an invisible world that must be there if what they see is to make sense. Part of this invisible world includes a reality they call God.

There is no way of proving objectively and conclusively that God exists. For centuries philosophers have tried to devise such proofs, but with little success. To perceive God, then, one has to (1) want to make sense of the world, (2) believe that this ultimate canvas is in fact one integrated whole, (3) believe that the world does cohere and make sense, and (4) believe that the reason it does cohere—in fact, the very principle of its coherence—is the existence of a reality we call God, and that this God can be "seen" in and through our experience of the world. This God may not be directly seen, but it can be "seen" as the ego is seen by the psychologist. Like the ego, God is not an object but more like a pattern that suffuses all things. Just as the ego is elusive, so is God; that's precisely why we need the range of metaphors to bring this God sharply into our consciousness, just as we use metaphors to bring the ego to life. A friend of mine once referred somewhat disparagingly to a mutual acquaintance of ours as having "the ego of a feather." That metaphor captured him perfectly!

Finally, like the psychologist, the believer must have a certain refinement, some education or training, a knowledge of what to look for. Without this training, all the looking in the world would not help. The entire task of religious education can be summed up this way: it is the attempt to train people to see the world as suffused with the presence of God, just as the psychologist is trained to see the ego in the behavior of a child. Believers, like psychologists, are members of a community that sees the world in a certain way. The community of believers has endured infinitely longer than that of psychologists, and—to use an admittedly pragmatic criterion—their way of seeing the world has worked remarkably well to help people in widely different ages and cultures make sense of the world and of their human experience. That conclusion may not be objectively true, but it is true enough to dispel any notion that God is a total human fabrication. That may be as much "proof" as we can ever attain in this matter.

To answer the question "Who is God?" is to study the twists and turns of the complex metaphorical system that Jews have used to try to make sense of the world and their lives, as this system winds its way through the generations.

Rabbi Lawrence Kushner is Rabbi-in-Residence at Hebrew Union College–Jewish Institute of Religion. He teaches and lectures widely to audiences of all ages, faiths and backgrounds, and has been a frequent commentator on National Public Radio's *All Things Considered*. In *Invisible Lines of Connection: Sacred Stories of the Ordinary*, Rabbi Kushner teaches us how everything "ordinary" is supercharged with meaning—*if* we can see it.

Federal Express

LAWRENCE KUSHNER

One of the last things you get to look at as an author, before your book goes to press, is something called "proofs." They are part of the error-checking mechanism.

Now people in the book business, like people in most businesses, are always looking for ways to make their jobs go quickly. So they often unceremoniously shorten the titles of books to just a word or two. Since the book which I had just finished would have one of the longer titles of any book ever published, it was an easy victim to such abbreviating. The full title was: *God Was in This Place & I, i Did Not Know.* Eleven words, which usually would get abbreviated to simply, "God Was in This Place." On at least one occasion, it has been further distilled by a mailroom clerk to just "God." This is all a roundabout way of explaining how the Federal Express package that arrived at my home from the publisher of the book was labeled, "God Proofs."

My kids, who were home to sign for the package, telephoned me at the office at once to announce—not without some mischievous glee—that what I had been working on and waiting for my whole adult life had just arrived via FedEx.

"It's finally here, Dad. 'God Proofs.'"

"Is there a return address?" I asked, wondering whether heaven had a zip code.

If a proof for God could come in the mail, what would it look like? It would be a book containing all the stories of your life. But because they are all holy stories concealing myriad lights, ordinary words cannot contain them. The stories are necessarily fluid because each new page redefines the meaning of all the previous stories—just as each deed ripples back through all the previous deeds. This is your life.

Dr. Eugene B. Borowitz, rabbi, is the Sigmund L. Falk Distinguished Professor of Education and Jewish Religious Thought at the New York School of Hebrew Union College–Jewish Institute of Religion. In *Broken Tablets: Restoring the Ten Commandments and Ourselves,* edited by Rabbi Rachel S. Mikva, Rabbi Borowitz teaches us how our interactions with the sacred texts serve as conversations with God.

I [Am the One]

EUGENE B. BOROWITZ

Someone is talking to me. I am not standing at Sinai and I hear no voice. All I have is a text, but that turns out to be not as inert as we might think letters on a page or screen are. As long as I can remember, the text has been read, chanted, for my (and others') benefit. Even when I am alone with the text, the voice of the reader/chanter dimly sounds in me, bringing the words to me as a living address. Mostly, I see/hear it in context, embraced in the story of the Jewish people's memory of what happened—and understood by them and me to be most sacred. Even read in utter silence, as happened just a moment ago when I prepared to begin writing these words, it came to me as address. (And were Jewishness not central to my being and were I only another reasonably sensitive participant in Western civilization, the words would still come to me as someone speaking to me.)

Who is talking? As yet, I don't know. Normally I would look to see where the sound is coming from or concentrate on its timber so that the first few syllables of this Hebrew "I" might identify the speaker. But while the very word "I" makes the act of address plain, there is no one to look at and no sound pattern to identify. And in all the times that I have read/heard this text, there has been no vision or sound connected with this "I" that I might now bring to this hearing.

Yet the word, which in its unadorned articulation seems so devoid of content, is, after all, the mysterious distance/nearness I/we share with You.

You—not Moses, not one of the other prophets—You Yourself speak. You present Yourself to me and to us, momentarily making the Far-Off-One the Here-Near-One, approaching as close as our retinas or eardrums. To have been so visited, even if only in paltry recapitulation, dignifies us unalienably.

You tell us Your name, and by it we come close enough to glimpse who You are and are thereby debarred from ever presuming to call you by it. We mean to cherish Your name by avoiding it, by calling You other things instead, none of them unproblematic. Our oldest euphemism, "Lord," now distorts our sense of nearness to You and is too gender-heavy to reflect the breadth of experience with You. Those today whose self-confidence disdains these old bounds and who assert their intimacy with ultimacy by readily calling You by name are nonetheless guessing how to pronounce it as, tradition says, the High Priest did each year in ancient Jerusalem. Yet just when the climactic moment of utterance came on Yom Kippur day, the Levite choirs increased their volume so no distinct sound could be heard. Nonetheless, the very notion that the High Priest was calling You by name shook us enough that everyone in the Temple threw themselves to the ground before You.

Though we are confined to English, Your name still puzzles and dazzles us. No hint of the sacred four Hebrew consonants is found in the Indo-European root *gheu* (to call, invoke) from which our Germanic-English "God" derives and it surely is more an abstraction than a proper name. Nonetheless, some today reflect their Hebraic awe in their English usage. Reverence for God suggests not fully spelling out the word, so "G-d" or "Gd" become distinctive signs of North American Jewish piety. With disrespect for God rife, believers can well cherish these signs of honest concern. Yet as with so many symbols, a shadow cannot be avoided. Deforming Your title/name seems a curious act of demonstrating regard for You. Does the *yetser hara* (the evil inclination, which is always in tension with our inclination for good) of otherwise inadmissible doubt here subtly infiltrate piety, and in every repetition do to "God" what the Rabbis said to do to idols so that, once they are defaced, statues might no longer be offensive to the Jewish soul?

"I, *ADONAI* YOUR GOD…"

"My" God? Surely *Adonai* is God of everyone and everything. Why then this surprising singular: "thy God"? Why this personal address to me—or not to me or any other individual, but to the people? Your reach here is clearly corporate, communal, national, but in all these Words, You address me/us individually. In pre-enlightenment days and certainly back in Bible times, people did not suffer from today's fearsome gap between the self-legislating I and its society. Rather the self and its group so imperceptibly merged into one another that modern scholars must speculate whether the biblical poet's "I" refers to a person, the nation, or, more likely, both at once in shifting emphasis. So by meaning me, you mean all the children of the covenant, each one preciously an individual to You.

Nonetheless, the singular "thy" comes as a two-fold imperative. The nation, in responding to *Adonai,* must not forget the supreme value of the single self. Only as individuals one by one, doing what *Adonai* requires of Israel, can the nation fulfill its covenantal responsibility. I must not forget that though the Jewish people has an existence independent of me, until I (and other individual Jews) carry out the commandments incumbent upon me (us) as one of all-Israel, it cannot be the Jewish people God is calling it to be. And that begins with knowing that *Adonai* is "my" God in a most personal and intimate way. Temperament, training, soul, experience, endowment—all mix to make me just who I am and the way I go about being/becoming me. You ask me, *Adonai,* by addressing me personally, to fulfill the common duty of all-Israel as just the me I am—that is, in terms of my unique self. To be sure, I speak here with some hesitation, knowing how much I have been affected by the special prominence modernity has given to the self. Yet our people has long cherished the many individualists and idiosyncratics who served You over its centuries, and it has lovingly transmitted their stories to us. I/we respond to Your evocative address to the nation as a collection of single selves by carrying on our uncommon Jewish blend of individualism and corporate concern.

"I, *ADONAI* YOUR GOD, [AM THE ONE] WHO…"

The English translation has now betrayed me badly enough that I must intrude upon its flow with bracketed words. Already in my problems rendering the sense of the previous Hebrew word, *Elohecha* (your God), the non-Hebraic soul of the English language made itself felt. Its "your" might well suggest a Hebraic ambiguity of singular or plural address. So I had recourse to the archaic "thy" to make the singularity of the Hebrew fully evident. Were it not for the Hebrew *asher*, which here means "who," the translation might have proceeded as the Hebrew does, without introducing a verb speaking of existence, "am."

What shall we make of the fact that, compared to Western languages, Hebrew seems to take existence for granted—or at least does not often see the need to introduce words to refer to being? Shall we say that existence does not seem so remarkable to the Hebrews that they find it worth mentioning? Or is it the opposite: Non-being is so contrary to their way of facing reality that the wonder of existence becomes almost as ineffable as God? Whatever the case, without *asher* I could have rendered the text without an interpolation this way: I, *Adonai* your God, brought you out of the land of Egypt, from a slavehouse. But by saying *asher*, the text stresses the connection between "I, *Adonai* your God" and "brought you out…" requiring something like my "[am the one]" to render its sense in English.

Shall I now simply pass over the fact that I have added some words to the Ten that the Torah declares God said directly to the people of Israel at Sinai? At least I have called my act to your attention, inviting you to join me in wondering about how much else I, in my

English-shaped thinking about Judaism, have reconfigured its message while transmitting it. Or should we be consoled that there has never been a moment when the Hebrew language stood still long enough to equip its words with some kind of prime, pure, essential meaning? Does not the biblical record show and our linguistic experience affirm that words and their combinations never fix into one perfect meaning that all else adulterates? Meaning abides in these shifting connotations in as obvious and mysterious a way as I remain me while going through the passages of my life. In translation as in life, we can only strive for ever greater integrity.

"I, *ADONAI* YOUR GOD, [AM THE ONE] WHO BROUGHT YOU OUT..."

Of course You did. But I mean no disrespect by quietly remembering that if I hadn't walked on my own two feet I might still be in the land of Goshen. And, while the text doesn't make much of the minutiae of the journeying—relying, I assume, on our great Jewish talent for complaining—it isn't difficult to imagine what daily activity was like when Your cloud lifted, signaling that we were to fold up our tents, repack the goods, get the family together, find our place in the march, and start another trudge. The daily mood, I would guess, was less the high that accompanied Your constant presence than the tedium of one foot after another and the hope against hope that today the ever-lurking problems wouldn't surface and further complicate our lives.

That recital in no way mitigates the wonder You did. Whenever we could lift our spirits so weighed down by each day's demands, we knew we could never have gotten out of Egypt solely on our own. It was as mighty an empire as the world had ever known. Why should they lose all our slave power so necessary for their awe-inspiring, slave-killing projects? Moses' charisma and group cohesion wouldn't have kept us going for very long. No wonder historians, pointing to the absence of confirming external evidence, have argued that although the exodus story is a marvelous national saga, it never happened: "History" doesn't work that way, at least not if you abide by the secular conventions of the academy that rule God out of their kind of "history." Our people, impressed by the continual improbabilities of what has happened to us over the centuries—not the least being that, against all odds, we are still around—knows that again and again God has showed up and, one way or another, brought us out. Not without our putting one foot in front of another, to be sure. Partnership, not unilateral action, has been our sense of God as taker-out but with no confusion over who was the Senior Partner in the process.

Not all the great faiths that call You "one" proclaim You, as do we, Bringer-out. They apparently believe that to involve You in history this way is to compromise Your purity or the fullness of Your being. We, who identify You not only as creator but as the one who called creation "good"—though flawed since the primal parents were chased out of Eden—know You only as the participating One. To us, one sign of Your greatness is that You are involved with us (and others) and by such interaction do not compromise Your superlative status. As the daily prayer epitomizes You: *Melech-ozer-umoshia-umagen* (King-helper-and saver-and shielder). The very one who is Most High is also the one who bends down low, not one without the other. And because You continue to be Bringer-out, we are a hoping people.

Not unproblematically so. If Your greatness rendered You neutral toward us, we would not have the problem of evil. Why should a universe indifferent to us not occasionally (or more often) erupt into evil? Why expect anything else? Our spirituality begins with wonder at how beneficent we find creation—that is, when we stop taking it for granted (as if there were no Grantor). That is particularly true when, after some depressing personal situation or historical calamity, Your help has brought us out once again. More than a hundred Jewish generations have wondered why You do not intervene more often or more quickly, how You can let the people of Israel suffer long years of Egyptian slavery before bringing them out. And the last couple of generations have brought us a new level of anguish over Your inscrutable time schedule. Yet we have also seen incomparable evidences of Your saving hand, though they cannot be said—vile thought—to compensate for the suffering that preceded them. A generation back some said You were dead, a curiously dated notion now that says more about human conceit than about Your reality. We, a generation seeking Your nearness, are more apt to pray that You heal our sick than that You explain clearly to us just who You are and why You act as You do.

"I, *ADONAI* YOUR GOD, [AM THE ONE] WHO BROUGHT YOU OUT OF THE LAND OF EGYPT, FROM A SLAVEHOUSE."

If You had only brought us out of the land of Egypt, *Dayenu* ("It would be sufficient for us," a recurring refrain in the Passover Haggadah's litany of God's blessings). Despite its plentiful leeks and cucumbers, its advanced culture and international status, Egypt was also where rulers were gods and idols were as much animal as human. At least the statues did not have the fallibility that made the Pharaohs' claims to divinity unbelievable, at least to the children of the children of Jacob, Leah, Rachel, Bilhah, and Zilpah. In such a country, to be created in the image of gods or to seek to imitate them could not lead to the society the Torah would envision and the Hebrews seek to establish. *Dayenu.*

Worse, Egypt was a slavehouse, literally the place where we were not free. Figuratively, it was a land where the Jewish spirit could not find itself. Literal slavery is not to be underestimated just because we no longer have enough of it in our world so that we have personal experience of slaves and slavery. The Torah, written for a world that took slavery as a human necessity, insisted that Jewish slavery must be limited to six years and extended only if the slave wished to stay with the master. Nonetheless, the Rabbis must have found even that institution sufficiently uncongenial since, while not abolishing Jewish slavery, they added severe restrictions on what the slave holder might do. It took a long time for economic reality to reflect religious idealism in this realm, but the outrage we feel when evidence comes to light of people anywhere who have, in effect, enslaved others is a testimony to what God began by bringing us out from Egypt. *Dayenu.*

But release from a slavehouse has its greatest effect on us today as a compelling metaphor for anything that releases us from any of the many bondages that impede our acting in proper freedom. The inescapable contemporary model of that exodus is what happened to our families as they went from the ghetto to emancipation. So when we now move from despotism to democracy, from ignorance to knowledge, from unemployment to a job, from discrimination to equality, from illness to health, from neurosis to maturity, from depression to hope, we know our lives have been touched by that same elemental force that so powerfully made its impact on our ex-slave forebears. And it is because God has not yet concluded all the taking out that humankind needs that we can believe that the long-ago promised days of sitting under vine and fig tree with none to make us afraid will one day come. And only when the great shofar sounds will we all be able to say the full, final, *Dayenu.*

"I, *ADONAI* YOUR GOD, [AM THE ONE] WHO BROUGHT YOU OUT OF THE LAND OF EGYPT, FROM A SLAVEHOUSE. YOU MUST NOT..."

Ah. So that is why.

Rabbi Miriam Carey Berkowitz is assistant rabbi at the Park Avenue Synagogue in Manhattan. In *The Women's Torah Commentary: New Insights from Women Rabbis on the 54 Weekly Torah Portions*, edited by Rabbi Elyse Goldstein, Rabbi Berkowitz teaches us about the relationship of women and the covenant.

Nitzavim: נצבים
Women and the Covenant

MIRIAM CAREY BERKOWITZ

> You are standing this day, all of you, before the Lord your God:
> your heads, your tribes, your elders and your officers, all the men
> of Israel, your little ones, your wives [or, "women folk"], and the
> stranger who is in the midst of your camp.
>
> *(Deuteronomy 29:9–10)*

After forty years of leading the Jewish people through the desert, Moses prepares them to enter the land of Israel, where, he hopes, they will become a proud people in their own land. It is not enough to be independent, though. Moses wants the people to be faithful to God, living according to the guidelines of the Torah. He wants them to affirm the covenant that God presented to them at Sinai, the covenant that they accepted with the words "All that the Lord has spoken, we will do" (Exod. 19:8).

What exactly is a "covenant"? What does it ask, and what does it promise in return? How do Jewish women in particular fit into the covenant set forth in *Parashat Nitzavim*? According to Anita Diamant, *Brit*, the Hebrew word for covenant, is the way Jews describe and define their relationship to God. A covenant is a contract—an agreement between responsible parties, a two-way street.

According to tradition, the document that spells out the rights and responsibilities for both sides in this agreement between God and the Jewish people is the Torah—the first five books of the Bible.[1]

Diamant enumerates four types of covenant found in the Torah: the rainbow, Shabbat, *milah* (circumcision), and the Torah itself. Are they separate covenants, or all part of the same encompassing pledge? And what are the repercussions for Jewish women today?

The covenant of Noah extends to all peoples, indeed to all living things. In the story of Noah, God promises never again to destroy the earth by flood. The rainbow is given as a sign of this pledge. God establishes this covenant "with you [Noah] and your offspring to come...and with every living thing on earth" (Gen. 9:9–10).

The covenant of circumcision, also called "the covenant of Abraham," is, of course, limited to male Jews—boys, who are circumcised, and their fathers, whose obligation it is to see that the mitzvah is done. Not only are girls spared any physical sign of entry into this covenant, mothers are not even commanded to have their sons circumcised. If for some reason a father is not available, the duty for making sure that the baby boy is circumcised passes to the *bet din*, the rabbinic court. Thus, women are not implicated in the covenant of Abraham in any way.[2]

The Sabbath, a covenant of cosmic significance, does address all Jews: "The people of Israel shall keep Shabbat, observing Shabbat throughout the generations as a covenant for all time. It shall be a sign forever between Me and the people of Israel, for in six days God made heaven and earth, and on the seventh day God rested and was refreshed" (Exod. 31:16–17). It seems clear from the context that, unlike circumcision, Shabbat is intended as a gift and responsibility for all Jews. Furthermore, the rabbis specify in the Talmud that women are obligated in all aspects of the Shabbat (see Babylonian Talmud, *Shavuot* 20b).

What of the covenant of Torah, the pact that demands the most of its parties, while promising God's protection and love in return? The covenant of Torah, which begins with the dramatic Sinai experience and is cemented in *Parashat Nitzavim,* once more affirms, despite mild ambiguity, God's commitment to the entire Jewish people and urges them all to accept the demands of the Torah, our side of the agreement.

At Sinai, the content of the covenant is inclusive, according to both Torah context and later rabbinic interpretation. God calls to Moses, saying,

> Thus shall you say to the house of Jacob and declare to the people of Israel: "You have seen what I did to the Egyptians, how I bore you on eagles' wings and brought you to me. Now then, if you will obey Me faithfully and keep my covenant, you shall be my treasured possession among all peoples. Indeed, all the earth is mine, but you shall be to me a kingdom of priests and a holy nation."
>
> *(Exod. 19:3–6)*

The rabbis interpret "the house of Jacob" as referring to the women, who not only receive the Torah but also learn it *before* the men, "the people of Israel" (Rashi on Exod. 19:3). Thus, in the rabbinic interpretation, not only are the women mentioned, they are mentioned first, because the women typically would be the ones to pass on Torah to the children, ensuring continuity of the heritage and the laws. We do not need commentary, however, to tell us that a pact made to safeguard the values, laws, calendar, and daily practices of a people necessitates involvement of all its members. Thus, the covenantal act, the promises and demands God makes to and of the people, encompasses the entire nation.

In *Parashat Nitzavim,* women's status is not quite so clear-cut, but the case still stands for women's inclusion in the covenant of Torah. Moses does speak specifically to the men: "You are standing this day all of you before the Lord your God: your heads, your tribes, your elders and your officers, all the men of Israel, your little ones, your wives [or, "women folk"], and the stranger who is in the midst of your camp" (Deut. 29:9–10). The women are portrayed as relational to the men, and, if anything is to be made of the order of listing, second to the bottom in the hierarchy. Women come after the children, above only the strangers. But women are clearly enumerated among those "standing this day." While referred to as adjuncts of their husbands (or fathers)—the common view of women in any patriarchal society—the women are definitely present and accounted for. The content of the message is unequivocal:

> [Y]ou should enter into the covenant of the Lord, and into the oath, which the Lord your God makes with you today, that God may establish you today as a people, and that the Lord may be to you as a God, as sworn to you and to your fathers, to Abraham, to Isaac, and to Jacob. I make this covenant, with its sanctions, not with you alone, but both with those who are standing here this day before the Lord our God and with those who are not with us here this day.
>
> *(Deut. 29:11–14)*

The covenant extends throughout time to men, women, and children in every generation; to those born Jewish and to those who will become Jewish; to those who stood at Sinai and to those for whom Sinai is but a distant collective memory. It is a demanding idea, but an embracing one.

What are the implications of being included in the covenant with God, of being bound by our ancestors' decision that fateful day four thousand years ago to say, "Yes, we will be your people"? Covenant enjoins with it responsibilities as well as rights. "I command you this day to love the Lord your God, to walk in God's ways, to keep God's commandments, statutes, and ordinances" (Deut. 30:16). Being covenanted means reaching out to grasp the Torah and incorporating it into your life.

Today, many women are embracing the "women's mitzvot," such as making Shabbat in the home, raising and educating children, and immersing in the natural waters of the *mikveh*. Other women are drawn to the more public roles that were once reserved for men: praying in a *minyan*, taking on the obligation of *tallit* and *tefillin*, becoming rabbis, cantors, and community leaders. Still others focus on the "mainstream mitzvot": keeping kosher, observing Shabbat and festivals, avoiding gossip *(lashon hara)*, giving *tzedakah* (financial contributions).

In our time, more and more women are taking their places in the covenantal community by studying Torah, in the hope that learning will lead to action, but also for its own sake *(lishmah)*. Whether it be in small groups of women teaching women in private homes, in mixed *yeshivot* or university classrooms, on rural retreats, in Israel or in their local synagogues or community centers, studying Torah and passing on this pillar of Judaism ensures that our participation in the covenantal relationship with God will be not only de jure, by right, but de facto, in fact—proved and sustained by our actions.

Now that many women have opportunities to study Torah, those opportunities must be seized and cherished. *Parashat Nitzavim* brings home this point forcefully. Moses summarizes his message to the people:

> For this commandment that I command you this day, it is not too hard for you, neither is it far off. It is not in heaven, that you should say, "Who shall go up for us to heaven and bring it to us, and make us hear it, that we may do it?" Neither is it beyond the sea, that you should say, "Who shall go over the sea for us and bring it to us and make us hear it, that we may do it?" But the word is very near to you, in your mouth and in your heart, that you may do it.
>
> *(Deut. 30:11–14)*[3]

Moses encourages even as he challenges. Only when a Jew takes the initiative to participate in the commandments and to learn does he or she become an active, deserving member of the covenant. The choice is up to her or him to make.

Our *parashah* opens with, "You are standing this day, *nitzavim* [inclusive plural, "all of you"], before the Lord your God" (Deut. 29:9). What clues does the word *nitzavim* give us about the essence of the people's attitude as they stood in preparation to hear Moses' parting words? An intratextual answer (from elsewhere within the Torah) proves fascinating.

When Miriam stood by the river to see what would become of her baby brother, Moses, the Torah says, "*vatetatzav* Miriam" (Exod. 2:4). J. H. Hertz comments that this means Miriam not just "stood by" but "took her stand."[4] *Vatetatzav* and *nitzavim* share the root *y-tz-v*, meaning "firmly planted, unshakeable, committed." This commitment of striving to forge a relationship with God, revere the world that God created, and learn about, internalize, and pass on Jewish ways of life is especially important to people who do not have a physical sign in their skin to remind them every day of their covenant. But by seeing ourselves as *nitzavot* (feminine plural), standing and firmly planted, eager, brave and proud before God, Jewish women can bring to life the spiritual covenant that, introduced at Sinai and reaffirmed in *Parashat Nitzavim,* has been engraved not physically, but metaphorically, on our hearts.

Rabbi Lawrence Kushner is Rabbi-in-Residence at Hebrew Union College–Jewish Institute of Religion. He teaches and lectures widely to audiences of all ages, faiths and backgrounds, and has been a frequent commentator on National Public Radio's *All Things Considered*. In *God Was in This Place & I, i Did Not Know: Finding Self, Spirituality and Ultimate Meaning*, Rabbi Kushner teaches us about the inspiring interpretations of Jacob's dream in Genesis.

Two Universes

LAWRENCE KUSHNER

"Once you acknowledge that bad things happen and that people do evil things, there are only two options," said Hannah Rachel, "Satan and God." She took a handful of pebbles and dropped them in two small piles before him. "Alternate worlds. In every way except one, these worlds of strewn pebbles are identical. In both worlds the sun shines, people make love, children play and people do astonishingly terrible things.

"In one universe, people maintain their 'selves,' their sanity, and God by giving evil its independence. Such wickedness, they reason, could not possibly have anything to do with God. There must be some other non-God power that makes it real and gives it vitality, and with whom God is in eternal conflict. In such a universe, where the source of evil is other than God, sooner or later, one way or another, you wind up with some kind of demonic force, *sitra achra*, Other Side, devil, or Satan.

"In the second world, God is somehow part of the evil, present even in its depths. This is the meaning of our assertion that 'God is One.'[1] A Oneness at the core of all being in whom everything—yes, even evil—ultimately converges. The source of all reality. If God is the source of all being and human evil is real, then God therefore must be in it also. The evil does not derive its being from some extra-Divine source. This is certainly what Job learns when God speaks to him from out of the whirlwind.[2] God does not cause, tolerate, or even forebear the evil, but God, as with everything else in creation, is in it."

IT'S ALL GOD

And if God is everywhere, God is also in the perverse things we plan and even carry out. To be sure, God is less evident and less accessible than in acts of kindness, for example, but in them nevertheless. In the words of Rabbi Tsadok Hakohen, a student of the school of Mordecai Yosef of Ishbitz, "God is present even in our sins." And rejecting our sins only postpones the ultimate task of healing and self-unification. Such an acceptance of all of our selves is another way of finding God. Dr. David Blumenthal of Emory University offers a similar teaching.

Evil, in its most profound sense, is contingent upon God for its very existence. There would be no shells [or, shards] if there were no sparks.... God is everywhere, even in the impulse to rebel against God. Reality is one. At this point, evil ceases to be grasped as an independent seductive force; it collapses ontologically and falls by the wayside psychologically. One's consciousness is, rather, filled with God.[3]

Aryeh Kaplan, the contemporary philosopher, explains it thus:

The Baal Shem Tov taught that God is actually hidden within all evil and suffering, but that God only hides when people do not realize that God is there.... Ultimately, there is no barrier between God and people except that of our own making, and if one succeeds in removing this barrier, then all evil is revealed to be an illusion.[4]

TALKING TO THE OCEAN

"Think of it this way," explained the Maid of Ludomir. "If the world is covered by an ocean, the ocean naturally would be implicated in everything that happened. But we would not blame the ocean for its currents, its waves, or its storms. The ocean simply is. In much the same way God's ubiquity does not mean that God is therefore in the business of causing, intending, or even tolerating human misery. Correcting those things is the business of human beings. That is why God made human beings in the first place."

"But can you talk to the ocean?" Jacob objected. "Can you have a personal relationship with it? Can you pray to it?"

"Of course you can. Anyone who has been near, in or on the sea knows that it can be addressed. But it does not answer, at least not in words that could be played back on a tape recorder."

"Still I wish it could speak in words like my father or my mother used to speak."

But even if God did—and we have a tradition that God's voice at Sinai was the voice of each person's parents—it is not the audible words themselves we crave. The content, the inflection, the sound of the voice—they all pale in comparison to the loving presence of the Holy One.

Dr. Daniel C. Matt is currently composing an annotated English translation of the *Zohar*. He was formerly a professor of Jewish spirituality at the Graduate Theological Union in Berkeley, California. In *God & the Big Bang: Discovering Harmony Between Science & Spirituality*, Dr. Matt teaches us about the sense of wonder and oneness that connects us with the universe and with God.

The Spice of Desire

DANIEL C. MATT

Yatsar means "to form or fashion"; *yetser* means "that which is formed or fashioned" in the mind. In other words, it is imagination, which is neither inherently good or evil, *tov* or *ra*, though it can be utilized in either way. In fact, in some Talmudic and midrashic passages *yetser ha-ra*, "the evil inclination," is seen positively: "'God saw everything that He had made, and behold, it was very good.' This refers to *yetser ha-ra*. But is *yetser ha-ra* very good? Yes. Were it not for *yetser ha-ra*, a man would never build a house, marry a wife, have children or engage in business."

Here *yetser ha-ra* is roughly the libido, expressing itself as desire, passion and ambition, all of which can create as well as destroy. In the words of an anonymous Talmudic sage, "Whoever is greater than another has a greater *yetser*." The challenge, as the Mishnah indicates, is to serve God not only with the good *yetser*, but with the evil one as well. Only in this way is God served "with all your heart." What this means is not spelled out. Presumably, simply rejecting the evil impulse is not the right approach. We must also try to transform evil into good. This is dangerous, of course, because in attempting such a transformation we may fail and succumb to the evil. Yet within our individual darkness lies an energy yearning to express itself, a spark of life. The libido can be channeled into creativity. As an eighteenth-century preacher said, "*Yetser ha-ra* is like fertilizer for the soul. As manure fertilizes the field, improving its produce, so the fruit of the *tsaddiq* [the righteous person], that is, *mitzvot*, are improved by *yetser ha-ra*. This accords with the well-known principle: 'with all your heart: with both your inclinations.'"

Without passion, life is flat, bland, static. The spiritual path involves more than merely obeying written commands. Genuine spirituality is vibrant. By drawing on the depths of one's being, even *yetser ha-ra* can become an essential ingredient of holiness. This radical recipe for a good life appears in a Hasidic interpretation of a passage from the Talmud: "The blessed holy One said to Israel, 'My children, I have created *yetser ha-ra,* and I have created Torah as its spice.'" The "spice" is an antidote to the poisonous effects of *yetser ha-ra*. But this utilitarian explanation is ignored in the Hasidic reading of the passage, which focuses on the relation between the spice and the main course: "The metaphor does not fit! Spice is added to meat, and the meat is the main dish, not the spice. Yet here God says that Torah is the spice! And so it is: *Yetser ha-ra* is the main thing. One has to serve God with the ecstasy drawn from *yetser ha-ra*."

The ecstasy of *yetser ha-ra* is wild and dangerous, yet indispensable. Constantly keeping it under control is one way to avoid evil, but the price of doing this is repression. Incorporating the *yetser* into our own halakhah means that the path we walk may become slippery. To the Hasidic master Nahman of Bratslav, the world is a narrow bridge and while we are on it "the most important thing is not to fear at all." Trying to transform *yetser ha-ra* makes the way even more perilous, like a tightrope. Here every step is a risk, and the first rule is not to lose one's balance.

The main component of *yetser ha-ra* is desire. Desire is not inherently bad; as we have seen, it has a positive function. The Midrash, in fact, mentions a special angel "in charge of desire." Desire keeps us alive. Hunger lets us know that we need to eat. The sexual drive ensures propagation of the species. The problem arises when desire for *more*—more material things, money, sex, food, attention, status—

becomes an end in itself. By fixating on desiring more, we prevent ourselves from enjoying what we already have and who we are right now. The insatiable desire that takes over becomes *yetser ha-ra.*

Since such desire can never be completely fulfilled, it leads inevitably to suffering and neurosis. But by realizing how enslaved we are to desire, we can identify our neuroses: the psychic strategies we have invented to excel in the game of desire. We encounter negative habit patterns and the dark sides of our personalities. Transformation begins when, instead of denying or rationalizing our neurotic behavior, we face it openly and with ruthless compassion. By stepping back and observing the tenaciousness of *yetser ha-ra,* we can loosen its hold on us. Examine it in the light of consciousness and it provides raw material for new growth; it turns from tyrant to teacher. "Who is wise?" asks the Mishnah. "One who learns from everyone." To which Hasidism adds, "Even from *yetser ha-ra.*"

Dr. Kerry M. Olitzky, rabbi, is executive director of the Jewish Outreach Institute, and was National Dean of Adult Jewish Learning and Living at Hebrew Union College–Jewish Institute of Religion. He is the author of many books that bring the Jewish wisdom tradition into everyday life. In *Jewish Paths toward Healing and Wholeness: A Personal Guide to Dealing with Suffering,* Rabbi Olitzky teaches us how the healing of the soul is an indispensable counterpart to the curing of the body.

The Meaning of Illness and Healing in Jewish Tradition

KERRY M. OLITZKY

Judaism seeks to find meaning for our lives in every human encounter, for Judaism is more of a religion of this world than it is a religion of the next. And Jewish spirituality is a spirituality of the mundane as much as it is of the transcendent. Thus, it is not surprising to find that Jews look to illness as a spiritual teacher rather than relegating it exclusively to a challenge of the body that needs to be beaten and overcome. Judaism teaches that we should embrace illness as part of who we are because it is an integral part of the world in which we live. As a result, I believe that Judaism teaches us that one spiritually suffers through illness only when one cannot find meaning in it. This is an essential message that emerges from the Jewish path toward healing. It is also the lesson that is at the heart of the book of Job. It is not merely that Job underwent trauma and tragedy; rather, it is that Job suffers for no reason. Or worse, Job suffered because he became a pawn in the game played between God and evil. This is what has troubled people for centuries. His illness had no meaning, no redeeming value to it. That is why he suffered—and we along with him. When we can find meaning in our illness, suffering is overshadowed and we are in a better position to find spiritual healing at the same time.

There are those who understand illness as punishment for one's sins. Others see illness simply as a mystery, one that, like God, is beyond human comprehension. Illness just seems to be a part of life's process, an inevitable part of living. We move between sickness and health throughout our lives. Writer Paul Cowan, who chronicled his struggle with leukemia in *The Village Voice* (1988), put it this way: "We are all going to enter the land of the sick at one time in our lives. The question is only when."

The world's population is not divided into people who are ill and people who are not. Rather, like most other aspects of our lives, we spend most of the time in the middle of the continuum and only deceive ourselves into believing that we are more fully on one side of the midpoint than the other. The goal of the healing process is to return to the center, rather than move fully over to one side, for that would not be in accord with human experience. Through the process of healing, one is brought back from the extremes and gains the feeling of being centered once again.

THE HUMAN DIMENSION

For me, the actual experience of illness is more important than is any theoretical construct in Judaism. The reality of illness undervalues any attempt to trace an understanding of illness in the history of Jewish thought; it's the human dimension that truly matters. However, I feel compelled to confront God as the source of suffering in a theoretical framework of a sound theological system. If I acknowledge God as the source of all life as I do, because of my faith, which has been bolstered by my direct experience with healing, I am more inclined to engage God as a healer rather than try to trace the root of anyone's illness necessarily to God. One seems almost irrelevant in the face of the other. The psalmist helps me here when teaching: "God forgives all your sins; God heals all your sicknesses" (Psalms 103:3). Thus, regardless of one's perspective on the cause of illness, the divine source for potential healing remains the same. Perhaps it does not really matter how classical Judaism or its pivotal thinkers look at illness. Instead, what is important is how Judaism considers the individual who is ill—and then helps him or her to galvanize resources to ameliorate the suffering.

THE BRIDGE BETWEEN
THE BODY AND THE SOUL

When you are seriously ill, few things really matter. Issues that may have seemed so important only days or weeks before hold little value at all. The only topics that become relevant are those forces that will drive the patient toward healing, a foundation of family love, and a new-found respect for transcendent values. On the other hand, the simple pleasures of daily life and its small details take on enormous proportions, even those that may have seemed trivial in the past. Getting up each morning, though sometimes in itself a challenge, is an affirmation of the rabbinic teaching that we are reborn each day. Activities in our daily routines, categorized in the daily blessings of the morning worship service, now carry profound significance. Each breath we take, the liquids we drink, the food we eat: Each sip or mouthful is filled with blessing. This is especially true for things that we suddenly cannot do for ourselves. People and relationships take on a new level of meaning. Values that transcend time and place become central. While our focus may be on the body, at the same time the world of the spirit dwarfs the material world.

For the first time perhaps, the prayer *Asher yatzar*, which is traditionally said shortly after rising each morning and performing our normal routines of bodily function, provides us with incredible insight about our bodies and souls. In the prayer, we marvel at the mechanical functioning of our bodies, something we might previously have taken for granted. Most prayer books attempt to translate the core elements of the prayer rather creatively, using phrases like "intricate network of finely tuned organs and orifices" for *"nikavim nikavim chalulim chalulim."* I prefer the Hebrew to speak for itself—"holes, holes, tubes, tubes." It presents the reality of bodily function in the most basic way. When they are not functioning correctly, we feel clogged, bloated, indeed unable to stand before God. The *Asher yatzar* is followed by an acknowledgment of the unique nature of our souls in the *Elohai neshama*. This prayer affirms our belief in the purity of our souls and its source in God. While some may want to separate our bodies from our souls to make a distinction between our mortal bodies and our immortal spirits, this is not the Jewish way. We are our bodies in a measure equal to our souls. Our entire self is created in God's image: *b'tzelem Elohim*. As the liturgist eloquently stated, "The soul is yours and the body is your handiwork." These two prayers are joined together in the morning liturgy, connected by a short prayer directing us to study Torah, for it is in the study of Torah that we come to understand the relationship between body and soul. In the liturgy for *selichot,* the penitential prayers that precede Rosh Hashanah, we add this sentiment, "Have compassion on your handiwork."

Spirit is the bridge between mind and body that makes us human. As a result of our illness, we may not be able to stand upright to praise God—or to do anything else. Because of the heavy burden that a serious illness lays upon us, we may not even have the desire to stand upright, and we may resist praising God even when we are able to. However, the daily recitation of these prayers helps pave a path toward healing. It offers a prism through which to view our entire day and forces us to assume a posture that might otherwise be overlooked in our quest for healing—the alliance between the body and the soul. I find these moments in the morning when I stand alone with God to say my morning prayers to be among the most powerful of the day, much more significant than the afternoon or evening service, or even the proclamation of *Shema Yisrael* before lying down to go to sleep.

Jewish tradition understands feelings of resentment, as well. We are beckoned to take solace from what our ancestors taught us from their desert experience. The shards of the broken tablets were carried along with the unbroken ones in the ark of the covenant because God allows for a shattered world and for a people who are cracked, broken, and scared. But God also insists on going forward, continuing with what is broken and what is whole. Rabbi Rachel Sabath, a colleague of mine with whom I have taught spiritual texts, suggests that from this experience, we can learn to hold gently those broken parts of ourselves and others so that healing and renewed trust can be established, for it is trust that is broken when we are ill. When trust is shattered, not only is the relationship between the individual and God broken, but the hearts of the individuals involved are also shattered. How can one heal? Trust does not emerge on its own; it has to be built and rebuilt. As the psalms teach, "God is the healer of broken hearts."

Tamara Green, an active founding member of the National Center for Jewish Healing and someone who struggles with her body each day, offers her insight: "There must have been at Sinai some children of Israel who, like me, were physically broken and saw themselves as I did in those broken fragments of the covenant." She may not be able to find a way to mend her broken body—just as mystics understand that the shards of the broken world cannot be gathered together to recreate the world—but, she says, "I can gather up the scattered light." With that light, she can be healed. Even as our bodies are ill, we can acknowledge the transcendent nature of our souls, and the light to find our path in the world.

THE PROCESS OF ILLNESS

While there are those whose experience with illness might suggest the sentiment that "One day I was fine and the next day I was sick," illness almost always includes a downward spiral that extends over time. Jon, a good friend of mine, told me recently that he was feeling well when he suddenly found out that he had cancer. Upon reflection, he began to realize that he had not been feeling well over the previous few months. That's what drove him to the doctor for a "routine check-up." Just as one does not suddenly awaken old, generally one does not suddenly wake up sick. It is the physician's label of illness that typecasts us so abruptly. However, the physician's words are only a description of symptoms. They do not change who you were prior to the diagnosis. We often have taken neither our bodily cues nor the spiritual cues of our souls seriously. We ignore them, and at some point, the illness becomes impatient and takes control. Often it goes like this: A lack of spiritual light (or awareness) brings on sickness. This sickness presents itself physically in what might be described as, and often actually is, a blockage. In turn, this physical blockage causes spiritual blockage. It is this spiritual blockage that prevents the individual from receiving God's light.

To break this debilitating cycle and find healing, the healer—and often that healer is one's self—must find a way to free the entrapped spiritual powers in order to access God's divine light and its inherent healing. As a physician and rabbi, the Rambam, Moses Maimonides, understood this: "Physical health is a prerequisite for spiritual health, but a healthy body does not in itself produce a healthy spirit" (*Hilkhot Deot* 4:1). The Baal Shem Tov, founder of Hasidism, put it similarly, adding another element: "When a person is sick, his soul may also be weakened and therefore he cannot pray properly, despite the fact that he may be free of sin. Therefore a person must take care of his physical health" (Keter Shem Tov #231). The Torah agrees: "Take care of yourself and treat your soul diligently" (Deuteronomy 4:9).

Whenever I counsel people, I often ask them to retrace their lives during the weeks and months before the manifestation of their illness. As these stories unfold, I often detect a common theme. I can usually even identify some of the elements with them that presage this illness through a series of questions, and these become cues for getting them back on the path toward healing. When relationships are broken, they need to be repaired. When self-esteem is destroyed, it needs to be nurtured. Nevertheless, even when I have seen a theme repeatedly played out in what I describe as a downward spiritual spiral, the person often does not recognize it. I hear the echo of the prophet Ezekiel who cried out, "they have eyes that do not see and ears that do not hear" (Ezekiel 12:2). Just as they are not ready to listen to the hints their bodies and souls are offering them, they are likewise not ready to hear what I might have to say. I say it anyway, and have always taught my students to do the same. It is what I call an aggressive form of pastoral counseling. The normal protocol of "wait and see" will not suffice if I am to try to help prevent the onset of illness by addressing the themes that threaten to overwhelm a person. An outside observer might be moved to ask why so many bad things are happening to that person. The individual might even wonder such things to him- or herself, even if unable to articulate it. It is difficult to realize what is happening when you are in the middle of it. One thing leads to another. They are not random, dissociated episodes; they are connected in a chain of events. If we want to help someone find healing, we have to discover the interconnections that create the chain.

Just before my wife, Sheryl, was first diagnosed with cancer, our lives had developed a certain frenzied rhythm, a pattern of living that was hard to keep pace with. We worked hard. We played hard. We arose early in the morning and worked until late at night. We seldom just relaxed—we were busy paving a foundation for our future. While struggling with being devoted parents to our then young sons in addition to doing what was necessary to build successful careers, things always seemed to rush ahead of us, even as we attempted to rein them in and direct them. Sheryl's illness gave us the opportunity to reflect on what was happening so that we might learn from it and change what we were doing wrong. We had to stop everything so that she could find healing.

Sheryl clearly remembers racing through an airport one day, trying to catch a late night plane so she would not have to spend another night on the road. She recalls consciously struggling just to place one foot in front of the other. Exhausted from her work, she said that it was as if she were telling her legs what to do because they did not know how to work on their own. While she believed, as our teachers have suggested, that when we hold the words of Torah in our hearts they will carry us, the burden she carried was manifest in her overstuffed and overweight briefcase. On top of all this, her grandfather had recently died, and we had just gone through a scary episode that threatened the health of our younger son. We both learned that the rabbis were right when they wrote: "Three things take away a person's strength: fear, traveling, and sin" (Babylonian Talmud, *Gittin* 70a). We learned that these are not three separate items. Instead, one simply emerges in the guise of the other.

THE SPIRITUAL STATE OF SICKNESS

The Hebrew word for sickness *(choleh)* is related to the word for emptiness or hollowness. That same word can also mean secular or profane. Thus, illness represents a state in which the lack of spirituality negatively impacts on the physical well-being of the individual. Sickness can ensue when the nonsacred side of one's life dominates and smothers the other side, potentially severing one's connection with God. The writer of Proverbs asks, "One's spirit strengthens oneself in one's illness, but who will lift up a broken spirit?" (Proverbs 18:4). The Malbim (Rabbi Meir Leibush ben Yechiel Michel) offers an answer: "It is the spirit that sustains the body. And even if there is sickness in the body, the spirit has great enough strength to support the illness, giving them strength to bear [the illness] and renew their courage. But if the spirit is broken [referring to spiritual sickness] who will lift it up? For then the sickness will affect the body too as it is written, 'A depressed spirit dries the bones'"(Proverbs 17:22). A psycho-spiritual commentary on the biblical texts, Metzudat David, adds this explanation: "But when the spirit is broken by sadness and depression, who will lift it up? For the body does not lift it up to strengthen it; rather, it is the spirit that supports the body."

When people read in the Talmud, "The best of physicians are destined to go to hell" (*Kiddushin* 82a), they think this is an indictment against the medical profession. Rather, as the Maharsha (Rabbi Shmuel Eliezer ben Yehuda Levi of sixteenth-century Cracow) explains, it is a criticism against those doctors who think they are the "best of physicians" and rely only on themselves—rather than recognizing their partnership with the Divine and the spiritual side—as they do their healing work.

REMEMBERING GOD

Each time I sit face-to-face with a person who is struggling with serious illness, a particular text from Exodus replays itself in my memory: "I am God your healer" (Exodus 15:26). I first studied it when I was a student rabbi and had to find the inner strength to make my first pastoral visits in the hospital. I was not sure that I had the inner spiritual reserve necessary, but this text became a *kavannah* for me, a sacred mantra that I repeated to myself each time I entered a hospital room, not knowing who or what to expect on the other side of the threshold. I continue to draw from it whenever I make such a visit.

In the midst of illness, it may be hard to remember how you felt before getting sick. Dr. Herbert Benson, a well-known leader in alternative or complementary medicine, suggests that the key to healing is to get the body and spirit to "remember (its) wellness," and he works with his patients to achieve this. Dr. Benson argues that if we can get ourselves to remember what it was like to feel healthy before becoming ill, we will then be able to move ourselves in the direction where healing takes place. At the same time, we have to block out everything that might prevent us from doing so. No negativity, no pessimism, only positive thinking. While this idea is still controversial in the medical community, it remains a leading idea in the area of alternative medicine. But what of the spiritual side of this "remembered wellness"?

Spirituality is focused on the relationship between God and an individual. Thus, the goal of spirituality is always to bring that relationship closer. Borrowing from the work of Rabbi Eugene B. Borowitz, North America's leading liberal Jewish theologian, it is called a covenantal relationship, one that mirrors the relationship established between God and the Jewish people at Sinai. In the midst of sickness, it might be difficult to remember the relationship one previously had with God, assuming that a relationship had been cultivated and nurtured at all. I believe that the key to remembering wellness, as per Dr. Benson, is to recall this original relationship with God. Here's how it works. I believe that all Jews possess "historical memory," the collective experience of the Jewish people that dates back to the covenant at Sinai. If so, regardless of whether or not they have ever accessed it, even if it has receded deep into the unconscious, then it may be possible to reach back into that memory and "remember" it. Pregnant women understand this idea rather well. Sarah, a neighbor of mine, told me that when she was pregnant, she kept misjudging how much room she would need to pass between two people or objects. She would constantly bump her belly into things, because she "remembered" her size before she was pregnant.

This is what the Passover seder attempts to accomplish in the family context. The Haggadah for the seder contains a step-by-step guide to help those sitting around the Passover table reach back and participate in the exodus again. It offers a model for the entire week of Passover and beyond. The Torah extends this idea: "If you listen to the voice of *Adonai* your God, and do what is right in God's eyes, and listen to God's mitzvot, and observe all of God's laws—all the diseases that I put upon Egypt, I shall not put upon you, for I, God, am your healer" (Exodus 15:26). For me, this "historical memory" is crucial to healing in Judaism. We bring the relationship with God back to the forefront of our consciousness by remembering it—and we bring healing along with it.

Rabbi David Zeller is a teacher and executive director of Yakar Institute, a center of Jewish textual learning and meditation in Jerusalem. In *Meditation from the Heart of Judaism: Today's Teachers Share Their Practices, Techniques, and Faith,* edited by Avram Davis, Rabbi Zeller teaches us about "a splendid way to live."

A Splendid Way to Live

RABBI DAVID ZELLER

The revelation at Mount Sinai, by all accounts, was an inconceivably incredible experience. It was not a lecture on the theory and practice of Judaism. It was an experience, and not just the experience of one "enlightened" master, but the experience of each and every individual who was at Sinai, each in their own way, differing only in accordance with their own personal level of receptivity.

According to tradition, the revelation lay in God's "speaking" the Ten Commandments, either with an outer voice or an inner voice. Some say it was just the first three of the commandments that were heard. Some say it was just the first commandment, *Anochi haShem,* "I am the Lord your God," that was "heard" by all. But to me, one of the most beautiful teachings about the revelation is that only the first letter of the first word was heard, and heard around the world. The first Hebrew letter of the word *Anochi* is *alef,* which has no sound. More accurately, it is the sound of silence, the Inaudible. *Alef* is the number one, not the integer that is followed by two, but the One of totality and all inclusiveness, the One of the Infinite.

If a computer printer had been plugged in at Mount Sinai, it would still be printing out the data, the understanding and interpretation of the experience. In fact, it is still printing out today through the fantastic, unbroken flow of oral tradition. But we tend to lose ourselves in the understanding and interpretation or in the argument whether it is God's revelation or man-written. And in almost all cases, the initiating experience is long forgotten.

PURSUING THE PRESENCE OF GOD

Eating from the fruit of the Tree of Knowledge of Good and Evil left us conceiving time as linear: What is past is past. We perceive Shabbat as the seventh day of the week. It follows the sixth day, Friday, and precedes the following first day, Sunday. But from the perspective of the Tree of Life, Shabbat is an ever-present dimension of time, the "ground" to the "figure" of the six days, just as the surface of my desk is always there though it is constantly covered up by the clutter of the everyday. So, too, the Inaudible Infinite *Alef* of revelation is eternal and ever-present but remains unheard and unseen and unknown due to the clutter of our minds.

But just as heart disease can be reversed by ceasing to ingest food that is high in fat and cholesterol, so too can we reverse spiritual heart disease by eliminating or at least by cutting down on the junk content of the things our eyes, ears, and minds take in, in our normal everyday diet of perceptions.

Judaism pursues the experience of the presence and revelation of God. Its primary practices of prayer, Shabbat, and learning are aimed at that. But without some ongoing connection to the nonlinear, the multidimensional, the Tree of Life, we forget about this other dimension of life. The real definition of being a slave, of being in exile, is learning about it but forgetting to experience it.

Rabbi James L. Mirel is spiritual leader of Temple B'nai Torah in Bellevue, Washington. Karen Bonnell Werth, a psychotherapist and psychiatric nurse, has worked extensively in the realm of body-mind-spirit with people of all ages and backgrounds. In *Stepping Stones to Jewish Spiritual Living: Walking the Path Morning, Noon, and Night,* they teach us that in every moment of each day, we have the opportunity to bring the sacred into our everyday lives.

Midnight:
Mysticism, Sexuality, and Creation

JAMES L. MIREL AND KAREN BONNELL WERTH

I arise at midnight to praise you.

—*Psalm 119:62*

There is a well-known legend that speculates on the many worlds that God created before this one. It seems that the Rabbis envisioned even God's creative process as a matter of trial and error. This idea is also a metaphor for the life of the individual. Spiritually, we ascend and descend every day searching for the proper balance in our lives. We suspect that we are, in essence, spiritual beings, but we are constantly being tugged by physical and ego needs. The journey of the human soul is the most exhilarating flight of all. What we fail to accomplish today may be realized tomorrow or the day after.

(jlm)

In the dark of midnight, we are freed from our normal vision so we can look within: Midnight is like the womb that envelops mystery and Creation. It represents a time when we can prepare to bring new life to old forms. To paraphrase Genesis (49:25), "Be blessed by the God of your father and mother who will help you, by God Almighty who will bless you with blessings of heaven above, blessings of the deep mysteries below, blessings of spiritual nourishment, and blessings of Creation." We now enter midnight—a time of gestation and promise, the time before awakening the dawn, before the birthing of a new day.

STUDY: MYSTICISM— TURNING PROPHECY INTO ACTION

Mysticism is the sum total of all the ways that we seek knowledge of God through insight or intuition, in ways other than ordinary sensory perception and logical reasoning. Mysticism often speaks in a language of poetry and metaphor, addressing the part of us that wants to transcend rational limits, that seeks to enter unbounded awareness and see from one end of the world to the other. This is the part that wants to soar—to dream of other worlds, to live with angels, to prophesy with Divine inspiration.

As Rabbi Lawrence Kushner has written, "We choose our truth by the scope of our vision."[1] The mystic sees the world through intuition, which is often called "spiritual sight," "symbolic sight," the "sight that comes from behind the eyes." Learning to see experiences as both physical and spiritual opens us to the intuitive self. Intuition helps us see the world differently and interpret cues on a spiritual as

Then the mystery was revealed to Daniel in a vision of the night. Then Daniel blessed the God of heaven. Daniel said:

"Blessed be the name of God for ever and ever,

to whom belong wisdom and might.

God changes times and seasons;

God removes kings and sets up kings;

God gives wisdom to the wise and knowledge to those who have understanding;

God reveals deep and mysterious things;

God knows what is in the darkness,

and the light dwells with God."

DANIEL 2:19–22

The king said to Daniel, "Truly, your God is God of gods and Lord of kings, and a revealer of mysteries…"

DANIEL 2:47

Such was the appearance of the likeness of the glory

of the Eternal One. And when I saw it,

I fell upon my face,

and I heard the voice of One speaking.

EZEKIEL 1:28

well as physical level. We begin to look at all interactions as learning experiences; we may "see" people differently (even seeing "auras" or energy fields or receiving pictures about them in our minds that give us insights into them); we recognize synchronicity as more than coincidence; and we honor the knowing that defies logic. Intuition is not reserved for a gifted few; it is a skill we can all develop. And over time and with practice and understanding, we see the miracle of Creation, and of God, everywhere.

An important mystical moment of the day might occur while sleeping or dreaming. "And God spoke to Israel in visions of the night, and God said, 'Jacob, Jacob.' And Jacob said, 'Here I am'" (Genesis 42:2). While waking visions may be rare, all of us have visions (which we call "dreams") in the night.

The ancient Hebrews had a great regard for dreams and sought the counsel of those who could explain them. However, the Israelites

The visions of my head as I lay in bed were these:

I saw, and behold, a tree in the midst of the earth;

and its height was great. The tree grew and became

strong, and its top reached to heaven, and it was visible

to the end of the whole earth. Its leaves were fair and

its fruit abundant, and in it was food for all. The beasts

of the field found shade under it, and the birds of the

air dwelt in its branches, and all flesh was fed from it.

DANIEL 4:10–12

were forbidden to let dreams and dream interpretation cross over into idol worship or magic.

The Bible has many accounts of dreams and their interpretations. Jacob dreamed and saw a stairway to heaven. Joseph dreamed and found his destiny. Some of these offer mystical insight into the nature of the universe; others are prophetic.

Dreams speak in symbolic language, which is the language of the unconscious, individual and collective. Like "symbolic sight," dreams provide inroads to our deeper thoughts and feelings. Dreams, even when strictly about ourselves, contain the seeds of mystical insight and prophecy. They are ours to interpret and learn from. As the *Zohar* says, "A dream uninterpreted is like a letter unopened." Pay attention to your dreams. Write them down. Discuss them. Contemplate them. In them, you may find answers you have been seeking, answers which may help you enter into a partnership with God to create our world that is constantly evolving. Following in the footsteps of the ancient prophets, Hillel said we are all "apprentice prophets." We are the ones listening, hearing, trusting, and following the Truth. We can be the ones who, through our work, fulfill the Eternal Laws of transformation and creation. According to Jeremiah (1:5),

And God said, "Hear my words:

If there is a prophet among you,

I the Eternal One make Myself known to you in a vision,

I speak with you in a dream."

NUMBERS 12:6

The Holy One called me from the womb,

from the body of my mother,

God named my name... "I will give you

as a light to the nations, that my salvation may

reach to the ends of the earth."

ISAIAH 49:1, 6

God said, "Before you were born I consecrated you; I appointed you a prophet to the nations."

Judaism is about translating ideas and beliefs into action. We can take the poetry of faith and mysticism, and apply its wisdom and insights to everyday life. To manifest the Mystery in the physical world, knowing is not enough; we must act in ways commensurate with our abilities to bring Light into the world. As Rabbi David Wolpe has noted,

> The normal mystic in the Jewish tradition was one whose life was devoted to the "repairing imperative," that things must be mended, a sense livened by the constant perception of God's presence and concern behind all things.[2]

Rabbi Lawrence Kushner is Rabbi-in-Residence at Hebrew Union College–Jewish Institute of Religion. He teaches and lectures widely to audiences of all ages, faiths and backgrounds, and has been a frequent commentator on National Public Radio's *All Things Considered*. In *The Way Into Jewish Mystical Tradition*, Rabbi Kushner teaches us the spiritual implications of Jewish mysticism.

Jewish Mysticism Reconsidered

LAWRENCE KUSHNER

A mystic believes that, beneath the apparent contradictions, broken-ness, and discord of this everyday world lies a hidden divine unity. Just beyond the radar screens of our five senses, all being is one lumi-nous organism. Religion is a system of sacred word and gesture designed to increase the likelihood we will remember that it's all one, or, as we Jews say, God is One. Or, as the Hasidim used to say, *Altz is Gott,* "It's all God!"

Consider the alternative: Can it be that reality is only what you can see and that nothing is connected to anything else? Is everything in life governed by chance, happenstance, a roll of the dice? Or, for those who believe in God's existence, is it possible that God is involved only in some things but not everything? No, for a mystic, God is not only involved in everything, God is everything. To borrow an ancient mystical metaphor: God is the ocean and we are the waves. The goal and the challenge of the mystic is to keep that awesome pos-sibility ever present in one's consciousness.

We all experience fleeting glimmers of this ultimate truth—when we're with people we love and with ones we don't, during solitary walks in the forest and while caught in rush-hour traffic, in the mar-ket or at a funeral. These little epiphanies make us grateful to be human, and they invariably make us also want to be better people.

There's no way to know exactly when these garden-variety mystical moments will occur. They last for only a moment or two and then, in the twinkling of an eye, they're gone. No spiritual fireworks, no Handel's *Hallelujah* chorus sung by angels—just a fleeting reminder that everything is connected, that we are part of something much larger than ourselves, something that overrides all our carefully laid plans.

Throughout Jewish history this yearning to experience and comprehend the unity within all creation has found myriad expressions: from Sinai and the psalms of the Hebrew Bible to the teachings of mainstream mystical talmudic sages like Rabbi Akiva. It exploded again with the appearance of the *Zohar* in thirteenth-century Spain and with Rabbi Isaac Luria of Safed three hundred years later. It reappeared in the Hasidic revival of the eighteenth century and continues all the way up to the nascent spiritual revival of our own day. Each one of these flowerings of the Jewish mystical imagination has added to Judaism its own overlay of imagery, vocabulary, and rituals. Indeed, we would be hard pressed to find any aspect of Jewish life that has not incorporated mystical elements. Gershom Scholem, one of the great historians of our generation, has observed that, for centuries, the average Jew on the street probably knew more *Zohar* than Talmud! From *Lekha Dodi* (a mystical hymn) in the Sabbath evening liturgy to *tikkun olam* (a cornerstone of Lurianic Kabbalah) of political action, the influence of our mystical heritage is ubiquitous.

BALANCING RATIONALISM AND MYSTICISM

If this is so, then why do so many modern liberals regard mysticism with suspicion? Why has liberal Judaism effectively expunged most, if not all, references to its mystical tradition? Until recently, it was hardly mentioned in religious school textbooks. It is rarely taught even to rabbinic students. Jewish seekers often get the impression that they would do better to search out the mysticism of Eastern religions than to bother looking in the temple library. Why have the pages on Jewish mysticism been torn out of the books?

The answer, in part, can be found in our origins. Liberal Judaism is the child of German rationalism. We proudly trace our roots to Immanuel Kant and Hermann Cohen and not, for instance, to the Hasidic master Yehudah Aryeh Lieb of Ger in Poland or Abraham Isaac Kook, the first Ashkenazi chief rabbi of Israel, both of whom were towering intellects, prolific writers, *and* mystics. Our liberal predecessors dismissed East European Jewish mysticism as unenlightened, irrational, and superstitious. This bias is plainly evident, for example, in the writings of Abraham Idelsohn, the great German-trained liturgist, who asserts that "in its very essence, mysticism is a negation of life, an escape from its realities and hardships"! Heinrich Graetz, arguably the nineteenth century's most influential Jewish historian, described Hasidism (the last great flowering of Jewish mysticism) as: "a daughter of darkness...born in gloom, [that] even today proceeds stealthily on its mysterious way." Lest there be any doubt about his assessment, this teacher of our teachers put it bluntly: "Mysticism and madness are contagious."

We now suspect that our German rationalist predecessors were perhaps too overzealous in their blanket condemnation. We understand that rationalism without mysticism is sterile. Mysticism is not escapist and madness but an essential and vital ingredient of a mature and balanced Jewish worldview.

In the opinion of many, mysticism connotes renouncing the world and ethical disinterest. While that may be true of some varieties of Eastern mysticism, such thinking has never found a home among the Jews. If anything, Jewish mystics are tediously rational. Far from ignoring the world, they embrace all creation as a manifestation of the Divine. For mystics, the task is to find God's presence everywhere and then act in such a way as to help others find it, too. Ethical behavior is inseparable from and, indeed, a central expression of the Jewish mystical enterprise. We have only to consider the courageous political activism of such contemporary mystical giants as Abraham Isaac Kook in Israel, who fought tirelessly for the inclusion of all Jews—including liberals and even secularists—in the Zionist dream, or Abraham Joshua Heschel, who marched for civil rights at the side of Reverend Martin Luther King, Jr. Indeed, the definitive manuals of Jewish ethical discipline, *Mesilat Yesharim* by Moses Chayim Luzzatto and the *Shulchan Arukh* by Joseph Caro (d. 1575), were written by practicing Kabbalists!

The Jewish choice is not rationalism or mysticism, logic or spirituality, but both. Just as early Reform's categorical rejection of all ritual as superstitious resulted in an antiseptic cerebralism, so too does the renunciation of anything mystical deprive us of poetry and mystery. Indeed, without this mystical dimension, liberal Judaism of our own generation is impoverished and tepid. Core religious experience is beyond words and reason. That doesn't mean that it's anti-rational, spaced out, or navel contemplating, but merely that the numinous transcends logic. To put it bluntly, if you can explain it, it ain't God.

EMERGING MYSTICAL METAPHORS

Permit me a few ancient, mystical metaphors that seem to have reappeared in contemporary liberal Judaism and hold high promise.

Probably the best known comes from Isaac Luria in sixteenth-century Safed, whose Kabbalah (or mystical tradition) promulgated a daring creation legend: that God underestimated the creative power of the divine light. The vessels God had prepared to receive the light shattered, leaving a world of brokenness, husks, and shards. The primordial light remains trapped, imprisoned within. The task—indeed, the purpose of—humanity is to repair creation, to free the sparks and literally put the world back together. This is called *tikkun olam*. It is much more than mere political action (although that is an indispensable element). It involves virtually everything a Jew does: through the performance of *mitzvot,* we are able to fix the world.

This brings us to a second and equally mystical metaphor: What we do in this world affects heaven. Our actions have cosmic significance. *Mitzvot*—even the *mitzvot* we do not yet understand—are not merely good deeds, or even divine obligations; they change the very workings of the universe. In the words of the kabbalists, "From awakening below comes awakening on high."

We liberal Jews share a growing sense today that the Torah—once only a document of enlightened reason—is, even more important, also an accurate manifestation of ultimate awareness. This is certainly not fundamentalism. (The *Zohar* itself says that the stories in the Torah could not possibly be about what they *seem* to be about, otherwise we could write better stories ourselves!) Rather, we are now beginning to understand that to call Torah sacred means that it is a uniquely potent mechanism for comprehending the very infrastructure of being. We may not be able to see it, but in the words of Proverbs, "She is a tree of life to those who hold fast to her." Or, to put it another way, there is more God in Torah than anyone can fathom. According to the Kabbalists, the Messiah will teach us how to pronounce the entire Torah as one long name of God.

This, in turn, leads us to another classical mystical idea: there's more to reality than meets the eye. Reality is layered, concealing myriad interrelationships and meanings. The Kabbalists went so far as to try symbolically to diagram reality or, as it were, the divine psyche itself. They envisioned a *sefirotic* tree (a diagram with ten circles). We today are more comfortable with the double helix of DNA or the unified field theory of modern physics, but they're all fundamentally the same: one awesomely integrated organism.

PSALM 19: ONE LAST READING

For the leader, a Psalm of David:

The heavens rehearse the presence of God, just as the firmament proclaims God's doing. Day after day speaking gushes forth, just as night after night wisdom is whispered. But of course there can be no speaking, nor can there be any words; indeed, the voices of the heavens and the firmament cannot even be heard. Still their voice reverberates throughout creation, their words to the ends of the earth. With them, God has made a tent for the sun. It is like a bridegroom emerging from his marriage canopy, like an athlete in prime, ready for the contest. He comes out at one end of the heavens and his course leads him to the other. No one can hide from the heat of the sun.

The Torah of God is really very simple, reviving the soul; the testimony of God is sure, giving wisdom to the fool. The statutes of God are right, rejoicing the heart; the commandment of God is clear, enlightening the eyes. The reverence of God is pure, enduring forever; the judgments of God are true and righteous altogether. More precious than gold, even than all the finest gold; it is sweeter than honey dripping from the comb. For this reason, your servant is eager to follow them; the reward is great.

Who could possibly be aware of every mistake? O let me be free from inadvertent wrongdoing. Keep your servant far from deliberate sins; let arrogance have no power over me. Only then will I be innocent and clear of great transgression. May these words of my mouth and the meditation of my heart be acceptable before You, O God, my rock and my redeemer.

We ask ourselves, how much God is in the world? Most of us were raised to believe that God resides beyond this world, trying benevolently (though not always successfully) to run it. In such a model, some things, some places, and some times are without the divine presence; evil, for instance, has nothing whatsoever to do with God. For mystics, on the other hand, God is everywhere and all the time. That doesn't mean mystics don't rail against injustice or try to make things better. But it does mean that even when they can't discern the presence of the Divine, mystics remain stubbornly convinced that God—the source, the ground, the font of all being—is somehow present. God is the ocean and we are the waves. *Shema Yisrael* (Deuteronomy 6:4)— "Hear O Israel, the Lord our God, the Lord is One!"

Rabbi Dannel I. Schwartz is spiritual leader of Temple Shir Shalom in West Bloomfield, Michigan. **Mark Hass** has been one of the staff of the *Detroit News* and the *Miami Herald.* In *Finding Joy: A Practical Spiritual Guide to Happiness,* they teach us how to use mysticism to enhance our own spiritual happiness.

Be Mystical. Be Happy.

DANNEL I. SCHWARTZ WITH MARK HASS

Mysticism and practical spirituality are not just harmless philosophical playthings. Traditional scholars treated the subject not only with great respect, but with tremendous caution. They strictly limited Kabbalah study to married men over the age of 40. Some teachers even required the equivalent of a graduate degree in Jewish studies before they let anyone open a book on mystical thought. Stories abound of defiant young men who ignored their elders' warnings and dabbled in the mysteries of the soul. Their reward was madness or death.

Practitioners of mystical Judaism weren't trying to maintain the value of their knowledge by making it a scarce commodity. Rather, they were trying to protect unsuspecting people from its power which was the equivalent of an open flame. In the hands of dilettantes, it would burn the user and those near them. But when practiced by a master, Kabbalah could provide light and warmth.

The reasons for the danger are obvious when you understand the functioning principle of Kabbalistic thought. Without the use of drugs, it can magnify and intensify every part of life and thought. Like radar set to detect even the slightest movement, we can be so flooded by sensation and experience that we are unable to process them meaningfully. We focus on the negative because it is so magnified that it becomes all we see. Properly managed, though, this sensitivity can let us see potential in people and situations, to focus clearly on what's around us. But more data about our world and our lives are not necessarily welcome if we have no method to sort it all and convert it into knowledge.

Kabbalists believed that when we reached a higher spiritual plateau, we gained a wisdom and a power to heal physical as well as spiritual ailments. Incantations and magical formulas, such as the Aramaic mantra *abracadabra,* were used by people of magic from many faiths to cure everything from a toothache to the common cold. Some believed that this word, later popularized in many children's stories, meant "the father, the son and the holy spirit" or was a corruption of the Hebrew words for "blessing," *bracha,* and for "word," *dabar.* The prescription had to be done so that first the whole word had to be written on the top line; then on each subsequent line the word had to be repeated with one letter less. Until finally at the very bottom of the triangle only one letter was left:

A B R A C A D A B R A
A B R A C A D A B R
A B R A C A D A B
A B R A C A D A
A B R A C A D
A B R A C A
A B R A C
A B R A
A B R
A B
A

Regardless, the ancients feared that these incantations might give the young and undisciplined enough knowledge about Kabbalah to be dangerous. The unstable might think it was based on sorcery, not belief. If the problem couldn't be cured with an immediate answer, incantation or spell, the immature might dwell even more on their own shortcomings, problems and pain. In a mundane sense, imagine the impact on the bald person who is already so conscious of his baldness that all he sees are people with full heads of hair. Or the overweight woman who lives in a world of flat tummies and well-proportioned waists. If the "magic" of mysticism fails to grow hair or reduce weight, will these people obsess even more? Instead of mini-mizing the negative, would just the opposite occur?

After all, fixating on the negative is not uncommon. Add a mis-understood belief system and facts might become meaningless and truth transformed into individual idiosyncrasies. The thin would sud-denly see themselves as fat and would exercise, purge and diet. The person with a pimple would look into a mirror and see no other attribute—only a pimple. Even the absolutely normal person might start exaggerating what is missing and ignore the intrinsic good beneath the surface.

Spiritual maturity means a problem is a potential opportunity. A spiritually mature person, a true mystic, views all problems as potential. The spiritual mind turns negative energy into positive results.

LET YOUR SOUL CATCH UP WITH YOU

Habitually focusing our attention on our positive qualities rather than on what seem to be our failings requires much concentration. It may be difficult, but doing so is crucial for those who aspire to be spiritually centered. Being focused is the essence of spirituality because it raises our sensitivity level. Kabbalah literally means "receiving," and students of mysticism believe that Kabbalah is based on our ability to make our entire being receptive to the wisdom and the divine sparks that surround us and are within us.

The sudden flash of insight that creates opportunities, the inspi-ration that comes in the middle of the night, the vision that trans-forms an all-consuming question into an all-encompassing answer are examples of spiritual receptivity. When our antennae are up and our inner radar is finely tuned, we can receive signals that we might not have otherwise received. Our maturity and wisdom help us interpret them into answers that are useful to us.

An ancient African legend describes why it is difficult to concentrate and focus on life's mystical possibilities. It is the story of Yameel, the fastest messenger and most reliable runner on the African continent. Myths abounded about Yameel's swiftness of foot, his sense of direction and his uncanny ability to find any location, from the most remote tree in the jungle to the largest village. Tribal leaders marveled at his speed and recounted tales of his quick sprints through the bush from one village to another.

So it was very strange that a village elder should encounter the runner on the road one day standing almost motionless. He asked: "Why have you stopped in the middle of a mission?"

Yameel looked down at the man and answered: "I have been running so fast that I have left my soul behind. I am standing here waiting for it to catch up to me."

Many of us move so fast that we have to stop and give our souls a chance to catch up to where we are. Whether by meditation, prayer, reciting a mantra, or just quietly walking in the woods, stopping ourselves is part of what we need to get ourselves in spiritual sync. The process is like calibrating an instrument or tuning a piano. The mystics felt that before we could be receptive to the possibilities of life, we had to be at peace within. Only then could we focus.

The Kabbalists realized that the best way to slow down and let our souls catch up involved meditation or, as they called it, *Devekut.* For centuries, meditative techniques were used for more than simple relaxation or stress reduction. They offered the ability to force everyday worry from the mind. By calming the concerns of the conscious mind, mystics could become one with the universe.

Some ancient scholars developed prayer wheels made of Hebrew prayers written in concentric circles. While trying to read the prayers, the reader would become mesmerized. Other scholars stared into the flame of a candle, believing they could dissipate their negative energy into the flame. Others stared for long periods into a basin of clear water to induce either a meditative or a hypnotic state.

Here are two techniques I encourage people to use, and that I use myself when I find that my body has outrun my soul. But first, two cautions: Never do these while operating machinery or driving a car. And some people may find that they don't work for them, although many will claim that ten minutes of these meditations make them feel better than a good night's sleep.

• Breathing Meditation

Sit in a comfortable straight-backed chair. Place your feet on the ground. Close your eyes, and become aware of your breathing. Spend three to five minutes relaxing. Tense your feet, count to five and relax. Tense your ankles, count to five, relax. Follow the same routine with your calves, your thighs, your stomach, your chest, arms and hands. Tense and relax your neck, your face and forehead. Finally, breathe deeply without consciously trying to alter the rhythm of your breathing. If your mind drifts, return your concentration to your breathing.

• Counting or Tones Meditation

Use the "tensing and relaxing" exercise described above. Then begin counting or saying key words aloud. Some people count to four in order to focus their mind as their breath goes in and out. Some prefer using words such as "God" or "love." For example, as you breath in, say "one"; as you breathe out, say "two." Jewish mystics used words like *"Hu"* (which means "he" in Hebrew), instead of the name of God. They would say the "h" while inhaling and the "ooo" upon exhaling.

According to the ancient mystics, meditation sharpens our ability to see that for which we should be thankful. Recall that Jewish tradition asks us to say one hundred blessings a day. Trying to see our blessings is most rewarding when our soul is in this highly receptive state. Saying thanks for anything makes us stop and become even more aware. As a Yiddish proverb says, "If you are going to be miserable when you are sick, be thankful when you are well."

The blessings need not be enormous. They should be things we ordinarily overlook. A gentleman once told the Kotzker Rebbe that he had nothing for which to be thankful. His business was losing money; his wife had died; his son was not talking to him; and his house was too small.

"Take your thumb and index finger," the Rebbe directed the man. "Take a deep breath, and then place those fingers on your nose and squeeze to the point that you will not be able to breathe out. Do not breathe from your mouth."

As the man started to turn red, the Rebbe cautioned: "Do not take your fingers away until you cannot stand it any longer." Finally, the man released his grip and inhaled deeply. "Ah," the Rebbe concluded. "The air is what you most take for granted, and suddenly you are grateful to have it. Now, look at the rest of your life that same way and see all that you have taken for granted."

We might give thanks for:

> Being able to see the sky and the stars.
> Being able to see our children.
> Having healthy, bright children.
> Having loving, supportive spouses.
> Being able to be with friends.
> Being able to make new friends.
> Being able to hear music.
> Being able to hear birds sing.
> Being able to hear great people speak.
> Being able to understand what they say.

Getting in touch with the blessings of our lives connects us with our souls. If Kabbalah sensitizes and magnifies what it touches, then it will also build self esteem, self-worth and a sense of well-being from the positive bricks and mortar we derive from reciting our blessings.

Don't be afraid to write down these blessings. This gives them a concrete feeling in our minds and gives them life. Hanging the list where it can be seen can help our souls keep up with us as we move through the day.

"GIVING AWAY" GRATITUDE CREATES WONDER

There will be days, of course, when none of these methods work. So when all else failed, mystics made a most effective and enchanting rec-ommendation: Give some gratitude away!

Telling someone how much they mean to us or the qualities we most admire about them creates wonderful feelings in both the giver of gratitude and the recipient. Being able to make people feel good about themselves makes us focus on something positive and forces us to look past ourselves. It magically does the same for the recipient of our compliment, who can focus on some personal strength and still feel gratitude toward us for pointing it out. This is a spiritual no-lose situation.

Tamar Frankiel, Ph.D., teaches the history of religions at Claremont School of Theology and at the University of California Riverside. In *The Gift of Kabbalah: Discovering the Secrets of Heaven, Renewing Your Life on Earth,* Dr. Frankiel teaches us about the history of Kabbalah.

A Note on the History of Kabbalah

TAMAR FRANKIEL

Kabbalah, the popular term for Jewish mysticism, comes from a Hebrew root that means "to receive"; thus Kabbalah is the received tradition. It originated, probably several centuries B.C.E., in the study of esoteric aspects of the written Torah (the first five books of the Bible), the contemplation of prophetic visions like those of Ezekiel and Isaiah, and apocalyptic traditions. Specific rabbis were known to be teaching mystical theology and practice in the first centuries C.E. Some leading scholars think that the Gnostics of the early Christian era (ca. 100–200 C.E.) developed their ideas from a core Jewish mystical tradition that existed by the first century. We have Jewish mystical texts that date back probably to the second or third century C.E., but we know very little about the transmission and interpretation of these texts. From the fascinating teachings that have come down to us, it is highly likely that the mystics limited their teachings to small circles because they were concerned about being considered culturally and even politically subversive in a variety of ways.[1] Yet in the long run, their thought was highly influential. The traditional Jewish prayer book, first compiled in the eighth century C.E., still incorporates important mystical ideas.

Whatever the reasons for the original secrecy, Kabbalah in a variety of interpretations became better known in the Middle Ages, even though its teachers still emphasized oral, teacher-to-student transmission. Among the best-known works circulating among the mystical masters of Europe were the *Sefer Yetzirah* (originally from the third century) and the *Bahir* (eleventh century). Major schools of mysticism existed in Germanic territory, in southern France, and in Spain, where the *Zohar* was published in the late 1200s. A major biblical commentator, Moshe ben Nachman, or Nachmanides (known in Jewish scholarship by the acronym Ramban) was one of the Spanish mystics; he frequently refers to mystical teachings in his commentary. After the expulsion of Jews from Spain in 1492, mysticism traveled with the exiles to Italy, the Balkans, and the Land of Israel.

By the mid-sixteenth century, a number of outstanding scholars and mystics had settled in Safed (pronounced *s'fat*), a small town in the Galil (northern Israel). Their presence attracted more individuals with similar inclinations, and soon Safed became the world center of Jewish mystical piety. When a remarkable rabbi named Isaac Luria arrived there in 1589, he quickly became the acknowledged master of the group and spent the next three years, until his death, consolidating, explaining, and elaborating the mystical heritage. "Lurianic mysticism" became the basis for most Jewish mysticism down to the present day.

Political and economic changes led to the decline of Safed in the next century, but teachings spreading from the village continued to engage the interest of more than a small elite. The next great eruption of mysticism came in the form of a popular movement in the 1600s led by Shabbatai Tzvi, an erratic teacher whose disciples believed him to be the Messiah, but who converted to Islam to escape death. After this debacle, many rabbis discouraged the teaching of mysticism to the general populace, and invoked again the traditional prescription of secrecy. Great mystics were carefully watched and sometimes forbidden to publicize their teachings. For example, about a hundred years later, Rabbi Moshe Chaim Luzzatto (whose acronym is the Ramchal) taught a devoted group of disciples in Italy, but when contemporary rabbinic leaders learned that he believed some of his students to be incarnations of great past leaders, and one to be a potential messiah, he was forbidden to teach. He moved to Amsterdam but again met discouragement. Nevertheless, a number of

Luzzatto's works were accepted and are today much respected in the history of mysticism.[2]

Most mystics stayed underground. According to one tradition, a circle known as the "hidden ones" carried on the teachings of the Ari—the "Lion"—Isaac Luria, for nearly two hundred years in Eastern Europe. In 1740 a member of this circle emerged into public view in the Ukraine, saying that it was now time to reinvigorate mystical teachings among the general populace. His name was Israel ben Eliezer, known as the Baal Shem Tov. His teachings, transmitted by his disciples and theirs in turn, sparked a flame of piety across Eastern Europe. The members of this movement were known as Hasidim (or Chassidim, meaning "the devout ones"). They taught love of God, joy in worship, and the ability of every Jew to be connected to God through prayer and service—whether or not a person was learned according to rabbinic criteria. Although this way of transmitting mystical teachings also had opponents, Hasidism grew to become a major influence on the piety of the Jews of Eastern Europe. In addition, many great non-Hasidic scholars continued to study Kabbalah. In the nineteenth century, even among the non-Hasidic groups, a young man who showed intellectual promise and a desire to inquire into esoteric meanings might be given a copy of the *Zohar*—one of the classic mystical texts—when he was still a teenager.[3]

Unfortunately, the persecutions and pogroms of late nineteenth-century Russia decimated many Jewish communities. Most dramatically, in the Holocaust perpetrated by Nazi Germany in the mid-twentieth century, ninety percent of Eastern Europe's rabbis were slaughtered. Still, the Hasidic traditions and some of the masters of Hasidic teachings survived and brought their message to the United States, in waves of immigration that began at the end of the nineteenth century. Until the 1950s, access to the traditions was confined mostly to the Orthodox enclaves of major cities, for all the Hasidim were Orthodox, as were Sephardic Jews who also maintained a strong mystical tradition. Martin Buber, who was originally from a Hasidic tradition, had begun to translate traditional tales and sayings, but it was the Lubavitch sect of Hasidim known as Chabad (tracing its roots to the town of Lubavitch in Russia) that began to spread the teachings to assimilated and non-Orthodox American Jews. Both through its official rabbinic representatives and through teachers who were trained in Chabad but left the confines of the group, mystical teachings became far more accessible even to Jews uneducated in tradition. The important Jewish Renewal movement, which attracted young Jews in major cities beginning in the 1970s, encouraged serious study of mysticism as well as other aspects of Jewish tradition. By the end of the twentieth century, a wide variety of Jewish groups had exposure to Kabbalah and were including mysticism, at least occasionally, as part of their teachings.

Meanwhile, the American public had demonstrated a growing interest in spirituality since the 1960s, an interest that increased dramatically in the 1990s. Most of that interest was directed toward Eastern thought, especially Hinduism and Buddhism, or to theosophical and occult traditions that had previously been of interest only to an elite minority. But non-Jews also became interested in Kabbalah. This was not entirely a new development; non-Jews have sought spiritual insight from kabbalistic traditions before. But as awareness of Kabbalah spread through the mass media, popular interest in Kabbalah grew larger than ever before.

At present, different approaches to Kabbalah are available. In traditional Hasidism, as well as in neo-Hasidic groups that deemphasize observance of Jewish law, mystical interpretations are incorporated as part of general Jewish learning. Studying mystical teachings while learning Bible, prayer, and Jewish law is the most integrated approach. I encourage everyone who reads this to incorporate that kind of study into their spiritual practice. But, for the beginner with a strong interest in mysticism, the relevant books are very difficult because they require familiarity with many basic Jewish texts and concepts, and often with Hebrew words and letters. Another alternative that has emerged in recent years is groups that specialize in Kabbalah for a general audience, but one must be careful because some of these groups are of doubtful authenticity and even use questionable methods to gain adherents. A third approach is reading books by non-Jewish kabbalists (note that many are older works, recently reprinted to satisfy current demand). Most of these are interlaced with intricate esoteric interpretations from other theosophical traditions and cannot be said to present Jewish Kabbalah. Finally, in very recent times a number of writers, including myself, have begun the effort of making the concepts of mystical Judaism available for the general reader who does not possess deep knowledge of Jewish tradition. Hopefully, these books will encourage dialogue among spiritual practitioners in Judaism and in other traditions as well.

Tamar Frankiel, Ph.D., teaches the history of religions at Claremont School of Theology and at the University of California Riverside. In *The Gift of Kabbalah: Discovering the Secrets of Heaven, Renewing Your Life on Earth*, Dr. Frankiel teaches us that Kabbalah is not only for Jews.

Is Kabbalah Only for Jews?

TAMAR FRANKIEL

God isn't only for Jews, so neither is Kabbalah. While there are some aspects of Kabbalah that are almost impossible to understand without absorbing a great deal of Jewish tradition, Kabbalah as a theosophy is primarily about understanding what God is (as far as we can understand) and who we are as refractions of the Divine image. Because of this, it is important for all peoples.

Yet, according to the popular conception among Jews, you couldn't study Kabbalah unless you were forty years old, married, and male—and, traditionally, Jewish. What these criteria meant was that a student should be mature, well grounded in the basics of Judaism (including Talmud), and stable in his personal life. Because a strong grounding in biblical and Talmudic texts was presupposed, women were not included. Women were taught the portions of Torah necessary to live a Jewish life, which was a considerable amount of learning, but they generally did not have access to Talmudic learning or extensive biblical commentaries. Rules also restricted certain kinds of kabbalistic interpretation and use of Divine names. All these restrictions would apply to non-Jews even more.

There were good reasons for the restrictions. If one studied kabbalistic texts without an appropriate background, one could easily misinterpret them. An uneducated interpreter would be like a person trying to fill a doctor's prescription without going to pharmaceutical school—even if you could read the writing, you wouldn't understand the code. Nevertheless, restrictions on some teachings were gradually lifted beginning around the twelfth century, and writings of masters of Kabbalah slowly became accessible to the literate Jewish population. At certain periods in the Middle Ages mystical teachings became quite widespread. Admittedly, widespread in medieval and early modern times did not mean what it does today. When books had to be copied painstakingly by hand, they were expensive and scarce. The writings of the mystical masters were more difficult than biblical Hebrew, and some were in Aramaic. Even after the printing revolution of the sixteenth century, the literate Jewish population who could read those languages well was largely limited to males. The subject matter of the mystical writings was highly esoteric, including many intricate interpretations of Hebrew letters and words and their numerical value. Nevertheless, over the centuries, the general concepts of Jewish mysticism gradually became available to those who sought them. The concepts of medieval Kabbalah were familiar to some Christian scholars and mystics. By the time of the Renaissance, those teachings were regarded as part of the general heritage of Western mysticism—some Christians even used them to support Christian doctrine! Kabbalah was also influential in the theosophical movements that emerged in nineteenth-century Europe and North America (and which may have influenced Robert Frost).

In short, Kabbalah in the general sense has not always been limited to Jews, and some of the basic concepts of Kabbalah can be understood without intensive Jewish education. More intricate teachings are difficult to access from outside of Judaism, and it is probably wise to be suspicious of anyone who says they are teaching deep mysteries to people without background in Judaism. It is also the case that many Jewish scholars still insist on limiting most Jewish teachings, including Kabbalah, to Jews. Some even teach, on the basis of certain mystical traditions, that Jews have a different kind of soul from non-Jews. While I don't subscribe to that viewpoint, I would be misleading my readers if I didn't acknowledge its existence.

Even if one could have defended such a viewpoint in earlier times, I believe that it is no longer relevant. We are part of one world, and we all need to understand each other at the deepest levels. Opening up the insights of our mystics can be a significant step in that direction. By learning something about Kabbalah, you can deepen your insight into the highest teachings of your own tradition, whether you are Jewish or a practitioner of another spiritual approach.

Ellen Bernstein is the founder of *Shomrei Adamah*—Keepers of the Earth, the first institution dedicated to cultivating the ecological thinking and practices integral to Jewish life. She currently works as Director of Community Building at the Jewish Federation of Greater Philadelphia. In *Ecology & the Jewish Spirit: Where Nature & the Sacred Meet*, Ellen teaches us about the role of "wilderness" in our spiritual lives.

How Wilderness Forms a Jew

ELLEN BERNSTEIN

> What I learned there…seemed to confirm the conjecture I had
> toyed with for so long that Natural Selection has designed us—
> from the structure of our brain cells to the structure of our big
> toe—for a career of seasonal journeys on foot through the blis-
> tering land of thornscrub or desert.
>
> —*Bruce Chatwin,* The Songlines

Wilderness plays a tremendous role in the story told in the Bible, but somehow when I was growing up, no one taught me that the wilderness experience was so fundamental to my tradition. If they had, I would have been much more enthusiastic about being Jewish from an early age. Instead I had to "back into" Judaism. My life experiences, my values, my sense of spirituality sent me, unwittingly, in a Jewish direction.

Since my youth, adventuring in the "great outdoors" has been as basic to my survival as eating and breathing. Growing up, I paddled, biked, skied, and meandered through the New England countryside. This penchant for the outdoors and the need to journey determined many of the choices I would make throughout my life.

My first extended wilderness journey was in the Trinity Alps in northern California when I was 19. My Free Clinic comrades Marc and George and I had planned a two-week hiking trek. I remember our lengthy days of food preparation: determining to the ounce the size of our portions, filling film containers with a variety of savory herbs, and squeezing peanut butter into plastic push tubes. I was preparing psychologically as well: psyching up to see bear, fox, wolves, coyotes. I was eager to be scared.

When we finally arrived in the Trinity Wilderness area, I recognized, somewhat sadly, there was nothing to be afraid of. Whatever big mammals were left in the American Northwest would not venture forth in the presence of people. Luckily Marc and George had lugged along an eight-pound hardcover book by Philip Munz, *A California Flora*. They knew that if it was wildlife we were after, there was a much better chance of finding it in the flowers.

Aside from wildlife, there was something else I would find in the wilderness that I didn't know I was looking for. Late one afternoon, having spent the entire day climbing, we reached a summit ridge. As evening descended, the three of us walked silently on a gentle trail, each absorbed in our own thoughts. I had been hiking for at least ten hours but wasn't tired. Even with a 50-pound pack, my steps were light and effortless. I was mesmerized by the panorama of oceanic mountains that surrounded me and propelled by the rhythm of my feet touching the ground. The soft golden light of the setting sun cast the forest in an emerald glow. I was captivated by the moment and felt lifted and humbled. Every breath inspired me. I had discovered the meaning of worship.

It was then that I began to take my wanderlust more seriously. I recognized that my adventuring resembled a religious quest. It was my chance to encounter life's mystery. It would usually take several days on the trail to leave behind the weight of my ego, my self-consciousness and all that is familiar and routine, and free my mind. In these moments, the world opened up to me; I felt an intimacy with the earth, I was more aware of the plants' special habits, I laughed easily and was eager to chat with strangers. I felt a profound generosity toward the world that comes too infrequently in my daily life.

Wilderness journeys also provided me a doorway to inspiration, to my vision and self-awareness. Usually, my mind is too cluttered for inspiration to find a way in. Yet in the state of deep relaxation I experienced on my journeys, my mind seemed to open up to new ways of thinking and new possibilities. I would come home from these journeys refreshed and with greater self-understanding. It is interesting to me that mystics use the *repetition* of particular words or the focus on the flow of breath in and out of the body over an extended period of time to attain a tranquilizing effect on the mind. Perhaps it was the constant *repetitive* motion of walking or paddling over a prolonged period that allowed my mind to relax and expand.

It is this sense of uplift and farsightedness that I recognize I craved on all those youthful journeys. My experience led me to believe that adventure—or something similar—must be a vital component of healthy identity development.

WILDERNESS AS PILGRIMAGE

I did not recognize any connection between my newly identified spirituality and the religion of my family—Judaism. As a youth, I had rebelled against what seemed to be a hypocritical, archaic, and dead tradition, and I gravitated toward the universal spirituality of my New England forebears, the Transcendentalists.

My observations about Jewish culture at that time concerned Jews, not Judaism. I found it curious that, although I was surrounded by Jews in social and academic settings, my fellow wilderness travelers—particularly the men—were almost all *not* Jewish. Wilderness adventure did not seem to be part of the repertoire of activities of the Jewish men that I knew. Rather, having chosen the fast-paced career track, they were weighted down by mortgages and too much ambition. Many seemed dispirited. I was curious about their lack of wanderlust and wondered if they might be substituting something less healthy (and perhaps addictive) to achieve the deep relaxation and inspiration I thought were necessary for life.

Given the off-putting Jewish experiences I had had while growing up, the last place I expected to find models for the spiritual journey was in Judaism. Yet, once I was able to drop my intolerance toward my heritage and yield to it, I recognized that my tradition embodied the most profound teachings about wandering. For, if anything, being a Jew is being a wanderer. Somehow what appears so obvious now took years for me to notice.

Many of our ancestors took to the wilderness. Abraham, Jacob, and Moses were all called to forsake their settled lives, their homes, and their communities to endure a period of uncertainty and unfamiliarity in the desert. It was only in the unknown that true self-knowledge could be obtained. There they would meet God, discover their sense of purpose, and become Jews.

Not just the biblical heroes, but the entire congregation of Israel embarked on a spiritual journey. Sinai, where our people received wisdom, the Torah, and became partners with God, was just a two-month trek from Egypt. Upon reaching it, the Israelites should have been able to proceed the short distance into the land of Israel and settle there. But Israel was promised to a free people, and this people was still in bondage. Although they had left Egypt, they carried their slavery—in the form of perceptions and behaviors—deep inside of them. It was the only way of life they knew.

It would take 40 years of traversing back and forth across the same wilderness for the Israelites to become free: to take responsibility for their own destiny, to believe in themselves, and to dream again. Only then would they be sufficiently prepared to receive the gift of the land. For these Jews, wandering was not an avocation; it was an occupation. It was a necessary initiation rite—part of the making of a Jew. Even one early name for the Hebrew people, *hapiru,* comes from a Semitic word for "wanderer."[1] Wandering was an essential component in the development of Jewish identity.

There were obvious differences between the pilgrimages that my ancestors made and my own. I had the luxury to choose my journeys; I arranged my trips so they would come when the weather was auspicious; I planned my route meticulously before leaving, knowing where I would camp every night; I prepared all the food and clothing I would need before setting out; I made sure to bring enough fuel for emergencies. My ancestors, on the other hand, did not know where they were going. They did not how they were going to get there, how long it would take, or if the journey would ever end. Often, they did not carry food or fuel. Although our circumstances were different, one thing remains the same: the heart of the journey was a voyage toward the soul.

THE INSPIRATION OF WANDERING

In the nineteenth century, Samson Raphael Hirsch, an Orthodox rabbi, wrote that God took us into the wilderness so that we could deal with our anxiety.[2] Hirsch suggested that anxiety was the true slavery; it is a condition that we perpetuate in ourselves by not claiming full responsibility for our lives. Anxiety results when we are dependent on others for our sense of our selves, when we blame others for the situations in which we find ourselves. I was charmed by Hirsch's reading of slavery and his understanding that a sojourn in wilderness could provide the context necessary for spiritual growth.

Hirsch wrote:

> The desert was the ideal venue for the revelation of His Torah because it was virgin soil, unpolluted as yet by egoism and ambition, undefiled by the pursuit of vanity. He chose the desert far from the cities, far from society and inhabited lands, far from an already corrupt society....

I have often noticed how my own perceptions and values change when I take to the wilderness. In the city, I am aware of myself and my individuality: my looks, my clothes, my car, my house, and all my possessions. In wilderness, my self-consciousness and inhibitions dissolve, and I am more conscious of the whole. In the city, I hurry through my chores joylessly so I can engage in more *important* things, like work. In wilderness, I find the greatest pleasure in fixing dinner, fetching wood, and bathing in an alpine lake. In the city, I always need *something*. My pleasure seems to derive in part from the goods I have acquired. In wilderness, I am content with what I have: the company of friends, the beauty of the place, the pleasure of walking.

I am not aware of wanting anything. Being resourceful and making do with what I have are part of the adventure.

In *The Songlines,* Bruce Chatwin connected the wandering life with inspiration and the settled life with resignation, boredom, and the accumulation of goods. He suggested that Cain and Abel were archetypes of these two contrasting character types: "The names of the brothers are a matched pair of opposites...." Abel wandered the mountains, tending his sheep. His name comes "from the Hebrew '*hebel*,' meaning breath or vapour: Anything that lives or moves and is transient." Cain was settled; he was associated with the development of city life. "The root of 'Cain' appears to be the verb '*kanah*': To acquire, get, own property."[3]

My point is not that the life of wandering is necessarily good and a more settled life is necessarily bad. Too much wandering can lead to problems just as too much settling can. I am arguing that a sojourn in the wilderness can fill a basic spiritual need that we all have. If our need goes unfulfilled, we will find other ways to satisfy it. Cain's way—the accumulation of possessions—has dominated our culture for generations. We have become heavy with the weight of owning things, and the spirit has too often been wrung out of us. It is time to bring the spirit of Abel back to feed our souls. It is time to take inspiration seriously.

The experience of wilderness was not just about the Israelites' relationship with the Divine. It was about their relationship with each other. Stripped of their physical baggage, their class and financial status, the Israelites had to get down to the bare essentials: the survival and development of the community.

Rarely are we so close to our neighbors for so long that we can even begin to imagine what spending 40 years homeless in the desert with thousands of other people must have been like. Living in such close quarters surely exacerbated tensions. Day in and day out, people were hungry, cranky, tired, sick; kids were crying for attention; mothers were giving birth; and old people were dying.

Under desert conditions, community can be forged because people are forced to rely on each other through boredom, fear, anger, depression, and pain. Today, we take pride in keeping our problems to ourselves. We build walls to keep the world out. But for the desert Israelites, there were no opportunities to get away from each other. The wilderness was the ultimate test of the sustainability of the community.

As in any community, the Israelites had a system of law to ensure order for its people. Jewish law developed to deal with the multitude of concerns that arose between neighbors. Confronted with the unknown in every moment, the law could provide some comfort and some code with which to ensure justice and harmony. Given that the Israelite people spent their lives walking, it is little wonder that *halachah,* the word for "law" in Hebrew, is linked to *holech,* the word for "walk." They both derive from the same three-letter root H-L-K. *Halachah* literally teaches us the art of walking. It teaches the boundaries of the path and lets us know when we have trespassed; it conveys the stance we should adopt for different occasions. It is the tool we were given to help us build community.

The experience of wilderness promises two of life's primary lessons: we find out who we are and where we belong, and we learn to live in community with other people. In the process, we have the opportunity to see our slavery for what it is, to purify ourselves, to receive a vision, to become proactive, to develop intimacy with each other and the land, and to participate in the process of community building.

Today, many people tend to view the biblical wilderness experience as a metaphor for the journey we must all take to confront the unknown side of our soul and gain self-knowledge. Given that almost the entire biblical story takes place in the context of the desert wandering, I am convinced that the experience of wilderness is more than a metaphor.

I have always thought that our relationship to nature was a lost part of Jewish culture. So, too, the experience of wandering and wilderness and the spiritual journey. Today, the term "Jewish identity" is a buzzword in many Jewish circles, but most people are still loath to attach identity to a relation with God, to self-discovery, to a deep personal journey, especially one that occurs in wilderness. We must recognize that we truly don't have any identity until we find ourselves. In Jewish tradition, a spiritual journey is the way.

Jewish practice affords us the opportunity to integrate the wilderness sojourn into our lives three times a year. The regular pilgrimage festivals that mark the Jewish year—Pesach, Shavuot, and Sukkot—provide us with the chance to regain our bearings and find our direction in every season, to leave behind our certainty and our arrogance for an experience with the unknown. It is no coincidence that these three harvest festivals, on which our ancestors traveled hundreds of miles from all over Israel to bring offerings to the Temple in Jerusalem, were collectively called the *shalosh regalim*, literally the three "on foot" days. Pilgrimage was a routine and necessary part of the yearly cycle. It would take weeks, even months for many of the Israelites to arrive and weeks to return home. I have to believe that the process of getting there was as important as the holiday itself.

Rabbi James L. Mirel is spiritual leader of Temple B'nai Torah in Bellevue, Washington. Karen Bonnell Werth, a psychotherapist and psychiatric nurse, has worked extensively in the realm of body-mind-spirit with people of all ages and backgrounds. In *Stepping Stones to Jewish Spiritual Living: Walking the Path Morning, Noon, and Night,* they teach us that in every moment of each day, we have the opportunity to bring the sacred into our everyday lives.

Study: Our Relationship with Community

JAMES L. MIREL AND KAREN BONNELL WERTH

All life is within community and each of us is inextricably connected to those around us. Community can have many meanings and many forms. Within community, we hope to be nourished and sustained so we can create, reach our goals, and be transformed. Within community, we may experience the "whole" becoming greater than the sum of the parts. The power of community has been an essential theme in the story of the Jewish people.

> And they shall be my community, and I will be their God.
>
> JEREMIAH 32:38

> And be ready by the third day;
>
> for on the third day the Eternal One
>
> will come down upon Mount Sinai
>
> in the sight of all the community.
>
> EXODUS 19:11

Our ancestors stood as a community before God at Mount Sinai, when the Eternal One honored the importance of sharing an experience with others and expressing communal support for the sustenance of the individual and the whole:

So Moses came and called the elders of the community, and set before them all these words which the Eternal One had commanded him. And *all the people answered together* and said, "All that the Eternal One has spoken we will do and we will hear." And Moses reported the words of the community to the Eternal One. And the Eternal One said to Moses, "Lo, I am coming to you in a thick cloud, that *the community may hear when I speak with you, and may also believe you for ever.*"

(Exodus 19:7–9)

Today, the importance of sharing experience and expressing communal support is personified in Judaism by the idea of *minyan,* the quorum of ten which is traditionally required for a prayer service.[1] Without a *minyan,* some prayers are not to be recited aloud. This is a metaphor for the void we feel when we are not fully supported by family and friends. God is not enough to overcome our existential loneliness. We need each other.

I will rejoice in Jerusalem [in holiness],

and be glad in my community...

ISAIAH 65:19

Jews often have a sense of comfort and security when they meet members of the Jewish community, whether they are home or halfway around the world. Finding out that someone is a Jew often breaks down barriers between people. When we travel and seek a synagogue or a Jewish community center or a Jewish museum, we seek comfort and familiarity in a strange place. Even in our everyday world, we may be attracted to cues that indicate that someone is Jewish. This elicits a sense of kinship, an understanding, a bond. Community may also provide comfort and security that reminds us of extended family. The Hebrew word for "family," *mishpacha,* derives from the root for the words "confluence" and "flowing": we *flow* together connecting one person to the next. We may experience *mishpacha* with all the Jewish people; and we spiritually long for a *mishpacha* with all humanity, since the universal river connects all Creation.

Community is also our context for *tikkun olam,* repairing the world. Here, our responsibility to others comes to bear. In our prayers we say, *Sh'ma Kolenu*—"hear our voice"—indicating *our* collective, communal responsibility and power. Whether we pray alone or with others, we pray *for* the community, which reminds us that we belong to community.

In Judaism, we recognize that communal empowerment is fueled by individual action, which is really individual responsibility coming together for the sake of the community. As Heschel wrote, "We must continue to remind ourselves that in a free society all are involved in what some are doing. Some are guilty, all are responsible."[2] The West was founded on principles of individual freedom; we may find it difficult to consider ourselves responsible for the actions of others in any way. Yet, as Einstein wrote, "To be a Jew means to bear a serious responsibility not only to his own community, but also toward humanity."[3]

The group that each of us shares our lives with is surrounded by the larger Jewish community, by the larger secular community, by a national community. All these are

> *Do not separate yourself from the community.*
>
> MISHNAH AVOT 2:5

surrounded by the global community, the cosmic community, and finally the Infinite Community. We belong. We are responsible. Our individual actions are not restricted to a select few, but extend to all humanity and to all God's Creation. Our soul's work keeps alive the community's Tree of Life, circulating the sap of life, and moving us toward the Days of *Shalom*, of Peace. As Abraham Isaac Kook wrote,

> There is one who ascends with all these songs in unison—the song of the soul, the song of the nation, the song of humanity, the song of the cosmos—resounding together, blending in harmony, circulating the sap of life, the sound of holy joy.[4]

The shadow side of "community" is cult. This occurs when we insist that each person in our group adopt the same thinking and behavior as the group norm, and when the group's certainty about truth cannot be challenged or changed. Judaism has a long history of challenging, disagreeing, adapting, changing, questioning, of wandering through the desert of uncertainty and searching for the Promised Land of understanding. As a dynamic religion, Judaism moves us forward toward the world that is constantly coming.

I will give them a heart to know that

I am the Eternal One;

and they shall be my community

and I will be their God,

for they shall return to me their whole heart.

JEREMIAH 24:7

In the face of challenging and questioning, Judaism has maintained certain traditions for thousands of years. This is every community's challenge: finding a balance in which growth constructively intertwines with essence, a balance which maintains tradition and purpose within the context of creation. Doing this requires tolerance and respect, pursuing justice and embracing the diversity of the Eternal One's family.

It is possible to have a path and a discipline that enhances spiritual progress without hierarchy, that does not create an "other" whom we perceive as "less than" or "bad." Rav Kook claimed that the highest sensibility of the Jewish soul is the quest for universality.[5] If so, then we must ask ourselves: Do any of us have the authority to exclude others from God's holy community?

Community does not come about spontaneously. *Pirke Avot,* "The Words of the Elders," tells us, "Find a Master, Acquire a Friend." We need to recognize our own responsibility in creating community. Often this consists of seeking out an already existing community and trying to be part of it; or we may need to create community for ourselves. At such times, we need to look inside for the courage to reach out, even when it may mean rejection.

And many nations shall join themselves

to the Eternal One in that day,

and shall be My community;

and I will dwell in the midst of you...

ZECHARIAH 2:11

To become a member of the Jewish community, we only need to follow the wisdom of Torah and God's Eternal Oneness: "Let not the foreigner who has joined the Eternal One say, 'The Eternal One will surely separate me from the

Eternal One's people'.... I will bring them to My holy mountain, and make them joyful in My house of prayer...for My house shall be called a house of prayer for all peoples" (Isaiah 56:3, 7). Becoming a Jew-by-choice involves deliberately deciding to walk the Jewish path. Spiritually, all Jews are "Jews-by-choice" since we must choose—moment-to-moment—how to live our lives as Jews.

Judaism is lived most fully with family and community. Yet, there are times when we are completely alone. It is important to develop spiritual coping mechanisms to be able to feel God's embrace at those times. Remember *Sh'ma Kolenu,* "hear *our* voice," and know that even when praying alone, we are in community. Prayer and meditation are the paths to God and wholeness, whether in the company of others or alone.

> *O that I had in the desert a wayfarers' lodging place, that I might leave my community and go away from them.*
>
> JEREMIAH 9:2

> *The Torah was given in public, openly, in a free place. ...it was given in the wilderness publicly and openly in a place that is free for all; everyone willing to accept it could come and accept it.*
>
> MECHILTA D'RABBI ISHMAEL

Rabbi Karyn D. Kedar is the regional director of the Great Lakes Region of the Union of American Hebrew Congregations. She was the first woman rabbi to serve in Jerusalem and lived and worked in Israel for ten years. In *God Whispers: Stories of the Soul, Lessons of the Heart,* Rabbi Kedar teaches us how the search for community is the search for shared responsibility.

Community

KARYN D. KEDAR

Hillel said:
Do not separate yourself from the community.
Do not judge others until you stand in their place.
Do not say that which should not be heard,
For in the end it will be heard.

(Mishnah Avot 2:4)

The desire for community is not necessarily the search for friendship. It is the search for shared responsibility. The word "responsibility" bids you to respond according to your ability: if you can, respond when I am sick, respond when I give birth, respond when I bury my father. When we have shared moments of celebration and sorrow, we respond by showing up.

In the hours before Hurricane Andrew struck the mainland in southern Florida in the year 1992, the sky was the color of mustard, and the stillness in the air made millions of people hold their breath. A 200-mile-an-hour wind was approaching the coast. My husband and I were renting a townhouse in Boca Raton. Our three small children were with us and I was scared. Around nine o'clock that evening, we walked outside. The neighbors were standing around. We didn't know each other, and nobody said a word. Never had my need for community been so great, and never had community been so absent. I wanted to reach out: What part of the house was the safest place to be when the storm struck? What were the chances of the eye of the storm hitting where we were? Instead, we were surrounded by isolation and silence.

Community comes from the word "common." The word assumes an awareness that we share in the most basic way: tears, loss, love, illness, joy, fear, birth, death, life. We are not meant to live alone. We are not supposed to ignore or deny what we have in common as human beings. That is the power of community. It is the acknowledgment of the universals of life, the sameness, the common ground. It is the knowledge that I will never be alone when I am sick; that I can share the mixed emotions I will have when my children go away to college; that when I pray for the secret desires of my soul, I will be joined by others doing the same. I live amid strangers, acquaintances, friends, and even a few people whom I don't like. What makes us a community is the sense of shared responsibility: when one is in need, the other simply responds.

I believe that to be fully actualized as an individual, you must belong to a larger community, a community that requires that you break down walls of isolation, a community that will respond to you—and that will ask you to respond in kind.

Rabbi Arthur Waskow founded and directs the Shalom Center, and is a Pathfinder of ALEPH: Alliance for Jewish Renewal, an international network. He is founder and editor of the journal *New Menorah,* and helped establish the Fabrangen Cheder and the National Havurah Committee. In *Godwrestling—Round 2: Ancient Wisdom, Future Paths,* Rabbi Waskow teaches us about our relationship to the Jewish community and about the Jewish community's relationship to the world.

On the Fringes

ARTHUR WASKOW

One Shabbat morning during Fabrangen's second year, we had just begun the Torah reading. Suddenly a young woman who had been a member from the earliest days walked up to the Torah table, looked around the circle of our puzzled faces, took a deep breath, and said in a clear, calm voice, "I have a grievance that I need the community to address. I invoke the ancient right to interrupt the reading of the Torah to ask you to address my grievance."

We gasped. Some of us knew that in medieval Europe, there was exactly such a custom. But—a grievance? Inside our community? We were such friends; how could there be?

The person who had been about to read the Torah covered the Scroll, turned to the woman, and said, "All right. What is your grievance?"

"At our Shabbat morning service three weeks ago," she said, "barely ten of us were present. Our davvening leader looked around and counted, and went forward with the prayers for which we need a minyan. But as most of you know, I was born into a Christian family. Although I have been living as a practicing Jew for several years, I have never taken part in any ceremony of conversion. I was one of the ten who was counted that Shabbat for a minyan.

"Just yesterday I learned that since that Shabbat, a number of you have been talking about whether I should have been counted. But you have all been too embarrassed to ask me to take part in that discussion. I have prayed here, studied Torah here, danced here. All of us have acted as if I were a Jew. *But—am I?*

"My grievance is simply that I have not been asked to join in this discussion. I am not embarrassed. I think the community needs to decide this question, and I can live with whatever we decide. But there needs to be a process, and I need to be part of it. So I ask you to begin."

So for the first time we publicly faced the question, "Who is a Jew?" For the rest of that Shabbat, and in special community meetings over the next few months, the Torah we discussed was the Torah of—"Who is a Jew? What is a Jew? When is a Jew?" Perhaps we should have realized that our interrupted Torah reading was a crystal of a larger truth—that over the next decades, Jews everywhere would have to pause from their accustomed rhythms to face that same question.

In our case, we decided that becoming a Jew was a process, with a beginning hidden in mystery and an end that was never completed, whether or not someone was born a Jew. But we also decided that someone not born a Jew who entered this process needed to cross a formal and explicit boundary to become a Jew. Immersion in the miniature ritual ocean of mikveh, we decided, was that boundary marker—just as ancient Jewish tradition had determined.

We also decided that we, as a community of Israel, were fully competent to carry out a conversion: That is, to decide whether a non-Jew had gone far enough into the process of inner conversion for us to authorize her to enter the mikveh and come out a Jew. We prepared to hold a meeting of the whole community that could function as a *beit din* (rabbinical court of judgment) to make this determination. We scheduled a trip to the mikveh. And then our Jew-in-process faced us with a new dilemma: During the months of study, she had concluded that she wanted to enter the people Israel through Fabrangen's gateway—and also through the gateway of an Orthodox *beit din*.

What a conundrum! There is no way to convert twice: Once it's done, you're a Jew. To do it twice would delegitimate one of the ceremonies: ours or the Orthodox rabbis'. What to do? Finally, we realized: The moment of conversion is the moment when the Jew-in-process says a blessing in the mikveh. Two different communities could authorize her to immerse herself; two different witnesses could witness. Yet the transformation would happen only once.

That is what we did. Our *beit din* did much more than ask some formulaic questions: We had a long, rich discussion of what it meant to be a Jew. What it meant for her; what it meant for the rest of us. By the time she was ready for the mikveh, each of us had become more fully Jewish than we had been before.

Even so, we did not see the implications of this experience in the larger world. Once we decided there were boundaries, we thought that what they were was clear enough: Anyone born to a Jewish mother or converted by any Jewish community was a Jew; others weren't.

Twenty years later, it is not so clear. There has been an enormous wave of intermarriages, and an enormous wave of conversions, the most since the days of Rome and the Talmud, when the Jewish people was rebirthing itself from the biblical to the Rabbinic form. Different Jewish groups are asserting different standards for conversion and for deciding whether particular individuals need a conversion ceremony or are already Jews.

And the boundaries of Jewish peoplehood have been softening in other ways as well. What about Buddhist Jews? Sufi Jews? Jews who celebrate with a Native American sweat lodge? Jews who believe that Jesus was the Messiah?

What are the boundaries of Jewish peoplehood? Who are part of the family and who are not? Is it a "family"? If so, in what sense?

Why is all this happening? Much of the agonized reappraisal has avoided saying out loud that the new intermarriage rates are rooted in the triumph of modernity. The Jewish people is not the only one profoundly affected by modernity, and we will better analyze our own situation if we keep that in mind.

Modernity has shown *all* those who walked the ancient life-paths, all the ancient communities and traditions, both ethnic and religious, that a "secular," "scientific" approach to the world has enormous power. Modernity has brought the various old spiritual traditions into much closer physical, intellectual, and emotional proximity with each other than before. The high fences between them have dissolved into semipermeable, uncertain, fuzzy boundaries. The boundaries are now more like fringes than like fences.

This has become true in three spheres of life:

First, the ideas mingle. Ancient traditions that used to be quite distinctive have all been listening to each other, absorbing bits of each other and of secularism—and have thus become more similar.

A poignant example: The Dalai Lama, head of a community of Tibetan Buddhists who are exiled from the homeland where they have lived for many centuries, asks to meet with Jews. Teach us, he says, how to keep a land-rooted religion alive in exile. And the Jews respond: Our people are searching for meditations, for spiritual "detachment." What, they ask, can you teach us?

One century ago, no such conversation would have been possible. The Dalai Lama was immured in Lhasa; his only teachers were other Buddhists. And most Jews would have viewed him as an idolater, proclaiming no god, bowing to the statue of a fat and laughing human.

Second, the peoples intermingle. The Jewish and Christian and Buddhist and Muslim and Native communities meet. Ghettos dissolve.

Third, actual membership in a tradition—the definitions of who belongs to, crosses over into, and actually lives with and rears children in the community/tradition itself—is far fuzzier than it used to be. *That* is intermarriage.

The first step in this process was secularization: Modernity itself was seen as an adequate, indeed powerful, life-path. Ethnicity and spirituality seemed impediments to personal and social progress. Many Jews welcomed this process.

CHOOSING THE JEWISH PATH

But we are already seeing a "post-modern," "post-secular" realization that spirituality and community are necessary if personal wholeness and the earth's survival are both to be protected.

Still, this does not automatically mean that individuals return to the communal and spiritual forms of their childhoods. Now, when people search toward community and spirituality, they may find themselves *choosing* a form that fits their individual needs, rather than replicating that of their childhood because they know nothing else. Indeed, some may so deeply identify the childhood patterns as merely "childish" that they can be satisfied as adults only by some form that they discover as adults.

Thus, in North America, more and more people who are born into households of one or two Jewish parents will choose whether to shape a Jewish identity for themselves or walk some other life-path. More and more people who are not born to Jewish parents will also be choosing their futures—and an appreciable number of them will choose Judaism. Those from *both* kinds of family backgrounds who see themselves as having consciously chosen a Jewish identity will become a large part, perhaps a majority, of North American Jewry.

Under these conditions, therefore, many North American Jews—perhaps most—will experience the Jewish community and Judaism as a spiritual/religious community of choice rather than an ethnic community in which membership is defined chiefly by birth.

It has been two thousand years since we faced the question of how to shape such a Judaism. That was when Hellenism (like modernity today) broke down our own and other communities' boundaries. The result was not only many conversions, semi-conversions, and intermarriages, but the very remaking of what Judaism was. What had been the biblical pattern of getting in touch with God by bringing offerings of food from a single land to a single place in that land, became a pattern in which a people scattered across Europe and the Middle East touched God through words: prayer, Torah study, and midrash-making.

As then, so today. This dynamic requires Judaism to transform itself. An ethnic community can survive by merely having children. For a spiritual/religious community to survive, it must not only survive but vivify: give people a sense of new life. Only a Judaism that is open, risky, spiritually alive and inviting will continue to keep non-Orthodox

Jews involved in Jewish community, and will attract non-Jews into the Jewish community.

GOOD FRINGES MAKE GOOD NEIGHBORS

One useful metaphor for the new Judaism can be drawn from the tradition that on the corners of our individual garments we wear carefully tied fringes, *tzitzit*. What would it mean to draw on this tradition at the level of the entire community?

What are *tzitzit*? They are a specially tied and knotted set of fringes that many male Jews and some women once wore on all their garments, and more recently wear on the ceremonial prayer shawl. They seem abstract, but not only is there a tradition of the meaning of the numbers of turns and knots, but as a gestalt the *tzitzit* honor and celebrate the fact that between individuals within a community there must be not high hard fences but soft and fading boundaries. These fringes are a mixture of "my" cloth and "communal" air.

In biblical tradition, this was affirmed by assigning the produce of the corners of "my" field to the communal needs of the poor, the stranger, the orphan. The field was "mine" (under God's ultimate ownership), but its corners faded away into communal space. In the new pattern shaped by the rabbis, the fringes of "my" garment played this role. Just as the shared communal use of the corners of the field betokened God's share in my property, so the communal fringes of the garment betokened God's share in my identity. God's representative, in both cases, was the community. If individuals were not open to and connected with other individuals, there would be no community—and no divinity. *Tzitzit* Judaized this assertion of connectedness: gave it a Jewish name, symbol, affirmation.

But while individuals had permeable boundaries with others in the same tradition, the community *as a whole* had high, strong fences in regard to other communities.

But now the fences between communities have become very leaky, fuzzy. There are in fact not fences but unclear boundaries between the Jewish people and other peoples, other societies. What do we do about it?

One option is to rebuild impenetrable fences. This is what the Hasidic and some other Orthodox communities try to do.

Another option is to leave the boundaries fuzzy. Until now, that has been the underlying assumption of the greater part of the American Jewish community. What is new is a deep sense of disquiet about this answer. But so far, there seems to have been an underlying assumption that there are only two possible options—sharp fences or fuzzy fringes. Back to the ghetto or a formless people.

But we might create a third option: Tying *tzitzit*. Recognizing that the boundaries are leaky, permeable, and turning that very permeability into a Jewishly affirmable fact. Some of us may view this permeability as a troublesome but valuable concomitant of moving out of the ghetto. Others may view it as a flaw or illness in the Jewish body politic, and so are reluctant to affirm the permeability in any way. But even on such a view, there may be Jewish ways of responding to the malaise. To use a physical analogy, we might say that Jewish experience recognizes that illnesses will come to the individual body and that some of these are in our present life conditions inevitable and incurable. Our community does not then throw up its hands in despair. We develop a Jewish response, *bikkur cholim,* a whole Jewish pattern of how to respond to sickness, drawing on Jewish paths and symbols. Similarly, we need to respond Jewishly to the new fact of Jewish existence that the boundaries of our community are permeable.

We must create *tzitzit* between communities. In other words, we need to bring the permeability of our boundaries into the purview of the community. We need to "own" the fuzziness itself, give it a ritual form that is our own, Judaize it.

Making *"tzitzit"* at the communal level means developing conscious spiritual and communal language—conscious *Jewish* language—for being open to people who are the community's "collective *tzitzit"*—our collective fringes, part "us" and part universal. This is true in regard to intermarriage and also to the spheres of life we call "political" or "intellectual."

Rabbi Sharon L. Sobel is rabbi of Temple Sinai in Stamford, Connecticut. In *The Women's Torah Commentary: New Insights from Women Rabbis on the 54 Weekly Torah Portions,* edited by Rabbi Elyse Goldstein, Rabbi Sobel teaches us about community as sacred space.

Terumah: תרומה
Community as Sacred Space

SHARON L. SOBEL

Let them make Me a sanctuary that I may dwell within them.
(Exodus 25:8, JPS Translation)

Have you ever noticed that when people walk into a sanctuary in a synagogue, their behavior changes, based on the physical characteristics of that room? If the sanctuary is a large, cathedral-like room with a vaulted ceiling, stained-glass windows, and a tall and remote *bimah* (podium), the immediate reaction is one of wonderment. People speak in hushed and reverential tones, as if they might disturb God by conversing more loudly. For many people, this type of sanctuary is an awe-inspiring and majestic place, a symbol of God's presence in their synagogue. If the sanctuary is a simpler kind of space, with wraparound windows looking out on a beautiful scene of nature, and a small, low-to-the-floor *bimah,* the mood it engenders is quite different. People enter the room talking and laughing. They don't hesitate to approach the *bimah* to speak with whoever is standing there before the worship service begins. For these people, God's presence is felt in their sanctuary by their closeness to nature and to each other. If someone who is accustomed to worshiping in one type of sanctuary visits the other, they have a tendency to feel uncomfortable praying, or they explain that they feel they can't connect to God, in any kind of space other than what they are used to at "home."

Why do we place so much emphasis on the sanctuaries of our synagogues? Can a physical space be holy in and of itself ?

Before the creation of the first *mishkan* (sanctuary) in the Torah, the Hebrews worshiped God on hilltops, beside streams, or wherever they felt moved to pray. Abraham and Isaac traveled to Mount Moriah. Rebecca confronted God in her own tent. Jacob encountered God in a lonely place in the desert and near the river Jabbok. Moses met God at an ordinary bush in the land of Midian and at the top of Mount Sinai in the wilderness. Miriam praised God at the banks of the Sea of Reeds.

It was only after the Israelites were liberated from slavery in Egypt, and after they accepted God's Torah at Mount Sinai, that they were commanded to build a sanctuary. The instructions for erecting this sanctuary are given in great detail in this *parashah* from Exodus, *Terumah.* This *parashah* provides explicit directions not only for the erection of the structure itself, but also for all of the objects and decorations inside. The sanctuary was to contain the Ark of the Covenant, with its sacred stones upon which the Ten Commandments were inscribed. It was to be placed in the Holy of Holies chamber, inside the inner tabernacle. The opening of the Holy of Holies was to be covered by a curtain. Outside that curtain, there was a special altar for the incense, a table for the shewbread, and a golden menorah (lampstand). In front of the inner tabernacle was another curtain, outside of which are the laver and an altar for burnt offerings. Clearly, the sanctuary was designed for performing sacred rituals, which included the offering of sacrifice, and prayer to God.

The Torah seeks to clarify the purpose of the sanctuary when God instructs Moses to tell the people, *V'asu li mikdash v'shachanti b'tocham,* "And let them make me a sanctuary that I may dwell within them" (Exod. 25:8). What do these words really mean? Was God telling the people that without a sanctuary, a building, a place for the Ark of the Covenant, or altars for sacrifice, they would not sense the Divine presence in their lives? Does God truly require a building in order to "dwell" among human beings? What does it mean for God to "dwell within" the people? What does this tell us about our relationship with God?

Commentators are intrigued by the notion that God will not dwell *in the sanctuary,* but rather, *within them,* within the people. It is the physical act itself of building the sanctuary that will cause God to dwell within the people. The sanctuary is not for God, it is for the people; it is to be a visible symbol of God's presence in their midst. God's promise to dwell among the people is a recognition of the limitations of human beings in trying to understand that God is everywhere. The tabernacle is a concession to humankind and provides a visible focus for the idea of God's indwelling.

Therefore, it is not the physical space itself that causes God's presence to come into our midst, and it is not the physical space itself that is holy. Rather, it is the involvement of the community, expending its labor on God's behalf. It is the act of the community joining together to make a sacred space. It is the rituals that take place within that space that bring God's presence into the midst of the people. The purpose of the involvement of all the people in building the tabernacle is, as Torah commentator Pinchas Peli explains, to "convert the people from passive participants in their relationship with God, as constant recipients of God's gifts, into active partners."[1]

The indwelling of God among the people cannot take place as long as the people are passive, doing nothing to help bring the sacred into the world. God is saying, "My dwelling among them is on condition that they make the sanctuary." *We* must do the building to glorify God. This is emphasized in the text by the Hebrew verb *la'asot* (to "make"). It occurs two hundred times in the story of the building of the sanctuary.

The indwelling of God among the people is not contingent only upon the people's active participation in the building of the *mishkan,* it is also contingent upon the participation of *all* members of the community—men and women both. It becomes clear that the instructions of *Parashat Terumah* are given to both men and women when we look at *Parashat Vayakhel* in Exodus 35. Exodus 35 is the parallel description of the actual construction of the *mishkan* that corresponds to the instructions given in *Parashat Terumah.* Exodus 35 explicitly states that the instructions given in *Terumah* are intended for both men and women.

This description of the construction of the Tabernacle provides the only biblical example of active female participation in an activity related to the official cult. When God states, "Let them make me a sanctuary," the word "them" refers to both men and women. In Exodus 35:1, Moses explicitly brings together all the community of Israel, which included both men and women. We see this in at least three statements in Exodus 35: "men and women, all whose hearts moved them, all who would make an offering" (Exod. 35:22); "all the skilled women spun with their own hands and brought what they had spun...; and all the women who excelled in that skill spun the goats' hair" (Exod. 35:25–26); "thus the Israelites, all the men and women whose hearts moved them to bring anything for the work that the Lord, through Moses, had commanded to be done, brought it as a freewill offering to the Lord" (Exod. 35:29).

Therefore, the Torah text itself tells us that it is necessary for the *entire community*, which includes men and women both, to be involved in trying to bring God's presence into their midst. If only half the population is involved, if it is only the men who are doing the work and participating, then God's presence will not be felt. The community is whole and the community is holy only when both men and women are involved in sacred tasks together.

The task of bringing holiness into the world, which is the main obligation of every Jew, has always been seen in the Bible as a partnership, a combined project of humans and God. The holy can be manifest in three dimensions: space, time, and the person. God desires to encounter human beings by meeting them halfway as partners: in time, for the Shabbat, which God sanctified (Gen. 2:3) and commanded us to sanctify (Exod. 20:8); in space, by the building of the sanctuary; and in each person, through the mitzvot (commandments) or the sacred rituals, which bring us into God's presence every time we perform them.

We must start out on the path towards God, both in time and in space, in order for God to meet us halfway as partners in the act of sanctification. From this understanding comes the focus on building the tabernacle for God in the wilderness, and the emphasis we place on our sanctuaries in our synagogues today.

But what does it mean that the building of the sanctuary will cause God to "dwell within the people"? What does it mean that this will start us on our path towards meeting God? Torah commentator Nehama Leibowitz points out, "Surely these words contain a message of Divine love, a promise of intimate contact with God."[2] The typical image of God as portrayed by much of the Torah is an image of a distant, transcendent, parental, authoritarian figure. This notion from our *parashah* that God can dwell within the people is a shift in focus from the earlier biblical model of God as distant or remote from the people. It shows us that different models of relationships with God are necessary in order for us to live out our lives as a holy people.

Some feminists have been troubled that the God of the Torah seems to be primarily a transcendent God, and that this is the model that our male commentators and rabbis have perpetuated. This description of God in our *parashah* as an "indwelling presence," however, shows another angle. God wants to live among us, and God wants us to feel that Divine love in an intimate way. Commentator Isaac Abravanel reinforces this when he says, "The Divine intention behind the construction of the Tabernacle was to combat the idea that God had forsaken the earth and that His throne was in heaven and remote from humankind. To disabuse them of this erroneous belief, God commanded them to make a Tabernacle, as if to say that God lived in their minds...in order to implant in their hearts His presence."[3] *Parashat Terumah* helps us to understand that the traditional notion of God as only transcendent is a limited notion. It shows us that for God to truly dwell among us, both men and women must embrace immanent images of God as well.

So as we sit in our sanctuaries, be they small or large, intimate or grandiose, we need to keep in mind that it is not a particular physical space that evokes God's presence in our midst. Rather, it is we who will bring God's presence into our midst by making sure we include everyone—men, women, and children—in the sacred acts in which we participate.

Rabbi Ira F. Stone, spiritual leader of Temple Beth Zion-Beth Israel in Philadelphia, began his spiritual odyssey as a para-professional social worker and street worker with drug abusing youth in New York City. He is a Visiting Lecturer in the Department of Jewish Philosophy at The Jewish Theological Seminary. In *Seeking the Path to Life: Theological Meditations on God and the Nature of People, Love, Life and Death,* Rabbi Stone teaches us about living in this life.

Living in This Life

IRA F. STONE

Living life after suffering the utter solitude of accompanying a loved one to the grave and then creating a new life which takes that lonely experience seriously requires that the way one lives with people change. Renewing and invigorating life comes only from being with people—not from retreating to the solitude of pain and despair.

This has been the most difficult part of my own journey. Prayer and study are easy. Loving is not. Confronting anger is not. Living with sadness is not. Moreover, just learning how difficult these things are almost inevitably heaps pain and hurt on those whose love one is seeking. Such has been my experience. The death of my infant sons, Hillel and Akiba, only exacerbated my tendency to withdraw from emotional encounter. After the shock of the abandonment caused by death, I insulated myself against further abandonment. I regret the pain this caused my wife and children. I am grateful that their prodding helped me to begin to learn that I was fleeing what I most needed.

I am also grateful to my experience in psychotherapy. I came to therapy highly suspicious, and I still believe that it rests on a truncated vision of human personality: it does not take seriously enough our need to submit before God. But despite these philosophic qualms, I found a gifted healer who nurtured those parts of my psyche whose very existence she may have doubted. Her acceptance of my pain and my fears (as well as her acceptance of my strengths and my talents) was vitally important to my attempt to discover these words. With her help, I began to trust my impulse to discover life after the experience of death. With her encouragement, I discovered the way moments-of-death in life clouded my relationships with others.

Thus I came again to God. And from God, I came to understand that the way to God was through people. I came to understand, also, that the way to God began with those people closest to me who were willing to love me, and whom I have only begun to allow myself to love.

Rabbi Karyn D. Kedar is the regional director of the Great Lakes Region of the Union of American Hebrew Congregations. She was the first woman rabbi to serve in Jerusalem and lived and worked in Israel for ten years. In *God Whispers: Stories of the Soul, Lessons of the Heart,* Rabbi Kedar teaches us about the importance of creating a sanctuary in our lives.

Creating Sanctuary

KARYN D. KEDAR

We must create pockets of hope, safe places where pain is softened because love abounds, places where God is invited to fill the void, where sparks of kind light banish the darkness. Once we find these places, we must surrender to their safety.

The desert: vast, loudly quiet, beautiful, dangerous. The desert journey: mysterious, endless directions, no clear path. The vast horizons of the desert make me dizzy and confuse me as to which way I should go. God says, "Build Me a Sanctuary so that I might dwell among you," and I get busy building a structure that will symbolize God's presence and love. I am commanded to focus on the details: blue, purple, and crimson yarns; acacia wood; pure gold, dolphin skins, and lapis lazuli. My focus gives me direction. It gives me hope that I will be guided out of the desert. I build this sanctuary, and I feel safe. As I approach the sanctuary, I feel God's presence, and I see the great cherubim guarding the entrance. I see their faces turned ever so slightly so that their gazes meet as I enter. "Where is God?" I ask myself. Perhaps God is in the place that their gazes meet.

I was searching for God in the numb stare of the thirteen-year-old girl in my office. She was about to become bat mitzvah, that rite of passage in which a young teen leads the congregation in worship and enters the community as a responsible adult. But before me was a sad, unresponsive, and aloof child. I had been hearing rumblings about her family. A recent divorce had left the husband stunned. Both parents agreed, however, to present a unified front when it came to the children, so both sat in my office with their daughter. I looked at Ivy's mother. She was beautiful, vivacious, filled with joy and life. I looked at her father. He was quiet, unsure, and terribly sad. I searched Ivy's face and saw both those forces living in her. She had not yet decided which would dominate her life. It was clear that she was not able to deal with the pressures of the approaching service and found the whole event terribly irrelevant to her difficult life.

I tried to engage Ivy in conversation, but mostly she stared blankly and gave me one-word answers. Occasionally, she would look at her parents and check their reactions against what I had said. I finally asked her parents to leave the room.

The door closed. I smiled at Ivy to assure her she was not "in trouble."

"Parents divorced this year?" I said in a matter-of-fact voice.

"Yeah." I could barely hear her.

"It's been tough, huh?"

"Uh-huh."

"This service doesn't mean much to you right now, huh?"

"I guess not."

I decided to continue with blunt honesty. "I suppose I understand that. It must be weird to be the center of all this attention when you feel your world is falling apart."

She looked at me carefully, trying to decide if she could trust me. She slid further into her seat and said, "Yeah, it's really weird."

"It's OK, Ivy. We'll get through this together. I'll be right by your side. You will get through this. You can't fail. I won't let you."

She slowly smiled at me, and I saw her beauty and sweetness. The day of the service arrived, and the guests were dressed in shades of elegance. Ivy was sitting by herself in my office, hiding from the turmoil outside. I sat with her and went over the last-minute details. She left the office to greet her guests, and I stood at the door and watched. Moments before we were to begin, people were entering the sanctuary, and Ivy's father came up to her to wish her well. As he leaned down to kiss her, she rested her head against his chest and burst into tears. Her mother saw what was happening from afar but was too stunned to react. As her father put his arms around her, she pulled away. I then took her by the arm into my office and closed the door.

I took both of her hands in mine. They were cold and fragile. I looked into her eyes and said, "Ivy, I want you to remember this moment. At this moment, you are loved and honored for who you are. You are not alone. I am here for you, and God is always with you. If you are ever in trouble, even ten years from now, you come to me. You are safe, Ivy. It will be OK. Let's begin the service."

Trembling, she did not want to pull her hands away. We had built a sanctuary of safety and invited God to dwell among us. We stared into each other's eyes, and in the place our gazes met, God brought us warmth, safety, and love. She surrendered to a moment of hope, and we left to lead the service.

In our sadness and fear of the future, we must find hope. We must be able to envision ourselves in a safer place, where we are loved for who we are and who we are meant to be.

Isa Aron, Ph.D., is Professor of Jewish Education at Hebrew Union College–Jewish Institute of Religion's Rhea Hirsch School of Education, where she directs the Experiment in Congregational Education (ECE). In *Becoming a Congregation of Learners: Learning as a Key to Revitalizing Congregational Life,* Dr. Aron teaches us about the community of a congregation.

The Community of a Congregation: The Congregation as Community

ISA ARON

Imagine two synagogues, located at opposite ends of a metropolitan area somewhere in North America. At first glance, the two look very similar. Both have impressive buildings with sanctuaries, social halls, classrooms, and offices. Both hold services on Shabbat and on holidays. Both offer religious school on Sunday mornings and weekday afternoons. But, looking more closely, one begins to notice significant differences.

The atmosphere at the first congregation is quiet and businesslike. Its schedule is regular and predictable. In the mornings the nursery school children arrive; in mid-afternoon they leave, and the religious school students begin streaming in, causing a momentary commotion until the they go into their classrooms. On most evenings small clusters of adults come in for meetings and classes; they sort themselves quickly, and rarely linger in the hallways. On Friday nights and Saturday mornings hushed murmurs can be heard in the sanctuary, where a group of 100 or so congregants assembles. Afterwards, in the social hall, there is polite conversation.

At first glance, this synagogue seems like any other—not particularly exciting, but certainly "good enough." But a closer look reveals the problem that lurks beneath the surface: Most of the adult activities are attended by the same small group of people, week in and week out. These are the synagogue "regulars." They are proud of the congregation, but, in truth, they feel a bit beleaguered. They wonder why most of their fellow congregants don't participate more often, and why these others don't seem to value the institution in which they have invested so much of themselves.

The second congregation, on the other hand, resembles a bee-hive. Everywhere there is a flurry of activity. All day long adults trickle in, sometimes with small children in tow. They head for the library, the resource room, the classrooms, and even the social hall, where art, music, and dance are scheduled. In the late afternoons and on weekends, schoolchildren arrive, joined by more adults. Though the children start out in classrooms, they don't stay put very long, spilling out into the rest of the building and, weather permitting, onto the grounds. On Shabbat the sanctuary is nearly filled; boisterous singing can be heard, and the laughter and chatter of children echo through the corridors. After services, people linger in the social hall and continue their conversations in the parking lot.

This congregation, like the first, has its own "regulars," but they are a larger and more diverse group. Though they too spend hours volunteering, they are hardly beleaguered, for they can feel their efforts bearing fruit. Together with the professional staff, they have created a vibrant community whose members are connected in multiple and overlapping ways. The parent with children in the religious school is in a study group with the senior citizen who works as a teachers' aide. The teenager who volunteers in the social action program sings in the choir with her friend's parents. People join this synagogue with the expectation that they will become active participants in some aspect of the community. They expect to volunteer in a variety of ways, and the synagogue is able to rely on their help. Although the membership is spread over a large area and many people see one another only at the synagogue, they feel connected. They know they will be there for one another when the need arises, whether it is organizing a blood drive or celebrating a *simcha* (a joyous event).

What enables the second congregation to flourish in this way? How might the first congregation become more lively, and more central in the lives of its members? For the last decade, leaders of the American Jewish community have been wringing their hands over the "continuity crisis," whose most obvious symptom is the rising rate of intermarriage, but whose ancillary symptoms include lower rates of affiliation and observance. In this discussion, synagogues have tended to be seen as part of the problem rather than as part of the solution. In the Jewish press and in community forums there is much talk of the promise of day schools, Israel trips, camps, and Jewish community centers, but very little said about synagogues. Of course, a vibrant Jewish community requires a panoply of institutions. We know that Jewish community centers bring in the unaffiliated and that day schools and trips to Israel can have a profound effect on many of their participants. But important as these are, it would be a mistake to dismiss the potential of a vibrant synagogue for enriching Jewish life.

Synagogues have an important role to play in linking Jews to their heritage and to one another. The synagogue is often the first point of entry into the Jewish community; approximately two-thirds of American Jews belong to synagogues at some point in their lives,[1] many more than will travel to Israel on a teen tour, attend a day school, or join a Jewish community center.[2] Synagogues have the potential for reaching people on a continuous basis throughout their lives and in the context of their families.

Unfortunately, much of this potential is not actualized for two reasons. First, the participation of many Jews in synagogue life is episodic rather than continuous. Jewish children typically begin attending synagogue when they enroll in religious school, where they remain through their bar or bat mitzvah and, perhaps, through confirmation at the age of sixteen or seventeen. Relatively few young adults participate in congregational life, but when they marry and have children of their own, many find their way back, if only to enable their own children to have a bar or bat mitzvah. Having reached this milestone, about a third of these families will drop out.[3]

More problematic is the fact that even those who remain members on a continuous basis rarely participate fully in a congregation's activities. Most synagogues attract members because of the programs they offer and amenities they provide, such as religious school, High Holiday worship, and rabbinic officiation at various life-cycle events.

Members pick and choose from the synagogue's offerings, but few see the congregation as important in their lives or as a locus of community.

It wasn't always this way. The traditional *kehilah kedoshah* (holy congregation) was a *bet tfilah* (house of prayer), a *bet midrash* (house of study), and a *bet kneset* (house of assembly) all rolled into one. But as Jews became more assimilated into American society, two of these functions dwindled and were supplanted by other institutions. Jewish learning for everyone devolved into secular learning for children, and became the province of the public school. A variety of social outlets developed: One kind of community could be found in the neighborhood, another in social halls and country clubs, a third in organizations like Hadassah and B'nai Brith. With learning and assembly taken care of elsewhere, the synagogue became, primarily, a house of worship. But in an era in which people questioned God's existence, more and more Jews grew ambivalent about prayer, showing up for state occasions, but feeling too uncomfortable to participate in prayer services on a regular basis.

To recapture their traditional place in the hearts and minds of their members, synagogues need to be rethought and reconfigured. Jewish *learning* is critical to synagogue revitalization because learning is at the core of our identities as Jews. For Jews, learning is more than an intellectual exercise; it engages our emotions and influences our actions. It is, by definition, communal; even when one learns alone, one is inextricably linked to Jews in other times and places.

A congregation of learners is much more than a collection of individuals that happens to learn. Learning will, inevitably, spill over into every other aspect of congregational life, changing people's approach to prayer, to ethics, and to social justice. Learning brings people together, creating the sense of community so many are seeking. When members of a congregation have a common understanding that Jewish learning is for everyone, and when they are provided with a range of engaging and stimulating opportunities for learning, that congregation will have become a congregation of learners.

III

The Times and Seasons of Your Life: When Does Spirituality Enter?

Go carefully:
Spiritual growth must proceed
slowly and steadily.
Too often we want to improve
ourselves and our relationships so
quickly that we make ourselves
frustrated and confused.

• • • •

Believe that none of the effort
you put into coming closer to God
is ever wasted—even if in the
end you don't achieve what
you are striving for.

— from *The Empty Chair: Finding Hope and Joy—*
Timeless Wisdom from a Hasidic Master,
Rebbe Nachman of Breslov

Rabbi Ira F. Stone, spiritual leader of Temple Beth Zion-Beth Israel in Philadelphia, began his spiritual odyssey as a para-professional social worker and street worker with drug abusing youth in New York City. He is a Visiting Lecturer in the Department of Jewish Philosophy at The Jewish Theological Seminary. In *Seeking the Path to Life: Theological Meditations on God and the Nature of People, Love, Life and Death*, Rabbi Stone teaches us how the choice of life defines time.

Time and Eternity

IRA F. STONE

The choice of life defines time. Every moment contained in that choice is connected to a past made up of choices made by ourselves and by our ancestors. And every moment contained in that choice immediately makes possible a future circumscribed by a death that, potentially, can be transcended.

Eternity consists only of God. Time is the quality of the sum of all the different forms of the relationship between us and God. Choosing life gives time meaning in this relationship. Choosing death-in-life destroys time. It leaves emptiness as the quality of the relationship between ourselves and God. The Eternal is alone outside of time.

By reminding ourselves of time's meaning, we imbue the passage of time with a nearly constant accumulation of choices for life. Reciting blessings, praying at appointed times, celebrating the Sabbath and festivals at their proper time are all part of our impulse to rescue time from emptiness and to befriend Eternity.

In this way, we gain a past. Jews, in particular, gain the past of Torah and Jewish history and of their family's heritage. We also gain the possibility of a future. Jews, in particular, gain the future of the Messianic world and the salvation of the world to come. And, we offer our friendship to a lonely God. Jews do this by living the life of Torah and halachah. Finally by giving life to time, we prepare ourselves to travel on the path that leads to transcendence and brings time and Eternity together.

Dr. Kerry M. Olitzky, rabbi, is executive director of the Jewish Outreach Institute, and was National Dean of Adult Jewish Learning and Living at Hebrew Union College–Jewish Institute of Religion. He is the author of many books that bring the Jewish wisdom tradition into everyday life. In *One Hundred Blessings Every Day: Daily Twelve Step Recovery Affirmations, Exercises for Personal Growth & Renewal Reflecting Seasons of the Jewish Year*, Rabbi Olitzky teaches us how the Jewish calendar is structured and how it relates to our lives.

How the Jewish Calendar Works

KERRY M. OLITZKY

Since biblical times, the months and years of the Jewish calendar have been established by the cycles of the moon and the sun. Included in Jewish law are guidelines which suggest that the months must follow closely the phases of the moon. These lunar months correspond to the seasons of the year which are determined by the sun.

When the Israelites were liberated from Egypt, the Torah teaches us "This month will be the beginning of the months, the very first of the month" (Exodus 12:2). The season of spring was the beginning of the year, according to the Torah, because it was marked by the rebirth of the nature and the liberation of our people.

The ancient Israelites had no real calendar. They knew of the cycle of the seasons, however, because of its relationship to planting and harvesting. In about the year 350 C.E., Hillel II helped to establish a permanent calendar for the Jewish people that adjusted the lunar year with the solar year. Since that time, this has become our calendar.

The Jewish calendar months are fixed by the cycles of the moon, while the days are fixed by the cycles of the sun. In this way, the Jewish holidays occur in their proper season, as specified in the Bible.

However, the dates of Jewish holidays on the secular civil calendar differ from year to year.

There are twelve months in the Jewish calendar. Each of these lunar months has either twenty-nine or thirty days, accounting for a total of three hundred fifty-four days. During Jewish leap years (approximately once every three years), a thirteenth month called Adar II is added.

The Jewish calendar numbers the years from the date of the creation of the world, as determined by ancient Jewish tradition. While many of us believe that the world was created millions of years ago, out of respect for Jewish tradition, we retain this method of numbering the years.

There are several synagogue celebrations directly related to the monthly renewal of the moon. *Rosh Chodesh,* the beginning of every Jewish month, is celebrated as a minor holy day for one day. The day of *Rosh Chodesh* is generally announced at the Sabbath synagogue service of the preceding week. This Sabbath, whenever it occurs, is called *Shabbat Mevarchim.* Although there is no work restriction on *Rosh Chodesh,* Jewish tradition has used it to honor women for their unusual piety by allowing them respite from their work. According to tradition, the Israelite women demonstrated this piety when they did not contribute their jewelry for the making of the golden calf. For many people, men and women, *Rosh Chodesh* serves as time for reflection and personal renewal. It provides us with an opportunity to look at the past month and suggest ways in which we might improve our lives (and our relations with other people) in the new month just ahead.

During the rabbinic period, the beginning of the new month was declared when two witnesses reported to the Sanhedrin that the crescent of a new moon had appeared. The declaration was relayed from city to city by lighting fires on hilltops. Often, fires were lit in error. This caused confusion and a delay in announcing the new month. To make certain that all holidays were celebrated on their proper day, an extra day was added to the prescribed number. Most communities outside of Israel follow this model. However, members of the Reform movement generally observe the holidays according to the original number because of the scientific exactitude with which the calendar is currently determined. The rabbis tell us that when the day of *Rosh Chodesh* was determined by the rabbinical court using the sighting of the new moon, people would assemble for a festive meal. Today, by astronomical calculation, the beginning of the new month takes place at the moment when the moon is exactly between the earth and the sun, and nothing is visible of the moon. It is at that time that the *molad* (or the birth) of the moon takes place.

It takes about twenty-nine and a half days for the moon to circle the earth. Since half days are awkward to count, some months in the Jewish calendar are always twenty-nine days and others are always thirty days. If a month contains thirty days, then the last day of that month and the first day of the next month *both* comprise *Rosh Chodesh*. If a month contains only twenty-nine days, then only the first day of the following month is called *Rosh Chodesh*.

The second celebration of the moon's renewal is called *Kiddush Levanah* or the sanctification of the moon. Several days after the emergence of the new moon, people assembled outside in an open space in order to offer a prayer of thanksgiving for the renewal of life and their hopeful optimism for the future.

The last celebration of the calendar occurs every twenty years. It is called *Birkat Hachamah,* the blessing of the sun. When the cycle of the heavenly bodies completes itself at the spring equinox every twenty-eight years, we give thanks to God for the sun.

HOLIDAYS AND FESTIVALS AT A GLANCE

Fall

Rosh Hashanah / New Year
Yom Kippur / Day of Atonement
Sukkot / Harvest Festival of Thanksgiving
Shemini Atzeret / Eighth Day of Assembly
Simchat Torah / Rejoicing of the Torah

Winter

Hanukkah / Festival of Lights
Purim / Festival of Lots

Spring

Pesach / Passover
Shavuot / Feast of Weeks

Dr. Lawrence A. Hoffman, rabbi, Professor of Liturgy at Hebrew Union College–Jewish Institute of Religion, is cofounder of Synagogue 2000, a trans-denominational project designed to envision and implement the ideal synagogue of the spirit for the 21st century. He lectures widely to Jewish audiences and people of many faiths. In *Israel—A Spiritual Travel Guide: A Companion for the Modern Jewish Pilgrim,* Rabbi Hoffman teaches us how to connect the sacred and the everyday.

The Sacred and the Everyday

LAWRENCE A. HOFFMAN

It has often been said that Judaism is a religion of the everyday. It is not that we are intent on transforming the everyday into the sacred. It is that the sacred exists around every ordinary bend in life's journey. Our daily prayer acknowledging the miracles of God, for instance, does not specify the spectacular instances of the hand of God. Instead, you find mention of "Your miracles which are with us daily, the wonders and goodness that occur all the time—morning, noon and night." On the great occasions that recollect God's miracles—Passover, for instance—we say a set of psalms called the *Hallel,* prayers of gratitude and awe at what God has done. But every day begins with such a set of prayers; the ordinary morning service starts with a lengthy section called *Hallel Sheb'khol Yom*—the Daily *Hallel.*

Jews are trained to look for God in ordinary places: faces on the street, blossoms on a tree, a simple loaf of bread. Remember Elijah as he heads to the wilderness to find God:

> Then, lo, the Lord passed by. There was a great and mighty wind, splitting mountains and shattering rocks by the power of the Lord. But the Lord was not in the wind. After the wind, an earthquake; but the Lord

was not in the earthquake. After the earthquake, fire; but the Lord was not in the fire. And after the fire—a still, small voice.

(1 Kings 18:11–12)

Blessings are our own still small voice, the best approximation we have to being Godlike ourselves. They are an act of creation, that convert the ordinary into the extraordinary, not because they are a kind of verbal alchemy turning leaden experience into gold, but because they reveal the sacred in the everyday.

Here is your first blessing. Try saying it now:

בָּרוּךְ אַתָּה יְיָ אֱלֹהֵינוּ מֶלֶךְ הָעוֹלָם
הַמֵּכִין מִצְעֲדֵי גָבֶר.

Barukh atah Adonai Eloheinu melekh ha'olam, hameichin mitsadei gaver.

Blessed is God who sets us firmly upon our way.[1]

Dr. Lawrence A. Hoffman, rabbi, Professor of Liturgy at Hebrew Union College–Jewish Institute of Religion, is cofounder of Synagogue 2000, a trans-denominational project designed to envision and implement the ideal synagogue of the spirit for the 21st century. He lectures widely to Jewish audiences and people of many faiths. In *Israel—A Spiritual Travel Guide: A Companion for the Modern Jewish Pilgrim*, Rabbi Hoffman teaches us the importance of blessings to spiritual expression.

Blessings!

LAWRENCE A. HOFFMAN

Blessings are a brilliant mode of spiritual expression designed by the Rabbis some 2,000 years ago. They are now so integral to Jewish spirituality that they are taken for granted, even though they are the key to Judaism's uniqueness.

The Rabbis followed the psalmist's view that "The earth is God's and the fullness thereof, the world and they that dwell therein." God is therefore everywhere, apt to break in upon us at any moment—in the fullness of a spring blossom, the raw force of a thunderstorm or a memory in the march of time. Rather than let such moments pass unrecognized, the Rabbis outfitted Judaism with blessings, a simple but eloquent genre of appreciation for life's special moments.

Blessings are immediately recognizable by their form. You probably know some of them by heart but have never considered how unique to Judaism they are, and with what genius they were invented. They are usually one-liners that recur so frequently in Jewish prayers that most Jews memorize their opening formula without even meaning to:

בָּרוּךְ אַתָּה יְיָ אֱלֹהֵינוּ מֶלֶךְ הָעוֹלָם...

Barukh atah Adonai Eloheinu melekh ha'olam....

The usual word-for-word translation is, "Blessed art thou, Lord our God, King of the Universe...." But it is often shortened to "Blessed is God...." Either way, the idea is that at moments that matter, we pause to acknowledge the presence of God.

That simple introductory formula is expanded to encompass the particular event we have in mind. We begin a meal, for instance, only after acknowledging God's gift of food in the first place (and, implicitly, the Rabbis say, by praying for food in abundance, some day, for all the world's hungry people).

בָּרוּךְ אַתָּה יְיָ אֱלֹהֵינוּ מֶלֶךְ הָעוֹלָם
הַמּוֹצִיא לֶחֶם מִן הָאָרֶץ.

Barukh atah Adonai, Eloheinu melekh ha'olam, hamotsi lechem min ha'aretz.

Blessed is God, who brings forth bread from the earth.

Similarly, when encountering a place where a miracle of history once occurred—maybe you should memorize this one; you will be using it a lot—we say:

בָּרוּךְ אַתָּה יְיָ אֱלֹהֵינוּ מֶלֶךְ הָעוֹלָם
שֶׁעָשָׂה נִסִּים לַאֲבוֹתֵינוּ בַּמָּקוֹם הַזֶּה.

Barukh atah Adonai, Eloheinu melekh ha'olam, she'asah nissim la'avoteinu bamakom hazeh.

Blessed is God, who performed miracles for our ancestors in this very place.

When Israel's poet laureate S. Y. Agnon went to Copenhagen to receive the Nobel Prize for literature, observers were surprised to find him conversing briefly with the Swedish monarch who presented him with the award. Careful rehearsal had impressed on the recipients the need to retain the strict formality of courtroom etiquette, whereby they were simply to march down the aisle, take the award, bow, and leave.

When questioned as to what he had said, Agnon explained, "I am a Jew. I have inherited many blessings from my ancestors, including one to be said in the presence of royalty. But I have never stood before a king or queen. Finally I got to say a blessing that has eluded me all these years, 'Blessed is God, who shares divine glory with earthly rulers.'"

Not all of us can be poets laureate or recipients of the Nobel Prize. But we all share Agnon's heritage of blessings, and visiting Israel gives us a chance to greet Israel's marvels with the same age-old formulas as Agnon drew upon to greet a modern-day monarch.

Blessings are a chance to get in touch with the sacred in an authentically Jewish way, inherited from 2,000 years of history. Reaching deep down into the collective memory of the Jewish people to find a genuine spiritual response to the sites of our ancient land is better than saying a simple, modern, succinct "Wow."

Dr. Lawrence A. Hoffman, rabbi, Professor of Liturgy at Hebrew Union College–Jewish Institute of Religion, is cofounder of Synagogue 2000, a trans-denominational project designed to envision and implement the ideal synagogue of the spirit for the 21st century. He lectures widely to Jewish audiences and people of many faiths. In *The Way Into Jewish Prayer,* Rabbi Hoffman teaches us the relationship between the seasons and becoming deeply human.

The Feel of the Seasons and Becoming Deeply Human

LAWRENCE A. HOFFMAN

Holidays cast their magic spell not just on the days when they occur but on the preparation period leading up to them and on the aftermath that lasts through the days or weeks that follow. Their traditional foods, rituals, and ambience provide a unique feel to the entire period in which they are situated.

I had a 90-year-old aunt, for instance, who had suffered a series of strokes that left her wheelchair-bound and unable to care for her daily needs. But she retained her sanity by regularly reminding her daughter of the time of year and the food that needed preparing. "Purim is over," she would say. "It is time to start preparing for Passover."

The autumn High Holiday period is a time of celebration but also of introspection. New Year prayers call Rosh Hashanah the anniversary of the world's conception. In Judaism, the first day of every new month, or Rosh Chodesh (pronounced rohsh KHOH-desh), is a time to start anew, and the first day of the first month is especially so. It culminates in prayers of atonement on Yom Kippur that wipe the slate clean for a new beginning, no matter how terribly we may have behaved in the year gone by. Sukkot, which follows, brings the flavor of Thanksgiving and is followed immediately by the joyous occasion of Simchat Torah, when Jews dance in the synagogue holding the Torah scrolls, the readings from which are completed and begun again.

The dark of winter is punctuated by fun: first Chanukah, which provides a festive spirit around the twin themes of light and freedom; then Purim, in late winter, a day of carnivals, masquerades, and parties. Passover ushers in the spring with a time for family and friends. It begins with housecleaning in preparation for the home celebration, called a *seder* (pronounced SEH-der or, commonly, SAY-d'r), the evening meal that celebrates freedom from Pharaoh and the birth of the Jewish people. During the next seven weeks, we literally count the days in preparation for Shavuot, when we will stand at Sinai once again. In the interim, we will remember the Shoah (the Holocaust) and celebrate the State of Israel's birthday as a nation.

There are other holidays, too, but these are sufficient to provide the Jewish feel of time.

In addition, however, we should ask ourselves how we become so fully human. How, that is, do we learn to grieve or laugh? How do we learn to value others and to appreciate our own innate potential for growth? The answer, in part, is that as prayerful people we learn to appreciate the calendar's flow of time. Do you want to know the joy of celebration? Dance with a Torah scroll on Simchat Torah. Do you want to know the power of a community that values freedom as our highest aspiration? Sit at a Passover *seder* year after year, remembering that "we were slaves to Pharaoh in Egypt." No matter how old you are, you can keep the child inside you from disappearing, just by showing up at Purim to read the book of Esther and enjoy the fun that accompanies it. I know what it is to give thanks because I celebrate Sukkot, and I know the joy of learning because I have a holiday of revelation called Shavuot. Yom Hashoah finds me grieving for the six million, and Yom Ha'atsma'ut binds me to a worldwide community of my people who look to Zion where it all began, and where I have my spiritual home. Chanukah finds me zealous for the freedom for others that my ancestors once attained for me, and the High Holidays never fail to thrill me with the feeling that I have been reborn along with the new year, permitted to hope for goodness and happiness in my life and in the lives of those I love.

On the Sabbath that anticipates every new month, I reread the prayer that reminds me of the things we all need and want and ought not ever to despair of having:

> May it be your will, Adonai our God, to grant us this month for happiness and blessedness. Grant us long life, a life of peace and well being, a life of blessing and sustenance, a life of physical health, a life of piety and dread of sin, a life free from shame and disgrace, a life of wealth and honor, a life marked by our love of Torah and awe before God, a life in which the wishes of our heart will be marked by happiness.[1]

And finally, there is the Sabbath itself, "a sanctuary in time," as Abraham Joshua Heschel called it. This singular day alone could have occupied a chapter. The brief discussion of it here is intended to illustrate not only the Sabbath, with its values of sanctification and rest, but the further fact that being a prayerful Jew means not just attending synagogue, and not just becoming aware of the sanctifying power of blessings each and every day, but also building a home where prayer is the norm. We saw that every meal is a sacred occasion bracketed with blessings that evoke hopes of eternity, but Sabbath meals are especially so. Friday night dinner, for instance, combines fixed prayers with spontaneous ones, for (it is important to note) prayerful people may make up their own words of worship and not depend only on printed texts composed by others. For centuries, parents have looked into the eyes of their children on Friday nights, put their hands upon their heads, asked (in the words of the priestly benediction) that God might "bless you and keep you," and then added their own words of blessing, freely composed and lovingly offered. Along with all the fixity of Jewish prayer, there is spontaneity, too, and in our homes especially, where we come most in contact with those we love, we can manufacture worshipful words of our own: on going to bed and on arising, on thinking through our greatest challenges, on confronting our deepest fears, and on pausing for our highest joys and our most grateful moments.

Dr. Arthur Green, rabbi, is Lown Professor of Jewish Thought at Brandeis University and former president of the Reconstructionist Rabbinical College in Philadelphia. He is a student of Jewish theology and mysticism who has combined scholarly career and personal commitment. In *These Are the Words: A Vocabulary of Jewish Spiritual Life,* Rabbi Green teaches us about the meaning of Shabbat.

Shabbat   שבת

ARTHUR GREEN

Shabbat or the Sabbath is the central religious institution of rabbinic Judaism. Observance of *Shabbat* is the practice that most defines membership in the traditional community of the Jewish faithful. The idea of a holy day, unlike any notion of sacred place, is seen by the *Torah* as existing from the beginning of the world. It started on the day after humans were created, on the day God rested. God sanctified the Sabbath from the very beginning of time (Genesis 2:1–4). This is a way of saying that human existence itself cannot be imagined in a world where there is no *Shabbat.*

The root of the word *Shabbat* means to "cease" or "desist." To observe *Shabbat* means to cease our work life and break our daily routine every seventh day, making that day holy. *Shabbat* is to be a day of enjoying God's world rather than doing battle with it; a day of relaxation rather than struggle, a time to live in harmony rather than to achieve domination.

Two events are celebrated each *Shabbat.* One is God's Creation of the world. Our rest is a way of taking part in God's rest, even re-entering for a while the perfect garden God created this world to be. *Shabbat* is known as bearing within it "the taste of Eden" and "something of the World to Come *('olam ha-ba),"* which is a renewed Garden of Eden. But *Shabbat* also commemorates the Exodus from

Egypt. Slaves are not able to choose their rest. The ability to create one's own balance of work and leisure is a sign of freedom. According to the midrash, Moses went to Pharaoh and demanded a weekly day of rest for the Hebrew slaves, thus instituting *Shabbat* even before they left Egypt. Part of each *Shabbat*'s celebration is based on our admitting that we are still slaves to work, oppressed today by the fast pace of our work lives and the pressures of living in a highly achievement-oriented society. Our taskmasters today may be electronic rather than human, tempting us rather than whipping us to work just a little faster and harder. Our ability to leave them behind once a week is our proclamation of freedom, a true cause for celebration.

The Torah gives almost no instructions about how to observe the Sabbath. "Work" is forbidden, but the nature of that work is not defined. A few details, including the forbidding of lighting fire and gathering wood on the Sabbath, are all the text provides. The rabbis, however, found an entire body of *Shabbat* law hidden in the Torah, based on a parallel between the *mel'akhah* ("work") prohibited on *Shabbat* and the work required for the building of the desert tabernacle *(mishkan)*. All the forms of work required for the building (there are thirty-nine major categories and many derivatives from them) are those forbidden on the Sabbath.

The tabernacle, of course, stands for the Jerusalem Temple. In ancient times the religion of Israel was Temple-centered and the most vital rites took place only at that sacred place. All the rest of the world, as it were, was situated around it. (Since Christians inherited this sacred geography from the Jews, it is no surprise that the earliest maps show Jerusalem as the center of the world.) The rabbis of the 1st and 2nd centuries, facing the loss of the Temple, somehow understood that it needed to be replaced. A portable sacred center, one that sanctified time rather than space, could serve equally well in exile as in the Land, and would not threaten their ongoing commitment to Jerusalem *(Yerushalayim)*. Ingeniously they tied the Sabbath to the Temple by employing the same set of rules. By doing this set of labors, we build sacred space; by *refraining* from the same list of labors, we hallow sacred time. *Shabbat* thus becomes a mirror image of the

Temple, a tabernacle-in-exile that serves over the centuries as the actual center of Jewish life.

Shabbat may still be the most important religious form that Judaism has to give to humanity. In our age of ever increasing pace and demand, the need for a day of true rest is all the greater. But the forms of *Shabbat* observance as they have evolved in endless detail are, for many Jews, overwhelming and even oppressive to the very spirit of *Shabbat* freedom. A contemporary *Shabbat* will have to be a simplified and streamlined one. This is necessary before *Shabbat* can be accepted by larger parts of the Jewish people, and also for the sake of any new message of *Shabbat* we might hope to extend beyond the borders of Jewry. Such a *Shabbat* will, of course, have to be entirely voluntary, without compulsion of any sort.

Rabbi **Lawrence Kushner** is Rabbi-in-Residence at Hebrew Union College–Jewish Institute of Religion. He teaches and lectures widely to audiences of all ages, faiths and backgrounds, and has been a frequent commentator on National Public Radio's *All Things Considered*. In *The Book of Words: Talking Spiritual Life, Living Spiritual Talk,* Rabbi Kushner teaches us about the primary words we use to describe the spiritual dimension of life and how rethinking what they mean can add power and focus to the lives we live every day.

Being   שבת

LAWRENCE KUSHNER

Imagine a day-long spiritual fiction suspending ordinary time. There would be neither past nor future. Our worldwork would be finished. By closing the books on the past week and refusing to think about the next one, we have nothing left to do. For this reason, on the seventh day there is only the present, simply being alive.

The heaven and the earth were finished, and all their array. On the seventh day God finished the work that God had been doing, and God ceased on the seventh day from all the work that God had done. And God blessed the seventh day and declared it holy.

GENESIS 2:1–3

On this day everything we do can be only here and now. If our worldwork is done, we cannot do anything about making it better later. Indeed, *there is no later.*

We quit planning, preparing, investing, conniving, evaluating, fixing, manipulating, arranging, making, and all the other things we do every day. All these things began in the past and will end in the future. We do them, not for their own sake, in the present moment, but with an ulterior motive, for the sake of some later time.

(shä•bäht´)   **The Sabbath Day**

We are obsessed with work. Six days each week we rest so we can go back to work. We play so that we can go back to work. We love so that we can go back to work. One ulterior motive after another. Worrying over the past, living in the future. We are either tied to the past through our uncompleted tasks or compulsively drawn to them through our need for completion in the future. But one day each week there is a day devoted to being present, the seventh day. On that day, we do not have to go anywhere or do anything. Everything is done and we are already here.

ABRAHAM JOSHUA HESCHEL

Technical civilization is [our] conquest of space. It is a triumph frequently achieved by sacrificing an essential ingredient of existence, namely, time. In technical civilization, we expend time to gain space. To enhance our power in the world of space is our main objective. Yet to have more does not mean more. The power we attain in the world of space terminates abruptly at the borderline of time. But time is the heart of existence.

LIVING SPIRITUAL TALK—*KAVANAH*

Before leaving for a vacation people usually are consumed with myriad minor tasks, all the little accumulated chores that now clutter the desktop. Unpaid bills, unreturned phone calls, letters to be answered, minor household repairs, things that were not a priority, and kept being postponed but never went away.

Each uncompleted task has its own claim on our freedom. And finishing them liberates us to begin our vacation. Indeed, finishing the last one may actually commence the vacation whether or not we ever leave home. The function of a vacation ultimately may be simply to get us to "clear off our desk."

Now obviously no one can ever complete all the little tasks. Sooner or later, as the vacation departure clock ticks down, we decree arbitrarily that whether or not they are done, we are done. We take whatever remains, stack it all in a neat pile on the comer of the desk, and renounce its claim on us. To do so requires great spiritual self-control.

Well, it is like that with the Day of Being too. Every seventh day we just clear off our desks. Of course we're not finished. And from the looks of our world, hopefully God isn't finished either.

Dr. Ron Wolfson is the William and Freda Fingerhut Assistant Professor of Education, the Director of the Whizin Center for the Jewish Future, and Vice President of the University of Judaism in Los Angeles. He is a co-founder of Synagogue 2000, an institute for the synagogue of the 21st century. In *The Shabbat Seder*, he teaches us the meaning and importance of honoring Shabbat in our lives.

Making Shabbes

RON WOLFSON

In Jewish English, the common phrase is *make Shabbes*. It seems logical enough: one person asks another, "Who's making *Shabbes* this week, you or your in-laws?" Immediately, it conjures up images of cooking, cleaning, shopping, organizing, etc. A whole progression of labor is involved in the creation of the day of rest. The idea of *making Shabbes* is a practical concept. It reflects a pragmatic social reality: in order to celebrate a day of rest, someone has to do a lot of work.

The idea of making *Shabbes* is really biblical. The Torah commands the Jewish people to "Guard Shabbat—making Shabbat throughout their generations" (Exod. 31:17). From the beginning, a Jewish vision of rest had little to do with a recreational use of leisure time. Starting with the beginning of the Torah, rest was defined as a process of RE-CREATION. God spent six days creating. Then the Torah says, שָׁבַת וַיִּנָּפַשׁ.... "God made Shabbat and God rested."

The word for rest here is וַיִּנָּפַשׁ, *vayinafash*. It is a form of the word *nefesh*, which means "soul." When God rests, the world has soul. When we are commanded to imitate God (living up to the image in which we were created), the expectation is that our rest, too, will be soulful. Creating that kind of rest is something at which we must work.

Scientists define "work" as something that burns calories. Their view is rational; labor is anything that uses energy. Something at rest uses no energy. When the rabbis of the Talmud looked for a definition of work, they viewed it differently They connected work to creation. Work was changing the natural (created) world. Rest was leaving that world unchanged—allowing it to change us. Mordechai Kaplan explained it this way: "An artist cannot be continually wielding his brush. He must stop at times in his painting to freshen his vision of the object, the meaning of which he wishes to express on his canvas.... The Shabbat represents those moments when we pause in our brushwork to renew our vision of this object. Having done so we take ourselves to our painting with clarified vision and renewed energy." Expanding on the same theme, Abraham Joshua Heschel said: "Six days a week we wrestle with the world, wringing profit from the earth; on the Sabbath we especially care for the seed of eternity planted in our soul. Six days a week we seek to dominate the world; on the seventh day we try to dominate the self...."

Shabbat is something we make. Ḥallot are bought. Meals are prepared. Tables are set. Children are herded to the table. We stand. We sit. Prayers are said. Rituals are performed. The execution of a Shabbat is the coordination of a myriad of small details and the application of a series of diverse skills. Yet the physical *making of Shabbes* is only the foundation on which we create Shabbat. The connection between a white tablecloth, the moisture collecting on the outside of a silver *Kiddush* cup filled with cold wine, the buildup of wax drippings on the candlesticks—and the "seed of eternity"—is at once both profoundly tangible and wonderfully mythic. The real world of Shabbat is made up of tablecloths stained with repeated use, family jokes that are so well-known that just a look triggers a laugh, hugs, and the feel and taste of warm *ḥallah*. It is this real-world Shabbat that bonds couples closer together, that creates significant family moments, that roots Jewish identity. These are the payoffs, the rewards of devoting a day to "dominate the self."

The Talmudic rabbis had a very simple principle: if you really want to know how something is to be practiced, go and look at what Jews really do. In crafting a book on how to *"make Shabbes"* we decided to do just that. We went to a number of Jewish homes and asked people about their Shabbat experiences. We learned a number of things, and all of these have helped to shape this work:

Shabbat is an art form. Every family creates its own Shabbat. While candles, *Kiddush,* and *ḥallah* were part of every Shabbat celebration (along with lots of other common elements), every family we visited had a very different Shabbat experience. The art of making Shabbat means finding your own way of using the traditional tools and practices to compose your own "picture" of the Shabbat ritual.

Shabbat is an evolving creation. Families change the way they celebrate Shabbat. New practices are often discovered and integrated. Eventually, children grow into and out of stages and needs, and families evolve through changing rhythms of expression. Also there seems to be a spontaneous and subtle process of constant change that simply marks growth.

You can start a Shabbat experience by just doing one or two things. Surprisingly, most of the families we interviewed did not come from strong experiences of Shabbat. Most had to develop their own sense of Shabbat and establish their own mode of practice. Usually they began by adopting just one or two practices as their weekly ritual process. Slowly, these families learned about and considered other options, evolving their own particular Shabbat practice.

The modern American experience has added to Shabbat. Wonderful new practices have been created because of our life-styles. Consider the practices of phoning a child at college every Friday afternoon to give him the traditional parental blessing, or baking three months' worth of *ḥallah* and filling the extra freezer.

Shabbat is a long-term investment. Not every single Shabbat is a great experience. Some weeks, celebrating Shabbat is a strain. Sometimes the experiences are less than ideal. Yet, wherever we found Shabbat taken seriously it had a profound effect. Every family we visited told us stories of individually difficult *Shabbatot* and all talked of the significant impact of the Shabbat experience on their home. Nevertheless, celebrating Shabbat seems to add up. This was an ongoing message. It is the sum total of *Shabbatot* that makes an impact.

Rabbi David A. Cooper has studied meditation and mysticism for over 30 years. In *The Handbook of Jewish Meditation Practices: A Guide for Enriching the Sabbath and Other Days of Your Life,* Rabbi Cooper teaches us about resting in the moment.

Resting in the Moment

DAVID A. COOPER

Rabbi Huna said: "If a person is in the desert and does not know which day is Shabbat, he counts six days and observes the seventh." Chayah bar Rav says: "The person should observe the first day as Shabbat, and then count six days." In what are they disagreeing? Rabbi Huna believes that it should be similar to the creation of the world [in which there were six days and the seventh was Shabbat], while Chayah bar Rav believes that it should be similar to the creation of Adam (who was created in the hours just before Shabbat, and thus celebrated his first day of existence as Shabbat].

(*Babylonian Talmud:* Shabbat 69*b)*

Judaism is built upon two fundamental wisdom teachings: (1) There is no separation between Creator and Creation, and (2) we need to "rest" from our normal, worldly activity if we wish to appreciate the truth of existence. Each of these teachings is in symbiotic relationship with the other. We learn the profound truth of the non-duality of creation when we are able to temporarily withdraw from our mundane lives. When we experience the true meaning of ultimate oneness, our everyday lives take on an entirely new meaning.

THE EXPERIENCE OF ONENESS

The first teaching, that of non-separation, is expressed in the quintessential Jewish prayer, the *Shema,* which interpreted mystically says, "Listen carefully at the core of your being, the part of you that yearns to go straight to the Source of Life; the transcendent unknowable God and all that we see in the material world surrounding us are, in fact, one and the same." It is all one. This truth is so important, according to Jewish law, that we are required to repeat it to ourselves at least twice a day so that we remember it. This means, in literal terms, to actually say the words *Shema Yisrael, Adonoy Elohaynu, Adonoy Ehad,* every morning and every evening.

In esoteric terms, the admonishment to repeat the *Shema* implores us to sink into the realization of the truth of non-duality, to keep these things "in your heart...when sitting in your home, walking on the way, lying down, or standing up..." In other words, we must rest in the understanding of oneness not just twice a day, but all of our waking hours as we engage in every activity of life.

Clearly this is not easy to do. Mundane life rapidly overwhelms us. Our minds are so complex and work so fast, we quickly succumb to believing that reality is what we "think" it is—disparate, material, and solid. Despite the fact that our own thoughts continue to swiftly evaporate, proving that they were never "real" or concrete in the first place, we persist in believing whatever is happening in our minds at any particular moment.

Attempts to answer the essential inquiries of existence are the driving force of knowledge and understanding. The early philosophers sought common denominators, basic elements out of which all things arise, such as earth, air, fire, and water. After thousands of years we continue to seek the fundamental building blocks, now conceptualizing them as mysterious subatomic energy bundles called quarks. Nobody has ever seen a quark, but mathematical systems are built on such ideas.

Other ideas have metamorphosed over the years. Past beliefs in the nature of space and the continuous steady flow of time have transformed into current beliefs of relativity, a kind of flexibility of time and space, that is almost impossible for most of us to picture in our minds. Relativity is an idea that challenges us on the deepest levels, for it affects our bedrock of belief that reality is something that can be seen, touched, measured, and eventually known with the proper tools. We are now taught that things work very differently than we can even imagine, and reality has multiple levels that rapidly transcend the grasp of human consciousness.

For example, we are no longer certain that there are solid building blocks upon which reality is constructed. At times, subatomic energy has the properties of little particles; at other times it seems to have properties of waves constantly in motion. More mysterious, when we set up experiments to look for particles, we find them; yet, using the same experimental method, if we are looking for waves instead, that's what we find. It is as if the observer influences the energy to behave in different ways. This has led modern science to conclude that we cannot separate a subject from an object, for the very act of observation affects that which is being observed.

This idea of inseparability casts an entirely new light on how we work with the primordial questions of what, how, where, when, and why as applied to the meaning of life, for we are compelled to reflect upon the source and nature of the question itself. Who, indeed, is asking the question? If there is no ultimate separation between subject and object, then we have a loop in which the answer and the question are intrinsically interconnected. Thus, rather than looking outward, as if the solutions to life's mysteries are somewhere to be found out there, we are being invited to look inward, to explore the unique energy of the creative urge that arises within each of us every moment of our lives.

There is yet another change arising in the way we look at things these days, far subtler than ramifications of the notion of inseparability. This change arises from the revelation that we can no longer precisely measure anything. The tools of measurement have their own limitations and those who are measuring, of course, have theirs as well. When the measuring stick is composed of the same elements as what it is used to measure, clear limitations arise. A measuring stick cannot measure itself! Moreover, the thickness of an electron is too great to measure another electron. Even worse, everything in the universe is constantly in motion, so there is never a static motion to measure it. Add to this yet another difficulty: That which is being measured reacts differently than when it is not being measured! Given all this (and there is more), we end up with never being able to measure anything exactly, and we can only come up with mere approximations.

As all measurement is approximate to some degree, then so-called ultimate truth is always unknown. That is to say, knowledge has limits. Not only are there things that we do not know, far more disturbing is the fact that *there are some things that will never be known.* This is not something easy to swallow. Humans are intrinsically optimistic when it comes to knowledge. We believe that with enough effort and the right tools we will ultimately know everything that can be known. The closer we look into this area—what can be known—the more we discover how little there is that is knowable. Moreover, knowing splits into that which is intellectually understood and can be communicated, and the much larger arena of transcendental knowing that extends beyond reason and expression. Wisdom is not something that fits easily into books, but is rather built upon foundations of direct experience.

Both science and philosophy in many ways have circled back to elementary teachings given by mystics in many traditions. They teach that we can discover basic truths by simply resting in quiet reflection in a way that will lead us to a direct experience of our innate nature. This experience is one of inclusivity, wholeness, and oneness, an interconnectedness of all things. When resting in this realization, we come to the essential Jewish wisdom teaching of *ehad,* oneness, the nonseparation between Creator and Creation.

This idea of resting quietly in the moment to more fully appreciate the oneness of creation brings us to the second fundamental Jewish wisdom teaching: to take contemplative time each week specifically to explore the meaning of life. Indeed, this is such an important tenet of the tradition that it is one of the Ten Commandments: Remember and observe the Sabbath day.

THE SABBATH AND HOLY DAYS

The admonition to remember and observe the Sabbath day is initially directed to the weekly Sabbath that in Judaism begins at sundown Friday night and ends at sundown Saturday night. But the idea of Sabbath also loosely refers to days that are referred to as *yomim tovim* (good days, or holy days), because the Jewish law applying to each of these days approximates, for the most part, similar restrictions as the Sabbath day itself. Thus, all holy days have the feel of a Sabbath, with only minor differences. This means that in addition to the fifty-two official Sabbath days every year, there are quite a few other times that require special attention. In addition to these are many minor holidays that have fewer restrictions, but still are treated with special awareness. Here are the best known of the major and minor holy days in the calendar, with brief descriptions of the special energy that can be the contemplative focus of each respective day.

Rosh Hashana

Rosh Hashana is the Jewish New Year. It falls in September or early October. Its main theme is "remembrance" and "return" to the Source of Creation. This is the time of the blowing of the shofar, calling to God, and it is required for all Jews to hear a shofar on this day. The esoteric teaching is that the shofar confuses the "accuser," the negative energy left behind by our unskillful behavior. So this is a time of reprieve, when we may be able to modify in some way the consequences of our actions. This is a marvelous idea and has deep connotations. In a retreat, on this day, we would want to spend time reflecting on the past, noticing any actions, words, or thoughts that were regrettable, and committing ourselves to more skillful behavior in the future.

Yom Kippur

Yom Kippur comes on the tenth day after Rosh Hashana. The intervening days are called the Days of Awe, a time of deep introspection. Yom Kippur is known as the Sabbath of Sabbaths, recognized as the most awesome day of the year. On this day we observe a complete fast, including drinking water, from sundown to sundown. It is a perfect time for retreat. The Kabbalah describes this day as a time when we have God's ear, so to speak, and can change our destiny. It is the most awe-filled day of the year. Out of time and space, one dwells completely in intimacy with the Divine. It is the day the High Priest within each of us enters the Holy of Holies, also within each of us, and speaks a special name of God only spoken on this particular day. If the mind goes astray in this moment, we die, metaphorically.

The practice throughout the day of Yom Kippur is to imagine that the heavenly court is in the process of determining what one's coming year has in store, based on previous actions, speech, and thoughts. This contemplation is the focus of many hours of reflection about oneself, one's family, associates, friends, and the world in general.

Sukkot

Sukkot comes four days after Yom Kippur. It is a seven-day holiday; the first and seventh days are special. The main mitzvah (commandment) of this period is to eat and sleep in a sukkah, a temporary dwelling with nothing overhead but a canopy of vegetation through which we can see the sky. On the esoteric level, the covering of the sukkah is equated with the skin of the Leviathan, the mythical monstrous beast upon which the righteous will feed at the time of messianic consciousness. The exposed sukkah carries a luminous reflection of the *Ohr Ein Sof,* the infinite light of awareness, and it draws visitors from other realms, particularly the patriarchs and matriarchs: Abraham, Sarah, Isaac, Rebecca, Jacob, Leah, Rachel, Moses, Tzipporah, Aaron, Joseph, and David. Each day different guests are welcomed to the sukkah.

For traditional Jews, Sukkot is a time of raising up four plants—an unopened, young palm branch *(lulav)*, a citron-like fruit *(etrog)*, three myrtle branches *(hadasim)*, and two willow branches *(aravot)*—all held together in a special way in the hands. Waving these in the six directions—east, south, north, west, up, and down—symbolically represents all of space. This is done while chanting praises and supplications. It is an elementary ritual of thanksgiving for the harvest and prayers for the rains and good fortune required for harvest to come the following year. This is an extremely rich and colorful ceremony that touches participants and viewers in deep primordial places.

On retreat we would try to spend most of the day outdoors, and even sleep out at night if feasible. Each day, we would not only commune with nature, but we would also esoterically connect with the archetypal energies of the biblical characters, each of whom represents an energy within us. This is a great opportunity to work on our personal character. Obviously, it is a wonderful experience to construct and live in one's own sukkah. Any Jewish bookstore can provide information for those who may be interested. This is a time of great joy and thanksgiving for the bounty of our sustenance and all the gifts of life.

Shemini Atzeret

The seven-day festival of Sukkot ends in a three-day series of special days: Hoshana Rabba, Shemini Atzeret, and Simcha Torah. Hoshana Rabba is celebrated the last day of Sukkot, when each member of the congregation circles around the Torah seven times and finally beats on the ground five willow branches that have been bound together. It symbolizes a final resolve to purify oneself in preparation for the year to come.

Simcha Torah is a joyous day when the Torah scrolls are carried through the streets accompanied by a singing and dancing congregation. It is a day of profound transition, when the last paragraphs of the Torah are read in public, followed by the reading of the opening sentences of Genesis, which signifies yet another cycle of completion and new beginnings.

Shemini Atzeret, the day that falls between Hoshana Rabba and Simcha Torah, is one of the most profound days in the calendar for Jewish mystics. It is a holy day, treated in the same way as a regular Shabbat, but it has a secret connotation for kabbalists: It is the culmination of all of the activities of Rosh Hashana, the Days of Awe, Yom Kippur, the preparation days for Sukkot, the week of Sukkot itself, and Hoshana Rabba, a rich and exhausting period of three weeks—the most intense twenty-one days of the calendar. It indicates that we are about to begin the new cycle of the Torah tomorrow. There is a great heavenly sigh when God says, "Wow! That was wonderful. But it has been so much, let's you and I spend some time together alone, just you and me."

Shemini Atzeret is viewed in this context as the day of greatest intimacy with the Divine, a day of resting in each other's arms, a time of enormous contentment that we have done everything possible to perfect our relationship and now we simply enjoy each other's presence without any particular expectations. On retreat, this is a time of essential communion, trust, and relaxation. In an esoteric sense, we are lovers with the Divine, caressing and being caressed in every move, sensually enjoying the unfolding of each moment. It is a wonderful time of quiet recognition and simple, uncomplicated delight.

Chanukkah

Chanukkah is a festival of light that comes in December. It is an eight-day holiday well known for its symbolic *menorah* and the daily lighting of candles. On the first day one candle is lighted, and a new candle is added each day until we light eight candles on the eighth day. From a mystical perspective, Chanukkah has kabbalistic significance in that it comes at the darkest time of the year (in the Northern Hemisphere), and our lighting of candles at this time has cosmic implications of creation and renewal. Thus, our contemplative practice would be focused on creativity and optimism, what it takes to bring the light of wisdom into the darkness of ignorance. Notice that only one candle will illuminate a completely dark room. This is the metaphor of Chanukkah, a light that continues to grow from day to day.

Tu b'Shevat

Tu b'Shevat comes in January or February. It is best known as the festival of trees and is a time when people plant trees in Israel. Mystically, it is a time when the will to live first finds expression, when the sap that will produce blossoms in springtime begins to flow. On retreat we spend extra time becoming very quiet so that we can explore the subtle quickening of our vital life force. Kabbalists celebrate this day by partaking in a special seder that includes a wide variety of fruits. Each fruit is classified in one of three categories, representing three of the Four Worlds of Kabbalah.

The lowest world of *assiyah* is represented by fruit that is protected in hard, inedible shells, like nuts. The next world of *yetzira* is represented by fruits with hard, inedible inner pits, like peaches or plums. Next, the world of *beriah* is represented by fruit that can be eaten whole, like grapes. Finally, the highest world of *atzilut* is too high for regular fruits. I usually represent it with maple syrup, which is the sap that the day is all about.

This seder uses four cups of wine, just like the Passover seder. But the difference is that red and white wine are mixed to represent the Four Worlds: full-bodied red at the bottom level of *assiyah*, mostly red on the second level of *yetzira*, mostly white on the third level of *beriah*, and full-bodied white on the top level of *atzilut*. Thus the seder celebrates different levels of creation manifesting, and our focus during the day is on developing our creative energies of rebirthing ourselves.

Purim

Purim comes in February or March. Traditionally, it is treated somewhat like carnival: People dress in outlandish costumes and imbibe intoxicating drinks. The Book of Esther is read at this time, describing when the Jewish nation was miraculously saved from total destruction. It is often noted that the Book of Esther at no time mentions any name of God in it. Yet, it represents one of the great miracles of the Jewish people. Thus, the mystery of the hidden God is a primary theme working on this day.

We are often grasping for the unknown and unknowable. When our minds take over, we can easily fall into despair. The secret of Purim is to come to grips with the possibilities of this hidden aspect of the Divine, which often is represented as holy sparks within hardened shells of mundane existence. We meditate on how to liberate these sparks in what seems to be the face of overwhelming odds.

Many people equate the archenemy Haman in the time of Esther with the modern archenemy Hitler. Retreatants at Purim usually focus on the paradox of life; they contemplate the presence of evil in the world and the miracle of divine grace.

Passover

Passover comes one month after Purim, in March or April. It is a seven-day holiday best known for the seder, which takes place on the first night and, for many, on the second night as well. Observant Jews have uncompromising dietary restrictions during the entire seven days. Next to Shabbat, Passover has the most complex body of Jewish law associated with it. The objective is to cleanse our lives of all *hametz* (leavening), which mystically is associated with pride and ego.

The story of the Exodus is retold at Passover to remind us of the relationship between enslavement and freedom. On retreat, we concentrate on understanding the areas in which we are enslaved—what has captured our minds, our beliefs, our sense of self-worth, our values—and how we might be able to attain new freedom. This is a perfect time to take the week and really explore the theme of freedom.

Passover has a wide spectrum of themes for personal reflection. It is not only a one- or two-day experience, but it also includes the thirty days leading up to it, and the forty-nine days of the Counting of the Omer that follow the first night of seder. Passover is an entire week of reflection, marked by the matzah we eat for seven (or eight) days. On the final night of the week, the esoteric celebration is focused on the crossing of the Red Sea, which symbolizes faith. Passover is the story of an escape when not really merited, of getting out of an impossible situation without deserving it.

Shavuot

Shavuot comes forty-nine days after the Passover seder, usually in May. It celebrates the giving of the Torah on Mount Sinai. Traditionally people study and learn the entire night of Shavuot, which is an excellent form of retreat. The mystical preparation for Shavuot occurs during the seven weeks between it and Passover. This is called the Counting of the Omer, and each of the forty-nine days is publicly enumerated during the first prayer of every day for seven weeks. The kabbalists added the idea that each of the forty-nine days represents an aspect of our being, our personality, and our deepest essence that needs to be fixed and uplifted so that when we receive the teachings of the Torah, we will be as pure and open as possible. Thus, cleansing and purification are the retreat practices of Counting the Omer, while the possibility of new levels of awareness is the retreat experience of Shavuot.

Tisha b'Av

Tisha b'Av occurs in the heat of summer, in late July or August. This is a fast day almost as strict as Yom Kippur. It is a day of observance that traditionally marks the destruction of the two temples of ancient Judaism. The temples represent the vehicle through which we can communicate with God. Thus, Tisha b'Av is a day of mourning that this communication is now much more difficult—almost impossible. On retreat, this is a time to reflect on the gap between our spiritual essence and our mundane lives, with the hope that we can close this gap and attain an expanded level of consciousness, sometimes called messianic consciousness.

Rosh Hodesh

Rosh Hodesh is the day each month of the new moon. It is treated as a special day by kabbalists, for the moon is viewed esoterically as the gathering place of souls. It is also the point when the quality of *gevurah*, constriction, gives way to *chesed*, expansion. The kabbalists look at midnight each day in the same way, as the end of the darkening process and the beginning of the enlightening cycle. Women also celebrate Rosh Hodesh in the context of moon cycles as a time of renewal and fertility, with great hope for possibilities unfolding anew.

Leora Tanenbaum is an editor in Hadassah's national department of Jewish Education. In *Moonbeams: A Hadassah Rosh Hodesh Guide,* edited by Carol Diament, she teaches us about the history and observance of Rosh Hodesh.

The History and Observance of Rosh Hodesh

LEORA TANENBAUM

I am sitting in synagogue on a Shabbat morning, in part savoring the peaceful pause from a hectic week, in part worrying that I don't have enough cholent[1] to serve everyone at lunch. The people sitting nearby are whispering in quiet conversation, keeping an eye out to make sure that the rabbi doesn't notice them. The Torah and *Haftarah* readings are over and we have just recited the Aramaic transitional prayer *Yekum Purkan.* I am looking forward to the next few minutes, when we will return the Torah to the ark and meditatively recite the silent *Amidah* of the *musaf*[2] service. But wait! Why isn't the cantor launching into the singsong *Ashrei?* What is going on? All of a sudden the realization hits: Rosh Hodesh, the mini-festival that marks each month's new moon, is coming up this week. That means that we recite an additional prayer today: *Birkat HaHodesh.*

Rosh Hodesh is a symbol of renewal. At the end of its monthly cycle, the moon becomes visually obliterated, only to reappear as a tiny, luminous sliver of light as it commences a fresh, new cycle. Likewise, we have the opportunity to take stock of our lives and revise our behavior, our commitments, our goals. We, too, have the power to start over.

Everyone rises; a hushed silence pervades the air. The cantor holds the Torah scroll for all to see. With pomp and fanfare, the cantor declares that a new moon will be "born" at the moment when the moon is hidden between the sun and the earth. (Six hours after the *molad,* the moon's birth, a crescent of light will reflect off of the moon, making it visible.) The cantor informs the congregation whether this Rosh Hodesh will last for one day or two. (When the preceding month is 30 days, Rosh Hodesh is observed for two days; and when the preceding month is 29 days, Rosh Hodesh is observed for one day.) The cantor is quite specific about the time of the *molad,* down to the exact *heilek* (part of a minute). (The lunar cycle is 29 days, 12 hours, and 793 *halakim,* and each *heilek* is equal to 3⅓ seconds; so an entire lunar cycle is equal to 29 days, 12 hours, 44 minutes, and 3⅓ seconds). The cantor concludes the prayer by requesting that God bless the new month and grant the people of Israel life and peace, joy and gladness, deliverance and consolation. Everyone in the congregation responds, "Amen." Only then do we begin the melodious *Ashrei.*

Birkat HaHodesh is the modern commemoration of the new moon. Today, though, as feminist Judaic scholar Blu Greenberg points out, if you "randomly ask one hundred Jews about this special day that comes eleven times a year, ninety of them will offer a blank stare. There are far more Jewish bird-watchers than there are moon-watchers."[3] But in ancient times, before the Jewish lunar calendar was fixed, the sighting of the new moon was cause for grand festivity alongside grave seriousness. Since every Jewish community was obligated to observe holidays at the same time, all Jewish communities needed to agree on dates, and dates were determined based on the sighting of the new moon.

During the Second Temple period, the new month began when at least two reputable witnesses observed the first sliver of moon. The witnesses were called before the *beit din,* the rabbinic court in Jerusalem, and the judges called each witness separately to testify about the precise location and appearance of the moon. If both gave identical testimony, the *beit din* declared the arrival of Rosh Hodesh. Then sacrifices were offered and incense was burnt. Special prayers were chanted, the *shofar* was blown, and a celebratory meal was eaten. The news of the moon's appearance was communicated to

Jewish communities throughout Israel and the diaspora by setting fires on the hilltops of Jerusalem, with each Jewish community that observed those fires then lighting its own fires to alert neighboring communities. Toward the end of the Second Temple period, the *beit din* instead sent messengers to outlying towns and villages to alert them to the appearance of the moon, because the Samaritans[4] had begun to deliberately set fires at incorrect times in order to mislead the Jews. By the middle of the fourth century, the rabbis had established a fixed calendar, and the examination before the *beit din* and the sending of messengers to publicly proclaim the new moon was discontinued.

Today we enjoy no festive meal nor do we blow the *shofar* on Rosh Hodesh. We do, however, continue to celebrate Rosh Hodesh with prayer. Besides reciting *Birkat HaHodesh* on the preceding Saturday, we recite a special *musaf* service on Rosh Hodesh itself. In addition, the *Kiddush Levanah* (sanctification of the moon) ceremony takes place outdoors on a clear night soon after Rosh Hodesh (usually on the first Saturday night that follows). We observe the new moon festival eleven times a year; we don't celebrate Rosh Hodesh for the month of *Tishrei*, which coincides with Rosh Hashanah, since the new year celebration incorporates the new month.

God first commanded us to observe the new moon just as we were ready to flee from the enslavement of Egypt. Rabbi Samson Raphael Hirsch, the nineteenth-century German scholar, noted that since we would soon be liberated from slavery, we could appreciate the moon's emergence from darkness to light. Through the moon's renewal, God is telling the people of Israel: "This is to be the model for your own conduct! Even as the moon renews itself by the law of nature, so you, too, should renew yourselves, but of your own free will."[5] God also commanded us to count the months, so that we could always calculate the amount of time that our people have been free.

Rosh Hodesh has long been considered a special holiday for women. There are a number of reasons. First, according to legend, the holiday was a reward given to the women of Israel because they refused to surrender their jewelry for the creation of the golden calf.

Because of their righteousness, the women were exonerated from working on Rosh Hodesh. Second, many people have pointed out that the menstrual cycle is similar to the monthly cycle of the moon. (The English word "menstruation" derives from the Latin word for "monthly.") Third, Penina Adelman, author of the first modern Rosh Hodesh ritual guide for women, points out that the words *Roshei HodshiM,* heads of the months, contain the same letters that form the word *ReHeM,* womb.[6]

Fourth, the status of the moon has often been compared to the status of women. The Talmud recounts a legend that the moon and the sun were originally of equal size and brightness, but the moon asked how two could rule equally; God responded by making the moon smaller. In ancient texts, woman likewise has a lesser status and is subservient to man. Furthermore, the *Zohar,* the authoritative work of the mystical tradition, frequently likens the moon to the *Shekhinah,* the Divine Presence, which mystics consider the feminine aspect of God.[7] Only when the world is redeemed will the *Shekhinah* reunite with the masculine aspect, the *Kadosh Barukh Hu,* the Holy One Blessed is He, and only then will the moon's light intensify.[8]

Rosh Hodesh has long been sacred to women. From the sixteenth to the early twentieth centuries, the women of Eastern Europe wrote special Rosh Hodesh *tekhines*—personal prayers in the Yiddish vernacular. Over the past three decades, Rosh Hodesh observance has been revived by religious feminists. The book *Miriam's Well: Rituals for Jewish Women Around the Year* by Penina Adelman, first published in 1986, presented the experiences of one of the first women's Rosh Hodesh groups, and provided a template for creative Rosh Hodesh rituals. Adelman describes, for example, an "anointing ritual…which invokes the messiah in each individual"; creating a small model of the gallows so that participants can hang "the Hamans of women's lives—sexual harassment, low pay, the beauty industry"; and "group wailing" to recall the wailing women in the Book of Jeremiah.[9] In addition to feminist groups focusing on personal spiritual growth, like those that began in the seventies, a wide variety of Jewish women—feminist and non-feminist—now meet to celebrate

Rosh Hodesh. Some groups are sponsored by synagogues, others by non-denominational organizations, and a few meet independently. Activities range from reciting the traditional liturgy and sharing a meal to discussing Jewish ethics and working for social change. Some groups, like those following Hadassah's *Moonbeams* guide, set aside Rosh Hodesh for Jewish study.

Sandy Eisenberg Sasso is rabbi, along with her husband, Rabbi Dennis Sasso, of Congregation Beth-El Zedeck in Indianapolis; they are the first practicing rabbinical couple in world Jewish history. She was the first woman ordained from the Reconstructionist Rabbinical College (in 1974), the first woman to serve a Conservative congregation, and the first rabbi to become a mother. Author of many books that enhance the spiritual life of children, in *Bar/Bat Mitzvah Basics: A Practical Family Guide to Coming of Age Together,* edited by Cantor Helen Leneman, Rabbi Sasso teaches us what to say to our children on the *bimah*.

What to Say to Your Child on the *Bimah*

SANDY EISENBERG SASSO

Sometimes the preparations behind a child's becoming bar or bat mitzvah do not allow us as parents to pause long enough to think about the meaning of the day. Of course, the occasion is first and foremost about Jewish learning and renewal, about family and celebration. But it is also about that fleeting moment as our sons and daughters stand poised between childhood and adolescence, holding on and letting go. What advice would we like our young people to take on their life's journey? It is not as though we haven't transmitted our values in the preceding years, by what we allow and what we prohibit, by how we live and how we do not. But this is a time for us to piece it all together and wrap a gift of words for them to carry into the future.

At this time of fragile self-esteem, a parental address is an opportunity to reinforce our children's positive self-image, to tell them why we are proud. This doesn't mean chronicling every accomplishment, from learning to walk to becoming the quarterback of the football team. But it is a chance to say what qualities you admire and hope that they will not lose as they grow.

If you can remember that your child is only thirteen, you will know to be brief, not to talk above them or down to them, and not to embarrass them. You want your son or daughter to hear you, not daydream. Neither a reminiscence nor a biography, a parent's talk should be a message.

Ask yourself some questions: What gift do I see in my child that a word of encouragement might enhance? What difficulty do I know that some wisdom might ease? What do I hand to my children when I hand them Torah? What elements of the Torah do I want them to carry in their hearts? What story do I want them to retell to become a part of its unfolding?

Some parents are reluctant to speak. Some say, "What we feel is private." Others say, "We are not good with words." But just as our children like to see us cheering them on at their performances or rooting for their teams, they also need to hear us tell them what we value and what we think. To give a good speech, you don't have to be a writer or an orator. You just have to be a Mom or Dad.

Some parents have told me that deciding what to say to their child was the most difficult thing they had ever done, and the most wonderful. As the b'nai mitzvah tell us, with their eyes and with their embrace: These words make a difference.

Feel free to borrow from the following speech excerpt, or let it inspire you to find your own words. A parental talk may be offered during the presentation of a special tallit, or just before or after the Torah service.

"STILLNESS AND TEARS"

Mother to daughter. By Rabbi Sandy Eisenberg Sasso and her husband, Rabbi Dennis Sasso, of Congregation Beth-El Zedeck in Indianapolis:

It seems like only yesterday that we stood with you on this *bimah* to welcome you into the covenant of the Jewish people and give you your Hebrew name. We were afraid then that you would cry. Now, I am afraid that I will.

What do I wish for you, my little girl becoming a woman, my daughter with the enchanted smile:

I wish for you to be a
person of character
strong but not tough,
gentle but not weak.

I wish for you to be
righteous but not self-righteous
honest but not unforgiving.

Wherever you journey, may your steps be firm
and may you walk in just paths
and not be afraid.
Whenever you speak, may your words
be words of wisdom and friendship.

May your hands build
and your heart preserve what is good
and beautiful in our world.

May the voices of the generations of our people
move through you
and may the God of our ancestors
be your God as well.

May you know that there is a people,
a rich heritage, to which you belong
and from that sacred place
you are connected to all who dwell on the earth.

May the stories of our people
be upon your heart
and the grace of the Torah rhythm
dance in your soul.

Zalman M. Schachter-Shalomi, a rabbi and teacher, is professor emeritus at Temple University. He is the founder of the Spiritual Eldering Institute in Philadelphia, which sponsors nondenominational workshops to help people grow into elderhood. In *A Heart of Wisdom: Making the Jewish Journey from Midlife through the Elder Years*, edited by Susan Berrin, Rabbi Schachter-Shalomi shows us how to understand and meet the challenges of the process of aging from a Jewish perspective.

From Age-ing to Sage-ing[1]

ZALMAN M. SCHACHTER-SHALOMI

Just as midwives help with natural childbirth and the hospice movement helps with dying, a framework is needed to help with one's initiation into spiritual eldering. Much of the physical and custodial care for the aged has—thank God—been humanized, but to date the preparation for eldering has essentially been ignored, even though the whole spiritual discipline for becoming serene is connected with this. "Growing" older demands that we look death in the face and accept our mortality.

Looking at our mortality and accepting our death is the door through which we each must pass. The key that opens this door is in the body, the heart, the mind, and the soul. We need to use all four of these to move through the gate marked "fulfillment" and "completion." With inspired imagination, it opens; and with that, comes light and guidance for the next stage. As long as the fear of death is considered part of the software for the preservation of life, one cannot begin to open the door to completion.

Until now, everything that threatened my life got an automatic, knee-jerk response that pumped adrenaline, urging me to run, fight, flight: "I've got to save myself." That response, which was essential in my earlier life, now blocks my walking through the door to eldering. Because the habitual, built-in response is to save one's life, one naturally panics and does everything to avoid facing death. This blind spot also blocks conscious and deliberate spiritual eldering.

The mystic Gurdjieff taught (as have most other spiritual teachers and philosophers) that "as long as you are a machine, you can't save yourself. It's only when you stop being a machine that you come to full consciousness." Full consciousness means you are conscious about how you are conscious.

This points to recognizing what drives the "fight and flight" response: a "program" that runs in the deep background of our consciousness and repeats, "I don't want to die. I don't want to die. I don't want to look at death. I don't want to look at death." Its life-affirming function says, "At all costs, save your life." Or as *halacha*, or Jewish law, says, "A human life is worth more than even the Torah." What is halachically expressed is also part of the biological program written into our body: "Save your life at all costs."

So I can't walk through the spiritual eldering door until I can separate myself from my ego's automatic avoidance responses. As one gets older these responses, which Buddhism calls *samskaras,* become less and less energetic. This is natural and as it should be. Our energy is running low and will eventually wear out.

Part of "fight and flight" is that I don't dare look at my death. So when my own death keeps coming up, I get anxious and distracted. I'll look in every direction to *not* face my death. But when I move beyond my fears, I begin to see a wonderful potential to complete and round out my life.

SEPTEMBER, OCTOBER, NOVEMBER

With our longer life spans, we can shape ourselves into the kind of elder we want to be. But someone who does not abandon his or her automatic response toward death does not graduate to sagehood. That person remains sidelined, stuck in the June, July, and August of life, rather than entering into the Fall and becoming an excellent September, October, November person. Part of awareness is realizing that we can't develop the September, October, November of our life if we don't look at death, and we can't develop the Fall of our life unless we look at October, November, and December. We must look from one phase into the next phase so our life's orientation is current and correct.

To perfect the knowing and becoming of a "sage," one needs to look past death. But this contemplative, philosophical, spiritual, intuitive piece of life needs to be learned. Most of us have learned how to run a computer, run a spreadsheet, write a letter, clip coupons. But we haven't learned to look at life contemplatively. Rather than displacing the condition of aging, we must meet it. We must live within the context and the condition of aging in order to maximize the parameters of our living.

A LIFETIME OF MONTHS

Asking myself, "What is eldering doing to me?" brought me to a vision of a lifetime organized into periods of seven years, with each seven years correlated to one calendrical month.

Imagine that from birth to age seven when our second teeth come in is January. From seven to 14 years and the onset of puberty is February. Then the time to 21 years, when we're more or less fully grown in our body, is March. April begins at that point, and ends when we reach 28 years. At 35 until 42, we set ourselves up as social beings, creating new families and new careers. We're in our prime from 42 to 49, from 49 to 56, from 56 to 63. These three "months" are when we do our major work in the world. They are our July, August, and September.

To have the prime of our life between 42 and 63, we need a vision of how we want to spend our October, November, and December.[2]

I am now in the October of my life. I search my soul and examine my conscience during the High Holy Days of September. When we take the year this way, Spring is when we're 21 years old and leaving Egypt. The Summer of our lives brings midlife crisis—Tisha B'Av, the destruction of the Temple. In this way, the liturgical year and our lives parallel each other.

I began to wonder about and pay attention to new internal processes. Earlier, my libido focused on sex, procreation, and acquiring material goods. My psychic energy is now concerned with preserving the distillate of my life's experiences. One day, I had a very strong insight. Moses, the Buddha, Lao Tsu and Confucius all reached a ripe old age; Jesus and Mohammed less so. Jesus was the youngest of them to die. Our North American culture, which is largely based on Christianity, doesn't have a good eldering model, perhaps because Jesus died before becoming an elder.

The Bible tells a very interesting thing. During biblical times, everybody served in the army from age twenty to sixty. At sixty, they were free. The Levites were also in service from 20 to age 60, but from 20 to 30 they had to learn from older Levites. The active Levite years were from age 30 to age 50, when they took the Ark apart and handled the altar. From age 50 to age 60, their job was to train the 20- to 30-year-olds.

Judaism has a wonderful eldering model in Moses. When he was 120 years old, he was still active. When the time came for him to die, he consciously left his body. In China, Lao Tzu and Confucius did the same kind of thing, as did avatars in India as well as the Buddha. But America is like the young, sequestered Buddha, Siddhartha, who was unable to see old people. America isn't especially concerned with developing a model for aging.

Another experience fed my insight about growing older. During a session with my Feldenkrais trainer, I fell asleep. I hope that when it is my time to die I can slip out of my body with that ease, with everything nestled and rested. Feeling that gentle wave wash over me made me realize that spiritual work is a necessary component to the process of aging and facing death.

A SENATE OF ELDERS

We have health maintenance organizations (HMO) for health. What if we created an HMO for eldering? The first level would include accountants and lawyers, who would help put our affairs in order. In the next level, a counselor would help us with relationships: "Who were your friends? Who were your lovers? What do you have to fix? How would you do that?" These counselors could help us put order to our affairs and leave the world, when the time comes, with ease.

Originally, the word "senate" referred to older people with greater wisdom and greater experience who would hear what lower courts had decided and comment on their rulings. Imagine a United Nations Senate of Elders where we would gather to meditate, hear, share, and counsel.

Several years ago, I participated in a gathering of about 150 Muslims, Sufis, Christians, Coptics, Palestinians, Israelis, Americans, Japanese, and a Native American. We gathered in the Sinai Desert and began to climb Mt. Sinai at 1:00 A.M. At sunrise we reached the summit, where we prayed and placed a stone that had been engraved with the inscription "*Dona Nobis Pacem,*" "Grant us Peace." It was an amazing moment.

Climbing up the mountain, an old Japanese man and I helped each other over the tough places. There was no need to talk because of the powerful presence of fellowship. I sat with the old Muslims, listening to them talk. What hit me was that just as the split between male and female is broader than the Sephardi-Ashkanazi split, so too is the younger-older split wider than the gulf between being Christian and Jewish. I realized that what was needed was a dialogue across the age barrier, an aging ecumenism which would foster a reciprocity in which older people would be inspired and revered while younger people would receive wisdom and counsel.

INITIATION INTO ELDERING

Staretz, in Russian, means the "old one," the "elder." Father Zosima, the *staretz* in *The Brothers Karamazov,* is a very patient, holy person. But even a *staretz* needs an initiation into eldering. Seminars I've developed to foster such a process emphasize growing old, not being old; growing into old age, but not being arrested by it. Growing old is a way to appreciate the process of aging. It is a celebration of our personal success story. We have achieved a greater maturity—and we deserve to be congratulated for that.

The seminars also teach the tools of contemplative life, such as meditation and centering prayer. We need to sit in deep silence and become mindful of the presence of God.

Another prime focus of the seminars is to teach us the basics of reviewing our lives, and observing what remains incomplete in our life. And finally, they introduce us to death and beyond. They teach us that at death, Moses received a "kiss" from God. The kiss of Death is like the waters of *mikveh:* the finite person merges with the great All and is flooded with the Universal Mind. Death is seeing the Indwelling of God, the *shechiniah,* before our last breath and melting into the White Light.

Each seminar helps prepare us for the work of being an elder and eventually dying. We create a sacred space and prepare for death and beyond. Spiritual eldering lets us accept the gifts of life and lets us give our bodies at death to the worms and our spirits to the Universal. It helps us flow into the Godstream not with the pain of an unfulfilled life but rather with a sense of appreciated completion. This model of late-life development enables older people to become spiritually radiant, physically vital, and socially responsible "Elders of the Tribe." It lets us transform the downward arc of aging into an upward arc of expanded consciousness that crowns an elder's life with meaning and purpose.

IV

Swords and Plowshares:
How to Forge the Tools That Will Make It Happen

Never miss an opportunity to
study the Word of God. It settles
the mind and calms the heart.

* * * *

God's Word is the source of all
true life. Know and understand it.
The Word can heal your soul
and unite it with its source.

* * * *

Sanctify your mouth through
prayer and study; your nostrils
through the long breath of
patience;
your ears by listening
to the words of the wise;
and your eyes by
shutting them to evil.

* * * *

It is not enough to know God
only in the mind. Bind understanding to your
heart so that the awe of
The Holy One's greatness results in
true devotion.

— from *The Empty Chair: Finding Hope and Joy—*
Timeless Wisdom from a Hasidic Master,
Rebbe Nachman of Breslov

Dr. **Arthur Green**, rabbi, is Lown Professor of Jewish Thought at Brandeis University and former president of the Reconstructionist Rabbinical College in Philadelphia. He is a student of Jewish theology and mysticism who has combined scholarly career and personal commitment. In *These Are the Words: A Vocabulary of Jewish Spiritual Life,* Rabbi Green teaches us about the meaning of the word *Torah.*

Torah   תורה

ARTHUR GREEN

Torah is Judaism's most sacred word, except for the names of God. It means "teaching," and it is derived from a Hebrew root that also means "to shoot" or "to reach the mark." Torah embraces a wide range of meanings. Sometimes it refers to the very specific teachings of ancient Judaism, while at other times it embraces any true teachings to be found in the world, all of which are said to derive from a single Source.

In its narrowest sense, the word is used to refer to the Five Books of Moses, the *ḥumash* or Pentateuch. But examining the first four books of the Torah, we find no indication that this is its title. The word Torah is used quite frequently in these books, but always to indicate a specific teaching concerning one practice or another. The frequently repeated injunction to have a single Torah for citizen and stranger (Exodus 12:49 etc.) is best translated as "way of doing things." Only in Deuteronomy (4:44, 33:4), the fifth book of the Torah, does one get a sense of Torah indicating a compilation, and there it seems to refer to this fifth book itself. The first references to Torah that include some version of the text as we know it may be those of Nehemiah 8, written after the return to Zion (from the Babylonian exile) in the 5th century B.C.E. This account reflects the earliest appearance of an edited and authoritative Torah text.

Rabbinic Judaism does not admit to that development. The rabbis understand the entire five-book Torah to be God's gift to Moses. In the early rabbinic or tannaitic period (1st to early 3rd centuries) there is still some debate about how and when this revelation took place. Some envisioned revelation as a single, transformative event: The heavens opened at Sinai and all was revealed. Moses was given the history of humanity since Creation and was told of Israel's fortunes through his own death, which concludes the Torah text. One legend has it that the last eight verses of Deuteronomy, beginning "Moses the servant of the Lord died there..." were written in Moses' tears rather than in ink.

But other, perhaps less apocalyptic, versions of revelation were also taught. Some said that only the Ten Commandments were given at Sinai. Other laws were revealed, bit by bit, throughout the forty years in the wilderness. In most of these cases the divine voice spoke only to Moses, not to all of Israel. (Might he have misheard, just occasionally?) Deuteronomy was indeed taught by Moses just before his death, as the text itself proclaims. The entire Torah text was authoritative, according to these views, but it was not the result of a single revelatory event.

These debates were set aside in the later rabbinic or amoraic period (3rd to 6th centuries), when the grandest notions of revelation were given full sway. Moses received not only the entire Written Torah at Sinai, but the Oral Torah, the tradition of interpreting the text, as well. "Everything a faithful student was ever to say was already given to Moses at Sinai," proclaims the *Talmud*. To deny that even a single word or letter of Torah was divine constituted blasphemy.

Judaism's openness to continuing religious creativity turns on the notion of the rabbis' authority to interpret the text. Since that authority itself comes from Sinai, it cannot be questioned. But the process of interpretation opens the text to multiple readings: Aggadic *(aggadah),* halakhic *(halakhah),* grammatical, philosophic, and mystical currents of thought have all been applied to Torah throughout the ages. These add constant new levels of richness and subtlety to our understanding of it. In this way Judaism remains a highly faithful text-based tradition without becoming fundamentalist, since each text is always open to a multitude of interpretations. "The Torah has seventy faces" is a well-known saying, meaning that there are a great many legitimate ways to understand the same verse. Literalism is generally not privileged over other ways of reading.

Mystical and Hasidic Judaism tend to emphasize the notion of continuing revelation. Sinai was not just a one-time historical experience, but is one that can be renewed at any time for the person who is properly attuned to hearing. "Every day a voice goes forth from Mount Horeb saying 'Return, O humans!'" Such revelation may not contradict *halakhah*, to be sure, but it may strengthen and renew the faith of those who seek it. For most Jews, the best place to seek further revelation is within the text itself, so that the processes of study, interpretation, discovery of new meanings, and "revelation" are quite inseparable from one another.

From earliest times the rabbis insisted that Torah existed in a cosmic dimension far beyond that of Sinai and human revelation. "God looked into Torah to create the world," says the midrash, reflecting still older traditions about Wisdom as the companion of God before Creation. The relationship between this eternal Torah (Did it have words? Letters? Where was it written?) and the text before us is also a matter of longstanding mystical speculation. Could it be that our Torah is only one of the "seventy faces" of God's teaching, which is itself beyond words and language? How do we trace the way back from revealed to hidden? How do we get from the very worldly concerns of *halakhah* back to the sublime yet elusive "perfect teaching of Y-H-W-H" (Psalm 19:8)?

Dr. Norman J. Cohen, rabbi, is Provost of Hebrew Union College–Jewish Institute of Religion, where he is also Professor of Midrash. Renowned for his expertise in Torah study and midrash, he lectures frequently to audiences of many faiths. He was a participant in Bill Moyers' *Genesis: A Living Conversation* series on PBS. In *The Way Into Torah,* Dr. Cohen teaches us about the study of Torah.

The Study of Torah

NORMAN J. COHEN

Most of us have not been exposed in an extended way to the study of Torah. We are like the Israelites who, after passing through the Red Sea and starting out on their desert journey toward the Promised Land, traveled for three days in the arid desert and found no water (Exodus 15:22).

One rabbinic interpretation, understanding water as a symbol of Torah,[1] stresses that the Israelites really thirsted for words of Torah, for it was their sole source of salvation. The message conveyed is that no Jew should be without water, that is, the words of Torah, for three days; and therefore the Rabbis instituted the public reading of the Torah, the Five Books of Moses, three times a week: on Shabbat, Monday, and Thursday.[2] The reading of Torah, *Keriat ha-Torah,* in the synagogue, in an annual cycle of weekly readings, each called a *parashah* (pl. *parashiyyot*), is seen as an act of ritual teaching and study.

At most, one who attends synagogue is exposed to a portion of the Torah and to a reading from one of the prophetic books, selected as the *haftarah,* which "completes" the Torah reading for that particular Torah portion. The Rabbis, however, often use the word *Torah* not simply to refer to the Five Books of Moses or even to the whole *Tanakh,* which is the Pentateuch plus the books of the Prophets and Writings, but also to the totality of the Jewish religious tradition.

Even most Jews who attend synagogue regularly on Shabbat have little contact and experience with this vast sea of Jewish knowledge.

Therefore, the texts of our tradition are generally perceived by many Jewish people as antiquated remnants of another time and place, which cannot possibly speak to us and our own life situations. Yet, many of us still feel aimless, rootless, searching for meaning beyond the material. Can we reclaim the texts of our tradition in an authentic and meaningful way for ourselves? Can we be energized and transformed by the words of Torah? Can we find ultimate meaning in Torah, though we will appropriate it in a modern way? How can we find a path back to the texts of old that will enable us to be moored in their values and world-view, yet reach creatively beyond the context of the time and space in which they were created so they can address the concerns of contemporary life?

Today, many people who live predominantly in the secular world would explore the ways that Judaism can relate to the central concerns of their lives, if only someone would help them find ways of accessing the traditional texts, of acquiring the skills to open the texts of our forebears.[3]

By learning how we can immerse ourselves in the Jewish people's sacred stories, whether we view them as divinely given or as the product of inspired human beings, we can gain a sense of our own baffling human dramas from a Jewish perspective. In turn, this can affect how we live our lives and the priorities we adopt.[4]

So let us together dive into this sea known as Torah, realizing that some of us are first learning to float, while others who are further along will be trying to improve their ability to swim. However, recognizing that the act of Torah study is not the same as reading a secular novel or even a beautiful piece of poetry, but rather a sacred task that places us in a chain of tradition that began millennia ago, we should pause to recite the traditional blessings for *talmud Torah,* the study of Torah. The traditional *Shacharit,* or morning service, contains the blessings for the study of Torah almost at the outset of the liturgy. Although many *siddurim* (prayer books) present them as three separate paragraphs, in reality there are only two blessings, the second of which also appears as the introductory blessing before the Torah reading. Since the commandment to study Torah is in effect all day long, these two blessings need not be repeated if one studies again during the day:

> Blessed are You, Adonai, our God, Ruler of the universe, Who has sanctified us with the commandments and has commanded us to engross ourselves in the words of Torah. Adonai, our God, please make the words of Torah sweet in our mouths and in the mouth of Your people, the house of Israel. May we and our offspring and the offspring of Your people, the house of Israel—all of us—know Your name and study Your Torah for its own sake. Blessed are You, Adonai, Who teaches Torah to the people Israel.
>
> Blessed are You, Adonai, our God, Ruler of the universe, Who selected us from all the peoples and gave us the Torah. Blessed are You, Adonai, Giver of the Torah.

These two blessings capture the meaning and grandeur of Torah study in a few words. They emphasize that the study of the words of Torah is a holy act, one that lies at the basis of our covenantal relationship with God. It is the very raison d'etre of the covenant. Torah study is a *mitzvah,* a commandment—in fact, the paramount commandment, since without it one cannot understand what God demands of us, and therefore it must lead to action, both ritually and ethically. It is not enough to study in order to merely gain knowledge; the study of Torah must affect our lives in every way.

We are commanded to be engrossed in the words of Torah, *la'a-sok be-divrei Torah.* The verb *asak* indeed means to "immerse," "be involved with," and "work at." Our challenge is to be totally involved in God's words; what is demanded of us is to continually be engaged with the words of Torah and to give our whole beings to the process. As we immerse ourselves in Torah in an ongoing manner, it comes alive for us in new and significant ways each time we study. Torah is not static; it is not given (or discovered) once and never to be added to or enhanced. Even though the tradition tells us that God gave the Torah to the Jewish people on Mount Sinai, the second blessing emphasizes not only that God gave us the Torah in the past (*natan lanu et Torato*—God *gave us* Torah), but also that Adonai is the Giver of the Torah *(Notain ha-Torah)*. Torah is ever expanding when we add to the interpretive tradition of our people as we ourselves engage with God's words.

Yet, the very prayerful second half of the first blessing, in which we ask that God make the words of Torah sweet for us, underscores what Torah study is all about. It must be uplifting and joyful, something that touches us emotionally as well as intellectually. We hope that Torah study will challenge our minds as it allows our hearts and souls to soar.

Dr. Norman J. Cohen, rabbi, is Provost of Hebrew Union College–Jewish Institute of Religion, where he is also Professor of Midrash. Renowned for his expertise in Torah study and midrash, he lectures frequently to audiences of many faiths. He was a participant in Bill Moyers' *Genesis: A Living Conversation* series on PBS. In *The Way Into Torah*, Dr. Cohen teaches us about the importance of Torah study.

The Importance of Torah Study

NORMAN J. COHEN

From the earliest times, the study of Torah has been the highest ideal toward which the Jewish people aspired. But when we speak of Torah from a Jewish perspective, what exactly do we mean? Is the word *Torah* synonymous with the word *Bible?*

WHAT IS THE BIBLE?

The term *Bible* comes from the Greek *Biblion,* a translation by Greek-speaking Jews of the term *Ha-Sefarim,* "The Books," which is how Scripture is referred to by the early Rabbis.[1] Another rabbinic term, *Kitvei Ha-Kodesh,* "Holy Writings," emphasizes the written nature of the biblical text, in contrast to the oral form in which the rabbinic tradition was thought to have been originally transmitted. Similarly, the term *Mikra,* "Reading," another rabbinic term for the Bible, underscores both the public reading of Scripture in Jewish liturgy and the fact that this written text could actually be read.[2] The most prevalent term, however, is the acronym *TaNaKh,* which is derived from the initial letters of the three divisions of the Hebrew Bible: Torah, *Nevi'im* (Prophets), and *Ketuvim* (Writings).

The earliest name for the first part of the Bible probably was *Torat Moshe,* the Torah of Moses.[3] Later, perhaps when the five parts of the Torah were transcribed on separate scrolls, it became known in

Greek as the "five-volumed [book]," which we know in English as the Pentateuch. In rabbinic literature, the Hebrew equivalent is *Chamisha Chumshei Torah,* literally The Five Fifth-parts of the Torah.[4] The first section is therefore called the *Chumash.* The English names for the five books of the Torah—Genesis, Exodus, Leviticus, Numbers, and Deuteronomy—are based on the titles in the Latin Bible, which were drawn from the Greek translations of the Hebrew names. These names—*B'reishit* (In the Beginning), *Shemot* (Names), *Vayikra* (And [God] Called), *Bamidbar* (In the Desert), and *Devarim* (Words or Commandments)—are the first key words mentioned in each book, but they also allude to the content of each one.

The second part of the Bible, called *Nevi'im* (Prophets), was later subdivided into the "Former Prophets" and the "Latter Prophets." The former are narrative-historical works: Joshua, Judges, Samuel, and Kings. The latter are literary creations from the oratory of the Prophets: the many-chaptered books of Isaiah, Jeremiah, and Ezekiel, and the Twelve Minor Prophets (simply an indication of size)—Hosea, Joel, Amos, Obadiah, Jonah, Micah, Nachum, Habbakuk, Zephaniah, Haggai, Zechariah, and Malachi.

The *Ketuvim* (Writings, also called the Hagiographa), the third section, is a potpourri of liturgical poetry (Psalms and Lamentations), love poetry (the Song of Songs), Wisdom literature (Proverbs, Job, and Ecclesiastes), and historical compilations (Ruth, Ezra, Nehemiah, and Chronicles, as well as the Book of Daniel, which is a combination of history and prophecy).

The tripartite division, *Tanakh,* as you can see, does not involve a categorization by theme, content, or style.[5] Rather, it reflects historical development, representing three stages in the process of the canonization of the Bible as a whole.

As we mentioned, the tradition associates the Torah with Moses, calling it *Torat Moshe,* the Torah of Moses. It is not clear, however, exactly what that means. On the basis of statements such as *"Moshe kibbel Torah mi'Sinai"* (Moses received the Torah on Mount Sinai),[6] some believe that God actually dictated the Torah to Moses. Others believe that Moses wrote the whole of the Torah text except for its ending, the final verses that describe his own death. More modern traditional readers may say that God did not dictate the Torah to Moses but rather that Moses was inspired to write it, since he possessed the divine spirit, *ruach Elohim*. All of these traditional stances, based on a sense of the infallibility of Torah, underscore the importance and power of the words of Torah, since it is somehow perceived as being God-given. Yet, at the same time, modern scholars and readers who approach the text from either a literary or a historical perspective also discover this beauty and power of the Torah. The personal meaning that Torah offers the individual reader can be enhanced by an understanding and appreciation of how it came to be put together by inspired individuals over centuries.

The traditional notion of Moses' authorship of the Torah is based on Deuteronomy 31:9–12 more than any other verses, since it is stated, "And Moses wrote the Torah." Yet, as mentioned above, most readers, even very traditional ones, do not understand this to mean that Moses wrote the entire Pentateuch. Two other biblical passages that help us understand where and when the Bible was written down are 2 Kings 22–23 and 2 Chronicles 34. They tell the story of the finding of the "Book of the Torah" in the year 622 B.C.E., which is recognized as authoritative by both the High Priest and King Josiah. The content of the book is not spelled out, nor is it identified directly as the product of Moses, although it is read publicly and accepted as binding upon the people. Since these biblical passages describe reform measures that can be identified with the Book of Deuteronomy, this "book" probably represents the formalization of Deuteronomy and the beginning of the formation of the Pentateuch.[7] The first report of the public reading of the Torah (as a whole) comes in a ceremony conducted by Ezra in Jerusalem nearly two hundred years later, in the mid-fifth century B.C.E., as reported in Nehemiah, chapters 8–10. It is clear that the Torah had already been canonized by this time, since the writer of Chronicles, dated slightly later, frequently mentions the "Torah of Moses" and knows each of the five books.

The canon of the *Nevi'im* was probably shaped in the Persian period, by the end of the fourth century B.C.E. This would explain why the prophetic books make no use of Greek words and make no mention of the downfall of the Persian Empire and the emergence of Greek hegemony. It is clear also from Zechariah 13:2–5 that prophecy waned around that time, after the return from the Babylonian exile. A tradition found throughout rabbinic literature is that Haggai, Zechariah, and Malachi were the last of the prophets, "the Divine spirit having ceased to be active in Israel with their death."[8]

Many of the works classified as the *Ketuvim* (Writings) were compiled during the prophetic period but were not included among the *Nevi'im*, since they were not seen to be prophetic in nature. Other works, like Daniel and Esther, were simply written after the close of prophecy and were not canonized until later, probably before the destruction of the Second Temple in 70 C.E.

However, there is ample evidence that the collection of the Writings as a whole was not closed until the second century C.E. The fact that at that time the Rabbis debated the status of the Wisdom of Ben Sira, which was not ultimately included in the canon,[9] shows that the collection of *Ketuvim* was still open.

WRITTEN TORAH AND ORAL TORAH

We have seen that the word *Torah* has two meanings. One is the first part of the Bible, the *Chumash*, which is read in the synagogue on the Sabbaths and holidays. Another is the entirety of the Bible: what was perceived to be the written record of revelation, in many literary forms, as it was grouped over several centuries. It is this larger category—the group that is also called *Mikra* or *Kitvei Ha-Kodesh*—that is also often referred to as the Written Torah, or *Torah she-Bikhtav.*

The word Torah, however, is used more broadly to mean not merely the biblical text but rather the whole of the Jewish religious tradition, which is seen as the subject of learning. The commentaries, interpretations, legal writings, and legends that students and teachers have woven around the Written Torah, starting even before the time of its canonization, are known as Oral Torah, *Torah she-Ba'al Peh,* because, as we shall see later,[10] unlike the Bible itself, they were thought to have been transmitted out loud rather than in writing. The Bible—the Written Torah—pervades all of these rabbinic works; the Rabbis presume that their readers also read and love the biblical text, and they refer to it often. But they also go far beyond it. Indeed, Torah in this broadest sense even supersedes the boundaries of these rabbinic books as well and includes the Jewish religious thinking and writing of our own generation. In that sense, to read this very book is not merely to learn about Torah but actually to engage in the study of Torah itself.

THE PRECIOUSNESS OF TORAH: THE ENTIRETY OF JEWISH RELIGIOUS TRADITION

It is with this broadest definition of Torah in mind that the Rabbis perceived Torah to be more important than belief in God, since if Israel forsakes the Divine, occupying themselves with Torah will cause the light that it contains eventually to lead them back.[11] Thus, the Rabbis even emphasized that the practice of all the laws of Scripture is worth less than the study of Scripture itself.[12]

Indeed, Torah study is more precious a crown—a greater source of honor—than the priesthood or royalty.[13] Maimonides, Rabbi Moshe ben Maimon, the twelfth-century Jewish philosopher and giant of legal scholarship, goes so far as to cite the sages who note, "A person of illegitimate birth who is immersed in Torah study takes precedence over the High Priest if he is ignorant of Torah,[14] for it is said, 'It is more precious than rubies' *(mi-peni'im)* [Proverbs 3:15]."

At first glance, it is not clear why this particular verse is cited as a text that proves the importance of study—as a proof text. How does Proverbs 3:15, which speaks about rubies, prove the point that the Rabbis, and Maimonides, are trying to make? The first step in the answer is to read the verse in its original biblical context, and when we focus on this Proverbs verse we see that its subject is Wisdom, which the Rabbis consistently identify with Torah. That explains why this verse glorifies the study of Torah. But what does it have to do with the priesthood? The answer lies in a rabbinic wordplay.

When we study Torah, we treat every word as a hook upon which meaning can be appended. Here, the difference between the *Ketiv*, the written form of the word, and the Keri, the way the word should be read despite its written form, provides the Rabbis with a golden opportunity. The text should actually read *mi-peninim*, since *peninim* means "rubies" or "pearls." Then the passage would clearly mean, "[The Torah] is more precious than rubies." However, the Proverbs text is written defectively, that is, with a letter missing, as *peni'im*, which means "those on the inside." As a result, the Rabbis can use this verse as if it were saying, "It [Wisdom, meaning Torah, and by extension, the person who studies Torah] is more precious than [the High Priest who] enters the inner sanctum of the Temple."

The study of Torah was frequently juxtaposed by the Rabbis to different aspects of Temple worship. Whether they emphasized that when the Temple no longer existed, atonement was possible through an occupation with words of Torah,[15] or that when scholars are immersed in Torah, it is as if they are engaged in the Temple service,[16] an underlying point was that Torah study is an act of religious worship.[17]

Dr. David Hartman, rabbi, philosopher and social activist, is the founder and director of the Shalom Hartman Institute in Jerusalem and Professor Emeritus at Hebrew University in Jerusalem. In *A Heart of Many Rooms: Celebrating the Many Voices within Judaism,* Dr. Hartman teaches us about the joy of Torah study.

The Joy of Study

DAVID HARTMAN

Our analysis of the joy of the Torah has so far dealt only with mitzvot, the joy of the commandments. The term "Torah" also denotes a body of material that is studied and analyzed. In the *beit ha-midrash* (study hall) of a yeshivah, one often finds people singing while studying Talmud. On seeing such people swaying and singing, one might mistakenly believe them to be praying, when in fact they are engaged in a profound intellectual activity. I have had the rare privilege of studying with a talmudic master who experienced total joy while intellectually grappling with Talmud and with the vast corpus of legal and aggadic material. Within the world of learning, often referred to as "the world of Torah," one discovers concepts of joy similar to those discussed above. The Judaic emphasis on study began with talmudic Judaism, with the oral tradition. The centrality of learning in rabbinic Judaism, as expressed in the saying *"talmud torah keneged kulam"* (Torah study above all else), has characterized Jewish values and practice throughout history.

The covenant experience truly emerges when Israel, the listener, turns the spoken Word into an open-ended creative word. The content of Torah can never be exhausted; it must be received and expanded in each generation. The student experiences the presence of God even in those aspects of Torah created through human interpretation. A student recites *birkat ha Torah* (the blessing over the Torah) even when studying the writings of contemporary teachers. Prophets are no longer the sole mediators of the word of God. Scholars and students of Torah are now the main actors in the ongoing drama of revelation.

The covenant, which is predicated on human responsibility, is strengthened when Israel feels adequate to expand the implications of the spiritual guidance that began at Sinai. Revelation at Sinai then becomes a *derekh* (a pointing, a way, a direction) and not the final consummation of the word of God. Intense intellectual engagement with Torah transforms the individual from a passive recipient to an active shaper of the future direction of Torah. Cognitive dignity and intellectual adequacy provide the foundations of the joy of Torah.

The tradition of Torah learning reflects a fundamental acknowledgment of human adequacy and dignity. Within this tradition, the importance of learning is closely linked to the model of God as the accepting, loving teacher. A student is encouraged and empowered to develop the implications of what was received. God's love liberates students of Torah to create, and to regard their creation as an elaboration of what the original teaching contained. The claim to originality is not the highest aspiration when love characterizes the teacher-student relationship. It is in this spirit that we should understand the talmudic ascription of all rabbinic and later creativity to the founding moment of Sinai.

> Scripture, Mishnah, Halachot, Talmud, Toseftot, Haggadot, and even what a faithful disciple would in the future say in the presence of his master, were all communicated to Moses at Sinai; for it says, "Is there a thing of which it is said: See this is new?" (Eccl. 1:10) and the other part of the verse provides the reply to this: "It has been already." (*Midrash Rabbah, Leviticus, Achare Mot,* 22:1)

> What relation does the Sabbatical Year [shmitah] have to Mount Sinai? Were not all the commandments stated at Sinai? Rather, just as [the laws of] the Sabbatical Year were stated in their general principles and in their specific details, so too were all the laws stated in their general principles and in their specific details. *(Sifra, Behar 9, parshata A)*

"Let him kiss me with the kisses of his mouth" (Song of Songs 1:2)—R. Yochanan said: An angel carried the utterances at Mount Sinai from before the Holy One, blessed be He, each one in turn, and brought it to each of the Israelites and said to him, Do you take upon yourself this commandment? So and so many rules are attached to it, so and so many penalties are attached to it, so and so many precautionary measures are attached to it, so and so many precepts and so and so many rulings from minor to major. The Israelite would answer him, Yes. Thereupon, he kissed him on the mouth. The Rabbis, however, say: The commandment itself went to each of the Israelites and said to him, So and so many rules are attached to it [etc.] and he would reply, Yes, yes. And straightaway, the *commandment* kissed him on the mouth. *(Song of Songs Rabbah)*

Instead of viewing rabbinic statements attributing halakhic discussions and interpretations to the founding moment of Sinai as attempts to provide authoritative foundations for the learning tradition, I believe these statements can be understood as expressing the experience of love of God that characterized the interpretive tradition, where the distinction between what is the Word of God and what is humanly derived loses all significance. Just as in human relationships of intense love, one often feels that all one is or has achieved is due to the beloved, so too a student intensely committed to a teacher may not always distinguish between what was received and what he or she has created.

It is important to differentiate between creativity grounded in love, which flows from an intense relationship, and the creativity of one who is conscious of separation and of individuality. Midrashic writers reflect the relationship of a lover to a beloved; the feeling that the Torah is a gift of love from God permeates all their writings. Because the Torah was given in love and is studied with love, it contains all that future generations will "discover" to have been "included" in God's message.

"The words of the Lord are...silver tried in the open before all men refined seven times seven" (Ps. 12:7). R. Yannai said: The words of Torah were not given as clear-cut decisions. For with every word which the Holy One, blessed be He, spoke to Moses, He offered him forty-nine arguments by which a thing may be proved clean, and forty-nine other arguments by which it may be proved unclean. When Moses asked: Master of the Universe, in what way shall we know the true sense of a law? God replied: The majority is to be followed: when a majority says it is unclean, it is unclean; when a majority says it is clean, it is clean.

(Midrash on Psalms, I, 12)

With the development of the oral tradition, Israel becomes a co-partner in the creative process of the Word; revelation ceases to be a Word given once and for all at Sinai, but becomes a Word that is continuously discussed and developed by students. The Word that mediates divine love becomes integrated with the human response. God's revelation at Sinai and the creative development of the Torah by Israel become one Torah. The written Torah and the oral tradition become one.

Dr. Norman J. Cohen, rabbi, is Provost of Hebrew Union College–Jewish Institute of Religion, where he is also Professor of Midrash. Renowned for his expertise in Torah study and midrash, he lectures frequently to audiences of many faiths. He was a participant in Bill Moyers' *Genesis: A Living Conversation* series on PBS. In *Voices from Genesis: Guiding Us through the Stages of Life,* Dr. Cohen teaches us how sacred stories help us make sense of our lives.

Midrash: Sacred Stories

NORMAN J. COHEN

Stories protect us from chaos, providing us with a foundation of memory and a potential for self-understanding. They are essential because they help us make sense of our lives.[1]

In particular, myths and sacred stories speak to the life journey that each of us makes. They embody events which take place in the psychic and spiritual life of all of us. Sacred stories also provide a sense of meaning to our own baffling dramas as they link us with past members of our community with whom we share a common destiny.[2] Perhaps few books can do this better than the Bible. By immersing ourselves in its sacred stories, whether we see them as divinely given or the inspired creations of human beings, we can find out about our own true natures; about who we are and who we can become.

According to the rabbinic understanding of the Bible, or Torah as it is traditionally known in Judaism, all human experience and knowledge is woven into its narrative fabric. The unfolding of history is evident in its sequence of events, just as all new, contemporary interpretations of the text are part of its original intent. All this was implicitly part of what was revealed at Sinai, though revelation is ongoing and mediated by the process of interpretation, which Judaism calls *midrash*.[3] Revelation is not something that occurs once—and never again. Every reader in every generation can draw new and poignant meaning from the biblical text.

The midrashic process is a dynamic interaction between the reader and the text, and the moment when the text and the reader meet is when meaning is born.[4] The reader doesn't merely read the biblical narrative, but rather *experiences* it. Its significance does not lie in the meaning sealed within the text, but rather in the fact that the text elicits what had been previously sealed within the reader.[5] What is hidden in the text is the reader's most essential and intimate life: his or her longings, fears, doubts, questions, and struggles.[6] It is these essential parts of ourselves which are uncovered when we become one with the text.

Reading the Bible, then, is about change. And this takes effort. Reading it involves one's entire being, and this forces involvement, response, passion, and self-reflection.[7] As readers open their hearts, minds, and souls to the biblical text, the text reflects back to them their own struggles and dilemmas. And the more they reveal aspects of themselves while reading and interpreting the text, the more the text will affect them. Ultimately, as we create new meanings in our engagement with the Bible, this process transforms us. The text does not merely mirror back to us who we are, but also shows us who we can become.

Since we change over time as our relationships and circumstances change, the particular meaning that we create as we engage with the biblical text at any one moment may be different than any previous meaning. As we go through a series of transformations at different times in our lives, experiencing at each stage different conflicts, challenges, and life issues, we are inevitably drawn to different aspects of the biblical narrative and to different characters. We might also be drawn to different aspects in the life of a particular biblical personality.

Rabbi Debra Orenstein is a senior fellow of the Wilstein Institute of Jewish Policy Studies and an instructor at the University of Judaism as well as a spiritual leader of Makom Ohr Shalom Congregation of Tarzana and Westwood, California. Rabbi Jane Rachel Litman serves Congregation Beth El in Berkeley, California. In *Lifecycles V. 2: Jewish Women on Biblical Themes in Contemporary Life,* Rabbi Orenstein and Rabbi Litman teach us how to create a contemporary midrash.

How to Create a Contemporary Midrash

DEBRA ORENSTEIN AND JANE RACHEL LITMAN

The more you study a biblical text on its own terms and in light of various techniques, the richer the *midrash* you will be able to create. By the same token, writing a *midrash* creates the opportunity and incentive for study, and, in both our ideal and our experience, generally returns a person to the text.

Midrash-writing, like more conventional forms of engagement with Torah, can be undertaken on your own or in a group. You can write a *midrash* on any genre—law, narrative, poetry, even genealogy. Choose something that moves you or makes you curious. Texts with a great deal of ambiguity or confusion especially lend themselves to *midrash*, since the best *midrashim* tell a story that is coherent in itself and implicitly answers a textual question or problem. A *midrash* is considered especially elegant when, in presenting a story or idea, it can solve several questions or problems at once.

Read your chosen text and supplementary sources carefully and repeatedly, with an eye to uncovering questions. List anything and everything that strikes you as unusual, puzzling, or provocative. Ask questions based on theological, literary, mythic, historical, Rabbinic, feminist, and other concerns. Even questions that at first seem "silly" can yield interesting discussions and interpretations.

Play the story out step by step, and isolate what is at issue and what the dynamics are in each beat of the scenario. What are the pivotal moments, and who is in control then? How are the "snapshots" of this episode related to the surrounding text? What are the moral problems and messages? How do men and women relate to each other and to God? What problem(s) and motivation(s) does each character have? What problem(s) is the larger story or law itself addressing, both on and below the surface? What would happen if a similar event transpired now or a similar law were in force? What situations are analogous to the one described? Review questions asked by traditional commentators and midrashists. What answers do they provide? What additional answers come to mind? What other questions would you ask?

One way of getting at interesting ambiguities and problems is to describe in detail what is happening (present tense) at a specific, pivotal moment in the playing out of a law, song, or narrative. For example, describe the motivations, expectations, and emotions of those involved, as Eve, incited by the snake, extends the fruit to Adam (Gen. 3:6). Or imagine the setting and feelings at the moment when the midwives, summoned by Pharaoh, open their mouths to explain why they have violated his orders (Ex. 1:18).

ENTERING INTO THE TEXT

Many traditional *midrashim* adopt the point of view of the various characters in a story. Try personalizing your *midrash* by using the first person singular to relate a story or law from the perspective of each person included in it. At first, be sure to mention only—and all—those parts of the picture to which your character has access. For example, "It was after these things that I, Abraham, was told to sacrifice my beloved son, Isaac" (Gen. 22:1). But "I, Isaac, suddenly found myself going along with my father, early in the morning, on the way to a destination I was ignorant of, without any explanation" (22:3). This will help you discern the narrator's voice and keep the various viewpoints distinct. It will also uncover gaps and discontinuous perspectives in the story, which your *midrash* can then fill or elaborate. For example, you might imagine a conversation between Abraham and Isaac (not reported in the Bible), after Abraham woke his son on the morning they set out together.

You can also report a law or narrative—again, in the first person—from the perspective of (1) animals or inanimate objects; (2) characters who are not present, though they appear in the larger story cycle; and (3) figures who are mysterious or underdeveloped. In the story of the binding of Isaac, these three types of perspectives are represented, respectively, by (1) the ram Abraham sacrifices in lieu of Isaac, along with the altar itself; (2) the absent Ishmael, Hagar, and Sarah; Satan, who dares God to test Abraham, according to *midrash;* and (3) the mysterious figures of God and the angel, as well as the relatively obscure servants who travel with Abraham and Isaac.

A similar technique, drawn from psychodrama, is to role-play different characters and speak their "secret thoughts," unarticulated in the text. Notice how the versions fit or don't fit together. Then, write a *midrash* that communicates one perspective, or somehow combines several, perhaps in a dialogue—another technique of traditional *midrash*. Or, play out what you would do—in the original setting or in a transposed, but similar contemporary situation—if you were in the same position as a particular character. Explore how you identify with different figures.[1]

Having studied the story of Hagar and Sarah, for example, you can enter into it by completing the blanks, below. (If doing this with a group, go around in a circle and let everyone fill in each blank a few times.)

I am like Hagar in that/because/when _____.

I reject Hagar in that/because/when_____.

I embrace Hagar in that/because/when _____.

I am like Sarah in that/because/when _____.

I reject Sarah in that/because/when _____.

I embrace Sarah in that/because/when_____.

This technique will help you understand the biblical figures—and yourself—better.

Another "right-brained" technique is synectics, a game of analogies. What are your associations to trees and "tree-like" qualities? How does this inform your understanding of Torah as a "tree of life" (Proverbs 3:18)?[2]

Poetry is also a wonderful tool for personalizing the themes and characters of the Bible.[3] Many women have written midrashic poems as part of an effort to reclaim women's stories.[4] Such poetry can emerge from group or individual interaction with the biblical text. When writing in/as a group, it is helpful to use specific structures and rules; these focus creativity, yield interesting poems, and decrease the pressure that some might feel. To explore Sarah and Hagar's relationship, each participant might write a single line of poetry from the perspective of either woman, using the format "I seem to...but really I...." and incorporating at least one verb other than "to be." Individual lines could then be ordered and juxtaposed so as to create a midrashic poem. Another simple, but powerful design is to begin each line of a poem about the Bible with the words "I wish." Imagine, for example, using this guideline to write a poem entitled "Sodom and Gomorrah." Other possibilities: Incorporate sensory elements, metaphors, colors, or geographic locations in an assigned pattern. Such techniques are drawn from the work of Kenneth Koch, who pioneered group poetry writing among children and the elderly.[5]

The primary goal is not to create beautiful poetry, though that often does emerge. Rather, the goal is to discover new avenues of creativity and interpretation, to link individual and communal stories of today with our ancient, sacred teachings.

Non-verbal expressions—especially drawing and dance—have also been used to produce midrashic interpretations. In a technique called "hand-made *midrash*," each participant creates a picture of a key concept or story in the Bible by tearing and pasting colored paper.[6] This levels the artistic playing field and, more importantly, encourages symbolic representations of relationships and ideas. Often, it is helpful to ask everyone to portray at least one figure who does not appear in the text. Thus, a representation of Esther jeopardizing her life by entering the king's court might depict other heros and (near-)martyrs from our history, the artist him/herself, Haman, Mordecai, and God (Esther 5:1f). By crafting and explaining pictures in a group, you can notice your own interpretive assumptions, literally *see* those of others, and invent new *midrashim*.

Dance is another group activity that can be used to create, explore, and express personal, midrashic interpretations. With dance, as with hand-made *midrash* and poetry writing, it is important to make the exercise user-friendly for those who are not experienced in the art form. In creating a dance *midrash* on the story of Isaac's birth, participants could move their hands to represent the way Sarah laughed when she heard she was to become a mother at age ninety (Gen. 18:12). Hands might shake dismissively, wave uproariously, or spiral upward prayerfully, in different interpretations of the story. Dancers might speak words from the Torah, the traditional midrash, or their own commentary as they move. This exercise is useful in itself. In addition, books and workshops on midrashic dance teach how such "motivating movements" as these hand-dances can be incorporated into a choreographed piece.[7]

With midrashic poetry, drawing, and dance, *text study should precede and/or follow the artistic activities,* and group discussion of the creative product is illuminating. New insights can be captured in written reflections on the artistic/group/interpretive process. Many times, a (group) poem, picture, or dance will "work" as an artistic and midrashic expression; if not, it may well inspire new poems, pictures, dances, or expository *midrashim.*

"ZIL GEMOR—GO AND LEARN" (BT SHABBAT 31A)

No matter what method is used in the creation of *midrash,* it is essential to connect the invention back to the biblical text. Otherwise, you may have created an interesting essay, poem, or performance, but not necessarily a *midrash.* "Connecting the invention back to the text" can mean using some of the Bible's language in your *midrash,* or even citing prooftexts for your interpretation, from the passage that gave rise to it or from another biblical text. If you generate a *midrash* from questions or perspectives that are textually based, you will not have difficulty "completing the circle."

In a particularly apt formulation, Paul Ricoeur provides a question and answer frequently discussed among literary critics. "What is indeed to be understood—and consequently appropriated—in a text?" Something much larger and more influential than we might assume: "The direction of thought opened up by the text...nothing other than the power of disclosing a world that constitutes the reference of the text."[8] The Bible is not just a text; it is a world. Indeed, for many students of the Bible, that world is the reference for *all* texts and experiences—not the Bible alone. Engaging in Torah study, therefore, can be a way of mapping the universe.[9]

Rabbi Daniel F. Polish, Ph.D., is Director of the Social Action Commission at Union of American Hebrew Congregations. In *Bringing the Psalms to Life: How to Understand and Use the Book of Psalms,* Rabbi Polish teaches us about the creative ways we can understand the psalms and use their power to enrich our lives.

The Power of Psalms

DANIEL F. POLISH

...With a clatter the trunk rolled right into the synagogue!

A near panic broke out among the worshippers. Their shrieks and screams were heard by the women and children, who came to see what was happening in the house of worship.

Strange voices were heard inside the trunk. Helm became frightened...surely the trunk was full of demons! The congregation stood petrified, and the Rabbi was about to begin reciting Psalms...[1]

What a strange moment, indeed, to begin the study of sacred text. Yet this is what is described in a well-known folktale. And in a recent news report we find the following account:

Some 33,000 Doenmeh, or secret Sabbateans, live in Turkey. Their calendar for secret religious observance includes conventional Jewish holidays such as Rosh Hashanah and Yom Kippur—and less orthodox ones such as the Festival of Light, when groups of married couples meet in a private home, slaughter a lamb, chant psalms, and then swap partners...[2]

Once again, a most unlikely moment for the study of scripture.

The fact is, of course, that Jews do not "study" psalms the same way we study other texts. Our relationship with this book is different from that with any other book in the Bible. Historically, it has been the custom for Jews to have copies of the Book of Psalms—often very small volumes—with them at all times to turn to in moments of trouble. These little volumes of *Tillim*, along with copies of the *Tanach* and the Prayer Book, were often a Jew's most precious possessions.

The Jewish people has always felt a special affinity for the Book of Psalms. The Talmud says that it was the will of the people at large that forced the Rabbis to formalize the practice of assigning a particular psalm to each day of the week. Thus it is now formal dictate, and not just popular custom, that gives every day its own psalm. *Mishna Tamid* 7:4 gives us the order that is followed to this day:

Sunday	Psalm 24
Monday	Psalm 48
Tuesday	Psalm 82
Wednesday	Psalm 94
Thursday	Psalm 81
Friday	Psalm 93
Shabbat	Psalm 92

Behind this practice lies the real question of why the people have, and have always had, such profound devotion to the Book of Psalms. Here is where we begin to confront the real power of the psalms. The power of the psalms is that they speak directly and personally to the human condition. In *Midrash Tehillim* (to Psalm 18:1) Rabbi Yudan says in the name of Rabbi Judah, "Whatever David says in his book pertains to himself, to all Israel and to all times." The same appreciation of the power of the psalms is articulated in the Christian tradition by one of the Church Fathers, Athanasius, Bishop of Alexandria (C.E. 293?–373):

> The Psalms embrace the entire human life, express every emotion of the soul, every impulse of the heart—[The Psalms speak for you] when the soul yearns for penance and confession, when thy spirit is depressed or joyous...when thy soul is yearning to express its thanks to God, or its pains...

Both Rabbi Judah and Bishop Athanasius identify that essential quality of the psalms that has made them so beloved, and so powerful. The psalms are remarkably human. They validate the whole range of human emotions. Psalms start with the recognition of just how tenuous life is: we suffer; we experience fear and exaltation; we meet with success and failure; we know contentment and anxiety; we experience betrayal, have enemies, even know rage and the desire for revenge; and we find vindication, comfort, new confidence. The psalms give voice to all of these emotions and help us put them in context. They help us marshal our resources so that we can move from hurt to healing, from the valley of the shadow back to the high places of life. The psalms hold out hope for us, even in our darkest hours. Above all, the psalms encourage us to give voice to our emotions and pour our hearts out to God.

SEEING GOD IN THE PSALMS

Human emotions are real and vibrant in the psalms, and so is the living presence of God. The psalms present us with a vivid sense of God's nearness. The nature of the experience of God in Psalms is congruent with the experience that most of us have in our own lives. In Torah and Prophets the story is almost always about God reaching out to people, something most of us do not experience directly most of the time. The psalms are about people reaching out to God, which is what we do experience, or what we can aspire to do. The psalms are a model for us of what our relationship with God can be. They show the close intimacy we can develop.

From another perspective, Psalms presents a compelling image of God. The God of the psalms is close at hand, listens, and is *chasid*—steadfast, reliable. The God of the psalms is a God who cares. We are assured that God cares about God's people (111:9) and that God cares about individuals. Religiously, this is the most compelling aspect of the psalms. God not only cares about the people as a whole, the great leaders, and the religious teachers, but also about individuals, average ordinary people, and perhaps especially, those who are cast down and hurting.

In Psalms, God is close by (34:19). God guards our going out and coming in—always (121:8). God listens (116:1). The ear of God is inclined to hear us. God is near to all who call on God (145:18). God champions the needy and downtrodden. God raises the poor from the dust (113:7).

Psalms assures us that God saves us, rescues us. Seventy-six times in the 150 psalms we are assured of God's ability and desire to save us. Because of this, the religious lesson of psalms is the lesson of hope—hope and *religious* patience: "I wait for the Lord, my soul doth wait, and in God's word do I hope" (130:5).

The relationship with God that Psalms models for us is intimate and intense. We can make demands on God, and be clear and explicit in what we want. Indeed, the closeness of the relationship even allows us to challenge God. As we pour out our hearts and our needs to God, we can even chastise God for the pains and difficulties that have befallen us.

Psalms teaches us that the greatest happiness is being in God's presence. Ultimately, the recitation of psalms becomes performative—that is, the very act of reciting them fulfills the goal to which they aspire. Reciting *tillim* puts us in contact with God, brings us into God's presence. The very recitation of psalms in itself brings us happiness.

USING PSALMS FOR SACRED MOMENTS

For these reasons, the psalms have become so precious to the Jewish people, and the recitation of psalms a customary part of sacred moments. Psalms are recited with a woman when she is in childbirth, and with a baby boy the night before his circumcision. When a child is given her or his name, it is the practice to take appropriate verses from Psalm 119—in which the verses are arranged in alphabetical order—and create an acrostic of the child's name. Among the Jews of Yemen, psalms are recited with a boy the night before he becomes bar mitzvah. Universally in the Jewish world, psalms are recited at the bedside of a person who is close to death. When a person dies, someone is assigned to remain with the body, reciting psalms, until it is buried. Psalms are the central part of the funeral service, and are recited as we accompany the body to the cemetery. You could say that whenever Jews hold a vigil of any kind, psalms are at the core of the experience.

In many parts of the world, it is customary to recite the entire Book of Psalms on the night of Yom Kippur. In describing this custom, S. Y. Agnon adds words of praise for psalms that can apply to all occasions on which psalms are recited. His tribute captures the special esteem in which psalms are held, and the devotion Jews feel to them:

> It is the custom in many parts of the Exile to recite all the Book of Psalms on the night of Yom Kippur. This is a good custom for those who are conscientious, for there is nothing more important than the Book of Psalms, which contains everything...and all the Psalms come from the hand of God.[3]

WHAT ABOUT "MAGICAL" USES OF PSALMS?

There is one other dimension of the Jews' devotion to the psalms that demands our attention. Much has been written about the relationship of religion and magic. It has often been noted that there is a continuum that runs between the realm of the strictly religious, and the realm of the "magical." Any specific act, under differing circumstances, can be placed at different points along that continuum. The same act can be performed for religious or for magical purposes—kissing the *mezuzah* in the Jewish tradition or doing honor to a statue of Saint Joseph in the Roman Catholic tradition. It should not surprise us that the psalms have become so central to the spiritual lives of Jews, that they are often put to use to serve purposes that might be described as magical.

Thus the reading of psalms in the two episodes described at the beginning of this chapter. The rabbi in the story about the village of

Helm was not engaged in study—or even prayer—when he began to recite psalms as he approached the presumably demon-inhabited trunk. Rather, he hoped to make use of the power of psalms to protect himself as he neared this fearsome object, and to protect his community from the effects of its presence.

Isa Aron, Ph.D., is Professor of Jewish Education at Hebrew Union College–Jewish Institute of Religion's Rhea Hirsch School of Education, where she directs the Experiment in Congregational Education (ECE). In *Becoming a Congregation of Learners: Learning as a Key to Revitalizing Congregational Life,* Dr. Aron teaches us how congregations and their members can re-dedicate themselves to learning.

What Is a Congregation of Learners?

ISA ARON

A congregation of learners is a center for authentic Jewish learning— learning that is viewed as a lifelong endeavor, that grows out of the life of the community, and which, in turn, strengthens the community. The congregation of learners is both a means to an end and an end in itself; it is an instrument for enculturating individual members into active participation in Jewish life, but it is also a model for Jewish community.

What does a congregation of learners look like? If one visited such a congregation, what would one see? First of all, one would see many people learning in many different ways. There would be formal classes, of course, but also informal discussion groups, arts workshops, and storytelling, as well as lots of one-on-one tutoring. Ideally, everyone in the congregation would be engaged in learning on a continuous basis. More realistically, learning would be seen as the norm, rather than as the exception. New members would be brought in with the expectation that they, and not just their children, would be engaged in learning in some form. It would be understood by all that Jewish learning extends throughout one's life, far beyond bar/bat mitzvah, and far beyond confirmation.

To accommodate its diverse membership, a congregation of learners would have to think in unconventional and creative ways about Jewish teaching. It is unlikely that funds could be found to provide truly professional teachers for everyone. Instead, teaching would be seen as a communal obligation, with the mitzvah of "teaching them [words of Torah] diligently to your children" expanded to include the entire community. In a congregation of learners, everyone would be a potential teacher, from the history buff teaching a course on the Golden Age of Spain to the teenager tutoring youngsters in Hebrew, and the amateur singers who lead song sessions. Everyone would be encouraged to assist someone else in learning, whether that involved becoming someone's study partner, leading an activity, collecting educational materials, reading aloud to preschoolers, or teaching a formal class.

A congregation of learners would be a congregation that acknowledges that there are many possible learning styles—that some people learn best through the arts, others through discussion, and still others through reading, listening to tapes, or surfing the Internet. Such a congregation would be committed to offering a variety of teaching modalities to its broad array of learners. Its goal would be to make learning both serious and enjoyable, accessible to everyone, but also challenging. Its educational programming would be conducted as a grand experiment, continually being evaluated and adapted.

Beyond the proliferation of learners, teachers, and teaching techniques, the hallmark of a congregation of learners would be what educators call a *culture of learning*. Learning would permeate every aspect of the congregation. To take just a few examples: Torah study would be incorporated into Shabbat services; the social action committee's work in a homeless shelter would be preceded by a study of texts related to *tsedakah* (which means both charity and justice); board members would study together, not simply as a perfunctory opening for a meeting, but as a way of grounding their decisions in traditional sources. Every activity and every space, from the bake sale and the Purim carnival to the hallways and offices, would be viewed as opportunities for learning. For example, items at the bake sale might come with tags that list the appropriate *brakha;* booths at the Purim carnival might actually teach something about the Purim story;

bulletin boards in the hallway could contain famous quotations, challenging questions, or the Hebrew phrase of the week. Tidbits of learning, whether in the form of a skit, a song, or displays on the wall, would become regularities, and would be seen as part of "the way we do things around here."

Moreover, these instances of learning would not be isolated fragments. Congregational leaders would see to it that discrete activities were set in an overall context. There might be a theme for the year or a more elaborate multiyear plan. Either way, a group of people, such as a learning task force or council, would be responsible for promoting learning and for creating a synergy between the various programs.

And what of the subject matter? *What* would members of this congregation be learning? This is a question every congregation would have to answer for itself. Four thousand years of Jewish history have yielded a vast body of culture and lore, more than anyone, even the most learned scholar, can master. Part of the task of creating a congregation of learners is the process of deciding what a curriculum of lifelong learning might look like. Some congregations might decide to coordinate their offerings, so that everyone would have a common core of knowledge. Others might prefer a cafeteria approach, encouraging personal exploration and a wide diversity of topics. Some might encourage the development of skills, such as leading prayers and reading Torah; others might prefer to focus on modern history and contemporary sociology. What would distinguish the congregation of learners is its commitment to open, informed discussion of the various possibilities, and to the tracking and feedback necessary to see that the programs chosen are succeeding.

It would be my hope that in every congregation, one type of learning would receive a special emphasis, and that is the study of Torah. Not only in the narrow sense, meaning the Five Books of Moses, but also in the broader sense of the canon of texts that have been essential to the Jewish people—including the remaining thirty-one books of the Bible, the many volumes of biblical commentary, the Talmud and other legal texts, and possibly even great works of Jewish philosophy and literature. While every congregation would have to decide for itself how much emphasis to put on text study, and while more general subject matters, such as Jewish history and Jewish art are also important, I would argue that text study—the most traditional form of Jewish learning—ought to be a central part of Jewish learning because it allows the learner to get inside the tradition while maintaining a critical stance. When conducted in pairs or in small groups, and with proper facilitation, text study creates community and promotes informed choice. The *brakha* over Torah study states that Jews are commanded "to engage in words of Torah," not simply "to study," and not even "to be Jewishly literate." In other words, the primary goal of learning is not the *acquisition of knowledge,* but rather the *process* of engaging continuously with texts.

Dr. Wayne Dosick, rabbi, is spiritual guide of the Elijah Minyan in San Diego, California, and an adjunct professor of Jewish studies at the University of San Diego. Author of many books on spirituality and living Jewishly, in *Soul Judaism: Dancing with God into a New Era*, Rabbi Dosick teaches us how Hebrew is the Jewish language and of its power in our prayers.

Hebrew Is the Jewish Language

WAYNE DOSICK

Surely, it is possible to be Jewish—to delve into Jewish learning and involvement, to have an appreciation of Jewish life, to create a personal relationship with God—in the vernacular, in English or Russian or Greek or in any one of hundreds of languages. But trying to experience Judaism without Hebrew is like trying to read a good book in a poor translation, or like seeing a beautiful painting in a black-and-white reproduction.

Hebrew holds the wonders and the secrets and the mysteries and the sweet pleasures of communicating with the whole of the Jewish experience and of intimate conversation with God.

We Jews need Hebrew because it is the key to unlocking the great storehouse, the great treasure house, of Judaism.

Yet, sadly, few contemporary Jews—we who have studied Latin, French, and Spanish; who do business in Japanese and Korean; who have become experts in Chinese literature—know Hebrew. Many "people of the Book" cannot read the Book in its original. Many are unfamiliar and uncomfortable with the chants of Hebrew prayer.

Many cannot understand a simple Hebrew greeting or a word from an Israeli newspaper.

It's not our fault that we don't know Hebrew. Hebrew school was boring; it wasn't relevant; the teachers were old-fashioned and mean. We had much more fun playing Little League or taking ballet lessons.

It's not our fault that we don't know Hebrew. But it is our loss. It is our loss because so much of Judaism is closed off to us. So much of Judaism remains untouchable, foreign and fuzzy, because, as much as we might like, we just don't have the words to speak or to understand.

The good news is that it is never too late. It is never too late to learn Hebrew.

Fortunately, Hebrew is a very concise and relatively simple language. It has an alphabet of twenty-two consonants with seven accompanying vowels. Each letter and vowel has its own distinct sound, and almost every Hebrew word is phonetically regular and consistent, making pronunciation and reading fairly easy. Certainly, like all other languages, Hebrew has its complex grammatical constructions and a few seemingly unfathomable irregularities. But we don't have to study for long or become linguistic scholars in order to acquire the basic Hebrew reading and verbal skills, vocabulary, and grammatical principles that will open the world of Judaism to us.

Many different and varied programs exist for studying Hebrew: videotapes, audiotapes, computer programs, and texts designed especially for the adult learner; courses emphasizing reading skills, modern conversational Hebrew, or more formal diplomatic Hebrew; courses to understand biblical Hebrew or prayerbook Hebrew or modern Israeli newspaper Hebrew. There are opportunities everywhere: at synagogues and Jewish schools and Jewish community centers; at colleges, universities, and community learning centers; in adult education programs in a variety of settings; by mail, by fax, and on the Internet.

Some courses take a year or a semester or an evening a week for ten weeks. Others are page-a-day texts that promise ability to read with simple comprehension in less than a month. One program even guarantees basic reading skills in a single twelve-hour-day marathon session. And, of course, as with all learning and personal growth, Hebrew study can fill a lifetime—a new word today, a new grammatical principle tomorrow, greater comprehension the next day, another new word the day after.

When we decide to learn Hebrew and to continually upgrade our Hebrew knowledge and skills, we pledge to ourselves to know at least as much Hebrew as that little dog in Israel. When we decide to learn Hebrew, we give ourselves the great gift of the Jewish tradition that can come only through the "holy tongue," only through the language of Sinai and Jerusalem. When we decide to learn Hebrew, we touch who we are. For, at the very depth of our beings, we know the truth that Chaim Nachman Bialik, the national poet of our people, taught, "Hebrew is our very flesh and blood, and each encounter with it is an encounter with our soul."

Rabbi Edward Feld is director of The Hillel at Smith College in Northampton, Massachusetts. In *The Spirit of Renewal: Finding Faith after the Holocaust*, Rabbi Feld teaches us how Jewish history is woven through the everyday.

History Today

EDWARD FELD

Even as we push forward in time and enter a new era history reverberates within us. The arguments of Job and Isaiah, the clashings of Talmudic discussion and the ethical debate which Jewish texts engaged in continue to speak to our generation, but in new ways.

We have come full circle.

Once again we take up the telling of the tale. Once again the Jewish people, as they contemplate their own history, must find a message within. And once again, amidst a hostile world, we listen to hear the call to witness the possibility of meaning and holiness.

Even as we move toward places we have never been, our roots search down to find nourishment in our past. Our post-modern consciousness discovers a connectedness with other generations. All Jewish theology is a conversation across time, each generation adding its own voice to the discourse. The questions that are the concern of our generation—the understanding of suffering, the meaning of redemption—are the eternal questions of Jewish history.

As we seek to find our own voice, voices of other Jewish times reverberate within us. To understand the present, we turn to the ancient past. There is a commonality that echoes across the abyss of time. Repeatedly, at each new articulation of Jewish history, the same

questions are raised. Each generation shatters its past with its questing; each new questing needs to articulate the divine speech in its own
voice. Yet even as the meaning we find cloaks itself in contemporary
language, we recognize the inherited frame that it enfolds. All of
Jewish thought seems to be an encircling around a pole that forms its
center. The circles widen, the radii enlarge, but the center always
remains the same. Each generation needs to find its own responses,
but the quest ultimately remains the same: to recover a vision of the
sacred amidst a tragic reality.

The initial responses to the quest achieve their first formulation
in the biblical canon, and anyone who wishes to understand these
questions must turn to those scrolls for a pristine vision that no subsequent generation can achieve. The biblical response is forever
uniquely fresh like all first times. Yet anyone who studies the course
of Jewish thought knows that the responses that Jews enunciate are
not limited to the biblical answers. Instead, they are ever again
renewed elaborations, exegetically—midrashically—expanding the
range of Jewish thought into a new time, into a new language. For the
past, whispering in faded voice, may yet signal the coordinates for
locating ourselves amidst our own uncharted time.

In the revival of Hebrew and the return to the land of our forebears, we rediscover our biblical roots where the call of God challenged those who would exercise power to act on the most primal
truths of religious understanding. That grappling with history and
existence in the world so characteristic of the Bible was, in part, cam-
ouflaged by the rabbis after Bar Kochba and by the Jewish experience
in the Middle Ages. The Holocaust and the return to the land uncov-
ers the primal confrontation between God's call and the world. So,
we awaken in ourselves that first exploration of religious quest even
as we reach toward a time that has never been known before. As we
move forward in time and discover new understandings, different
ways of viewing God, humanity, and Israel, yet we also find that we
continue the vocabulary and the argument that has been at the center
of our existence.

Torah will not be an end for us; it will not constitute the experience of time out of history, but it can keep alive in us the sensitivities found in the resources of our past. Torah represents one of the few ways we have of assuring the weighing of values necessary in these new and dangerous times.

We will not look to the tradition for law, for an absolute guidance, for our circumstances and theology are conditioned new events and understandings, but we can be sustained by vocabulary that the tradition offers us for self-knowledge.

We will not receive singleminded direction from our study of the tradition, but in engaging in open-ended argument regarding what we must do, we will be bounded by the values of survival and otherness, of the knowledge of evil and the will to do good, of the needs of the self and the need to reach out to the other. We will go out to create a new life, one that will reveal through its existence the divine calling. As much as the return to the land is an expression of a new Jewish story, it is equally an expression of continuity, of a determination to continue Jewish life as a witnessing, as a message aimed equally at the inner life of Jews and all humanity. In an unredeemed world, our task is to be a blessing to ourselves and to others.

Once this people was called to witness, to give its message to humanity and now yet again. This new calling has within it, for all its innovation, a deep connectedness with that earlier one. The quest for holiness amid a violent and tragic world is still our task.

We have traveled far, only to continue walking on the way.

As Martin Buber taught in a series of lectures delivered after the war:

> Creation is incomplete because discord still reigns within it, and peace can only emerge from the created. That is why, in Jewish tradition, he who brings about peace is called the companion of God in the work of creation.[1]

The word is spoken, the silence becomes articulate, but the mystery is not dispelled; it only beckons us to move on.

Adam lay with his wife again. She bore a son and named him Seth [the one who is placed before us] "for," she said, "God has granted me another son in the place of Abel because Cain killed him." Seth too had a son whom he called Enosh [humanity]. At this time people began to invoke the Lord [YHVH] by name.

(Genesis 4:25–26)

We stir toward each other. We reach out. In the darkness, we see only a profile. Having borne rage, having known violence, having witnessed fratricide, we have no expectations for what will come. What will be is a gift. We shall treat it as a mysterious treasure. Perhaps that is the secret of our humanity. Perhaps that is what is meant by the sacred...Such thoughts can only last a moment...And then the terror, the emptiness will be upon us again...I touch the face of the one beside me...

Anne Brener, L.C.S.W., a psychotherapist and teacher, leads workshops that explore the connection between spirituality and psychology, particularly as they relate to grief, mourning, and healing. In *Mourning & Mitzvah: A Guided Journal for Walking the Mourner's Path through Grief to Healing,* she teaches us about satisfying spiritual yearning with prayer.

Spiritual Yearning and Prayer

ANNE BRENER

If we have spiritual yearnings, it is hard to identify them as such. These things are seldom named. Often we lack the vocabulary to articulate our spiritual yearnings. Sometimes we are too busy to even notice them. Many who feel a profound existential emptiness that might be alleviated by spirituality pursue distractions to fill that emptiness that is so hard to name. This is acknowledged by treatment programs for substance abuse and other addictions, such as Alcoholics Anonymous, which focus on spirituality.

Indeed, if we can name that emptiness as a spiritual craving, we are often embarrassed, since people who search for the spiritual are often dismissed as naive or aberrant. In fact, given what we know about the condition of the world and our understanding of the God of the Bible, it can be embarrassing to admit that we struggle to encounter something higher and deeper than our familiar, concrete human existence. Our concept of the Divine stifles our need for It. Prayer becomes impossible.

CONFRONTING YOUR DOUBTS TO EXPLORE THE POSSIBILITY OF PRAYER

All these doubts are my own doubts. Throughout my life I have struggled to obtain a concept of the Divine that could account for the variety in our universe. But the word *God* did not work for me. It throws me back to my childhood experiences of counting the light bulbs in the dome of my synagogue rather than connecting with the words of the prayerbook.

I used to avoid the word *God* completely. When a participant in a workshop I led on prayer asked why I never spoke of God, I had to question myself. I responded by saying that I wanted to make it easier for people who do not believe in God to find the healing that I believe is present in the universe. "Healing," I thought, perhaps that's my concept of God. For in conceiving of healing, I feel a connection to something greater than myself, something that I feel I can tap into in the process of working to heal myself and to heal the world.

Still, I realized that I am uncomfortable saying the name of God. It may be the inhibitions I wrote about earlier, but it is not just that. When we have a name for this infinite mystery that is the source of it all, we begin to limit it. By naming it so often, we wear it out; it becomes familiar. We think we know it. It diminishes the mystery, the way electric lights can dim the stars. By having such an immutable name for The Source, we fix that which is holy and beyond definition; in trying to quantify the ineffable, we deny the flow of mystery. Perhaps that is why the Hebrew name for God—יהוה—is never pronounced, or why many observant Jews put a hyphen in place of the *o* when writing the word *God.*

I struggle with the word *God,* but I can experience the Holy Presence. And I do believe in prayer as a way of aligning myself with that Presence and basking in Its light. I learned that the biblical word for prayer means to intercede or intervene and that there is even an ancient Arabic word that may be related that means to cut oneself with the notched edge of a sword. I feel that I can intercede in Divinity. I can place myself in the midst of Holiness. I don't believe that I need to wait for some power far away to take responsibility for my life, but that I am empowered to open up to the Divine and bask in its holiness. Sometimes in order to let the Divine enter, I must cut myself open, find my wounds, and let them speak.

Rabbi Nancy Flam is director of The Spirituality Institute at Metivta, a retreat-based learning program for Jewish leaders. She co-founded the Jewish Healing Center in 1991. In *LifeLights: Yearning for God,* Rabbi Flam teaches us about our spiritual needs.

Yearning for God

NANCY FLAM

I grew up in a household that didn't talk about God. When I entered adolescence, my yearnings for depth, connection, and truth began to intensify. Only later did I come to understand that these yearnings were part of a search for God's presence in my life and that I was not alone in my search. When I began to study religion in college, I found others who were eager to talk about their ideas and experiences of God's reality. Somewhere in my sophomore year, I dared to consider that my growing sense of wonder, mystery, beauty, and compassion had something to do with God. I began to believe that, in fact, I had a very strong connection to God. Exploring, cultivating, and deepening this relationship with God has been at the center of my life ever since.

I can't say that the path is easy. There are times of great disconnection, times when I feel spiritually asleep, times when I question my own experience of God's reality. And yet, despite the challenges, I find that my central desire is to know God's presence: to cultivate an open, responsive heart; to be alert to the vitality within and around me; to experience myself as part of an interconnected whole; and to recognize the beauty and mystery of creation.

> Three things conspire
> together in my eyes
> To bring the remembrance of
> You ever before me:
> The starry heavens,
> The broad green earth,
> The depths of my heart.
> SOLOMON IBN GABIROL

RECOGNIZE YOUR YEARNING

We experience yearning for God in many ways. Sometimes our yearning begins with an underlying sense of emptiness or shallowness. We may feel that we are lost or that something is missing. There sometimes grows in us a desire for a greater fullness and vitality in our lives. We seek to fill an emptiness; many of us try to fill ourselves with excessive food, alcohol, drugs, or distraction of one kind or another (such as TV, movies, computers, excessive sex). Often, we are unaware that our deeper desire is for a relationship with God: a relationship in which we might discover profound beauty, worth, and meaning.

For many of us, our yearning for God is activated at a particular crossroads in our lives: when our physical or mental health is challenged, after the loss of a loved one, or in the midst of a life change such as marriage, divorce, or the birth of children. We yearn for God as a source of comfort, hope, or perspective. We seek the assurance that our lives make sense and that, on some ultimate level, everything will be all right.

Sometimes, our yearning is tied to remembering a "peak moment" that we may have once known but from which we now feel distant. We remember the deep peace we may have felt after a long hike in nature, the sense of union we knew with a beloved, a fleeting insight we had in which our lives and all of creation seemed coherent and meaningful. We seek to reconnect with a time of wholeness, purpose, or fulfillment. Our yearning is a sign that we are already in a relationship with God.

EXPLORE LOVE AS METAPHOR AND
MANIFESTATION OF GOD

Jewish mystics (and mystics of all traditions) have described human yearning for God as the intense desire of the lover for the beloved. In *Yedid Nefesh,* a sixteenth-century poem that has been incorporated into the Jewish prayer book, Rabbi Eliezer Azikri seeks to be reunited with his Beloved. His heart is breaking. He remembers or imagines the pleasure of God's nearness; he can almost taste it: "To Your servant, Your friendship will be sweeter than the dripping of the honeycomb, and any taste [imaginable]...Majestic, Beautiful, Radiance of the universe—my soul pines for Your love. Please, O God, heal her now by showing her the pleasantness of Your radiance. Then she will be strengthened and healed, and eternal gladness will be hers." The soul (or *neshamah,* which, in Hebrew, is in the feminine form and therefore referred to as "her") is lovesick. Only the presence of the Beloved can heal her. This is the soul's one desire: to be near God.

Being near God can be awesome and overwhelmingly frightening. When the Israelites stood at the foot of Mount Sinai and witnessed the thunder and lightning at the beginning of God's revelation, they fell back, asking that God not speak to them directly, but rather that Moses speak to God and then tell them what God said. They needed to protect themselves from coming too near. We experience a similar sense of awe when we ourselves lie awake during the loud cracking of a thunderstorm, when we walk beneath the trees in a redwood forest, when we stand before death or witness the birth of a child.

But being close to God can also be incomparably sweet, pleasant, comforting, and beautiful. It can feel like being in love. Love dissolves the boundaries of the self. Love relaxes the ego's defenses, permitting penetrability. One is able to extend beyond one's sense of self.

Yearning for God expresses the desire to connect with something that is bigger than the self. Ultimately, being near God can give us a sense of the interconnection of all being and of all creation and of the unity that underlies it. At such a "rare eternal moment," writes

> *God, you are my God;*
> *I search for You, my soul*
> *thirsts for you, my body*
> *yearns for You, as a*
> *parched and thirsty land that*
> *has no water.*
>
> PSALM 63:2

Daniel Matt, a professor of Jewish mysticism, "[t]he part yearns to rejoin the whole.... [T]he self realizes it is no longer a fragment. It discovers a consciousness that is transpersonal: the entire universe becoming aware of itself. The image of a personal God gives way to oneness."

This sense of connection, the part becoming aware of the whole, happens in different ways: in nature, in intimate personal relationships, in prayer, in meditation, and in religious ritual. These moments can fill us with a sense of belonging, with satisfaction, with comfort, and with meaning. When we experience our yearning for God, we need to take the time to focus on those activities that might help us find God's presence. Ultimately, we need to develop practices of regular spiritual discipline to help us cultivate and maintain our relationship with God.

BEWARE OF THE DIFFICULTIES OF LANGUAGE

As I write these words, I am aware of the difficulty of using language to talk about God or about my experience of God. In particular, I am torn between talking about God as an "other," as a "You," as something separate and outside myself, and talking about God as the totality of being, oneness, something of which I am an integral part. These different conceptions lead me to two different kinds of religious experience and consciousness. Each is valuable. Each leads to a kind of truth. And my yearning takes me in both directions at different times.

AWAKE, YOU SLEEPERS!

Yearning for God can be experienced as a desire for greater awareness of life, deeper appreciation for its blessings, and keener sensitivity to its spiritual demands. Sometimes, we simply fall asleep. We go through our days on "automatic pilot," barely noticing the miracle of our breathing, the gift of our food, the cosmic carnival of the earth rotating around the sun, which allows for our existence at all. For this reason, the rabbis invented a series of blessings that can help us stay spiritually awake.

For instance, there are blessings to say upon awaking in the morning, in recognition that our bodies and souls are joined for another day of life. There are blessings to say in gratitude for opening our eyes, stretching out our bodies, for standing upon the firm earth. There is even a blessing to say after using the toilet, in gratitude for the body's proper functioning. Nothing is to be taken for granted. The rabbis knew that we tend toward spiritual dullness; we need reminders to rouse our sense of gratitude and wonder.

As part of the shofar service on Rosh Hashanah, a most visceral call to spiritual and moral alertness, many congregations read Maimonides' words: "Awake, you sleepers, from your sleep! Rouse yourselves, you slumberers, out of your slumber! Look at your deeds! Turn back to God! Remember your Creator, you who are caught up in the daily round, losing sight of eternal truth!"

> *Where is God? Wherever you let God in.*
> HASIDIC SAYING

The practice of meditation is another wonderful tool for staying awake. By quieting the mind and opening the heart, we train ourselves to be aware of the present moment: its textures, tones, pleasures, and challenges. Meditation helps us slow down so we can enter a place of stillness; in such an internal environment, life is less likely to whiz by in a torrent of stimulation. Instead, we are more likely to notice each moment and enter it fully.

RECOGNIZE THE EBB AND FLOW OF YOUR RELATIONSHIP WITH GOD

Our yearning for God does not get sated once and for all. We all know periods when our relationship with God is best characterized by a flat absence. At such times, our hearts resonate with the words of the psalmist who wrote, "I am weary with calling, my throat is dry; my eyes fail while I wait for God" (Psalm 69:4). At these times, God is simply eclipsed from us. At other times, often by surprise, we feel God's presence gracing our lives with meaning, clarity, vitality, and gentleness. We open to the beauty of the world; our hearts soften and bring us into blessed relationship with all that is within and around us. But inevitably, such moments fade. We find ourselves again yearning to sense God's nearness. Perhaps it is out of a recognition of the ebb and flow of our relationship with God that the Psalmist wrote,

"One thing I ask of God; only that do I seek: to live in the house of God all the days of my life, to gaze upon the beauty of God and to meditate in God's sanctuary" (Psalm 27:4).

TAKE HEART

The following are among many ways that we can listen to our yearning and grow in our relationship with God:

- *Explore the resources of your local synagogue.* Many synagogues offer courses and retreats focused on spirituality. You might consider finding a few other similarly minded individuals with whom to start a spiritual support group for mutual support, learning, and exploration. Synagogue 2000, a transdenominational project for synagogue renewal, can help synagogues establish such a group.

- *Find a spiritual guide with whom you can talk about your spiritual life.* This person might be a rabbi, pastoral counselor, or wise elder. Set up regular times to meet for the sole purpose of discerning ways in which God is present (and absent) in your life. Such a relationship helps us to grow in our awareness of God and to find direction in deepening our sense of God's presence.

- *Find a spiritual friend.* Agree to listen to one another on a regular basis about your spiritual lives to provide witness and support for each other.

- *Most importantly, cultivate a personal spiritual discipline.* Such a discipline might include daily meditation or prayer, regular study, or the taking on of a particular mitzvah that you sense might lead you to a deepened spiritual life.

Our spiritual yearning takes us on a journey toward greater insight, love, wisdom, and compassion. *Baruch Atah Adonai, Eloheinu Melech Ha'olam, hamechin mitzadei gaver.* "Blessed are You, Eternal our God, who guides us on our journey."

Dr. Lawrence A. Hoffman, rabbi, Professor of Liturgy at Hebrew Union College–Jewish Institute of Religion, is cofounder of Synagogue 2000, a trans-denominational project designed to envision and implement the ideal synagogue of the spirit for the 21st century. He lectures widely to Jewish audiences and people of many faiths. In *The Way Into Jewish Prayer*, Rabbi Hoffman teaches us that all the world is a place for prayer.

All the World Is a Place for Prayer

LAWRENCE A. HOFFMAN

Beyond the prayers of synagogue and home, which could be planned because the times for them were fixed, there were the events of everyday life that evoked blessings, often unexpectedly. Indeed, though often hard, the workaday world was conceptualized not as a daily grind but as an opportunity for prayers that celebrate creation and our human place within it. Still today, the performance of commandments like illuminating a home with Shabbat candlelight, for instance, evokes the words "Blessed are You, Adonai our God, ruler of the world, who has sanctified us with your commandments and commanded us to kindle Shabbat lights." But God's presence was likely to become evident not just in the moment when a divine commandment was being performed but at any time or place, like the breathtaking surprise of coming across a desert landscape or a redwood forest, for which one says, "Blessed are You, Adonai our God, who created the universe." The thinking behind these blessings that celebrate nature—not just its extraordinary manifestations but even such ordinary beauty as a tree in blossom—is especially instructive.

North American culture divides human activity into simple oppositions. We are either at work or at play, on vacation or on the job, in school or at recess. We instinctively treat prayer, therefore, as what you do when you are in synagogue (or church) but not in the office, the garden, the playground, or the car. Judaism takes just the opposite point of view. Though not all of life is holy, the holy can come bursting through the everyday at any time. Jews were therefore to be ready for such occasions by reciting appropriate blessings for happening upon the sacred: a rainbow, a flower, thunder and lightning, an ocean, a wise teacher, hearing good news (or even bad)—all of these occasions evoke a blessing from Jews, who know that prayer is an inherent part of life, not something reserved just for specific days of the week or year and for certain places but not others.

> It is written (in Psalm 24:1), "The earth and its fullness belong to God." But Psalm 115:16 says, "God has given it to human beings." There is no contradiction. The first verse reflects the situation before we say a blessing; the second verse describes the case after the blessing has been said.[1]

Our rabbinic aphorism indicates that appreciating the universe without saying a blessing is a sin, because it is like pillaging God's universe. But if we pause to say a blessing over a wonder of nature, thereby demonstrating our appreciation of whatever we are saying a blessing over, God releases it into our care.

As we can see, Judaism has three kinds of fixed prayer: the daily synagogue service; prayers to be said at home, chiefly around the table; and a lexicon of prayers for special occasions when God's presence bursts in upon our daily routine. No wonder prayer is a discipline. It involves being in certain places at certain times, and practicing the art of saying certain things when the occasion calls for them. Becoming a prayerful person is like becoming a marathon runner or a world-class chef. It takes regular practice. And it presupposes failures along the way to ultimate success.

But it is important to know what counts for success. People who think of prayer solely as a way to ask God for favors miss the point. People who carp at the literal meaning of words without appreciating the grandeur of the human position that makes speech possible in the first place miss the forest for the trees. A very old prayer we say on

Yom Kippur, our Day of Atonement and widely regarded as the holiest day of the year, recounts the gravity of human sin but then concludes, "You distinguished human beings from the beginning: you recognize us when we stand before you." The word *recognize* here has the sense of "the chair recognizes the woman with her hand up," the idea being that human beings are recognized to speak up before God in a way other animals are not.

We are gifted with speech, not just elementary speech but complex ways of becoming conscious of the world and then reflecting that consciousness in language. The medieval philosophers categorized the human species as *m'daber*—literally, "the species that speaks." Contrary to the popular adage, talk is not cheap. Judaism insists that we use our words wisely. Jewish law, for instance, calls slander a sin on the metaphorical level of murder, since injuring someone's reputation is like killing part of that person. Jewish ethics looks askance at *d'varim batelim* (pronounced d'-vah-REEM bah-tay-LEEM), mere idle chitchat. Jewish wisdom urges human beings to act as if their words matter, and that means dedicating time regularly to two disciplines, both of which are allied to each other: the study of Torah and the practice of prayer. Unless we have managed to dull our sense of the incomparable mystery of life, words of prayer come naturally to us, just because we are alive. It is what happens automatically as long as we view the world with what Heschel called "radical amazement." By contrast, he says, "The surest way to suppress our ability to understand the meaning of God, and the importance of worship, is to take things for granted."[2] Judaism reserves regular moments to regain our sense of amazement, and it celebrates those moments with words that link us to thousands of years of tradition. Prayer in the Jewish mode, then, is like painting with oils or playing the violin. We may have a natural talent to respond to the universe with awe, but that talent needs to be nurtured to the point where it becomes an art.

Rabbi **Lawrence Kushner** is Rabbi-in-Residence at Hebrew Union College–Jewish Institute of Religion. He teaches and lectures widely to audiences of all ages, faiths and backgrounds, and has been a frequent commentator on National Public Radio's *All Things Considered*. In *The Book of Words: Talking Spiritual Life, Living Spiritual Talk,* Rabbi Kushner teaches us about the primary words we use to describe the spiritual dimension of life and how rethinking what they mean can add power and focus to the lives we live every day.

Script   תפילה

LAWRENCE KUSHNER

> When you enter the land that the Lord your God is giving you as
> a heritage, and you possess it and settle in it, you shall take some
> of every first fruit of the soil, which you harvest from the land
> that the Lord your God is giving you, put it in a basket and go
> to the place where the Lord your God will choose to establish
> God's name. You shall go to the priest in charge at that time and
> say to him, "I acknowledge this day before the Lord our God
> that I have entered the land that the Lord swore to our parents
> to assign us."
>
> *(Deuteronomy 26:1–3)*

Prayer only sounds as if you're talking to God. In truth prayer is reciting the words of a script evolved and evolving over the centuries that gives form to the inchoate yearnings of your innermost being. There is nothing new to say in prayer. Surely God has "heard it all before." What you need to do in order to pray is surrender your own expressions of gratitude and petition to the syntax of tradition. Only one who can allow the annulment of his or her self is capable of being transformed through the words of prayer, the lines of the script. As

(t´fee•läh´)   **Prayer**

264

long as you cling to your discreet selfhood, you will be unable to transcend your self and your prayers will go "unanswered." For this reason the key to unlocking our most important songs is the script recorded in the prayer book.

Of course, like any good actor, occasional *ad libs,* inflationary modifications, and even forgetting one's lines at times are part of the business. Even the sensation of improvisation has a place, as long as you remember that your "new creation" has already been recited by the Heavenly retinue since before the creation of the world. The script, in other words, is present whether or not the "play" is performed in a human prayer hall.

DOV BAER OF MEZRITCH

You need to think of yourself as nothing. Forget yourself entirely. Pray only for the sake of God's Presence. Only then will you come to transcend time and attain the "World of Thought." No contradictions. No distinctions between life and death or sea and dry land. All the same.... This can only happen if you forget yourself entirely. But it cannot be the case while you are attached to the tangible reality of this world. Fixated on the distinctions between good and evil and mundane creation. How otherwise could one possibly transcend time and attain ultimate unification. Thus as long as you remain convinced that you are "something," preoccupied with your daily needs, then the Holy One cannot be present, for God is without end, that is, "nothing," no vessel can contain the One. But this is not so when you think of yourself as nothing.

LIVING SPIRITUAL TALK—*KAVANAH*

You cannot set out to put yourself out of the way, any more than you can set as your goal the attainment of love or a sense of community. Such gifts are a coincidental side effect of working with others toward a common goal, caring for a partner through difficult times, or praying regularly. In prayer, of course, the trick is to balance the routine with novelty. You need to know the "script" so well that you can recite the words on "auto pilot" but not so well that the words are habitual. You must know them well enough so that you do not really need the prayer book, yet maintain enough "presence," that the words stream forth fresh, as if you have never spoken them before. In this way you remain balanced on the edge. It does not have to be the entire liturgy; even a single prayer, recited each morning, can serve as a proper beginning. In this way you can make a prayer your own that has been recited for centuries.

Dr. Lawrence A. Hoffman, rabbi, Professor of Liturgy at Hebrew Union College–Jewish Institute of Religion, is cofounder of Synagogue 2000, a trans-denominational project designed to envision and implement the ideal synagogue of the spirit for the 21st century. He lectures widely to Jewish audiences and people of many faiths. In *My People's Prayer Book, Traditional Prayers, Modern Commentaries—Vol. 1: The Sh'ma and Its Blessings*, Rabbi Hoffman teaches us what to look for in the liturgy service.

Introduction to the Liturgy: What to Look for in the Service

LAWRENCE A. HOFFMAN

Liturgy can seem confusing, more like a shapeless mass of verbiage than a carefully constructed whole; a jumble of noise, not a symphony; a blotch of random colors, hardly a masterpiece of art. But prayer is an art form, and like the other arts, the first step to appreciation is to recognize the pattern at work within it.

There are three daily services: morning *(Shacharit),* afternoon *(Minchah),* and evening *(Ma'ariv* or *Arvit).* For the sake of convenience, the latter two are usually recited in tandem, one just before dark, and the other immediately after the sun sets. All three follow the same basic structure, but the morning service is the most complete. It is composed of seven consecutive units that build upon each other to create a definitive pattern. Though the words of each unit remained fluid for centuries, the structural integrity of the service has remained sacrosanct since the beginning.

Services are made of prayers, but not all prayers are alike. Some are biblical quotations, ranging in size from a single line to entire chapters, usually psalms. There are rabbinic citations also, chunks of Mishnah or Talmud that serve as a sort of Torah study within the service. Medieval poetry occurs here too, familiar things like *Adon Olam* or older staples marked less by rhyme and rhythm than by

clever word plays and alphabetic acrostics. And there are long passages of prose, the work again of medieval spiritual masters, but
couched in standard rabbinic style without regard for poetic rules.

Most of all, however, the Siddur is filled with blessings, a
uniquely rabbinic vehicle for addressing God, and the primary liturgical expression of Jewish spirituality.

Blessings (known also as *benedictions,* or, in Hebrew,
b'rakhot—sing., *b'rakhah*) are so familiar that Jewish worshippers
take them for granted. We are mostly aware of "short blessings," the
one-line formulas that are customarily recited before eating, for
instance, or prior to performing a commandment. But there are "long
blessings" too, generally whole paragraphs or even sets of paragraphs
on a given theme. These are best thought of as small theological
essays on such topics as deliverance, the sanctity of time, the rebuild-
ing of Jerusalem, and the like. They sometimes start with the words
Barukh atah Adonai... ("Blessed are You, Adonai..."), and then they
are easily spotted. But more frequently, they begin with no particular
verbal formula, and are hard to identify until their last line, which
invariably does say, *Barukh atah Adonai...* ("Blessed are You,
Adonai...") followed by a short synopsis of the blessing's theme
("...who sanctifies the Sabbath," "...who hears prayer," "...who
redeems Israel," and so forth). This final summarizing sentence is
called a *chatimah,* meaning a "seal," like the seal made from a signet
ring that seals an envelope.

The bulk of the service as it was laid down in antiquity consists
of strings of blessings, one after the other, or of biblical quotations
bracketed by blessings that introduce and conclude them. By the
tenth century, the creation of blessings largely ceased, and, eventually,
Jewish law actually opposed the coining of new ones, on the grounds
that post-talmudic Judaism was too spiritually unworthy to try to
emulate the literary work of the giants of the Jewish past. Not all
Jews agree with that assessment today, but the traditional liturgy that
forms our text here contains no blessings dated later than the tenth
century.

The word we use to refer to all the literary units in the prayer book, without regard to whether they are blessings, psalms, poems, or something else, is *rubric*. A rubric is any discrete building block of the service, sometimes a single prayer (this blessing rather than that, or this quotation, but not that poem), and sometimes a whole set of prayers that stands out in contrast to other sets: The *Sh'ma and Its Blessings*, for instance, is a large rubric relative to the *Amidah*. But considered independently, we can say that the *Sh'ma and Its Blessings* subsumes smaller rubrics: the *Sh'ma* itself, for instance (a set of biblical readings); some blessings that bracket it; and the *Bar'khu*, or official call to prayer, that introduces the entire thing.

At the liturgy's core are three large rubrics, not only the two already mentioned (the *Sh'ma and Its Blessings* and the *Amidah*—known also as the *T'fillah* or *Sh'moneh Esreh*), but also the public reading of Torah. The *Sh'ma and Its Blessings* and the *Amidah* were recited every day; Torah is read on Monday and Thursday (market days in antiquity), when crowds were likely to gather in the cities, and on Shabbat and holidays, of course. The *Sh'ma and Its Blessings* is essentially the Jewish creed, a statement of what Jews have traditionally affirmed about God, the cosmos, and our human relationship to God and to history. The *Amidah* is largely petitionary. The Torah reading is a recapitulation of Sinai, an attempt to discover the will of God through sacred scripture. Since the *Sh'ma and Its Blessings* begins the official service, it features a communal call to prayer at the beginning: our familiar *Bar'khu*. We should picture these units building upon each other in a crescendo-like manner, as follows:

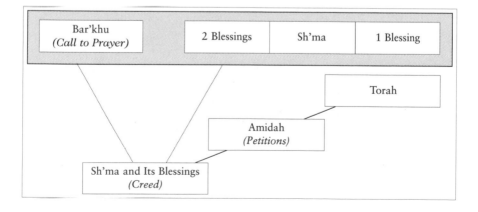

It is, however, hard for individuals who are normally distracted by everyday concerns to constitute a community given over whole-heartedly to prayer. Already in the second century, therefore, we hear of some Rabbis who assembled prior to the actual Call to Prayer in order to sing psalms of praise known as a *Hallel;* and even before that—at home, not the synagogue—it was customary to begin the day immediately upon awakening by reciting a series of daily blessings along with some study texts. By the ninth century, if not earlier, these two units too had become mandatory, and the home ritual for awakening had moved to the synagogue, which is where we have it today. The warm-up section of psalms is called *P'sukei D'zimrah*—meaning "Verses of Song"—and the prior recital of daily blessings and study texts is called *Birkhot Hashachar*—"Morning Blessings." Since they now precede the main body of the service, gradually building up to it, the larger diagram can be charted like this:

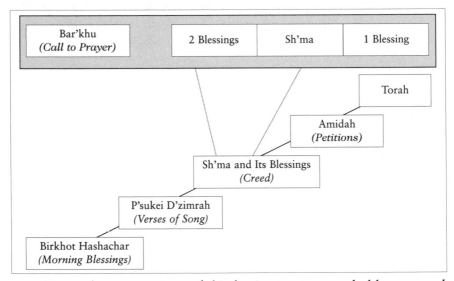

Two other expansions of this basic structure probably occurred in the first two centuries C.E., although our evidence for their being that early is less certain.

First, a Conclusion was added. It featured a final prayer called the *Kaddish* which as yet had nothing to do with mourning, but merely followed the Torah reading, and therefore closed the service, by looking ahead to the coming of God's ultimate reign of justice. Eventually other prayers were added to the Conclusion, including the *Alenu,* which had originally been composed as an introduction to the blowing of the Shofar on Rosh Hashanah, but was moved here in the Middle Ages.

Second, the Rabbis, who were keenly aware of the limits to human mortality, advised all Jews to come to terms daily with their frailty and ethical imperfection. To do so, they provided an opportunity for a silent confession following the *Amidah,* but before the Torah reading. In time, this evolved into silent prayer in general, an opportunity for individuals to assemble their most private thoughts before God; and later still, sometime in the Middle Ages, it expanded on average weekdays into an entire set of supplicatory prayers called the *Tachanun.*

The daily service was thus passed down to us with shape and design. Beginning with daily blessings that celebrate the new day and emphasize the study of sacred texts *(Birkhot Hashachar)* it continues with songs and psalms *(P'sukei D'zimrah)* designed to create a sense of community. There then follows the core of the liturgy: an official call to prayer (our *Bar'khu*), the recital of Jewish belief (the *Sh'ma and Its Blessings*), and communal petitions (the *Amidah*). Individuals then pause to speak privately to God in silent prayer (later expanded into the *Tachanun*), and then, on select days, they read from Torah. The whole concludes with a final *Kaddish* to which other prayers, most notably the *Alenu,* were added eventually.

On Shabbat and holidays, this basic structure expands to admit special material relevant to the day in question, and contracts to omit prayers that are inappropriate for the occasion. On Shabbat, for instance, the petitions of the *Amidah* are excluded, as Shabbat is felt to be so perfect in itself as to make petitioning unnecessary. But an entire service is added, a service called *Musaf* (literally, "Addition"), to correspond to the extra sacrifice that once characterized Shabbat worship in the Temple. Similarly, a prophetic reading called the *Haftarah* joins the Torah reading, and extra psalms and readings for

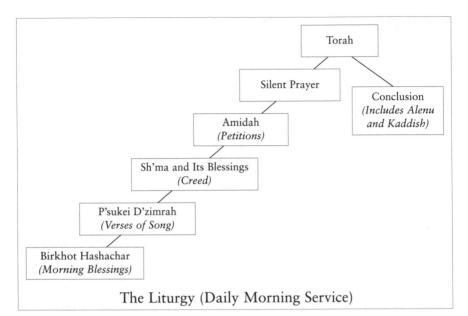

The Liturgy (Daily Morning Service)

the Sabbath are inserted here and there. The same is true for holidays when, in addition, numerous *piyyutim* (liturgical poems) get said, especially for the High Holy Days, when the sheer size of the liturgy seems to get out of hand. But even there, the basic structure remains intact, so that those who know its intrinsic shape can get beyond what looks like random verbiage to find the genius behind the liturgy's design.

Dr. Daniel C. Matt is currently composing an annotated English translation of the *Zohar*. He was formerly a professor of Jewish spirituality at the Graduate Theological Union in Berkeley, California. In *God & the Big Bang: Discovering Harmony Between Science & Spirituality*, Dr. Matt teaches us about the sense of wonder and oneness that connects us with the universe and with God.

Silent Prayer, Breathing Prayer

DANIEL C. MATT

We need more silence in prayer. The words have been piling up for millennia; there are simply too many of them. This tendency toward wordiness reaches a crescendo on the High Holy Days, when Jews throughout the world read a thick volume of prayers over three days. Half the book is read on *Yom Kippur* alone. Words can be powerful, but an excess of them burdens the soul. The traditional Sabbath service is so long that to complete it in less than two and a half hours, the text must be read or scanned so quickly that anyone praying can easily suffer spiritual indigestion. The same applies to the daily morning service, which is briefer, consigned to about forty minutes. This service often turns into a communal race, punctuated by furious page-flipping, so that the ten or so loyal congregants, who have gotten up half an hour earlier than they might have otherwise to go to *shul*, can get to work on time.

We need fewer words—and more room for silence. We need fewer prayers—and more time for reflection. The prayers selected should be prayed slowly; a single verse can be chanted again and again. The best lines of prayer lend themselves to meditation.

If we limit ourselves to spoken words, we never taste the richness of silence. Incessant verbal prayer, with its duality of "we" and "You," maintains a mental barrier between us and God. In silence, we can contemplate the possibility that the barrier is an illusion.

Such epiphanies are rare since oneness so infrequently intrudes on the self. Undeniably, especially in our culture, we are steeped in language and in the mental language of thought. So we need words of prayer to express our pain and our joy, our longings and fears and hopes. With words, we can cry and sing and bridge the divide between God and us. Even while crossing the bridge and sensing that we are part of what seemed "other," the part can still sing to the whole, addressing it personally and poetically as *You,* even if, ultimately, we are not separate from You. Consider, for example, these lines selected from different parts of the morning service: "My God, the soul You have breathed into me is pure." "In Your light we see light." "With Your Torah, open my heart."

Precious words of prayer should not be rushed into oblivion. Allowed to last for a while, they lead to meditation. You can move back and forth between contemplating the personality of God and Its infinity. Meditative prayer overcomes the apparent dichotomy between the two, enabling us to develop intimacy with the abstract.

The *Qedushah,* one of the holiest moments of Jewish prayer, contains a question that lends itself to contemplation: "Where is the place of God's presence?" But the site of God can't be pinned down, as the continuation of the prayer implies: "Blessed be the presence of *YHVH* from its place." The Hasidic answer to the question is also conducive to contemplation: "Wherever I let God in." Or, the question can be left unanswered, as a Zen koan, a *kavvanah,* a focus of meditation. In the words of one kabbalist, "Concerning everything that cannot be grasped, its question is its answer."

Meditative prayer links us with the cosmos. The *siddur* proclaims that God "out of His goodness renews the act of Creation every day, constantly." Chanting these words, I imagine the cycles of life on Earth. Expanding my awareness, I envision the creation of new solar systems in the Milky Way. Somewhere out there right now a star is being born. A clump of matter has attracted gas and dust, grown larger, drawn matter to itself more efficiently until finally the temperature and pressure within are high enough that hydrogen atoms are jammed together and thermonuclear reactions begin. The star turns on and the surrounding darkness is dispelled. Matter turns into light.

About once a month, somewhere in our galaxy, out of a pitch-black cloud of gas and dust a new solar system forms. And the observable universe may contain 100 billion galaxies; so perhaps 100 solar systems are forming every second. In that multitude of worlds, many are barren and desolate. Others may be lush, fertile, and animated with forms of life unknown to us but exquisitely adapted to their environment.

With creation unfolding moment by moment, there is no rush: We don't have to read every word on every page. Better to move *slowly* through prayer. With no one counting how many words we have said or not said, our first step is to slow down. The next step is to fully and completely stop—to linger in silence, to bask in it. This is difficult for most of us because silence makes us uneasy. Usually our immediate response to silence is to fill it up with anything we can. Even when we are alone, we tend to avoid silence: We turn on the TV, the CD player, the radio. If we are with someone else and a moment of silence arises, we immediately squash it with whatever comes to mind, no matter how trivial or inane it may be. We prefer that to the awkwardness of silence. Even lovers rarely share silence for more than a few moments.

But silence can be more profound than words. No words of prayer can adequately praise God, and even the Psalmist, that master of words, said, "To You silence is praise," *Lekha dumiyyah tehillah.* Silence and God share infinity and a pregnant nothingness.

Most of the time, my mind is on the move, responding as quickly as it can to all the busyness surrounding me. To begin to fathom the depths of the divine requires a different approach, a ceasing. "Only toward God is my soul silent," *Akh el elohim dumiyyah nafshi.* Entering this silence, I realize it is not mine. It is God's. It envelops and soothes me, dissolving the strident ego, eroding the story I keep telling myself. The sheer, subtle silence has a texture all its own.

One way to ease into silence is to put aside the book of prayers for a few moments and simply sit and breathe. Become aware of your breathing. Each breath partakes of the breath of creation, the primordial divine breath through which "cosmic space expanded."

Just as God breathed the world into being, so we rejuvenate ourselves through breathing with *kavvanah,* with awareness. There is no need to think profound thoughts. Just to breathe, to inhale an elixir of oxygen and exhale carbon dioxide. Imagine yourself flowing in the stream of life, in the rhythm of the cosmic breath.

The biblical word for "breath" is *neshamah,* as in *nishmat hayyim,* "the breath of life" that God breathed into Adam. But *neshamah* also means "soul." The awareness of breath opens up the dimension of the soul. The soul is not confined within us; rather, we dwell within the soul. Surrounding and permeating us, it is our interface with oneness.

By becoming aware of *neshamah*—breath and soul, soul-breath—we see ourselves more clearly. The *neshamah* exposes what we have hidden away: our secret thoughts and favorite regrets, the pain that we suffer and cling to, the panoply of psychic strategies for propping up the ego. "The human *neshamah* is a lamp of God, searching all one's inmost chambers." In this verse from Proverbs, what does *neshamah* mean? Soul—the powerful beam of awareness, a searchlight into the depths of self. But "breath" also fits—breath as a powerful diagnostic tool. Gentle, deep, relaxed breathing helps you sense where you feel tight and constricted so you can begin to untie the knots—mental, emotional, and physical. As the knots loosen, energy flows more freely and efficiently through the nerves and cells of the body, through the 100 trillion synapses of the mind.

In meditation, thoughts and mental images do not stop, but you let them pass without fixating on them, without becoming attached. Between thoughts, there arises a moment of emptiness, the creative emptiness of *ayin.* Usually, we rush in to fill this emptiness with words and thoughts; in meditation we savor the gap, "contemplating a little without content, contemplating sheer spirit." A moment of pure awareness, of just being—without thought or action. "Though you do not grasp it, do not despair. The source is still emanating, spreading."

Meditation requires practice and patience. Its fruit, an expansive peace of mind, ripens unexpectedly. Kabbalists call meditation, which is often practiced alone to minimize distractions, *hitbodedut,* "seclusion, aloneness": the temporary separation of the self from the frenetic bustle of daily life.

But meditation is also appropriate for the communal life of the synagogue. Rabbis should be trained in meditation, so that they can introduce their congregants to spiritual silence. If the rabbi is not a meditator, then a qualified congregant can take the lead.

Silent meditation is appropriate at various points in the traditional service. At the beginning of the service, it can calm us down and usher us into prayer. After a song or a *niggun,* a wordless melody sung over and over, silence lets the music reverberate within us. Various powerful phrases and prayers invite contemplation. As the mind wanders, it is helpful to come back to such phrases, refocus, and begin again.

One of the central prayers of each morning and evening service is the Sh'ma. Its opening line proclaims God's oneness: "Hear O Israel: *YHVH* our God, *YHVH* is One." For centuries, this line has served as a Jewish "mantra," or what is called in Hebrew a *yihud,* a "unification." What does it mean to unify God? Kabbalists conceive of a contemplative unification of the *sefirot,* the various divine qualities. Hasidim are more simple and direct: "When reciting the word *one* in the unification of the *Sh'ma,* you should intend that there is nothing in the world but the blessed holy One, whose 'presence fills the whole earth.' Your essence is the soul within, part of God above. Thus only God is. This is the meaning of *one.*"

From a mystical perspective, the command of the *Sh'ma* means: "Hear O Israel: God is oneness." After chanting these words, a few moments of the service should be devoted to meditating on the word "one," on oneness.

In the Torah scroll, the first line of the *Sh'ma* is written with two of the letters enlarged: *ayin,* which is the final letter of the word *Sh'ma,* and *dalet,* which is the final letter of the word *ehad.* Among the reasons that have been proposed for this oddity is that these two letters spell *ed*, "witness."

Meditation helps us witness oneness, pause and appreciate the interwoven wonders of existence. If we dedicate part of the worship service to meditation—to listening to the *alef*—the synagogue will become a spiritual oasis and those praying will discover their own openings to silence, whether these are words from the prayer book or from their own hearts. Some in the congregation may feel slightly uncomfortable and fill in the silence with whispers or banter or by flipping through pages of the *siddur,* but most will gradually shed their nervousness and try out this new, yet ancient form of prayer.

The Mishnah describes how "the *hasidim* of old used to wait an hour before praying so that they could focus their mind on God." As the synagogue welcomes meditation back, the words between the silences will breathe more freely and resound, spread new wings of meaning and soar. Prayer will become less rote and less boring. It will recharge us, inspiring us to live out the harmony we have tasted in prayer, to play our part in harmonizing the world.

Just as silence and words enrich one another and need each other, so do stillness and movement. To spend an entire service just sitting down and standing up borders on the sacrilegious. As the Psalmist sings, "All my bones will declare, '*YHVH,* who is like You?'" As the Talmud teaches, one should bend and bow often during prayer "until all the vertebrae of the spine loosen."

Tamar Frankiel, Ph.D., teaches the history of religions at Claremont School of Theology and at the University of California Riverside. Judy Greenfeld is a Certified Fitness Trainer. In *Entering the Temple of Dreams: Jewish Prayers, Movements, and Meditations for the End of the Day*, they teach us about recovering the sweetness of sleep.

Recovering the Sweetness of Sleep

TAMAR FRANKIEL AND JUDY GREENFELD

Just as the moon is sometimes seen negatively, sleep also is sometimes seen as a spiritually negative state. This is a limited viewpoint, but some of its proponents have been prominent in Jewish tradition. They hold that waking consciousness is "expanded consciousness" (although one can also be spiritually "asleep" during the day!) and sleep is "constricted consciousness."[1] Accordingly, one should sleep as little as possible. The saintly person (a *tzaddik*) in Judaism has been described as "the one who is constantly consumed by love for God to the extent that he is unable to sleep at night, so agonized is he by the fear of losing conscious contact with the Beloved." To minimize sleep was frequently upheld as the ideal, because for a holy person, the "expanded consciousness and the holy thoughts of the whole day disappear, and on the following day you have to begin again and make great efforts to regain that level once again." Of course, such a person didn't stay up late just to run a business; the purpose was to learn Torah or say prayers. As a result of this spiritual tradition, many devout Jews have the custom of rising at midnight to say psalms and/or to pray for the restoration of Jerusalem and the Holy Temple; this is called *Tikkun Hatzot* (Mending [the World] at Midnight).[2]

This viewpoint is based on two traditions: one from the Talmud, which says that King David's harp woke him at midnight to sing God's praises; and a later one from the mystics, which states that holy souls join with God at midnight. The *Zohar* mentions both:

Every night the souls of the righteous mount on high, and at the hour of midnight the Holy-One-Blessed-Be-He comes to the Garden of Eden to disport himself with them.

With which of them? Rabbi Jose says, with all—both those whose abode is in the other world, and those who are still in their dwellings in this world....

At midnight all the truly righteous arise to read the Torah and to sing psalms, and we have learned that Holy-One-Blessed-Be-He and all the righteous in the Garden of Eden listen to their voices.... Hence it is that the praises that are sung at night constitute the most perfect praise.

See now, King David too used to get up in the middle of the night.... He did not remain sitting or lying in his bed, but he literally rose and stood up to compose psalms and praises.... He, as it were, awoke the dawn, as it is written, "Awake, my glory, awake, songs and harp; I myself will awake very early."[3]

(Psalms 57:9)

It would seem that the less sleep the better, so long as the nocturnal waking hours are spent in prayer. Yet rabbinic advisers did not recommend this for an ordinary person. Holy individuals, who had disciplined their passions and devoted virtually all their time to study and prayer, could do with little sleep because they did not expend energy in the same emotional struggles as the ordinary person did, and did not need to recover that energy in sleep. Some sages also felt that the tradition of staying awake might easily go too far. As one great rabbi said, a person should have "his mind clear and bright and undimmed, and his body vigorous.... Staying awake too much is very harmful."[4]

We follow a different rabbinic viewpoint: that we can actually do spiritual work while sleeping. For example, the Hasidic Rabbi Tzvi of Ziditchov said that if he accomplished in sleep only what he does while he is awake, it was not a good sleep. In his view, the service of God during sleep could—and should—be higher than during waking hours, because the soul is then freed from the body. The great Rabbi Chaim of Volozhin said that his teacher, the famous Vilna Gaon, had stated that God created sleep so that we could attain insights that were unattainable in our waking state. Some of our greatest teachers—including the Baal Shem Tov, who was the founder of Hasidism, and Joseph Caro, the great legal scholar—were taught by spiritual beings in their sleep.[5]

From this perspective, we sleep so we can dream, and dreams are ways to heal and sources of information. If we sleep well—whether for short or long periods, and in accordance with our own patterns and with the sort of spiritual preparation provided by the Bedtime Prayers—sleep is not spiritually negative or neutral. It is positive. The *Zohar* illustrates this with a story of Rabbi Isaac, who went to Rabbi Yehudah despondent because he expected to die soon. Rabbi Yehudah asked him why he thought so. Rabbi Isaac responded, "My soul has lately been leaving me in the night and not enlightening me with dreams as it used to do."[6] Dreams are part of living fully the soul's life on earth.

> "With my soul have I desired You in the night, yea, with my spirit within me will I seek You early" (Isaiah 26:9). Rabbi Shimon said, "The inner meaning of this verse is as follows: When a man lies down in bed, his soul leaves him and begins to mount on high, leaving with the body only the impression of a receptacle that contains the heartbeat. The rest of it tries to soar from grade to grade, and in so doing it encounters certain bright but unclean essences. If it is pure and has not defiled itself by day, it rises above them...and there they show her certain things that are going to happen in the near future. (Sometimes they delude her and show her false things.) Thus she goes about the whole night until the man wakes up, when she returns to her place. Happy are the righteous to whom God reveals secrets in dreams!...[7]

If God joins the souls of the righteous in the heavenly ceremonies at midnight, we do not all have to awaken ourselves to join them. If our souls are ready, they can travel to the Garden while we are asleep. We will bring back their messages in our dreams. That allows the imagination, guided by the soul, to bring potential into form. This literally brings light from darkness.

Sleep, then, is not only physical rest for the brain but also an opportunity for the soul.

Rabbi Sheldon Zimmerman, Executive Director of Birthright Israel U.S.A., Inc., was spiritual leader of Central Synagogue, New York City, and Temple Emanu-El in Dallas, Texas, before becoming president of Hebrew Union College–Jewish Institute of Religion. In *Healing of Soul, Healing of Body: Spiritual Leaders Unfold the Strength & Solace in Psalms,* edited by Rabbi Simkha Y. Weintraub, Rabbi Zimmerman helps us pray.

A Prayer for Prayer

SHELDON ZIMMERMAN

O My God
My soul's companion
My heart's precious friend
I turn to You.

I need to close out the noise
To rise above the noise
The noise that interrupts—
The noise that separates—
The noise that isolates.
I need to hear You again.

In the silence of my innermost being,
In the fragments of my yearned-for wholeness,
I hear whispers of Your presence—
Echoes of the past when You were with me
When I felt Your nearness
When together we walked—
When You held me close, embraced me in Your love, laughed with me
    in my joy.
I yearn to hear You again.

In your oneness, I find healing.
In the promise of Your love, I am soothed.
In Your wholeness, I too can become whole again.

Please listen to my call—
    help me find the words
    help me find the strength within
    help me shape my mouth, my voice, my heart
so that I can direct my spirit and find You in prayer
In words only my heart can speak
In songs only my soul can sing
Lifting my eyes and heart to You.

Adonai S'fatai Tiftach—open my lips, precious God,
so that I can speak with You again.

Dr. **Arthur Green,** rabbi, is Lown Professor of Jewish Thought at Brandeis University and former president of the Reconstructionist Rabbinical College in Philadelphia. He is a student of Jewish theology and mysticism who has combined scholarly career and personal commitment. In *These Are the Words: A Vocabulary of Jewish Spiritual Life,* Rabbi Green teaches us about meditation in Jewish spiritual life.

Hitbodedut   התבודדות

ARTHUR GREEN

This word literally means "self-isolation" or separating oneself from the company of others. Historically it has come to mean doing so in order to be alone with God.

The practice of *hitbodedut* is first described in this language by Rabbi Bahya Ibn Pakuda, a philosopher and mystic of the 11th century. He lived in a society where Sufi practice, including meditation, was popular among the Muslim majority. His Judaism reflects the great awe in which he held this practice, one he enthusiastically recommends for his readers.

But if the term is a later one, the practice of solitary prayer and silent standing in God's presence is biblical in origin. It is widely reflected in the Psalms, in such tales as Abraham's wanderings through the desert and Moses and Elijah's forty days at Horeb, the mountain whose name means "desolation." Jeremiah and others among the prophets also felt the calling to a lonely life of dedication in order to seek God's word. The biblical practice was continued among later Jewish groups, especially communities such as that at Qumran, the "Dead Sea Scrolls" community, where individual pursuit of God and communal life each had their place.

Practices of *hitbodedut* have varied over the centuries. The followers of Rabbi Abraham Abulafia, from the 13th century onward, had techniques of visualized meditations that they developed with great skill. For them, *hitbodedut* came to mean "concentration" on the images before the inner eye. Some Hasidic leaders continued in this path, especially that of visualizing the letters of prayer.

Others see *hitbodedut* as a time for private, but not necessarily silent, prayer. The followers of Rabbi Nachman of Breslov (1772–1810), in fact, insist upon the spoken form. These regular practitioners of *hitbodedut* seek to pray this way for one hour each day, pouring forth spontaneous personal prayer, in whatever language the heart knows best. The purpose of this prayer, they say, is to break the heart, for only in the wholeness of knowing our broken heart can we truly come into God's presence.

Meditation is being revived in our day as a part of Jewish spiritual life. Ancient Jewish techniques are being simplified and updated. Methods of concentration and mindfulness are also being brought into Judaism by those who have learned them elsewhere. All this is for the good, a part of our generation's effort to make the Judaism we hand on to the future richer in this area than it has ever been.

Nan Fink Gefen, Ph.D., is co-director of Chochmat HaLev, one of three U.S. centers devoted to teaching Jewish meditation, where she has trained hundreds of students and has led many meditation retreats. In *Discovering Jewish Meditation: Instruction & Guidance for Learning an Ancient Spiritual Practice*, she teaches us what Jewish meditation is.

What Is Jewish Meditation?

NAN FINK GEFEN

Over the years you've undoubtedly had experiences that were spiritual in nature. Perhaps they took place while you were reading a poem, or holding a sleeping child. Or walking in the woods, or watching the sunset. Or while you were praying.

These experiences—and more—have helped you know that something exists beyond your regular, everyday reality. This "something" is what I call "the silence within." To many of us this state seems both familiar and mysterious. It has the quality of spaciousness, and it appears to have no boundaries.

Like a pregnant pause before a sentence, the silence within contains all possibility. It is the raw material of creation, the formlessness that exists before the concrete emerges. When we enter into this state, we have our most intense spiritual experiences and receive our most significant moments of understanding.

WHAT IS JEWISH MEDITATION?

Most simply, Jewish meditation is a spiritual practice found within the Jewish tradition.

The best way to describe it is to consider its name. The word "Jewish" is included because meditation has been—and is—a part of Judaism. Traditionally it exists alongside other aspects of Jewish observance, such as prayer and Torah study. Less traditionally, it is done alone as a spiritual practice.

Jewish meditation uses images, words, and symbols that come from the Jewish tradition. The meditations themselves, and the teachings that go along with them, reflect Jewish understanding. Because of this, people who are introduced to Jewish meditation will not mistake it for any other meditative practice.

Now we move on to the "meditation" word in Jewish meditation. Meditation is a specific kind of activity that involves directing the mind. It follows a prescribed order, and it uses techniques different from ordinary thinking or daydreaming. The activity takes place during a prescribed time period, and thereby has a beginning and an end. Although the contents of Jewish meditation are unique in many ways, it joins other meditative traditions in directing the mind to the silence within.

Jewish meditation can be further described as an organic practice that has grown and changed through history. Although it is part of Judaism, it nevertheless has absorbed elements from other traditions, such as Sufism, Gnosticism, and Buddhism. The practice contains a great variety of teachings and meditations. At different times creative bursts of collective insight into the use of meditation have taken place. One, in fact, is going on right now.

Nan Fink Gefen, Ph.D., is co-director of Chochmat HaLev, one of three U.S. centers devoted to teaching Jewish meditation, where she has trained hundreds of students and has led many meditation retreats. In *Discovering Jewish Meditation: Instruction & Guidance for Learning an Ancient Spiritual Practice,* she teaches us how the practice of Jewish meditation can lead to a deeper connection with the Devine.

The Practice of Jewish Meditation

NAN FINK GEFEN

Who among us doesn't want to become more focused, more aware, more spiritually attuned and closer to the Divine? But you might be wondering what this has to do with being Jewish.

Many Jewish meditators are completely secular when they begin to practice. They may have investigated other meditative traditions in their search for spiritual meaning. However, they still yearn to be connected to the tradition of their people. Jewish meditation offers them this possibility.

Secular people can enter Jewish meditation without feeling that they are violating their values. The practice does not require a belief in the traditional patriarchal God, nor membership in a synagogue or temple. Meditators' experience with other traditions only adds to their ability to do Jewish meditation, because certain meditation skills are transferable. Once they've started a practice, they often become enormously interested in Judaism. I've known many such meditators who end up committed to the Jewish path—much to their surprise. However, they still value and retain what they've learned elsewhere, and bring it into their renewed Jewish lives.

Sometimes it takes a period of time for people to feel comfortable exploring the roots of Jewish meditation. They need to get beyond their ambivalence about Judaism as a religion. Many still are angry about being forced as children to go to Hebrew school or sit through boring services. Others are upset that Judaism historically is a patriarchy. Once they begin to see that this inequality is changing in dramatic and significant ways, they discover that they can relate to the tradition. They take from it the parts that are meaningful and discard those that are unacceptable.

Jews who are already religious also are drawn to Jewish meditation. When they realize that it has been a part of Jewish tradition for centuries, they accept it as legitimate. They would not explore Buddhist meditation, but they are open to learning Jewish meditation since it is grounded in their own tradition. They usually are pleased to discover that it supplements their already established Jewish religious practice. Many report that their prayer life deepens as they integrate meditation into it.

Jewish meditation appeals to many non-Jews. For those interested in learning about Judaism or exploring conversion, meditation is a good entry point. The practice contains universal attributes found in other meditative traditions, thus making it appear accessible, even familiar.

People from all kinds of backgrounds practice Jewish meditation. They do it together, without the usual problems of religious Jew versus secular person, or learned Jew versus neophyte. Jewish meditation is an equalizer within the Jewish world: The familiar divisions between people disappear. Anyone can practice it, and no special group claims it as its own.

Will Jewish meditation bring you closer to Judaism? Probably. But this will come about because you desire it, not because it is imposed upon you.

Dr. Daniel C. Matt is currently composing an annotated English translation of the *Zohar*. He was formerly a professor of Jewish spirituality at the Graduate Theological Union in Berkeley, California. In *Meditation from the Heart of Judaism: Today's Teachers Share Their Practices, Techniques, and Faith,* Dr. Matt teaches us about the sense of wonder and oneness that connects us with the universe and with God.

Why Meditate?

DANIEL C. MATT

What is Jewish meditation? Does the meditator make it Jewish? Or is there a technique in itself that can be defined as Jewish?

There are Jewish meditative techniques. In Kabbalah, many techniques focus on Hebrew words, on names of God, on various *sefirot*. There is a technique of meditating on *ayin*, or "nothingness," which is traditionally seen as especially demanding and dangerous. It is also certainly the most open-ended of all the meditative techniques, since its goal is simply to surrender the self to the Divine Oneness, to that nothingness that transcends all Jewish symbols. But the Hasidim and Aryeh Kaplan, a twentieth-century writer and meditation teacher, say that *ayin* is not recommended as a place to start.

MEDITATING ON *AYIN,* ON "NOTHINGNESS," AS A MEANS

I prefer to meditate on *ayin* rather than most other specific names, formulas, images, or symbols. There's something attractive to me about this, perhaps the deep immersion in a boundless Divine energy. At times, it seems to be the essence of spiritual experience, and everything else pales. But I know from my own experience and from others, too, that you can't live in the realm of *ayin*. We have to function in the world. So it's useful to have other techniques that you can use if you're stuck in a traffic jam or if you can put aside ten minutes in the morning.

The best way to get a handle on *ayin* is to compare it to Buddhism. The Buddhist concept of *sunyata* (emptiness) is similar to *ayin*—not identical, but very close.

Being born into a tradition places a demand upon us. It's useful to explore all of the spiritualities of the world, to learn from the insights of each. On the other hand, there's a natural connection we feel with the faith in which we've been raised, and that should be honored, too. Learning how to balance the particular and the universal, the Jewish and the non-Jewish, is one of the challenges on the spiritual search.

Immersion in *ayin*, though, is not the ultimate goal. Such immersion is meant to recharge our batteries. It's an immersion for the purpose of emerging, an immersion to enable us to express ourselves in a constantly "renewed form." It's useful to immerse in *ayin*, in nothingness, but it would be very bad to be stuck there, since this could easily lead to delusions or to extreme withdrawal from the daily give-and-take of life.

ENLIGHTENMENT

A permanent state of enlightenment seems to be the model in the East. Once you attain enlightenment, you never lose it or fall from it. But in the West and in Judaism, it's somewhat different. I'm not going to rule out the possibility that a Jew who is enlightened can be enlightened just as spiritual seekers are in the East. But the West and Judaism are more engaged in community and in history than is Buddhism. And the commitment to transform the mundane into the divine, to transform the "potentially" holy into the holy, is profoundly Jewish. We're engaged in the world; we cannot flee from it. Acknowledging this is a sign of the success of our meditation.

SILENCE

American Judaism profoundly needs group meditation and communal silence. This is a productive, rich kind of silence. Today, a number of rabbis are introducing this around the country, but still in a limited way. Yet, it is one of the most significant developments in contemporary Jewish spirituality.

Traditionally, parts of the worship service are silent, but words dominate, even if they are read silently. True silent meditation will help people appreciate the words. There should be fewer words and more room for silence. Then, when the words do appear; they will be more powerful. The silence will enrich the words.

Of course, a fair amount of people don't believe meditation has a place in the regular service. But there are ways to introduce meditation gradually and gently, such as a minute of pregnant silence after a *niggun,* a special wordless melody. Try this and see how the group responds.

VARIETIES OF JEWISH MEDITATION

There are different meditative techniques and traditions in the Jewish contemplative world. Traditionally, one distinction is between ecstatic Kabbalah and prophetic Kabbalah. Abraham Abulafia meditated on the Hebrew letters and on Divine names to "short-circuit" the workings of the mind. He used a technique he called "cutting the knots," which was meant to break through various mental and psychological constrictions by whirling these combinations of letters around mentally. This technique is still practiced.

Another technique is meditating on the words of the prayers with what I call "*sefirotic* correspondences." This means that certain words will resonate with certain *sefirot* (qualities of God's infinity made manifest in a finite world). In moving through a *berachah,* a blessing or a prayer, you contact the realm of the *sefirot.* This kind of meditation functions as part of the liturgy and ritual, expanding their meaning.

NOTHINGNESS IS EVERYTHING

The Western mind focuses on substance; the Eastern mind focuses on the interrelationship between everything. Nothing has independent being in and of itself. That's the basic insight of *sunyata*, whereas in Western mysticism, nothingness is still the ultimate essence. The West seems locked into the notion of substance. It may be pure Divine being, but it's also something. The East would criticize even this ultimate substance or essence and try to see through the illusion that there is any existent thing in and of itself.

You could say that these are two ways of describing an underlying reality that, presumably, is one and the same. But whereas *sunyata* is central to Buddhism, most Jews have never heard of *ayin*. Even in Kabbalah, it's talked about very rarely. In Hasidism, it's further developed, but of all the Hasidic teachings, maybe one percent is devoted to *ayin*.

Yet, *ayin* is central because it represents the moment of transition from Infinity *(Ein Sof)* to the *sefirot*. *Ayin* is how God unfolds. Creation is rooted in nothingness. There are roots for this positive sense of nothingness within Judaism. The Talmud, for example, states; "The words of Torah do not become real except for one who makes himself as if he is not." Job asks rhetorically, "Where is wisdom to be found?" The word *ayin* in this verse is a question: "Where?" But already in the Talmud, *ayin* is interpreted as a noun: "Wisdom is found in nothingness." In Kabbalah, it becomes Divine nothingness. Its roots lie in rabbinic literature, but Kabbalah expands this.

STARTING YOUR MEDITATION PRACTICE

When starting your meditation practice, the most important thing is discipline: "Make your study of Torah at a fixed time" (*Pirke Avot* 1:15). Sit for ten minutes and create openness. Moshe de Leon, composer of the *Zohar,* describes meditation in these words:

Thought reveals itself only through contemplating a little without content, contemplating sheer Spirit. The contemplation is imperfect. First, you understand, then you lose what you have understood. Like pondering a thought: The light of that thought suddenly darkens and vanishes. Then it returns and shines and vanishes again. No one can understand the content of that light. It is like the light that appears when water ripples in a bowl. Shining here, suddenly disappearing, then reappearing somewhere else. You think that you have grasped the light when suddenly it escapes, radiating elsewhere. You pursue it, hoping to catch it but you cannot. Yet you cannot bring yourself to leave. You keep pursuing it. It is the same with the beginning of emanation. As you begin to contemplate it, it vanishes, then reappears. You understand, then it disappears. Even though you do not grasp it, do not despair. The Source is still emanating, spreading.

Sitting for five minutes or ten minutes or even two minutes is very demanding. And to not think of anything while doing this? We can't do that. Thoughts will come, so let the thoughts come and don't hold on to them. The thought will then move on. You're then left with a gap of *ayin,* of emptiness. You contemplate just the mental process itself, without being attached to any particular idea or image or desire that pops up.

Or you can sit outdoors near a body of water and watch the light reflecting off the water. See the ephemeral nature of the mind in front of you and experience it mentally. The water itself becomes a mantra. Seeing that helps recall to you what is going on mentally.

A simpler way to start a meditation practice is just to open the siddur and find one word, one phrase, one line that's moving, uplifting, inspirational, spiritual, colorful, intriguing—and meditate on it. Start with something that attracts you in the tradition. Or take a melody, preferably one without words, or a chant, and then enter silence.

OBSTACLES TO MEDITATION

Common obstacles to meditative practices are boredom, pride, and laziness. Pride is an obstacle when you've actually made some breakthrough. You can be proud of meditating. You can be proud of being nothing.

Some *Musar* (ethical) literature can help you overcome these obstacles, as can Yitzhak Buxbaum's book, *Jewish Spiritual Practices*.

INTEGRATING MEDITATION WITH YOUR LIFE

If I approach life with the bit of clarity that I can gain through meditation, then my life will be less secular and more spiritual. You integrate meditation and life just by being sensitive to the possibilities that arise: the possibilities of relationship, the possibilities of creativity that we often miss. Starting the day with a little bit of tranquillity can help you identify those opportunities and engage them.

One of the benefits of meditation is that it enables us to surrender the images we have of God and self. Meditation is an opportunity to melt these down and refashion them.

The Bible demands that we smash the idols. We can extend this idea from the physical idols of stone to the mental concept of God. Each smashing of an image allows for a more expanded image, which itself must be expanded until we have smashed all the images. That's what happens in the laboratory of meditation. Then we confront God anew every moment.

Rabbi David A. Cooper has studied meditation and mysticism for over 30 years. In *The Handbook of Jewish Meditation Practices: A Guide for Enriching the Sabbath and Other Days of Your Life,* Rabbi Cooper teaches us how to reclaim the healing power of self-reflection with Jewish meditation.

The Roots and Fruits of Meditation

DAVID A. COOPER

Language, the tool of rationality, is often inherently in conflict with mystical teaching. Meditative techniques are designed to help spiritual "aspirants" achieve altered states of consciousness. When this in fact occurs, the results often transcend rational explanation. Throughout history, mystics have been unable to directly communicate their experiences. Rather, they have found ways to transmit experiences indirectly through metaphor, poetry, or enigmatic wisdom teachings. Each mystical teacher finds his or her expression through the cultural structure in which he or she lives, with the culture's beliefs, values, attitudes, and opinions, all of which are molded by the era, surrounding communities, and general historical perspective in those times.

The teachings of these mystics, although not particularly rational, have profoundly influenced the history of humankind. They have birthed many spiritual traditions and have caused these traditions to branch into various directions. The mystics give us pause to reflect on the possibility of something more than life as we see it in front of us. They inspire us to seek more deeply, beyond appearances. In many ways, although from widely diverse backgrounds and even though they use their own distinctive languages, they speak about a common theme.

The metaphor for this is that whereas there are many paths up the mountain, there is only a single peak, higher than all others.

Obviously, each person on the spiritual journey has his or her own natural dispositions and characteristics. Different paths up the mountain will be more readily accessible to some than others. For some, a path will seem to be a dead end; for others, the barriers they encounter are simply obstacles that need to be surmounted to get higher up the mountain. The mysteries of these spiritual paths defy explanation, and many spiritual adventurers spend their lives exploring a path and its divergent tracks with remarkable patience. In the end, however, no matter what path we take, the highest peak of truth remains the same for all who seek it.

Judaism is an extraordinary path for spiritual growth, as we shall see. It is a rich tradition with a long history. It is not really one path up the mountain, but many trails that occasionally are parallel but often go on totally different routes. With limited perspective, one might think that the result is that these paths will never meet again. But, when standing back, we can still see that there is only one highest peak and all paths ultimately lead to the One.

Often, people ask, "If they all lead to an ultimate truth, how do we choose our path?" This question raises many issues. It suggests that we have total free choice, but this is not completely true. We are constrained in many ways. We have our parentage, our character, our physical, emotional, and intellectual makeup, our society, our culture, our ancestry, our language, and so forth. All of these set parameters and incline us one way or another.

Clearly, Eastern spiritual and meditative traditions during the past century have become more accessible in the West. In absorbing some of these teachings, the West has modified, redefined, and remolded the practices to fit a more Western model. This simply is the way it works. So whatever path we "choose," we will adapt it to meet our needs.

As Eastern teachings, particularly in the arena of meditation, have grown in popularity, an interesting phenomenon has developed in the past twenty years. Under the influence of strong meditative practices, Westerners have increasingly been returning to their root traditions. When one is immersed in altered consciousness, it overflows into everyday life. Seen through these eyes, we discover that many elements of our lives and many aspects of our root traditions are meditation practices in and of themselves. It is out of this phenomenon that an entire new appreciation for the potential of Jewish meditation has dramatically evolved over the past decade.

While Jewish meditation as an identifiable collection of teachings is a relatively new phenomenon, meditative practices have been deeply rooted in Judaism for thousands of years. The essence of meditation is an integral part of traditional Jewish daily life, ritual, prayer, study of Torah, Talmud, and celebration of the Sabbath and the holy days. Indeed, meditation techniques are so fully integrated into traditional Jewish life that they were never separated out as unique practices of themselves. Today, many practitioners of traditional Judaism are highly skilled meditators in one way or another but they don't give this a name.

While very few Jewish teachers over the past two thousand years emphasized meditative techniques, per se, they often described how one can achieve higher states of consciousness through prayer or continuous study. We must keep in mind that until only the last couple of centuries, traditional Jewish life assumed certain daily activities had the potential for regular periods of self-reflection and contemplation. It was a given that people would have periods of quiet, that the Sabbath would be a day of rest, that time for prayer would be made each day, that one would pay close attention to food preparation, that, indeed, every facet of one's life would be under close scrutiny. The ideal was to live impeccably. This was what life was about. This impeccability by its nature requires experiencing many opportunities for meditative awareness in the context of expanded consciousness.

The most distinctive transformation Judaism has undergone in the past couple of hundred years is the way in which modern Jews live their daily lives. It is not surprising that the farther away we get from a traditional life style, the less meaningful we find the elements of Jewish practice. Each part loses something when separated from the whole. The complaint of a large number of people who want to be connected with their Judaism is that individual practices, like prayer or occasional Torah study, a Sabbath morning in a synagogue, or the celebration of a ritual, are primarily devoted to a form but lack a spiritual content.

On the other hand, many who have been discontented with Judaism have been drawn to simple practices of sitting quietly, chanting a few words in repetition, or singing to God while focused on basic thoughts of lovingkindness, forgiveness, gratitude, generosity, and so forth. The plain truth of the matter, of course, is that all these basic practices are within the repertoire of Judaism, but are often hidden, obscured by layers of a tradition originally designed for another way of life. The reason Jewish-oriented meditation has become popular so quickly is that it provides a foundation in a subtle but profound way upon which these individual practices can link with the heart of the tradition. In this way, there is a new opportunity for modern practitioners to access a deep spirituality through elements of Judaism that are bonded in some way with an inner pulse that has continued over the centuries, and will continue for centuries to come.

The roots of Jewish meditation have often been hidden in the oral tradition passed directly from teacher to student, or in kabbalistic writings that are difficult to decipher. However, many Jewish meditative techniques have been common knowledge and were widely practiced in various ways over the centuries. There are many different Hebrew words for these techniques.

For example, the word *hitbonenut* usually refers to a type of contemplation in which one focuses one's thought on a subject that has an intrinsic potential to alter one's consciousness. Another word used in a similar context is *histakkelut,* which is a type of contemplation that involves visualizations. *Hitbodedut,* often used to describe meditation, means to seclude oneself physically, to separate oneself. The term *kavannah,* which means intention, is also used to describe a meditative, focused state of mind. The term *hishtavut,* meaning equanimity, is viewed as foundation for attaining higher states of awareness. The idea of *bittul ha-yesh,* literally to nullify the sense of "is-ness," is descriptive of letting go of one's self-awareness, also viewed as an essential element of expanded consciousness. So, too, the term *meserit ha-nefesh*, sacrifice of the vital soul, is a way of referring to the state of selflessness.

Aryeh Kaplan, the most prolific modern writer to discuss the Jewish contemplative approach, lists several types of Jewish meditation in his books *Jewish Meditation* and *Meditation and the Bible*. One is called *suach*, a state of prayerful elevation in which the meditator communes with the divine Source of Life. Another is called *hagah*, or *higayon*, in which the meditator uses repetition—much like a mantra—to enter a state of altered consciousness. A third method, *ranan*, involves drenching the emotions until the meditator attains a level of ecstasy. In the East this is referred to as *bhakti*, in which one attains a connection with the Divine through concentrated devotional practice.

Yet another method of Jewish meditation is called *shasha*. It is one of the higher and more difficult forms in that the meditator is continuously pressing the limits of the mind. It is as if there were a sphere of light—called *awareness*—that seems always out of reach. The meditator dances on the periphery, not quite absorbed in the sphere and yet not really outside it. On this edge of awareness, one attains a deep state of rapture. At a higher level, however, one comes to the ultimate realization that there never was an edge in the first place, and one transcends rapture into yet a more inclusive state. This is the state of *devekut*, being at one with all.

MEDITATION AND THE TALMUD

Judaism has a long history of contemplative and meditative practice. A well-known reference to the mystical side of Judaism is recorded in the Talmud (*Berachot* 32b) in a discussion about prayer. It says that the first *hasidim*, ancient pious practitioners, meditated an hour before prayer and an hour after. Because the Talmud itself is an old document, the ancient ones to whom it refers must have lived well over two thousand years ago.

The Talmud notes that if these practitioners did the required three prayers a day lasting an hour each, they would have spent nine hours a day in meditation and prayer. It then inquires, in typically talmudic fashion: If these people spent nine hours a day in contemplative activity, how could they keep up their studies of Torah, and, moreover, how could they earn a living? The answer it provides is that these contemplatives did not have any difficulty in learning because they never forgot anything, and they did not have to work so hard because, for them, a little effort went a long way. The important point here is that the Talmud gives clear support to the contemplative life style, and it suggests that a strong commitment to inner work will be rewarded in mysterious ways.

In another section (*Hagigah* 11b), the Talmud gives detailed instructions about teaching the secrets of Judaism's hidden mysteries. For example, there was a profound and esoteric teaching called the mystery of "descent into the Chariot." The mystical Chariot was the means by which one could use contemplative techniques to be transported to higher realms of awareness. In this section of the Talmud, it is written that a teacher was not permitted to discuss anything regarding the Chariot unless the student was already accomplished on the highest level. Today we might call this "postdoctorate" spiritual education.

Throughout this same talmudic section, the great masters are reluctant to answer their students' questions regarding the mystical underpinning of the creation. Indeed, the Talmud discusses at great length the dangers of esoteric exploration. It is here that the famous story is told about four sages who entered the *pardes*—the orchard or garden of mystical awareness. Three of the four were not well prepared for the shock of experiencing the overwhelming light of expanded consciousness. One died as soon as he looked around him, another instantly went mad, and a third became a disbeliever. Only one, Rabbi Akiva, came out unharmed. As Rabbi Akiva is one of the most important figures in the Talmud, it is of great significance that his mystical and contemplative character is a point of considerable distinction. Clearly, the talmudic scholars had extraordinary respect for contemplative practice.

Rabbi Jonathan Omer-Man is the founder and director of Metivta, a school of Jewish wisdom and meditation in Los Angeles. In *Meditation from the Heart of Judaism: Today's Teachers Share Their Practices, Techniques, and Faith,* edited by Avram Davis, Rabbi Omer-Man teaches us how to understand meditation from a Jewish perspective and how to bring its practice into our lives.

Noble Boredom:
How to View Meditation

JONATHAN OMER-MAN

The English writer C. Day Lewis once said that the reason he prayed was because he had to. For some people, the contemplative life is an absolute necessity. You can assuage the need for going to the movies by smoking dope or by getting involved in a thousand and one other endeavors. But at a certain point, the point when you discover the contemplative path, it is clearly your path. Contemplative practice is a method of discovering one's path and how to progress along it and how to be less consumed by diversions and distraction.

Ultimately, a contemplative life is a way of being in the world. For those who have this predisposition, it is extremely valuable. It isn't a way for everybody. It's very important to acknowledge that, for most people, the contemplative is irrelevant. For some people, it is more important than anything else.

Contemplative practice is not like an addiction, though. It is an innate path. It isn't just that persons must find what their soul needs, but almost as if there are different kinds of souls and each proceeds along different kinds of paths: *This* is the path for my kind of soul. This is the way my life unfolds. This is the way that, whatever my task is in this world, it is more likely to be fulfilled.

One of the problems of our time is the excessive development of the sense of the individual. This really has nothing to do with a sense of path, but more the sense of striving and of expansion. The distinction between them is the same distinction between creating and discovery. Discovery is uncovering what is already there. But creating is building something that was never there. One example in music would be Bach, who discovered patterns that were there, whereas romantics are people who create things that were never there.

A few years ago, I had dinner with some friends who were scientists at Cal-Tech. One of them talked about the Galileo Space Program, which sent space probes twice around the moon and the earth, then to Mars and beyond. The phrase used about the people working on it was that they had "discovered" the trajectory of the outgoing orbits. For me, this was an incredible validation of discovery of uncovering hidden patterns. Someone who contemplates is a discoverer. The ecstatic is a creator.

AVOID BECOMING ADDICTED TO THE "HIGHS"

I look at meditation fairly narrowly. Ultimately, it is a daily practice that is boring and that is transformative and doesn't necessarily offer you incredible experiences. The "highs" are not the goal. When we are twenty, we define a relationship by the intensity of the orgasm. Then you get a little bit of life in you and realize that marrying someone because of the intensity of orgasm is really very naive. And one doesn't always even marry the person with whom one has the best sex. Such things are incredible gifts, and we wouldn't want to think about life without them. But they are simply a high.

For many years, I wanted to be an ecstatic. Then, I regarded myself as a failed ecstatic. I could never do what my Sufi friends could do or what my ecstatic Jewish friends could do. Finally, I realized that ecstasy wasn't really a central part of my path. And that I could do pretty well without it.

The ecstatic is a person who has transformative moments of very high intensity. It is relatively easy to bring someone to ecstasy.

But what do you do afterwards? The contemplative path is slower and steadier and concentrates more on ongoing awareness than these very intense flashes. Contemplatives have had ecstatic moments, and ecstatics, I assume, have contemplative periods. But we must beware of an addiction for the high. This is especially true in American society because Americans worship high events.

Ultimately, the contemplative knows that life is boring. Aristotle distinguished between noble boredom and ignoble/base boredom. It is very important that we cultivate a sense of noble boredom, of being without the need for action, without the need for something to happen.

Noble boredom means no anticipation of action. It means having the ability to be present without needing something to happen. This is one of the most important things in meditative practice. I have a great suspicion of pyrotechnics and explosive sparks. Seeking these is not really meditation. They may have value and their place, but they are not really meditation. To illustrate this, I would like to draw on the image of marriage. A good marriage is when the two partners know that there is an element of boredom with which they must live. They ultimately accept the richness of the boredom. This allows for occasional high peaks. But the need for more excitement is dangerous and a diversion from the essence of the practice.

I question whether meditation can be fit into mainstream Jewish practice because it's ultimately a minority practice. In synagogues, a rabbi will start doing meditation, and half the people there don't want it, perhaps a quarter do, and the rest are curious. Meditation is not a "main sanctuary" activity. It is not something to be added to services precisely because many people don't want or understand it.

I don't know how this will be worked out. There is a problem of size, which is very significant in contemporary American Judaism. We need large institutions to pay rabbis, to have dayschools and afternoon schools, and to have educators. A group of fifty meditators are not going to be able to build a school for their kids or to maintain Jewish services. They cannot even maintain a building. So one of the tragedies of the modern temple is that it has become a coalition of many different needs and often sinks to the lowest common denominator.

For a small percentage of people, meditating is the most natural thing in the world. They move directly into it. For most of us, it's a struggle. This is why the group is important: it reinforces our desire to meditate. In many ways, learning to meditate is changing the way we use our minds. Of course, there are profoundly different kinds of meditation, but common to each is observing how the mind works.

THE VALUE OF BOREDOM

There are many models of mind in various civilizations. Plato defined the mind as a rider of a chariot with two horses, one white and one dark. Spiritually, understanding the mind is a way of promoting and deepening one's spiritual work and understanding the nature of one's path. It is a true understanding of the unfolding of our life.

There is no easy way to integrate this. A practice like Shabbat is very helpful, since this one day can affect the rest of your life. Sitting in meditation for twenty minutes every morning is the same. But it's a slow process and can take months or years.

For many people, the main difficulty of meditating is that it's scary to open the closets of the mind. You don't know exactly where you're going and you don't know whether it is worthwhile. But if you belong to a meditation group, you can discover these difficulties with others and realize that they are remarkably banal and ordinary and that everybody has them. My own meditation has led me to a certain amount of equanimity and helped me to become a more responsive and a less reactive person. Not a less spontaneous person, but a less automatically reactive person.

Another common obstacle to practice is how to carry on in a dry period. How do you have the momentum to carry through when nothing happens? Then one must seek external reinforcements, such as group practice.

Another difficulty is loss of meaning. At a certain point during their meditation career, everyone thinks, "Why am I bothering with this?" Then you must rediscover meaning. An aspect of difficulty is the difficulty itself. The chatter and the reactiveness of the mind are all-pervading. But one thing I've always found with meditation is that the difficulties are the major part of the course.

You must make the leap forward from difficulty, and this can't be done with ease. The obstacles themselves are points of transformation. This is a very hard truth.

Another aspect of this is that one component of a spiritual practice is becoming a better person. This is true transformation of self, but it is very hard. It is similar to the difference between turning around a 250,000-ton tanker or a rowboat. A rowboat can be turned around in a moment, but a tanker takes three days. We are much like this. Patience is key.

So, an example: A particular politician makes us angry. He might be a self-righteous liar. A spiritual practice demands that we be alert to when we ourselves are being drawn into an inner drama of anger or fear and so on. As we observe it, we become more truly responsive and less reactive. A red flag comes up in the mind, as it were, denoting an obsessive reaction. From this, I learn to budget my energies more effectively and pay far less attention to this politician.

THE REWARDS OF DISCIPLINE

My own spiritual practice became more formalized when I was in my midthirties because that was when I found some meditation teachers. In my forties, it became integrated into a Jewish practice. I have a strong regular practice, but there are times when it just disappears. I understand the disappearing within the context of the whole of the practice. It isn't that I have a practice—and then I don't have a practice, but rather that my practice includes periods in which I lose my practice. For me, this is an important distinction. It isn't that I have a relationship with the Divine that I sometimes lose. But sometimes my relationship includes periods of profound doubt, or my practice is boring. It's just sitting, yet it's an incredibly rich part of my life. I feel it has changed my path in the world and is something I very much want to share with other people.

Part of my life's work is to make Judaism more hospitable to people like me. This is, I think, occurring. But there are dangers, as well. For example, a number of people who can't meditate are actually teaching meditation. This is very disturbing. Very often, these folks who can't meditate teach kabbalistic meditations that induce a high. Another concern is what I call "medicalized meditation." People who offer this strip meditation of its spiritual components and say, "Do this; it will make you feel better. It will reduce your anxiety, and your blood pressure will drop twenty points." But the spiritual component is the doorway to true transformation. Without it, progress cannot be achieved.

Ultimately, enjoy your successes, but do not get too excited by them. Just keep plugging away.

Sylvia Boorstein is a cofounding teacher of Spirit Rock Mediation Center in Woodacre, California, and a senior teacher at the Insight Meditation Society in Barre, Massachusetts. Author of many books on meditation, in *Meditation from the Heart of Judaism: Today's Teachers Share Their Practices, Techniques, and Faith,* edited by Avram Davis, she teaches us about mindfulness.

On Mindfulness

SYLVIA BOORSTEIN

Early on in my mindfulness meditation practice, I spent several weeks in intensive retreat in a monastery in Massachusetts. In the weeks just before that retreat, the entire country had followed the story of a young child with leukemia whose parents, dedicated to alternative healing, had refused to accept conventional treatment for him. The child died. Since childhood leukemia has a high cure rate with modern medicines, I was very upset about what I considered the parents' "attachment to New Age views." I was more than upset; I was mad. "How could they do this?" I thought. I was infuriated, by extension, at everything that I associated with "New Age." I was mad at newsletters and magazines and books and diet regimens and health food stores—I was mad at anything I felt had colluded in forming these parents' attachment to a view I thought had cost the child his life. I also felt righteous in my anger, since I was, at that time, a vegetarian, a yoga teacher, and a meditation practitioner, and I thought I had made my choices wisely, while other people's narrow-mindedness and rigidity were giving my choices a bad name.

I arrived at the retreat troubled by my anger. It continued for days in spite of my attempts to develop composure. I'm fairly sure that the level of my anger was probably also sustained by my fear about what I considered inadequate parenting. At that time, I had young children of my own, and the idea that parents might be so trapped by views that they could make decisions that had such dire consequences frightened me. Every time I remembered the story, my mind filled with anger and indignation and, finally, resentment that these parents, strangers to me, had "destroyed my retreat by their behavior." I felt so burdened that I prayed, "May I be *free* from this painful anger," asking that no reminder of the incident would arise in my mind to trigger another attack of anger.

One afternoon, sitting quietly, in a moment in which my mind was completely resting, an entirely new thought arose: "Those parents must be in terrible pain!" And then: "How are they going to live with themselves?" I was startled to find that my anger had disappeared. I still believed the refusal of medicine was a wrong choice, but I felt sad instead of mad and, at last, compassionate. "What if I made a terrible mistake—even a well-intentioned terrible mistake—with my children? I couldn't bear it."

At the moment of my change of heart, I was so grateful that I didn't think about how or why it had happened. I was just glad to have been set free. It felt like a miracle. I later discovered it is really not a miracle. It's the grace of mindfulness. Mindfulness meditation does not change life. It changes the heart's capacity to accept it. It teaches the heart to be more accommodating, not by beating it into submission, but by developing wisdom.

CULTIVATING A BALANCED AWARENESS

Mindfulness is a natural capacity of mind. It's balanced awareness of the truth of present experience. Our habitual responses to challenge are often flurried and create confusion. Mindfulness *practice* calms and steadies the mind so that confusion is recognized and clarity maintained.

I think of mindfulness as a practice that develops over time, as well as sufficient unto itself in every moment. It's *becoming* wise and *being* wise at the same time. The becoming wise aspect happens gradually. By paying attention calmly, in all situations, we begin to see clearly the truth of life experience. We realize that pain and joy are both inevitable and that they are also both time limited. We discover, more and more often, that struggling with what is beyond our control is extra. It creates suffering. We also discover that kind, considered responses make life manageable and leave room for compassionate response. The being wise part of mindfulness is balanced, alert, non-embittered responsiveness. Each moment of nonstruggle is a moment of freedom, a moment in which the mind, at ease, is able to access the truth of the moment clearly.

Although mindfulness is a natural capacity of the mind, the pressures of daily life often present challenges to seeing clearly. A retreat provides a special opportunity to practice. When I began my practice twenty years ago, I had a family and a professional life that would not support extended periods of intensive meditation, so I incorporated shorter retreat periods into my life. Retreats are simple, nonsectarian, and open to students who are at all levels of experience, since the instructions remain the same throughout practice. Retreatants in a traditional mindfulness retreat spend their days alternating periods of sitting and walking meditation. Students are encouraged to bring calm attention to each moment of experience without adding to it. Often, they are given preliminary instructions that encourage focusing attention on the breath during sitting meditation or on physical sensations while walking. This particular attention to the essentially neutral activities of breathing and walking develops composure in the mind, which then supports the ability to pay balanced attention to the entire range of body and mind experience. When I finally understood that, years after I began meditating, my life became my practice.

MINDFULNESS AS WISDOM PRACTICE

My experience is that mindful awareness provides the context for religious expression. As I have been increasingly able to stay alert and balanced from moment to moment, the truths of impermanence, suffering, and the interconnectedness of all things have been revealed as "insights." As my insight developed, my suffering lessened. As it did,

I became kinder, my prayers became more meaningful, and I have been sustained in my capacity to bless.

Mindfulness cultivates compassion. As I practiced, I saw how the painful habit of clinging mind is very strong. I watched the way my mind made up extra stories, complicating my life and upsetting me unnecessarily. I also saw that even *awareness* of attachment causing suffering did not necessarily end it. I recognized that must be true for everyone and understood that the pain of the world is *enormous*. For some period of time, I was depressed with what seemed to me the inescapable sadness of life, and I felt heartbroken. The result of the heartbreak is that I became more compassionate to myself and to the other people in my life.

I first met Rabbi Mordechai Sheinberger in Jerusalem five years ago. I told him I was a meditation teacher. He asked about my practice and about what I taught. I explained mindfulness. He said, "Well, I'm not a meditation teacher. I teach the path of *mitzvot*." On his suggestion, I read *The Path of the Just*, by Moses Chaim Luzzatto, an eighteenth-century Kabbalist, and found it an elaborate and inspiring framework of guides for behavior, all rooted in kindness. It seemed obvious to me that dedication to *mitzvot* practice requires *incredible* impeccability and scrupulous attention to the intention motivating every act, the basics of mindfulness meditation.

MINDFULNESS, PRAYER, AND MOMENTS OF BLESSING

I trust that prayer is the natural, legitimate, effective response to realizing the incomprehensibility of cosmic design. My prayer life became more real to me as I recognized that the things that made me happy were fundamentally a gift and beyond my control. All my previous hesitations, all my "logical" questions about prayer ("To whom?" "Does it work?") fell away. Prayers—prayers of gratitude and even of supplication—became the voiced (silent or aloud) expression of the truth of my heart.

Judaism is a blessing religion, and mindfulness supports the capacity to bless at all times. Pleasant, fortunate situations inspire automatic blessing as thanksgiving. Painful situations are more challenging. The visceral response to acknowledging pain is recoil, aversion. The *mindful* response is compassion based in the wisdom that in a precise, just cosmos, *everything* is revelation of lawful order. A blessing practice holds the mind steady. A steady mind supports mindfulness. Mindfulness maintains clarity. Clarity reveals the truth of the cause-and-effect structure of creation's interconnectedness, awesome enough to inspire spontaneous blessing. Wisdom is the realm, I believe, in which blessings are kept alive.

Dr. Avram Davis is the founder and co-director of Chochmat HaLev, a center dedicated to Jewish spirituality and meditation. In *Meditation from the Heart of Judaism: Today's Teachers Share Their Practices, Techniques, and Faith,* he teaches us practical ideas and techniques to help us begin to meditate.

Best Practices: A Distillation of Techniques and Outlook

AVRAM DAVIS

Meditation from the Heart of Judaism: Today's Teachers Share Their Practices, Techniques, and Faith is full of many wonderfully cogent and wise ideas and techniques to help us begin to meditate and to orient us along the path of meditation. From these, I have extracted the following list that essentially divides a successful meditation discipline into two key components. The first is developing the right attitude; the second is using the right techniques, especially those that are appropriate for your present state of discipline and practice and your readiness to experience different realms of consciousness. Knowing which techniques to use is most important if you are a relative newcomer to meditation.

Attitude means the way in which we frame our questions and how we answer them or seek answers to them. Without a proper attitude, no technique, no matter how valuable or potent, will have long-lasting worth. And since every technique is essentially anchored in attitude (hopefully a proper one), for that attitude to be strengthened and perpetuated, it must be linked to a strong technique that we practice again and again.

ATTITUDE: OPENNESS, DILIGENCE, HUMOR

- One basic question that helps shape proper attitude is the question of self. When we ask ourselves major questions of life, we should ask, Who's talking and who's listening?

As Lawrence Kushner points out in his teaching, "Silencing the Inner Voice(s)," "The fact that we can hold these interior conversations with our 'selves' means that we are fragmented, alienated, broken. If we were whole, then there could be no conversation because there would be no one else in there to talk to.... Menachem Mendl of Kotzk, a nineteenth-century Hasidic teacher deliberately misreads Deuteronomy 5:5, ...'I stood between God and you.' Menachem Mendl teaches that it is your I, 'your ego that stands between you and God.'"

Since ego is what separates us from God, we must lose ego if we are to make progress in meditation and a spiritual life.

- Divinity can be found in this world, and the mundane can be found in Divinity. Rabbi Rami M. Shapiro, in "The Teaching and Practice of Reb Yerachmiel ben Yisrael," points out that ultimately these two worlds are one, though they often do not appear to be so. Reality is sometimes perceived as being "out there" and other times as "in here." Both are valid. They are simply aspects of the same ultimate reality, and both point to ultimate meaning.

- Trust yourself. The understanding and wisdom brought about by meditation is useful only to the degree that you experience it. It says in the Psalms, "Taste and know that it is good." That is, experience the benefits of meditation yourself before believing anything. Rabbi David A. Cooper forcefully makes this point in his teaching, "The Promise of Jewish Meditation." He writes, "Religious traditions are not built on *intellectual* revelation. They're built on something that happens in the *kishkes* (gut).... Any faith—Judaism or Islam or Buddhism—is based on a personal revelation that profoundly changed someone's life." Trust yourself and your experience. Everything else will follow from this.

- Many of the teachers in this book view Jewish law not as a straitjacket but as a liberating force. One way to think of the law is like art. Shaul Magid, in "Piety Before Ecstasy," writes, "One model to reformulate and renew *halachah* is '*halachah* as art.'"...

Halachah should facilitate the expression of the creative impulse of the Jewish will." Jewish law is not the enemy. Let it become an extension of your will, nothing more. It will serve you well.

- God is *ayin,* nothingness. Nothingness is God. Soul is God, a synonym for nothingness. In his teaching "Why Meditate?" Daniel C. Matt helps us incorporate in our practice the concept that God is nothingness, which is ultimately a synonym for soul. By bringing the mind to a realization of *ayin,* nothingness, we perceive our true self. This true self is the ground of being. It is ultimate reality. Realizing this is essential. First, we realize this in our mind. Then we realize this in our practice. Eventually, the knowledge becomes part of our soul.

- There is a need in meditation, and indeed in one's daily practice, to surrender and let go. There is no way around this. While it is true that we are pressured by the imperative nature of our busy lives, meditation practice insists on a discipline of surrender. In "Meditating as a Practicing Jew," Rabbi Sheila Peltz Weinberg points this out very forcefully: "Meditation is...about letting go: letting go of preconceived ideas and gently bringing oneself into the presence of what is, not what we imagine or remember or desire." This teaching is both an attitude and a technique, for it presumes a constant effort of surrender.

- The ultimate reality is intimate and personal. It is not distant, removed, or mechanical. Many of the teachers in this collection reiterate this point. Andrea Cohen-Keiner, in "Go to Your Self," emphasizes that the universe is found within our own, personal body, only writ small. As she writes, "Meditation can help us get a handle...from which to watch ourselves so we can be more aware about how we react to things." This attitude of self-awareness is an inherent part of the universe. The more we cultivate it within ourselves, the stronger our practice becomes.

- We are what we practice. If we become angry a lot, then essentially we are practicing anger. And we become quite good at it. Conversely, if we practice being joyful, then a joyful person is what we become. We are what we practice. Each of us consciously must decide who and what we want to be—or the circumstances of our life will choose for us.

One way to make such a choice is to calmly be aware of life's situations. By doing this, we begin to clearly see that both pain and joy are inevitable and time limited. We discover that struggling with what is beyond our control causes suffering. We also discover that kind, considered, compassionate response makes life manageable.

- The essence of God's reality is joy and blessing. Rabbi Shohama Wiener, along with several of the other teachers, stresses this teaching. While some spiritual paths say that the world is suffering, this is not the perspective of the Jewish path. It is true that there *is* suffering in the world, but the beauty and joy of God are the more fundamental reality. This is not to discount the pain, but underneath even this is joy.

- Rabbi Rami M. Shapiro teaches in "The Teaching and Practice of Reb Yerachmiel ben Yisrael" that the Infinite is already here. God is outside so that we can draw the Divine inside. God is inside so that we can let the Divine merge with the outside.

- Don't be pretentious. Meditation is not brain surgery. In "Notes from a Beginning Meditation Teacher," Nan Fink gives us permission to experiment with our practice—to take it on a bit at a time or to completely immerse ourselves in it, but to guard against too much self-aggrandizement. The practice is, after all, only to benefit us. The speed by which this occurs is completely up to us.

- Wherever you are, that's where you need to start. As I point out in "Jewish Meditation Today and Its Obstacles," it is important not to get hung up on definitions. Many things are "meditation." Many things help us in the transformation that we need to accomplish. At the same time, give yourself time and space to sit and delve inwardly.

- Be diligent. Practice with humor. Much of the Torah deals with life situations. Many of these are amusing, at least in retrospect.

Try to keep this humor close to hand. But, also practice your meditation with great resolve.

- Meditation does not negate the cognitive. In their teachings, both Susie Schneider and Rabbi Laibl Wolf strive to make this point. The mind informs us and helps direct our actions. But our intellects are not the end-all.

- Problems arise when we seriously engage in a spiritual practice like meditation. There may be such obstacles as feeling a loss of meaning or wondering why you are even bothering to meditate. Rabbi Jonathan Omer-Man points out that this is inevitable and that the difficulties are part of the work. The obstacles themselves, as Omer-Man says in "Noble Boredom," can become "points of transformation." But patience is the quality we must cultivate. Patience with your obsessions, with your foolishness, with your difficulties. Patience to keep on with the work.

- This whole meditation business is really very communal. Rabbi Alan Lew, in "It Doesn't Matter What You Call It," rightly points out that too much solitary meditation opens us to delusions of Self. We can get overly caught up in our own ego machinations. In a group, we are part of a collective, self-monitoring system, and our mistakes will be fewer, our insights deeper.

- Rabbi Lew believes meditation to be, in its deepest sense, a "leave-taking." Feel free to gain insight from meditation, and try to incorporate this insight into your day-to-day living.

- Rabbi Rami M. Shapiro teaches meditation is part and parcel of everyday life. "Doing everyday things with a clear and attentive mind awakens us to the fact that we are both apart from and a part of everything else. We discover that from the perspective of *yesh,* we are unique, irreducible, irreplaceable manifestations of God. We discover from the perspective of *ayin* that we are totally interconnected with and dependent upon all other manifestations of God. We are awake to our being and our emptiness simultaneously. And from this we awake to God, the Source and Substance of both."

TECHNIQUE: DISCIPLINE, STUDY, TRADITION

- Time is a key factor in developing, keeping, and strengthening your spiritual path, as Rabbi David Zeller stresses in his teaching "A Splendid Way to Live." Shabbat, which is a one-day-a-week withdrawal from technology and work, is a very important time to cultivate one's practice in terms of sitting meditation. It is a time to cultivate *midot,* or personal qualities.

  All the teachers in *Meditation from the Heart of Judaism* believe in the need to observe Shabbat gradually, but steadily. Shabbat is all about time, and all meditation, all spiritual practice, and all spiritual improvement ultimately involve time.

- In quiet meditation, let your consciousness ascend into the all-pervading light of the Divine. In his teaching "The Hierarchy of Jewish Meditation," Rabbi Alan Brill directs us to bring this infinite light down, letting it grow and give energy, letting it fill our minds and bodies and wherever we may be. Channel this slowly to avoid being overwhelmed. The purpose of this meditation is to unify the Divine and the mundane.

- The use of specific sounds contributes to advancement of our practice. Repetition of these holy words and sounds is a strong technique. In "Opening the Inner Gates," Dr. Edward Hoffman recommends using the commonly known word *shalom,* which means "peace" or "wholeness." As Hoffman writes, "Begin by saying *'shalom'* aloud a few times, gradually elongating its syllables. Now, find a rhythm that feels comfortable, yet empowering, by adjusting the length of the 'shhhhaaa,' 'lo,' and 'mmmmmm' sounds to your preference. They do not have to be of equal length; each can have varying durations." At the end of this exercise, record your thoughts in a journal. While doing this technique, hold on to a feeling of reverence "for the holiness of our inner world."

- Chanting works. Rabbi Shefa Gold, in her teaching "That This Song May Be a Witness," introduces us to the ecstatic power of chant. Chant has a unique power to open the heart. As Gold writes, "Repetition [of a chant] became a way to still the mind and open the heart so widely that it felt as if the sacred phrases were planting seeds there."

- Rabbi Rami M. Shapiro offers a ten-point outline of practice: meditation, recitation of a sacred phrase, study, focused attention, daily self-assessment of behavior, generosity, random acts of loving-kindness, dream study, ethical consumption of food and other products, and finally, Shabbat.

- A straightforward beginning way to meditate is given by Mindy Ribner in "Keeping God Before Me Always." She suggests that you first sit quietly, regulate your breath, and calm your mind. Tell yourself that this meditation is meant to unite the *yod heh* with *vav heh*, the Divine letters of God's Name. Let yourself picture the connection you are making with all the generations of 5,000 years of Jewish people. All these holy teachers are helping you link together the disparate aspects of God. A beautiful variation on this meditation is to begin with the same relaxing preamble, then open your heart and let the presence of the Divine dwell there. Let yourself feel this presence. Reflect on whether what you want in your life is the same as what God wants for you. From this meditation will arise insights on how to bring God more into your daily life.

  As you sit, thought fragments of the day and emotions will begin to surface in your mind. Perceive each of these clearly, and embrace it with affection, for the mind is not your enemy. Then, let the thought fragment go. In the moment that follows the letting go, there will be an opening and a deepening of consciousness. Dov Baer of Mezritch called this "in-between." It is the doorway to *ayin*, to nothingness. As we deepen this in-between space, true wisdom arises. This wisdom we may call "soul." In her teaching "On Mindfulness," Sylvia Boorstein calls this the place of mindfulness. It is a powerful place. Its cultivation is invaluable for a strong meditation practice.

- Rabbi Alan Lew embraces the insight of direct seeing. For a moment during the day, try to see whatever it is you are dealing with without barrier or illusion. By doing this, "suddenly the street is beautiful and the quality of light is extraordinary...." This is the practice of insightful seeing.

- Rabbi David Zeller in his teaching "A Splendid Way to Live," urges us to see the Divine in the everyday. This is an essential component of meditation: the everydayness of perspective. Each of our emotional traits needs to become "a channel for the highest aspect of that trait—its Godly aspect...." This perspective is not a detachment from the world, but a passionate attachment to all the beauties put on the earth.

- A key teaching from Rabbi Shohama Wiener is to bless what you eat, bless what you drink, bless what you wear, bless your relationships with other people and with nature. Make many blessings every day, Wiener advises in "Healing and Meditation." Jewish tradition says we should make one hundred blessings a day. Saying blessings unites the spiritual and the mundane.

- Tell stories. This deceptively simple recommendation from Rabbi Lynn Gottleib in "Meditation and Women's Kabbalah" is a striking bit of advice. It is simple but goes straight to the root of practice. As Gottleib says, "Telling a story can be compared to building a home or sacred lodge for the imagination. This lodge is a place of giving witness to one's truth, of opening one's voice and body, of surrendering to the story's own transcendent wisdom." Learn the stories of the tradition, and tell them with your own words. Make them your own, and through them your own stories will become avenues of understanding.

- Words have power. Just as there are power "spots" on the planet, so are there power objects or especially powerful images. Words have great power and so do their building blocks, the letters. The Hebrew letters are a powerful lens of meditation. We can use them, each individual, as a meditation object to strengthen our concentration and deepen our insight, for each letter has a resonance unique to it. The tradition considers the letters to be the building blocks of the universe. Rabbi Steve Fisdel is acutely aware of this in his teaching, "Meditation as Our Own Jacob's Ladder." He writes, "The Kabbalists…taught that each of the twenty-two letters of the Hebrew alphabet represents a primal cosmic force that is a fundamental building block of Creation. Each letter is a different light, a different energy. The combination of any group of letters is understood to be an interaction of primal energies, the result of which is the emergence of some specific reality within the universe." Under the tutelage of a trained teacher, use the letters as meditation foci.

- Edward Hoffman and other teachers recommend this beginning meditation: First, relax and let your mind's eye perceive a point of light. Inhale slowly, and draw this light into your body. Feel it circulate through all of your limbs; feel it vitalizing your spirit and emotions. The light will begin to increase in clarity. Inside of your body, let it travel where it will, especially allowing it to fill the places that need healing.

  Exhale, and sense the light leaving through your feet. As it leaves, it removes any tensions and negativities that you may have been harboring, either consciously or unconsciously. Feel yourself becoming refreshed and cleansed.

  Breathe a few more times. With each breath, feel connected to God.

- Meditation does not necessarily mean sitting still. You can meditate standing, walking, dancing, or lying down. It can be done through emotions, thinking, learning, and contemplating and through art, music, or song. The variety of practice exists so everyone can find their own way (or ways) to transform themselves and the world.

- Studying holy texts lets your mind directly access that intense revelation of light and consciousness that happened at Sinai.

Study hard, but deeply. The point of study is not memorization or clever argumentation but to bring you closer to the Divine.

- Sing. Eat. Love. Embrace. Laugh. Cry. Give. Surrender. Sit and contemplate Self. You will find that you will finally be drawn into the silence, a silence that is always singing.

V

So What Do You Do with It?
Why Spirituality Should Be Part of Your Life

Be strong-willed and stubborn
if you want to get closer to God.
How else will you survive all
the difficulties that are sure
to come your way?

• • • •

Don't be frustrated by
the obstacles you encounter on your
spiritual journey. They are there
by design, to increase your desire
for the goal you seek.
Because the greater your goal,
the greater the yearning you'll
need to achieve it.

• • • •

Always remember:
You are never given an obstacle
you cannot overcome.

— from *The Empty Chair: Finding Hope and Joy—*
Timeless Wisdom from a Hasidic Master,
Rebbe Nachman of Breslov

Dr. **Arthur Green**, rabbi, is Lown Professor of Jewish Thought at Brandeis University and former president of the Reconstructionist Rabbinical College in Philadelphia. He is a student of Jewish theology and mysticism who has combined scholarly career and personal commitment. In *These Are the Words: A Vocabulary of Jewish Spiritual Life,* Rabbi Green teaches us about the concept of "repairing the world."

Tikkun 'Olam תיקון עולם

ARTHUR GREEN

Tikkun 'olam, which means "mending the world," is an ancient Hebrew phrase that has taken on new life in the past few decades. Its verbal form is found in the *'alenu* prayer, which concludes every service in the traditional synagogue. There *le-takken 'olam* means "to establish the world in the kingdom of the Almighty *(shaddai),*" or to bring about God's rule on earth. In contemporary usage it refers to the betterment of the world, including the relief of human suffering, the achievement of peace and mutual respect among peoples, and the protection of the planet itself from destruction.

While associating these ideals with *tikkun 'olam* may be a recent innovation, the values themselves are deeply rooted in Jewish tradition. Spreading our most basic moral message—that every person is the divine image *(tselem elohim)*—requires that Jews be concerned with the welfare, including the feeding, housing, and health, of all. The Torah's call that we "pursue justice, only justice" (Deuteronomy 16:20) demands that we work toward closing the terrible gaps, especially in learning and opportunity, that exist within our society and undermine our moral right to the relative wealth and comfort most of us enjoy. The very placing of humans on earth "to work and guard" (Genesis 2:15) God's garden, as well as the *halakhah* forbidding wanton destruction of resources, tell us that protecting the natural order is also a part of that justice.

The rediscovery of ancient spiritual forms in recent decades has paralleled an age of activism for political and social change. In some cases these have been quite separate from, or even opposed to, one another. Many of those attracted to seeking spirituality have given up on the possibility of any serious improvement in the human condition altogether. In the case of Judaism, such a bifurcation of spiritual and sociopolitical concerns is hardly possible. Anyone who tries to undertake it ultimately has to deal with the prophets of ancient Israel, still the strongest and most uncompromising advocates for social justice our world has known. If you try to create a closed world of lovely Jewish piety and build it on foundations of injustice and the degradation of others, Isaiah and Amos will not let you sleep.

Dr. Neil Gillman, rabbi, is Professor of Jewish Philosophy at The Jewish
Theological Seminary in New York, where he has also served as Chair of the
Department of Jewish Philosophy and Dean of the Rabbinical School. In
The Way Into Encountering God in Judaism, Rabbi Gillman teaches us that
we are partners with God in repairing the world.

Partners in Redemption

NEIL GILLMAN

God does not work alone. God depends on humanity for the full
manifestation of God's power. In historical time, God and humanity
are partners in redemption, as in creation and revelation.

The most striking expression of that theme can be seen in the
teachings of the sixteenth-century mystic Rabbi Isaac Luria. Luria,
who lived and taught in the city of Safed in Palestine in the wake of
the expulsion of the Jews from Spain at the end of the fifteenth century, wove ancient rabbinic and mystical traditions into a highly original myth of redemption for a generation of Jews that had once again
tasted the bitter reality of exile and national trauma. These Jews were
confronted, in the starkest way possible, with the fact that the world
that they inhabited was profoundly flawed. Where indeed was God's
redemptive power?

Luria's answer, far too complex to be traced in detail here, centers on the notion that from the very outset, God's entire creation was
flawed. God created the world by emanation out of God's own being,
so to speak, from an original "God-stuff." This emanation was
designed to be contained in "vessels" that God had created so that the
created world would emerge ordered or structured. However, those
vessels were not strong enough to fulfill their assigned role. They
shattered in a primordial catastrophic event, and the sparks of God's
creative impulse came to be scattered throughout the cosmos. This

scattering of the divine sparks accounts for the presence of all evil in the world, both natural evil and historical evil. In effect, the world was born flawed; it emerged broken from God's very hand.

The implication of that creation myth is that God is responsible for the evil in the world, but Luria's theory is even more radical. Since creation occurred as an emanation out of God's own being, the created world, with all its flaws, is at the same time an inherent part of God. Therefore, the flaws in the world are at the same time flaws within God. The world is broken, and so is God. Luria posited that there were two faces to God: God in God's intrinsic essence, which he dubbed *Ein Sof* (literally, "Infinity" or "Without End"), the transcendent or hidden God; and *Shekhinah* (literally, "Presence"), God as immanent, manifest or present in creation. In that primordial catastrophe, these two faces of God were split asunder. Luria called that dislocation in God's being "the Exile of the *Shekhinah*." If Israel is in exile, then so is God.

REPAIRING THE WORLD

To this creation myth Luria now added a myth of redemption. The world needs to be mended or repaired, and so does God. The responsibility for mending the world is assigned to Israel, and the means of accomplishing this mending are the mitzvot, God's commands to Israel. Every mitzvah performed by a Jew, accompanied by the proper inner focus, is redemptive, an act of repairing the world. Since the world and God together form one cosmic system, as we repair the world we also repair the split within God. To use another metaphor, the entire cosmos is one giant pool. Drop a pebble in one corner of the pool, and the ripples affect the entire pool. The material world in which we live is but the outermost edge of this cosmic pool. Performing one simple command affects the entire system, up to and including God.

The Hebrew term for what we call "inner focus" is *kavanah*. Lurianic mystics composed brief liturgical statements, also called *kavanot* (plural for *kavanah*), to be recited before the performance of the commandments to ensure that we will indeed perform these commands with the proper intent—namely, to repair the split within God; reciting the words of these brief prayers serves to focus our thoughts. Before donning the *tallit* (the shawl Jews wear during prayer), for example, Jews were to say: "For the sake of the unification of the Holy Blessed One and His *Shekhinah,* in trembling and in love, to unify the name *Yod Heh* with *Vav Heh* in perfect unity, in the name of all Israel."

This is an incredible statement. First, the name "Holy Blessed One" (in the original Aramaic, *Kudshah Brikh Hu,* or in Hebrew, *Kadosh Barukh Hu*) is one of the traditional names for God. In kabbalistic thought it becomes a synonym for what we called *Ein Sof,* "Infinity," God in God's essence, the transcendent or hidden God. *Shekhinah* is God's presence in and through creation. They are now split apart, but we are about to perform a commandment that will repair or mend that split and unify God.

As the text continues, that responsibility is given even greater emphasis. The four Hebrew letters *Yod, Heh, Vav, Heh* form the Tetragrammaton, the unpronounceable, four-letter name of God, usually rendered in English as YHWH or YHVH (as in "Yahweh" or "Jehovah"). The split in God's nature is reflected in the split between the first two and the last two letters of God's holy name. By performing the command of donning the *tallit,* now with the proper inner focus or intent, we are helping to reunify God's name and, symbolically, the two faces of God.[1]

The conclusion is inescapable. Not only are Jews partners with God in redeeming the world, they are also partners with God in redeeming God. God too needs redemption. There is no more powerful statement of God's dependence on humanity.

Now place this myth of redemption in its historical context. In a very direct way, Jews had just experienced, once again, the full reality of a deeply flawed world. In this context, Luria provides them first with a measure of consolation: you are in exile, but so is God. Second, he provides them with the resources to mend the world and God. These resources are immediately at hand: they are the familiar, day-to-day responsibilities of every Jew, the divine commandments, such as donning the *tallit*. Testimony to the effectiveness of the myth is the fact that within a few generations, it led to one of the most traumatic events in Jewish history, the messianic movement centered on Shabbatai Zevi.

Shabbatai Zevi (1626–1676) was a Turkish Jew who proclaimed himself to be the Messiah, inflamed the Jewish people with his vision that the long-awaited end of days had finally arrived and that redemption was finally at hand, then converted to Islam and plunged the Jewish world into a renewed despair that took generations to overcome. The story of this failed Messiah is long and complex.[2] What is important to us here is its implicit testimony to the effectiveness of Luria's redemptive myth: Jews were fully prepared to believe that their work of repairing the world had accomplished its goal. That Shabbatai Zevi turned out to be a false or failed messiah is another story. The Achilles heel in all myths of redemption is the risk that they may be falsified by history. Myths of this kind are effective as long as they remain visions or dreams, always slightly out of reach. When they become so concrete that they lie within our immediate grasp, they inevitably disappoint. Redemption is always around the corner. The main purpose of the vision is less to forecast events that lie ahead than to make the here and now bearable. The redemptive myth must remain a dream deferred.

Luria's Hebrew term for "repairing" or "mending" the world was *tikkun*. That term has achieved renewed popularity in our own day in the phrase *tikkun olam*—literally, "repairing the world." It is used to characterize social and political activities undertaken by Jewish groups that have the general purpose of making the world a better place. The term itself is ancient. It appears originally in the *Mishnah*, where it is used to justify a series of legal enactments that were promulgated for the public welfare—literally, "in order to repair the world." To give one example, *Mishnah Gittin* 4:3 teaches, "Hillel ordained the *prozbol* in order to repair the world." According to Deuteronomy 15:1–3, in every seventh, or sabbatical, year, all debts are to be remitted. However, the Bible also warns us lest, as the sabbatical year approaches, we avoid lending money to the poor (Deuteronomy 15:9–11). To avoid that eventuality, Hillel, the first-century C.E. rabbinic master, enacted a procedure whereby on the eve of the seventh year the creditor may make a declaration before the court that would insulate his loans from the law of remission. That declaration was called *prozbol* (from the Greek for "before the court"). The purpose of the declaration, then, was broadly redemptive; it was designed to guarantee the availability of loans for the poor.

The phrase occurs in another rabbinic passage, that same closing paragraph of the daily Jewish worship service that concludes with Zechariah's prophecy. The paragraph begins with these words:

> We hope in You, Lord our God, soon to see Your splendor, when You will sweep away idolatry so that false gods will be utterly destroyed, when You will repair the world under Your kingship, so that all of humankind will invoke Your name.

That text, together with its opening paragraph, also dates from the rabbinic period; it was composed as an introduction to the recitation of the passages proclaiming God's sovereignty, part of the High Holiday *musaf* ("additional")—an additional service in the daily morning worship on Sabbaths and festivals. Here, it is God who will in time "repair" the world. In the case of Hillel's *prozbol,* we act to perfect the world. Luria's use of the term takes us far beyond these earlier references. Now repairing the world also effects a repair within God's very being.

THE POWER THAT MAKES FOR SALVATION

For Mordecai Kaplan, redemption defines God. Kaplan was far from enamored of Jewish mysticism. He was far too hard-headed and rational a thinker. However, note two aspects of his thought. First, Kaplan's characteristic definition of God is that God is the power that makes for salvation. Second, recall that Kaplan was a naturalist theologian. God is not a being located in some supernatural realm. Kaplan placed God, this salvational impulse, precisely in the world, in people, in nature, and in history.

Here is one of Kaplan's many definitions of salvation:

> Man, once his physiological needs are satisfied, begins to experience the need to overcome such traits as self-indulgence, arrogance, envy, exploitation and hatred, or to bring under control the aggressive forces of his nature. That constitutes man's true destiny. Therein lies his salvation.[3]

Kaplan characterizes the next step in his argument as "no blind leap into the dark":

> The next step is to conclude that the cosmos is so constituted as to enable man to fulfill this highest human need of his nature.... *The fact that the cosmos possesses the resources and man the abilities—which are themselves part of those resources—to enable him to fulfill his destiny as a human being, or to achieve salvation, is the Godhood of the cosmos.*

The entire world—literally, all there is—is pervaded with an elemental power, force, or impulse that Kaplan likens to a magnetic force and that drives all things to achieve perfection. That power is itself God; it is not caused by God, not created by God; it *is* God. This God is most immediately experienced within us—within our hearts, our minds, and our behavior—precisely at those moments when we strive to banish "those aggressive forces" of our nature. True, that very same power exists outside us, where it serves to complement human efforts, but without our efforts there is no salvation. The world may furnish us with the resources to conquer disease, but without scientists to work with these resources, cures will never result. The resemblance to Luria's mystical myth is uncanny.

The parallels between Luria and Kaplan are even deeper, for in the present time, in history, Kaplan's God's redemptive power is not yet fully manifest. Kaplan's God is not all-powerful. The world may well be infused with this power that makes for salvation, but other powers are also at work in the world: counter-salvational impulses, the powers of chaos and anarchy. We may have found a cure for polio, but what about AIDS? Kaplan's God needs redemption, too. Again, it is humanity that can help to achieve God's own redemption.

We are left with the inescapable conclusion that the image of God portrayed in Jewish sources is very different from the popular conventional image. We were all trained to believe that God, at least, has it all together. This is not so, say our sources. In theory it may be true, but in practice it is not. The God that we experience is a God who needs humanity to achieve God's own purposes. This is a God who is frustrated, who dreams for humanity and the world, who is rebuffed but returns again and again, with infinite yearning, pleading for our help to achieve God's purposes and our own as well. That may well be God's most striking tribute to us.

Rabbi Levi Meier, Ph.D., clinical psychologist and biblical scholar, is chaplain of Cedars-Sinai Medical Center in Los Angeles. In *Ancient Secrets: Using the Stories of the Bible to Improve Our Everyday Lives,* Rabbi Meier teaches us about the concept of the choices we make in Judaism.

Choices

LEVI MEIER

Moses continues, *"and you shall love the lord your God with all your hearts, and with all your soul and with all you have."*

Wait a second. Did Moses say "hearts"—plural? His words in Hebrew are next to impossible to translate accurately into English. But to anyone who knows Hebrew, the Bible's unusual spelling of this word is arresting and puzzling.

The Hebrew word for "heart" consists of two letters—*l'v*—not coincidentally, I think, related in sound to the word "love." But in this passage the word is written *l'vv.*

What could that possibly mean? A human being has only one heart. What is Moses really trying to say with "all your hearts"?

Yes. In truth, he means something even deeper than that. Moses is talking about a single heart that has two sides: one in the light and one in the shadow, one inclined to good, one to evil. These two sides constantly remind human beings of their gift of free will and the inevitable struggles that accompany it. So it has been since the dawn of human history.

Even as he is speaking to the people in what is to be the final year of his life, Moses thinks back to the beginning of all that has been written in the five books. He thinks back to the story of creation.

Everything on this earth was created with a dual aspect. Ever since human beings experienced that split, they have struggled to understand both it and its reason for being. The famed philosopher Georg W. F. Hegel expressed it in terms of "thesis" and "antithesis." Hermann Hesse wrote about it beautifully in his *Narcissus and Goldmund*:

> All existence seemed to be based on duality, on contrast. Either one was a man or one was a woman, either a wanderer or a sedentary burgher, either a thinking person or a feeling person—no one could breathe in at the same time as he breathed out, be a man as well as a woman, experience freedom as well as order, combine instinct and mind. One always had to pay for the one with the loss of the other, and one thing was always just as important and desirable as the other.

This is what Moses is reminding us. At the first moment of human history, when man and woman were placed in the Garden of Eden, they were confronted with two trees—and a choice. Ever since then, such has been the human condition. Temptation—the serpent—always plays a role. And we live and die by our choices. Spiritually speaking, we choose life or death at every juncture.

We might ask, then, Why is it so hard to make the right choice, since the Bible instructs us to choose life every time? If it were that simple, it would not be a real choice. The choice the serpent presents is, on its face, always very appealing, very attractive. Only when we think about the *consequences* of following the evil inclination do we pause, and it is that pause that initiates the struggle.

No one is immune to this struggle, and no one succeeds in making the right choice each and every time. Indeed, it has been said that there is no great person who hasn't made a mistake. I would add that there is no great person who hasn't made a great mistake. This is simply because great people choose to take great risks, and implied in each great risk are choices, one or more of which are sure to lead in the wrong direction.

Often the choices we are called on to make are subtle. The evil inclination doesn't always masquerade as a seductive sex partner. Sometimes the evil inclination even masquerades as a good deed.

When a husband invites company to dinner without first checking with his wife, is he responding to the good inclination to love his neighbor or to the evil inclination to disregard his wife's feelings? Scratch the surface of a dilemma like that, and you are bound to find that the people invited to dinner were likely to advance the husband's business or perhaps that he needed to make himself feel good by his spontaneous invitation—at the expense of his wife's feelings.

As a psychologist, I am not immune to this dilemma. There is a joke in my profession that we would all rather work with a "YAVIS," an acronym that describes a patient who is young, attractive, verbal, intelligent, and successful. No one wants to struggle with an "OUNDUF," a patient who is old, ugly, nonverbal, dumb, and a failure. Yet quite possibly, the latter is the one who needs a psychologist more.

How do you see the good in what appears unattractive and the evil in what is sexy and seems good? When you recognize and embrace that which is not so good and not so appealing within yourself, when you learn to love yourself, you will see those around you through different eyes. This is because recognizing the good and the evil inclinations has a great deal to do with how you perceive things.

Moses is well aware of this reality. Some in his audience, who have seen only the worst in everything, will never reach the Promised Land as a consequence of their complaints and lack of faith. He is well aware that many of those who will be reading his words in the generations to come will be like these people. For reasons of their own making, or perhaps due to circumstances beyond their control, they will also be far from the Promised Land. So he is trying to teach that how you see things is everything. Again, there is a choice. And the choice of what you perceive and how you perceive is yours. It is an important choice, because your perception of the reality around you determines how you will act.

I try to teach patients that the duality that defines all creation extends to reality as well. We all operate in two realities. There is the physical reality based on our five senses: touch, sight, hearing, taste, and smell. And there is the psychic reality based on our inner selves: imagination, intuition, and soul. When the physical reality is unbeatable, it is possible for us to call on the psychic reality to get us through.

The wonderful thing about the psychic reality is that it travels with us wherever we go. It is just as real as our physical reality. A Promised Land of the imagination has no geographic boundaries. It is not like a house, filled with many possessions, that cannot be picked up and transported along with us. Possessions can be stolen or destroyed, but the psychic reality can never be taken from us.

One of the great lessons that Moses is teaching us is that, like the psychic reality, religion is portable. The Ark of the Covenant, which held the tablets on which were written the Ten Commandments, was designed and built with handles so that it could be carried along as the people traveled through the wilderness. Even after the destruction of the Temple, when the Ark disappeared, the loss was not insurmountable. By then, everyone had committed the Ten Commandments and their meaning to memory. The words of God, as spoken to Moses, were indelibly engraved in the psychic reality of his descendants. All that remains is making the choice to access the inner sanctuary, where the Ark is stored.

So the point is made: Life is about choices. But there is more to this biblical lesson. Choices make us aware of the duality in which we live, in which we were created. But we also know that God is one. So we learn that our mission is to make this duality into a unity, a oneness. The task implied in Moses's instruction is to love God with both sides of your heart. We are somehow to love God with both our good inclination and our evil inclination. We are charged to remember that both were created by God and that both have a purpose.

The Jewish festival of Purim celebrates this idea. On Purim, one is commanded to get so drunk that one doesn't know the difference between "Blessed be Mordechai" (the hero of the Book of Esther) and "Cursed be Haman" (the villain). Why? Because evil has a purpose. Pain and death often cause us to think more deeply about who we are and what we are doing with our lives. Were it not for evil, how many of us would be stirred to action? Most of us would sit around in comfort, luxuriating in our apathy. Were it not for the visible presence of evil in the world, how many of us would work to combat it, whether in our world or in ourselves?

The challenge of loving God with our evil inclination is to find a way for it to serve good. If you are a hot-tempered person, why not use your anger to fight injustice? Your hot temper will find itself turning to passion for the cause you advocate.

That is what it means to serve God with all your hearts. That is what it means to serve God with all you have. All you need to do is set your imagination to work to figure out how you, too, can accomplish this within your own reality. The first step is making a choice to do so. I can't put it better than Moses did himself: *"I have put before you life and death, blessing and curse.... Choose life!"*

Dr. Avram Davis is the founder and co-director of Chochmat HaLev, a center dedicated to Jewish spirituality and meditation. In *The Way of Flame: A Guide to the Forgotten Mystical Tradition of Jewish Meditation,* he teaches us that spirituality and life are one.

Confronting Our Borders: Spirituality and Life Are One

AVRAM DAVIS

Each of us places borders around the vision of the Infinite. For borders help us to say what a thing is by their ability to also say what it is not. For example, every day in a traditionalist's life, a prayer is recited. This is the *Sh'ma Yisroel Adonai Elohenu Adonai Echad:* "Hear, O Israel, the Lord Our God the Lord Is One." The *Sh'ma* seeks to help trigger a deep awareness that all of the world is interwoven and without division, in spite of what our senses tell us. That is, the God (the totality of things) is One. Indeed, the *Sh'ma* is a meditation that insists ultimately that separation is illusion.

Yet even illusion has reality, and recognizing this forces us to recognize that our visions always contain borders. That is, as members of society we do live according to divisions we have created. We act based on choices concerning right and wrong, good and bad. But the Jewish tradition insists we should not accept these divisions as the deepest reality; they are, rather, a *disguised* reality. These guises are the *klippot,* the shells masking the inner reality of endless light.

And because our borders are ultimately *klippot,* they need to be tested regularly. The Nikolsburger rebbe would often use the sacrifice of Isaac as a teaching tool. "Look here," he would say. "God spoke to Abraham and commanded him to sacrifice the boy. So what's the big deal that he went and tried to do it?" The assumption being that if the Force of the Universe speaks to you and commands you, how can you possibly refuse?

Then the Nikolsburger rebbe would pause theatrically and answer, "All the previous enlightenment Abraham had achieved meant nothing at that moment, for every person constantly is confronted with their own limits. It does not matter whether we are on a high rung or a low one. Our test will be directed at exactly the place we are. This was the test for Abraham. All of his past holy deeds helped him not at all. Stripped of everything, each serious test forces us to confront the Force that makes the tests in the first place."

This is the nature of *avodah,* of constant practice.

We may become discouraged by our limits from time to time. My father used to tell me a story that may be helpful here. There was once a minister of state whom the king ordered to be executed. The minister threw himself at the king's feet and told him of a wonderful wooden horse he had that with the proper preparation could be made to fly.

"Bring me this magic horse," thundered the king, "and have him fly!"

"Oh, I cannot, Your Majesty," replied the minister, who explained that he needed a quiet place to make this miracle occur. "Lock me in a tower for safekeeping, if you wish, Your Majesty," he said, "but for peace of mind I need the food and companionship I am used to."

"And how long before the horse flies?" asked the king.

"About seven years, Your Majesty." And so the king ordered it done. The minister's friends came to visit him in the beautiful and sumptuous tower that was his new home. "What are you doing?" they asked incredulously. "There is no way you can succeed at your work."

He replied, "Within seven years the king may die; there may be a revolution. And who knows—I might make that damned horse fly!"

Indeed, we may be able to make the damned horse fly! This is the vision of the Infinite, without borders. There is no end to what is possible, given a passionate and God-intoxicated heart. And to let this awakening to the Infinite happen to us—this is certainly within our power.

Each soul, reflected in the personality, has its bright gifts as well as its limitations. Our goal is to integrate both our strengths and weaknesses into our practice, to direct them toward enlightenment. Each of our borders, each of our *klippot,* must be woven with every other piece of the self. This weaving together of body, mind, and heart is part of the task of our *avodah.* No part of our soul can be cut off or discarded, no part of the deep structure that makes us *us* can be torn away. Each part must be *coaxed* into the weave of the whole. It must be *caressed* toward a greater and more proper use of its talents. It must be seduced. Then the borders we have placed around enlightenment will naturally expand, leading us further and further toward the Infinite.

We can so easily get caught up in our distinctions, in the borders we draw around the Infinite One. There is a Yiddish expression: *A grosser bord makht nit a Yid,* a big beard doesn't make a Jew. Modern life tends to see a split between everyday life and the eternal. Religion stands against this splitting. For it is also possible to see the great harmony, the great interweaving. Spirituality and life are one. Our *whole life* is the dance! The Rebbe Shlomo Carlebach often shouted at his Chasidim in the room, "Drunken! You must be drunk! It's in your heart! I need Chasidim who are drunk with love!" Drunk with love, we open our hearts, and love spills across the borders, across the splits between self and other, everyday and sacred.

Just as the infinite is borderless, there is no limit to the amount of love we can give and receive. The Torah path commands us to love. It is the second statement of the *Sh'ma:* "And you shall love God with all your heart and might and strength...." But this is a strange command, really. How can we be commanded to love? We can be asked, cajoled—but ordered? Yet it is considered the fundamental principle of Torah. "You shall love your neighbor as yourself." But what if your neighbor is a fiend, a horror? We can answer this only with the admonition to look deeper. Every soul is a fragment of the Infinite. Each soul is a candle flame lit from the great sun of the Infinite One.

And as it has been said, should we not love and feel compassion for such a pure thing that has become lost amid the shells of illusion?

Love your neighbor as yourself. This is a command to test the borders. It is a very active command. It seeks to reaffirm the fundamental connection among all aspects of creation. But this is not to say, Be passive in the face of oppression!

The Jewish path is neither passive nor pacifist. One must respond to oppression and cruelty. We live in the universe of *Assiyah*, the realm of making, and we are called upon to be co-creators with God in this creation. Creation may require destruction—that is, proper and forceful action. A story illustrates this: Once a young woman came to her teacher and told him that every morning, as the group went into prayers, a young yeshiva student would get behind her and grope her. She was uncertain how best to deal with this. The master stroked his beard for a moment. "My friend," he said, "you should fill your heart with love, then turn around and deck him!"

BEYOND THE BORDERS

The Jewish tradition has defined enlightenment in many different ways. There are aspects of the tradition that understand it supernaturally, as outside everyday consciousness, and other aspects that describe it purely psychologically, as an inner process. These definitions are not always kept separate; the psychological is often seen as an attribute of the supernatural and vice versa.

The Baal Shem Tov used to teach that where our mind is, that's where we are. This is a statement he repeated many times. His meaning was straightforward. We create a heaven or a hell every moment. But this creation arises from our own perception.

When the sage Hanina ben Tradyon was being martyred, his disciples gathered around him and pestered him. "What do you see, master?" they cried.

Hanina ben Tradvon had been wrapped in scrolls of Torah and was being burned. He called out, "The parchment burns, but the letters fly up to heaven!"

We know that during the Holocaust, many Chasidim sang and danced on the way to the gas chambers. Where did this spirit come from? What was their motivation? I do not mean to advocate senseless frivolity in the face of pain or anguish. But these stories point out that the world has many layers. Where we place our consciousness is the key to where we ourselves *are*.

To put it differently: The Baal Shem Tov, in teaching that we are where our minds are, was saying that in one moment we can be totally enlightened. And in the next moment we can fall away from it. Life's distractions are many, but the rewards are great. One may fall away from enlightenment in an instant, but it takes only another instant to regain it.

There is a story: Once there was a fish who started wondering, where was the ocean? She had heard all her life about the ocean and how we are born and die in it—how it surrounds us and how, when we surrender to it, we gain enlightenment. All this sounded very exciting to her, and she was determined to find it. So she swam from sea to sea, asking everyone she met whether they knew where to find the ocean. As far as I know, she is swimming still.

Finally, all that is required of us is to open ourselves to the ocean around us—to taste it and know that it is good. All viewpoints within the Jewish tradition agree to this. Enlightenment is; all we have to do is open up to it and let it fill us.

It has been described in our tradition that God is the infinite light and our soul is like a prism. Hold a prism up to the sun, and it will fill with innumerable permutations of light. Each prism moves light in different ways. In the same way, each person catches the Infinite differently. And this difference, from person to person, is very important to keep in mind.

I believe the Torah calls us to reunite with the Infinite Mother, the *Ayn Sof*. By opening ourselves to God, we are linking our drop of divinity with the Infinite One. The Jewish path advocates a life—and ultimately an enlightenment—in which a person lives fully in the world, savoring it, loving it, engaging *passionately* with it. Our task is not to remove our attachments to the world but to strengthen them—strengthen them in a true way, not simply in a way that increases the power of the ego. Each obstacle and each joy are equally gifts of the Infinite. For we have it within our grasp, through our own effort, to elevate our souls and open them to the grand and sweeping melody of God.

Dr. Wayne Dosick, rabbi, is spiritual guide of the Elijah Minyan in San Diego, California, and an adjunct professor of Jewish studies at the University of San Diego. Author of many books on spirituality and living Jewishly, in *The Business Bible: 10 New Commandments for Bringing Spirituality & Ethical Values into the Workplace,* Rabbi Dosick teaches us spiritual techniques to transform our work and our working environment.

Managing and Leading

WAYNE DOSICK

As a manager striving to be a true leader, you accomplish the most when you *walk humbly,* when you are modest and unpretentious, when you leave pride and arrogance and power trips at the front door.

A man who pursued honors came to Rabbi Bunam and said, "My father has appeared to me in a dream and told me that I am to be a leader of men."

Rabbi Bunam listened to the story in silence.

Soon afterward the same man returned to the rabbi and said, "I have had the same dream night after night. My father appears to me to announce that I am destined to be a leader of men."

"I understand," said the rabbi, "that you are ready to become a leader of men. Now if your father comes to you in a dream once more, tell him that you are prepared to become a leader of men, but that he should now also appear to the people you are supposed to lead to tell them."

No memo from headquarters, no unilateral declaration, no interdepartmental power struggle, no office coup, ever created a true leader.

You can never become a true leader by foisting yourself on others, by flaunting power, by demanding loyalty.

Rather, you can rise to leadership through quiet determination, gentle persuasion, humble presence.

You can become a true leader when you *earn* the respect, the allegiance, and the admiration of those you seek to guide.

You can become a true leader when you truly understand that your power comes not from those who appoint you, not from your own sense of self-importance, but from the permission, acceptance, and grace of those you lead.

You can become a true leader when you understand the wisdom of the ancient sage who said, "I have learned much from my teachers, even more from my colleagues, but from my students, I have learned the most."

One day a recently appointed vice president was called into the office of the chairman of the board.

The chairman said, "I have some troubling news to tell you. Your people have been complaining about you. They say that you are aloof and unreachable; they say that you do not listen to their ideas; they say that you do not make time to work with them and help them. They say that you just sit in your office, talk on your telephone, and go out for long lunches with your friends."

The vice president was stunned by the accusations and began to protest his innocence.

So the chairman of the board took the vice president over to the window and said, "Look out there. What do you see?"

The vice president looked and replied, "I see people out on the street."

Then, the chairman took the vice president over to a mirror hanging on the wall. "What do you see now?" he asked. The vice president looked into the mirror and said, "Now I see myself."

"Ah," said the chairman. "In the window there is glass, and in the mirror there is glass. But the glass of the mirror is covered with a little silver. No sooner has the silver been added—no sooner do you have position and power, some fame and some fortune—then you cease to see others, but see only yourself."

When you walk humbly, you understand that the very best leader is, in reality, the very best servant.

And you can be the best manager, the best leader, when you serve selflessly and with a full heart, when you care for and cherish your people, when you meet their needs as if they were your very own.

One of the greatest leaders who ever lived was Moses.

Following the dictates of God, Moses confronted Pharaoh, brought the ten plagues upon Egypt, freed his people from bondage, and led them across the Red Sea. He stood with them in battle against foes who tried to destroy them. He climbed to the top of the mountain to receive the Law. He guided his people on the long journey in the wilderness.

Through it all he patiently listened to the cries of the people when they complained about lack of food, lack of water, lack of comfort.

One day the people cried out more bitterly than ever before. They were thirsty, so thirsty, and there was no water. They came to Moses. "Find us water," they cried, "lest we die here in the desert."

Moses turned to God. "What shall I do?" he asked. "Where will I find water for these thirsty people?"

And God said, "Speak to that rock over there, and it will bring forth water."

But Moses did not speak to the rock. Instead he hit it with his staff. Water gushed forth, and the people drank and were satisfied.

But God was very angry. He said to Moses, "I told you to speak to the rock, but instead you hit it. You must be punished. Moses, you will not be able to enter into the Promised Land."

Not enter the Promised Land? Just for hitting the rock? After all he did for his God and his people, Moses is to be denied the prize, the payoff, the reward for all his labors?

It seems grossly unfair.

But the real problem was not that Moses had hit the rock, or even that he had disobeyed God's instructions.

What happened was that Moses was exhausted, "burned out," angry, from the people's constant complaints and never-ending demands. Rather than being able to speak to the rock—as he knew he should do, and as he knew would bring result—he struck out at it in frustration and fury.

Moses could not lead the people into the Promised Land, not because he had hit the rock but because he no longer possessed the qualities of leadership. He had forgotten to do justly, love mercy, and walk humbly.

You are a Moses. For you—like every person—want to enter the promised land of your own desires in your own lifetime.

Like Moses, you can be denied the ultimate prize of satisfaction and fulfillment in your work if you forget what it takes to be a real leader.

Or you can lead the way into the promised land of accomplishment and success—bringing with you all the people with whom you work—if only you will remember the words of David Wolpe, in his book *The Healer of Shattered Hearts:* "For each of us, the question is not how we slay the dragon, but how we tend the sheep."

The promised land awaits you. The sheep await their shepherd.

Rabbi Jeffrey K. Salkin is spiritual leader of The Community Synagogue in Port Washington, New York. In *Being God's Partner: How to Find the Hidden Link Between Spirituality and Your Work*, Rabbi Salkin teaches how we can smuggle religion into work.

Smuggling Religion into Work

JEFFREY K. SALKIN

The greatest window into the rabbinic way of understanding work is through the rabbis' vocabulary. One word, *avodah*, came to mean not only "work," but also prayer, Torah study, and sacrifices in the ancient Temple in Jerusalem. What all these meanings had in common was their potential ability to lift each of us out of ourselves and to let us touch something deeper and higher in the world.

Maimonides, the great medieval sage, taught that we should equally divide our time among (1) studying Torah; (2) earning a livelihood; and (3) necessary physical activities, such as eating and sleeping. He never questioned that studying Torah took precedence over the other two.

The ancient rabbis elevated work to the level of a *mitzvah* (a holy obligation) since the Torah commands "six days you shall labor" before it demands that we rest on the Sabbath. They said that a father was obligated to teach his son a trade: "Whoever does not teach his son a trade has taught him robbery." These sages had "real" jobs: Hillel was a woodcutter; Shammai, a builder; Rabbi Joshua, a blacksmith; Rabbi Hanina, a shoemaker. They understood the scruffy, gritty, workaday world because they worked in it; they recognized its limits and their responsibility to it. When, for instance, some rabbis were discussing how the world had been created, they said, "Let us go ask Rabbi Joseph the Builder, for there is no one better versed in these matters."

They found the rabbi working on some scaffolding. "I cannot go down to answer," he said, "for I was hired by the day and my time belongs to my employer."

Rather than answering obscure questions about the origins of the cosmos, Rabbi Joseph knew that his job—*at that particular moment*—was to be engaged in the seemingly mundane world of work. Rather than engage in games of intellectual speculation, as a builder he could imitate and complete, in his limited way, God's work of creation.

The way of Shimon bar Yochai—the way of the cave and of withdrawal from the material world—never became the way of Judaism. *Parnassah,* or material benefit that is honestly gained and never placed at the center of one's being, is part of the Jewish people's spiritual vocabulary. To them, money and possessions were never a curse, as they were considered by more mystical religions in the ancient Near East. Instead, Judaism taught that money, possessions and work were essentially *neutral,* yet eminently powerful in their ability to transform or destroy. All three could be used to improve the world. Even on Yom Kippur, the holiest day of the year, Jews reflect upon the material world. And even as God opens the Book of Judgement, the Holy One also opens the *sefer parnassah,* a book of economic and material welfare, and Jews pray to be inscribed in it as well.

> The ineffable Name of God: We have forgotten how to pronounce it. We have almost forgotten how to spell it. We may totally forget how to recognize it.
>
> *(Abraham Joshua Heschel)*

For many people, "work" and "spirituality" negate and contradict each other; they are polar opposites that come from two entirely different universes.

Such individuals may be well-versed in the concept of "work": They do it almost every day. But they do not properly understand the concept of "spirituality." To them, "work" is wholly practical, rooted in the necessities of this world and geared toward providing for self and family. "Spirituality," on the other hand, is otherworldly, ethereal and has little bearing on what seems to be one of the most mundane, demanding and unavoidable aspects of our lives: Our jobs and our professions.

For them, the concept of spirituality has to be reconstructed, almost from the ground up. These doubters have to reorient themselves to spirituality's surprising practicality, to its broad applications to every facet of our lives, and to the surprising symmetry it has with work.

But this is hard for many of us to believe. That difficulty arises because of our preconceived notions about the nature of spirituality, work, and "the real world."

As a rabbi, I have heard many misconceptions from lay people about spirituality. Below are some of the most frequently voiced opinions about spirituality—and how I respond to them.

Work is about being active. Isn't spirituality basically a passive stance towards the world?

Sometimes, but *only* sometimes.

By "passive" spirituality, I mean those moments when God's light and grace seem to flow almost on their own volition into our lives. Some of this is admittedly "foxhole" theology, a faith that comes upon you in the midst of a crisis or an emergency: "I was almost run over by a car, but God saved me" or "I was sure my baby would die of pneumonia, but something stronger than medicine saved her."

Such a moment of faith is very Jewish. It is the faith of Moses, who, upon asking God, "Let me see your glory [*kavod*]!" hears God responding, "I will let all my goodness pass before you." *Kavod* is usually translated as "divine glory," but a better translation is "a moment of divine, ineffable wonder."

This is also the faith of the Psalmist, who often speaks of God's miraculous redeeming presence. On a communal level, it is the events that we commemorate on a holiday such as Passover (and to a lesser extent on Purim) when the entire Jewish people felt God's power in history.

But spirituality is more than feeling that you have been temporarily lifted from the mundane world. Spirituality is *active* as well as *passive*. This means that we search for and intentionally *create* moments and possibilities in which our eyes open to a reality that is beyond us, yet very much part of us.

No wonder many of us have trouble relating spirituality to work. If we think that work is active, and that spirituality is passive, how can work be spiritual? But *if* we realize that we can be active agents of God in the world, then we can fulfill some of our Jewish duties even while we're on the job.

I've had spiritual experiences and feelings, but I only know about them after they've happened. You can't really plan for this to happen—certainly not in your work.

This is 20-20 hindsight spirituality. *Something* may have connected us to a higher and deeper reality, but the experience came, it went, and now it's gone. The next time it comes will be truly wonderful, but one can't really make it happen.

Yet, it is possible to create a mindset, an attitude, a posture that will help us experience the world anew—and not merely *ruminate* upon a past experience that was uplifting. It is also possible to *plan* to experience something, such as work, spiritually.

One thing we can do is to *reframe* our experiences. This means that we choose to interpret our experiences so that we see them as pathways to God. I believe that Judaism wants it no other way. Hasidic masters inserted meditations *(kavannot)* throughout the texts of their prayer books. These were intended to focus worshippers' minds and souls on the essence of the immediate spiritual task. Everything we do is subject to contemporary *kavannot* that can help us focus on the higher implications of our actions.

Such focusing, of course, means being radically open to such experiences and having a vivid, creative imagination. Abraham H. Maslow, the pioneering humanistic psychologist, called mystical, illuminating, transcendent moments "peak experiences." Spirituality brings peak experiences to everyday life; it is the ability—and the desire—to find those junctures where our reality and God's reality intersect; it is learning how to feel God in every part and every moment of our life.

How can we talk about God being in our work if spirituality happens in the "other" world, not in this world?

"Spirituality" is not the opposite of "worldliness." We should not let our heads soar into the clouds if our feet are not anchored on the ground. To do so is to lose any sense of mundane reality—a reality that we need to survive in this world. We do not need to flee to other worlds to feel the presence of God: Holiness exists in *this* world and in the rhythms of daily existence.

Hasidism teaches the doctrine of *avodah be-gashmiyut*, of worshipping God through such physical acts as eating, drinking, sex, and even through the way we conduct business. Consciousness about such seemingly mundane acts lets us redeem the sparks of holiness that are present in the world; it prevents us from succumbing to the dangers of an overwrought spirituality that distances us from the realities of existence.

Perhaps the most potent lesson of Jewish spirituality is that redemption resides in *this* world. As the late Jewish theologian Abraham Joshua Heschel wrote, "God will return to us when we shall be willing to let Him in—into our lands and our factories, into our Congress and clubs, into our courts and investigating committees, into our homes and theaters." Heschel found spirituality in political action. Walking alongside Martin Luther King, Jr., in Selma, Alabama, he felt, for example, that "my feet were praying." Deuteronomy 30:12 also tries to keep our spiritual feet on the ground: "It [the Torah and God's teachings] is not in the heavens." *It* is in every moment of our lives, in our every action, in our work.

Isn't spirituality about emotion? And isn't work about the rational mind?

Some people define spirituality as "religion *plus* emotion." *Religion* in one's work is hard enough. But *emotion?* Many people believe that work can't be about emotion. As a doctor told me, "You'll lose your mind if you do nothing but *feel* all the time at work. Sometimes work just *has* to be routine." Moreover, in the compartmentalized way that we sometimes view the world, *work* is the rational arena and *religion* is the place where emotions take over. Mixing the two would be a categorical violation of the highest order.

Some people might argue that totally severing our emotions from our work would make us even more effective in our careers. But would it be worth it?

I don't think so. Such a severing of emotions from the work world would only further contribute to the mind/body split so common today. Jewish spirituality asks us to strive to be like God, to be *echad,* "one," just as God is One. By attempting to experience God in our work, we affirm that no sector of everyday experience is aloof from the divine.

I could find spirituality in "the real world," but it's a little scary.

As a doctor once told me, "You can find spirituality in your work. I do all the time. But a lot of people fear being *overwhelmed* by spirituality, and they automatically detach themselves from the potential spiritual experience in their work. Let's face it: Your ability to function credibly at work means leaving spirituality behind. You must set limits for yourself, or that spirituality will truly devour you."

Almost from its beginnings, Judaism acknowledged this fear of being spiritually overwhelmed. When Moses encountered God's presence in the burning bush, he "hid his face because he was afraid to look at God" (Ex. 3:6). Elsewhere, God told Moses: "No one can see My face and live" (Ex. 33:20). To be in God's presence was frightening. It still is frightening. We cower at the possibility at the same time that we seek it.

But can we *increase* such moments of closeness? And can they occur not only before bushes that burn, but also in the office?

WE CAN RE-BUILD MEANING IN OUR LIVES

Our ultimate mission is to become what Judaism calls *hamavdil beyn kodesh la-chol:* To make a difference between that which is already holy and that which, with a little effort, can become holy.

Some of the best, most powerful religious stories are paradoxical tales of people finding non-religious ways to express their faith. The Jewish theologian Martin Buber told of the little boy who brought his flute to play in the synagogue to show his devotion to God. It was the only thing that he knew how to do well. Some people can only work and make money. It is not the worst thing in the world to offer to God. Work, indeed, can be a very worthy offering to God.

After the Romans destroyed Jerusalem in 70 C.E., the sages of the beleaguered Jewish people fled to Yavneh, a small town in western Israel. There, they had a saying: "I am God's creature, and my fellow is God's creature. My work is in the city, and his *[sic]* work is in the country. I rise early for my work, and he rises early for his work. Just as he does not presume to do my work, so I do not presume to do his work. Will you say I do much and he does little?... One may do much or one may do little, it is all one, provided he directs his heart to heaven."

The ancient sages sought a place in which to re-create Judaism and re-build meaning in their lives. But they also knew that *all work*—not just theirs—can be a source of holiness and that everyone has a task in God's divine plan.

Today's Jews are also living after a great destruction: the Holocaust. But the modern world knows of another destruction, one less bloody but no less traumatic: the destruction of meaning and value. Today, meaning itself must be reconstructed by finding spirituality in everyday experiences.

"Where is God?" asks a Hasidic teaching. "Wherever you let God in," comes the answer.

God wants to be allowed into our lives. Not only that, but God *needs* to enter the many hours and the many thoughts and the many worries that we devote to our work. Our careers consume much of our strength and our time and our creativity, but they must never consume us. If that occurs, we are dead to ourselves, to our colleagues at work, to our family at home.

One way to wake up to ourselves, to be truly alive, is to ask ourselves, as the Hasidic rebbe had the night watchman ask him, "Who do you work for?"

When the answer is clear, we will still work—for that is our purpose in life. But we will do it with a pure heart and with a more playful (and a more prayerful) soul.

Lee Meyerhoff Hendler is a popular and inspiring lecturer on leadership, Jewish identity, and intergenerational philanthropy. Formerly president of her congregation, she serves on several local and national Jewish organization boards, and is involved in her family's philanthropic activities. In *The Year Mom Got Religion: One Woman's Midlife Journey into Judaism*, she teaches us the practical aspects of leading a spiritual life.

Spirituality, Schmerituality: Getting There through Deeds

LEE MEYERHOFF HENDLER

Effort is its own reward. We are here to do. And through doing to learn; and through learning to know; and through knowing to experience wonder; and through wonder to attain wisdom; and through wisdom to find simplicity; and through simplicity to give attention; and through attention to see what needs to be done....

(Pirke Avot V:27)

I admit it. I don't like the word "spirituality." I mistrust it. I'm not even sure what it means, but I know I resent it when people assume their understanding of it is the same as mine. "Oh, Lee's on a spiritual quest," they declare, as if they were describing an adolescent's attempt to "find herself." Consigning me to that category conveniently explains my engagement with Judaism, making it intensely personal and, therefore, entirely capricious. They exile me to the land of self-absorption, when, in fact, what I think I am doing is the exact opposite of exile and self-absorption.

I admire precision in language. When we settle for ambiguity, we forego mastery and deny the crucial impulse to make meaning of our lives. The purpose of all language is to create—and to communicate—meaning within a particular context. So we ought to be able to assume consistent definitions for critical words, words that communicate something significant about need or place. "Spirituality" strikes me as one of those words. But I haven't the faintest notion what most people mean when they use it. Is their imprecision intentional or unavoidable? Or is it that no one word can possibly capture all the nuance and complexity of this complicated idea?

Are they talking about some sort of out-of-body experience, a way to escape the constraints of time and place? Are they thinking about a moment when they lose their sense of self, a temporary loss necessary for them to experience a higher level of "being"? Are they referring to a moment of awe, usually triggered by some natural phenomenon that stops us dead in our tracks? Are they referring to the possibility of encountering divinity: catching a glimpse of God or finding that God's purpose for them has suddenly been revealed?

My sense is that people mean all of the above and more: what we mean depends on the occasion. We are not only talking about an experience, but a possibility, about "spirituality" as a means of getting from one place to another. We're also talking about spirituality as a goal, the place we will know when we get there. We use the two applications interchangeably without regard for distinctions. It's become a catch-all term to encompass all that's elusive in our lives— our deepest emotions, yearnings and impulses—and its indiscriminate use obscures the very meaning we're struggling to establish.

The one thing I'm certain of is that spirituality is not something I can *seek*. It's something that comes to me when I am purposefully pursuing the knowledge and acts that grant life meaning. Going in search of it is as fruitless as setting out on a journey to "find" myself. If that's all I'm after, that is all I'll find: a self-contained universe; a biosphere of one. Individuals "in search of themselves" bore and annoy me. They have so little to share, so little to contribute from all those hours spent on themselves. They are as narcissistic as fitness fanatics and seldom as pretty to look at. When I encounter one of them, a refrain from my parents goes round and round in my head: "Don't bother looking in your belly button. All you'll find is your belly button." While their folk wisdom wasn't intended to encourage soul-searching introspection, they did teach me to be ruthlessly honest with myself and to value deed over intent—to be spirited, but not spiritual. My whole upbringing—and my natural disposition—inclined me to learn by doing, to seek meaning by exercising whatever gifts I've been graced with, to trust in them enough (because they are *God's* gifts and only on loan to me) to go where they lead me. In his book *Flow,* Mihaly Csikszentmihalyi, a professor of psychology and education at the University of Chicago, describes a unique state of being. "Flow," as he defines it, is the pinnacle of human experience. Athletes, writers, dancers, artists, women in labor all experience it. It occurs when we are so deeply focused and concentrated on a task that we lose all self-consciousness. We transcend self by creating, doing, being. Unanticipated interruptions, heightened self-consciousness, pain, and time constraints all disrupt "flow," depriving us of the uniquely gratifying (perhaps holy) energy and sense of well-being that "flow" creates. But when we experience the *full* effect of "flow," it is the nearest we ever come to discovering our essential humanity, our reason for being.

This is the closest enunciation of spirituality I have encountered—and the most sensible one. For me, spirituality is what happens when mind, body and soul are all in the same place at the same time; when these three elements of self are so fully present and integrated that internal boundaries dissolve, and we suddenly "see" in a different way. It is that rare moment when we turn to face life utterly whole and complete—totally capable of being in *that* instant. It is a moment of sacred coherence. This is not, as some might suggest, a mindless exercise. Rather, it comes from being mind*ful,* from vigorously exercising our intellectual and creative powers to the point that we can stop thinking about them. It is that state where purpose displaces desire, like riding a bike and getting beyond the aching in your legs to the point where you can pedal painlessly, persistently. It is that moment when you can glory in the ride and no longer *think* about it.

THE JEWISH SOUL I DIDN'T KNOW I HAD

What does this definition of "spirituality" have to do with Judaism? It gives me a framework for understanding not only the profound attraction, but the deep satisfaction I have found in Judaism. It explains almost every form of joy and growth I have experienced in the past four years: all those times I have lost myself in learning, doing, praying—and felt energized and almost exalted. This is an odd thing to admit since I have steadfastly maintained that I am *not* on a "spiritual journey." I didn't want to be pigeonholed and stuffed into some cramped space of another's imagining. That possibility inferred that much of what was happening was happening *to* me rather than *because* of me and my active engagement with Judaism. If that's what "spirituality" meant to others—a kind of holy passivity—then I didn't want it pinned on me or on Judaism. That wasn't what I sought when I started out, and it's not what I'm after now that I've moved a tiny distance from my initial point of embarkation.

I certainly did not understand this at the outset. Ironically, it took a conversation with a Christian to force me to rethink my take on "spirituality." My good friend, Peter, invited me for one of his famous "teas" on a weekday afternoon in the fall of 1993. Peter is the only American male I know who can issue an invitation for tea without sounding affected. Approaching sixty, he has a lanky, thin body and an appealing boyish face. I've known Peter for seventeen years since I first served on the board of Center Stage, the theater where he has been managing director for over three decades. Peter and I may be kindred spirits in our love of theater, and our faith in the essential goodness of people. Yet for the many years we've known each other, I didn't know how deeply religious he was. It had never come up. What Peter wanted during our two-hour tea was to explore how I felt about Judaism and what my experience meant to my family. We sat at a table in his kitchen, slowly sipping our freshly brewed iced tea.

"Do your children have any sense of what you are going through?"

"Only in the way that kids sense everything: by how it affects their lives. Mom's not available for errands on Saturday mornings any more. We can't do soccer league."

I laughed, then dug a little deeper. "No, that's not entirely true. Sam is paying attention. He says he is learning from me that adults can keep growing. And the girls are now enrolled in religious school. Alex is quiet. He's watching and taking it all in. I expect to hear his reaction about four years from now."

He laughed and then asked me about "spirituality." I rolled my eyes. Like a car accidentally turning onto a dead-end street, Peter backed up and looked for another way around. He wanted to know *when* I experience spirituality.

"Peter, I'm not even sure I know what that *is*! I think I may have seen it in some Christians, but I don't know if it's really possible for Jews."

"Well then, do you feel the presence of God when you study Torah?"

I smiled. "You flatter me. Not yet. I haven't studied enough. In fact, I've hardly studied at all. And I may never experience it. Not even then."

"Do you feel God when you're out in nature?"

"Yes, there I feel God. There, I can make myself empty, but that emptiness doesn't feel to me as if it's particularly Jewish—or rather *specifically* Jewish. I think it's natural. The universal response of any human being who's paying attention."

"Do you know the presence of God anywhere else?"

That one stumped me for a moment. This was the first time I had reflected on "spirituality" other than to vigorously deny it when people suggested I was pursuing it. Somehow I was willing to do with Peter what I had refused to do with anyone else. Peter was not so easy to dismiss for he wasn't trying to pin me down: He was trying to understand me. That realization let me take his question seriously and honestly consider it for the first time. I idly stirred my drink, then finally looked at Peter. "I sense God when I'm writing and an idea goes *through* me. It doesn't come *from* me. That's a moment of inspiration. Maybe," I whispered, "it's the feeling of God breathing on my neck."

I became excited as I realized I was suddenly saying something that was true, not speculative: "When I'm no longer thinking but *doing,* I become the vehicle through which an idea moves. I don't feel like I can take any credit for what comes out then, only for being there. And even if I could leave, I wouldn't be able to. Something much bigger than me holds me there. I have to *stay* with it. In some way, it is a holy moment."

RELATIONSHIPS ARE ALL WE'VE GOT

Now nearly four years later, I am less impatient when people use the word "spirituality" around me. I'm more willing to hear what they mean, not so trigger-happy and ready to either denounce or trounce them. My study of Genesis and my growing understanding of *halachah,* Jewish law, and the role it plays in our lives have gradually expanded my notion of Jewish spirituality. Today, I believe there is such a thing as "spirituality," but it's different than what my friend, Peter, and other people were after. It's about a oneness that we spend all of our lives trying to achieve—or, perhaps, trying to recover. It's not the Christian notion of reversing the fall from grace or trying to redeem ourselves afterwards. It's an impulse deeply embedded in Jewish texts and reaffirmed through our liturgy: A sense that there once was—and can be again—a state of universal harmony, one that each of us can know and experience. It will directly inform us about why we were put on earth and how to fulfill that purpose. We will know it because the din of ugliness and corruption ("The earth became corrupt before God; the earth was filled with lawlessness," Genesis 6:11) will no longer drown out the possibility of hearing God. We will know it because we will be attracted to good, not continually distracted by evil. We will know it because everyone and everything on earth will be performing from the same score—in their own style, to be sure, but with the shared intent of making music together—less an orchestrated symphonic performance than a spontaneous jazz riff. And we can achieve it *by working to get there*.

Genesis contains two Creation stories. One story tells us that we are made in God's image, *b'zelim elohim*. This principle still grounds Jewish relations with all of humanity and with our fellow Jews. The second story (we are meant to connect the two) gives us the remarkable notion of God breathing life into the first human, who is, according to rabbinic legend, at that point, male-female. The first story seems to be saying: Remember that we are all made in God's image; that we all came from the same gene pool; and that a long, long time ago, we all spoke the same language and lived in harmony with all of creation. The ancient idea of our coming from one place in time and space may explain the enduring human fantasy to return to that place where chaos is banished and peace prevails. The myth gives us a guide for present behavior—and a dream to work on for our future.

The guide? If we are all made in God's image then all our interactions contain the possibility of a divine encounter, a possibility that must frame our actions and elevate our ethics from the realm of "it would be nice" to the world of "shalts" and "shalt nots." Ethical behavior, as an expression of our original and continuing divinity, can invest our lives with Godliness—continuing divine meaning and purpose.

The dream? The notion of paradise is a universal fantasy—a recurring archetype expressed by every culture in one way or another. Judaism reinterprets this archetype in a specifically Jewish way by saying that the paradise of Genesis manifests a divinely ordained hierarchy which derives from God's oneness. It also says that God's judgment of goodness ("and God saw that it was good") relies on a planned, innate balance (day-and-night, heaven-and-earth, crawling-and-flying creatures) and relates the power of language directly to creation. With words, we may create worlds. With words we may dream of improvements we would like to make. Through deeds, we make those improvements.

Is it possible that the second Creation story taps into an almost ineffable yearning to *be* inspired, to have life breathed into us by a divine source, to know from the inside out that our life is divine? And couldn't the route to that inspiration in Judaism be *through* Torah? If Torah is the word of God and if we keep Torah alive in our lives and minds and hearts, isn't it then possible to continually reaffirm God's original role in our creation by drawing divine inspiration from Torah? As a Jew, the way to do that is by bringing Torah into our lives through study, prayer, and action. These activities correlate directly to mind, soul and body. The quest to understand and unify these elements of our humanity leads us to a life of wholeness and sacred coherence. Together, study, prayer and action help to organize, focus and steady us in the midst of a chaotic world that constantly threatens us with distractions, temptations and distortions.

The point, of course, is to fulfill the ancient commandment to be holy like God, to individually and collectively fulfill the original promise of being made in God's image. That is what I seek. I am not looking for a spiritual recovery program to reclaim my lost inner self. I don't care to give voice to my primal scream because I don't think it would be a very pretty sound. I don't want to get in touch with "the child within" because I'm an adult who got there by going through childhood. I'm interested in forward movement, not self-indulgent back-pedaling. I'm trying to bring prayer, study and action, meaningfully, sincerely and fully into my public life *and* my private life: to live them, believe them and breathe them. Then perhaps one day, the breath of God I once felt on the back of my neck will be the breath of God in my own lungs, inspiring me with every inhalation to do good deeds, to stand for the right things, to love humanity and to work to make the world a better place than when I found it.

I can't do that by sitting around and examining my belly button, as my parents so gruffly maintained. I can't do it by communing with trees and birds and hoping for a glorious, "natural" moment of divine revelation, although that doesn't mean that God is absent from nature. God *is* in the physics of a raindrop and the design of a daffodil. Anyone who cares to look can see that. But God is also in the vortex of a tornado and the thorn of a rose. Neither recognition requires much of me unless I'm a meteorologist or a botanist or have the bad luck to be standing in the path of a funnel cloud or to have carelessly clutched a sweetheart bouquet. Certainly, I can relate to God through nature—and I do. But I can't have a *full* relationship with God there unless I choose to set up housekeeping in a cave and live off the land. I like my creature comforts. I love electricity and furniture and indoor plumbing and telephones and computers. I love my family. I love my community. I love this world we live in, awful as it sometimes is. And I love my God. In every instance, my love requires me to have a relationship with the other: home, family, community, world, God. And when you have a relationship with someone or something you have to take responsibility for your share of it.

SEEING WHAT NEEDS TO BE DONE

For me, spirituality is the natural byproduct of taking responsibility for those relationships. It is not a state of transcendence we achieve through passivity, because taking responsibility for something requires us to *do*. Antoine de St. Exupéry captures this idea exquisitely in his timeless children's tale, *The Little Prince*. In the story, Antoine, a downed airplane pilot, encounters a mysterious little boy in the desert who recounts his interplanetary adventures and the instruction he's received from a variety of teachers. An extraordinarily gentle but wise soul, the child finally learns from a fox the lesson that lets him make sense out of his trials and end his self-imposed exile: "It is only with the heart that one can see rightly, what is essential is invisible to the eye…. It is the time you have wasted for your rose that makes your rose so important. Men have forgotten this truth, but you must not forget it. You become responsible forever for what you have tamed. You are responsible for your rose…."

I don't know of any other way to maintain or sustain a meaningful relationship of any kind except to take responsibility for it. I know that *thinking* about my responsibilities, engaging in quiet, honest reflection, may help me better hold up my end of the bargain. I know that what I feel often influences what *I* do. But since I have yet to master the art of telekenesis I have yet to see my feelings change a single thing or a single soul outside of myself. Feelings seldom change the world, but actions *always* do. I don't want to live in a world in which I have to depend on my neighbor's *feelings* to predict her behavior. I do want to be part of a community in which everyone feels *obligated* to behave in a certain way. With obligation as the prevailing rule of conduct, I can count on others to do the right thing and they can count on me to do the same, regardless of how we feel, because safeguarding the sanctity of the community is *more important* than our individual emotional needs at any point in time. How can there be a community of common intention and integrity if everyone does what they think is right *only* when it "feels" right for them or *only* when it makes them feel good about themselves? How can we know what will make one person feel good about themselves and another awful? How can we measure human conduct by that standard? How can we depend upon each other if we are all hostages to mood and motivation? The simple answer is that we can't. Torah acknowledges that truth. We wouldn't need commandments if we all *felt* like doing them. It's precisely because we don't always feel like it that we *need* them. That's why we're *commanded* to do them. We are obliged, and that means "have to"—*not* "may—if I feel like it that particular day." Obligation is just another word for responsibility and responsibilities don't go away simply because we grow tired of them or find them too difficult to assume. Our ability to shoulder responsibility willingly, kindly and wisely is the litmus test of our continuing growth and development as human beings. Obedience as a manifestation of responsibility is a profound expression of our respect for other people and our reverence for God; a recognition that all our actions have consequences and that all our relationships have a holy dimension. The law of cause and effect is immutable whether in physics or human behavior.

I can discover the wholeness of spirit, the fullness of purpose, the exaltation of coherence—the spirituality that *I* seek—when I pursue every relationship I have with all my heart (which is "mind" in the rabbinic tradition), with all my soul and with all my might (which is "body"). Judaism commands me to seek those relationships *in* community and to link heart, soul and might to study, prayer and action through Torah. The moments when I get the linkages right will be moments of "spirituality." If I can string the moments together one after another and learn to sustain and connect them, I will be living a life of *Jewish* spirituality. Torah will tell me how to do it. But the pursuit requires, as *Pirke Avot* reminds us, that I do, *"and through doing to learn; and through learning to know; and through knowing to experience wonder; and through wonder to attain wisdom; and through wisdom to find simplicity; and through simplicity to give attention; and through attention to see what needs to be done...."*

Rabbi Jack Riemer was spiritual leader of Congregation Beth Tikvah in Boca Raton, Florida, and the head of the National Rabbinic Network, a support system for rabbis across all denominational lines. He has conducted many workshops to help people learn about the inspiring tradition of ethical wills and to prepare their own. **Dr. Nathaniel Stampfer** is Dean/Vice President Emeritus and Professor of Jewish Studies at Spertus College in Chicago. In *So That Your Values Live On: Ethical Wills and How to Prepare Them,* they teach us the importance of writing an ethical will and how to do it.

Writing an Ethical Will

JACK RIEMER AND NATHANIEL STAMPFER

Why don't more people write ethical wills nowadays? Many do, of course, but why don't more people keep this tradition? I think that there are at least three reasons.

One is that in order to write an ethical will, one must come to terms with one's own mortality. If you think that you are going to live forever, you need not write one. The trouble is that everyone understands in their minds, but no one really believes in their gut, that they are mortal, and so it is hard for us to contemplate a time when we will no longer be.

Judaism is not a morbid religion, but it is a realistic religion. So Jews would buy plots and prepare their shrouds and write their ethical wills just in case, just so as to be ready. They lived with their emotional bags packed. They understood that death is a constant companion and possibility within life, that we live all our days in the shadow of death. We moderns use a host of different devices by which we try to deceive ourselves about the coming of old age and the inevitability of death. Dr. Heschel once said that in our society it is less rude to ask a person about his income or about the intimate details of his sex life than it is to ask his age. We have a multi-million-dollar industry devoted to helping us cover up the signs of aging. We have memorial gardens instead of cemeteries. We have rouge and makeup with which we paint the dead, and we have many other techniques by which we try to deny the reality of death—futile ways in which we try to deceive ourselves.

There is a story told about the tourist who came from America to visit the renowned scholar and saint who was known as the Chafetz Chaim. He came in, and he saw a bed, a chair, a table, a cupboard, a closet, and a bookcase. The tourist was shocked, and asked the sage:

"Where are your possessions?"

The Chafetz Chaim replied: "And where are *your* possessions?"

The tourist said: "What kind of a question is that? I'm a visitor here."

The sage replied: "I am too."

Jews lived with the awareness that we are all strangers and sojourners on this earth, we are all visitors here. This is one of the reasons why they were able to write ethical wills, while we find it difficult to do so.

There is a second reason why we have trouble writing an ethical will. We live in a relativistic culture. Everything is a matter of opinion. You are entitled to your opinion, and I am entitled to mine. I have no right to impose my values on you, and you have no right to impose your values on me. I may happen to like carrots and you not. You may happen to be in favor of abortion rights and I not. You may like being a cannibal and I may not—but each of us is entitled to our own opinion. If this is the way you feel, then you have no convictions, and therefore you cannot write an ethical will in which you share your convictions with whose who come after you.

The mentality that says that everything is a matter of opinion, and that all opinions have equal value, has to have some limits. If the teacher asks the class: "Who was the first president of the United States?" you cannot say: "Let's vote on it." Some things are simply not up for voting. They are either right or wrong.

In Judaism, some things are right and some things are wrong, and to be a Jew is to know some truths, to affirm them and care about them so passionately that you want to persuade those whom you love to affirm them too. We do not want to cripple our heirs by imposing a burden of guilt. We do not want to impose our beliefs and values upon them by threats or by manipulating their emotions. That would be wrong. But we do want a vote, if not a veto, in their lives. We want the chance to convey to them, in words as well as by our deeds, who we are and what we stand for and what are the things that mean the most to us. To do this is our right as parents, and our duty too.

There is one more reason why ethical wills are not as widely known in our time as they should be, and that is because all of Judaism is so little known and understood in our time. This truth came home to me in an extraordinary experience that I had when my first book on this subject came out. The congregation that I served was kind enough to have a reception in honor of the event, and there was some publicity about it in the local newspapers. An hour before the dedication party was to begin, a man came knocking at my door, obviously distraught. He introduced himself to me this way:

"I am a therapist. And I make use of this very technique of having people sum up their innermost values and their convictions by writing a letter. I use it in my work with terminally ill patients and in my counseling with married couples. Why didn't anyone ever tell me that this was a part of Judaism *BACK WHEN I WAS JEWISH?*"

That therapist's question has haunted me ever since I heard it. This man did not really reject Judaism—*he never had it to reject!* He may have had a smattering of Jewish education at a child's level, but he was never really exposed to it in any serious or substantive way as a grown-up. As Dr. Heschel used to lament: "Judaism is one of the world's least known religions," and the question this therapist asked me is proof of that.

Writing an ethical will is not an easy thing to do for these reasons and for many more, and yet I would urge you try it. If you do, you will leave a gift to the future, and the not-yet-born children of your children's children will thank you and bless you for it.

A GUIDE TO WRITING YOUR
OWN ETHICAL WILL

There is no one way in which to write an ethical will. Feel free to write yours in whatever style or tone you want to. But as every writer knows, the hardest thing is to get started. These are only a number of topic headings under which you can structure what you wish to say; you may choose other topic headings as you wish. The topical index will help you to see how many famous and ordinary Jewish people have dealt with ethical issues in their lives and in their ethical wills.

Step I: How to Decide on Topics: Some Suggestions

Getting started can be challenging. Here are some introductory sentences to help you enter this rewarding effort.

- These were the formative events of my life...

- This is the world from which I came...

- These are some of the important lessons that I have learned in my life...

- These are the people who influenced me the most...

- These are some of the favorite possessions that I want you to have and these are the stories that explain what makes these things so precious to me...

- These are causes for which members of our family have felt a sense of responsibility, and I hope you will too...

- Some of the Scriptural passages that have meant the most to me...

- These are the mistakes that I regret having made the most in my life that I hope you will not repeat...

- This is my definition of true success...

- This is how I feel as I look back over my life…

- I would like to ask your forgiveness for…and I forgive you for…

- I want you to know how much I love you and how grateful I am to you for…

Step II: How to Organize and Write What You Want to Say

Having selected and completed some of the topics suggested above, and/or written down a number of your own, write each of these at the top of a separate sheet of paper. Treat each statement as a topic sentence and expand it into a paragraph or develop it into a section of any number of related paragraphs. Many or all your topics may warrant such development. Some topics may require more than one page. In that case, attach same-topic pages to each other. (An alternate plan for organizing your writing is on the following page.)

Arrange the pages in sequence, that is, in the order in which you wish the parts to be in the final form. Rearrange the parts until you arrive at the sequence you desire. Read all the parts through for coherence, making needed changes or corrections. If you have used quotations, now is a good time to check their accuracy.

Rewrite or type the entire manuscript. It is recommended that this be considered a *draft* of the final document. It is useful to set it aside for a few days or weeks then re-read and edit it from the perspectives presented in the next section.

Step III: How to Personalize and Strengthen the Links

Special Words

Some words are worth a thousand pictures. Are there such words and expressions, loaded with special meaning, for you and your family? Your use of these in your ethical will are bound to resonate for

ALTERNATE PLAN FOR
ORGANIZING YOUR WRITING

Briefly fill in some or all of these statements, or others you wish, on a single sheet. This serves as an outline for expansion on separate sheets of paper. Then proceed as suggested in Step II.

OPENING I write this to you, my _____ , in order to _____ .	**THE FAMILY** 1. My parents, siblings, antecedents were/are.... 2. Events that helped shape our family....
RELIGIOUS OBSERVANCES, INSIGHTS 1. The ritual(s) of most meaning to me.... 2. Specific teachings from Jewish source(s) that move me most....	**PERSONAL HISTORY** 1. People who strongly influenced my life.... 2. Event(s) which helped shape my life....
ETHICAL IDEALS AND PRACTICES 1. Ideals that found expression in my life.... 2. I would like to suggest to you the following....	**CLOSING** 1. My ardent wishes for you.... 2. May the Almighty....

your loved ones. In re-reading your draft, therefore, consider including some of these to evoke important memories and insights. If some of these like Bar Mitzva, Seder, Shabbat, Brit, Kiddush, Confirmation, Israel, are associated with specific events in the life of the family, perhaps these special events ought to be remembered in your ethical will.

Favorite Sayings

Are there favorite sayings often used in the family that should be preserved? One family recalls that their mother used to tell the children at meal time *Est Kinderlach, vet ihr hobn koyach tzum lernen.* (Yiddish for "Eat, children, so you can have strength to study well.") It is for them a deeply cherished recollection which they have in turn transmitted to their children.

Anecdotes

Do you have or wish to find a suitable anecdote to help illustrate a point you have made in the draft of your ethical will? Here is an example:

> A skier, separated from his comrades in a blizzard, became lost and disoriented. He fought valiantly to stay awake and moving, against the bitter wind and the blinding snow. But after several hours, his strength ebbing, feeling his struggles to be in vain, he lay down to comforting sleep but certain death.
>
> But as he moved to lie down, he stumbled over an object in the snow. Glancing at the object that had made him fall, he realized to his surprise that the object was a *man*. He cleared the snow from the face and body, placed his ear to the man's chest, and detected a heartbeat. Quickly, he began massaging the limbs of the other vigorously to restore circulation, and in so doing, he restored his own. When the man returned to consciousness, he helped him to his feet.
>
> Supporting each other, the two walked on...until they reached safety together.

This story has appeal in the context of an ethical will because it underscores the ethical view that brotherly love demonstrated by kind deeds, charity, encouragement, volunteerism, etc., is as basic as any necessity for maintaining human life and preserving the human image in man.

How Much Is Enough?

How much or how little to elaborate on any idea is an individual matter. There are ethical wills that are brief; they simply list the ideas dearest to their writers and of motivating force in their lives. Others are longer because they expand the major ideas and explain how they were expressed in the lives of their writers. If you choose to list several ideas or principles, however, keep in mind that they should be able to stand alone. Here are several examples:

- Reality can be an extension of our dreams

- What each of us does is significant and makes a difference.

- Collectively and individually we are always *emerging* and are capable of becoming more than we are.

- Each of us can find his and her human-Jewish fulfillment and personal perfection only in concert with others in a community of action.

- We are all responsible, ultimately, for one another.

- When we identify with the ideas and causes of the Eternal People and with the institutions which give them continuity, a touch of immortality becomes our own.

Note that each of these statements is a complete sentence and expresses a single idea. Each can, of course, be elaborated upon and discussed. But whether to do so or not is up to you. Although it is often true that "more is less," it is not always true. It is not true of an ethical will if you have the desire to elaborate.

Important Dates—Yahrzeit

If there are Yahrzeit dates which you wish to have observed, you may want to request this in your ethical will, as some of the writers of wills found in this book have done. Surely, reciting the kaddish on the anniversary of a relative's death and at Yizkor memorial prayers are among the links that bind the generations.

If some of these elements are to be added to the draft, it may be possible to do so without rewriting or retyping the entire draft. When you feel the text is ready, consider the section that follows.

Step IV: How to Prepare the Ethical Will Document in Other Formats

The great majority of ethical wills are prepared in written or printed form, on paper. Although some have been audio or video taped, the favored mode has been the written. In this form it is durable, easily reproduced and framed. Keep in mind, too, that even if taped, your text needs to be written out first.

If written or typed, it is advisable to use acid-free paper. Many documents written on acid-free paper have remained in superb condition for hundreds of years. Such papers are widely available in specialty stores. Also, if the ethical will is to be written by hand, a fountain pen should be used rather than a ball point because the ink in ballpoint pens is usually oil-based and very often causes the ink to "bleed" through the paper. These precautions will help preserve the valuable document against time and environmental factors.

In this vital process of linking the generations, however, there is an important place for a taped format after the ethical will has been written, that is, preserving and transmitting cherished songs, poems, stories and beloved *zemirot* (Sabbath table songs) that might otherwise be forgotten. These can be prepared with home recording equipment or in a professional setting. Today, compact disc recordings give promise of coming into use as widely as tape players are at present; and no doubt still more sophisticated equipment will be developed in due time. But the coming generations can be depended on to transfer the cherished recordings into the new modes.

Step V: How to Convey the Ethical Will

Each individual can decide when it is the right time to present an ethical will to loved ones. Some prefer to present it soon after writing; others prefer to review and revise it over time, even over a period of years. Some leave this spiritual legacy to be given after their death, often as a codicil to the material will. Some do both—presenting one while alive and a second loving message as a codicil. Either way, the will should be reviewed and updated over a period of time.

Step VI: Some Other Considerations

If you have written a *living will,*[1] tell your children what is in it and where it can be found. If you have made a decision about donating your organs after death, they should be told about it. In both these matters you should first discuss the details with rabbinic authorities or the clergyman of your faith.

If you have divided your goods among your survivors, you may want to explain to them the reasoning behind your distribution.

And if there is any more unfinished business between you and them, this is the time to resolve it and make peace.

Rabbi Lawrence Kushner is Rabbi-in-Residence at Hebrew Union College–Jewish Institute of Religion. He teaches and lectures widely to audiences of all ages, faiths and backgrounds, and has been a frequent commentator on National Public Radio's *All Things Considered*. In *Invisible Lines of Connection: Sacred Stories of the Ordinary,* Rabbi Kushner teaches us how everything "ordinary" is supercharged with meaning—*if* we can see it.

Field of Dreams

LAWRENCE KUSHNER

A few years ago, our temple administrator told me I should see a new film called *Field of Dreams*.

"It is a spiritual movie," she said. "It's about impossible things that remind you of something else. It makes you feel better about life."

Since I try never to miss a chance to feel better about life, I took her advice.

Essentially, the film is about an Iowa farmer who keeps hearing a voice that says, "If you build it, he will come," only to learn that the "it" refers to a baseball stadium in the middle of his farm and the "he" refers to "Shoeless Joe" Jackson and other long-dead members of the Chicago White Sox accused of throwing the 1919 World Series. It is also about how the farmer resolves his differences with his estranged (and also long-dead) father with whom he used to play catch.

The farmer docs what the voice says and sure enough, from the standing corn just beyond right field, people who years ago had left this life with unfinished business come walking out and finish the game.

Don't get me wrong. I may write books with the word *spiritual* in the subtitles, but I don't really believe such things are possible. A pillar of cloud or fire? The sun standing still? The Red Sea splitting? Piece of cake. But resurrected members of a baseball team? No way.

And yet, I bought it. I left the theater with the mischievous, reassuring hunch that such things were possible. That may be why the film was so gratifying.

* * * *

Yehuda Aryeh Leib of Ger, a nineteenth century Hasidic master, taught that "through the power of performing a religious act, some spiritual power is awakened. And so it is with everything a person does." In other words, we can only light the matches, but we cannot keep them burning. We can kindle a match, but we cannot sustain a fire. For we have no real power of our own. We have only the capacity to initiate light. The rest is up to God.

Anything accomplished by the power of a human being sooner or later must stop. But when the power of the Holy One is awakened, this kind of power continues forever. The whole idea behind performing religious deeds is to set things in their proper places until they are joined to their source. In the language of the Kabbalistic maxim: "By means of the awakening below, comes the awakening on high."

* * * *

What *Field of Dreams* said was that by doing what you believe you must do, you can sometimes awaken something in another universe and rouse a power far beyond anything you could ever hope to understand. At the end of the film, the eye of the camera slowly moved higher and panned out into the evening distance to reveal thousands of headlights silently winding their way toward the grandstand in the corn field. The message for me was that there are a lot of people driving around out there looking for someone who listens to "the voice" and is willing to do something about it, even if it doesn't make sound business sense.

You cannot force the hand of that kind of power. But through quiet, usually faltering, but faithful diligence, you can awaken it in yourself, in your long-dead parents, and maybe even in the players of the 1919 Chicago White Sox.

Rabbi Debra Judith Robbins is the associate rabbi at Temple Emanu-El in Dallas, Texas. In *The Women's Torah Commentary: New Insights from Women Rabbis on the 54 Weekly Torah Portions*, edited by Rabbi Elyse Goldstein, Rabbi Robbins teaches us about achieving our dreams.

Miketz: מקץ
In Search of Dreamers

DEBRA JUDITH ROBBINS

> Pharaoh...gave Joseph Asnat, daughter of Potipherah, priest of On, for a wife.
>
> *(Genesis 41:45)*

Dreaming. With a pillow under her head and the moon high above, she dreams. Sitting at her desk, eyes wide open, with the sun shining through the window, she dreams. Dreams are visions, fantasy and exploration, glimpses of the past and the future. Some dreams need interpretation while others offer clear insight into our hopes and aspirations. Dreaming is a wonderful blessing. But not everyone has the luxury of paying attention to dreams.

Studies have shown that women, and especially teenage girls, are not always able to dream and fulfill their dreams. Thirty-five percent of teenage girls believe that they are not smart enough or good enough to achieve their dreams. Women, and especially young women, often feel devalued by our culture; they feel that they don't have the right to their dreams, or if they achieve them, they feel undeserving.[1] Jews believe in dreaming. Our tradition embraces dreaming by celebrating and studying the story of Joseph, the most famous dreamer in the Torah. Today's teenage girls need a variety of dreamers to emulate if they are to defy the statistics and embrace dreaming in their lives.

If only Asnat, Joseph's wife, who is mentioned only in *Parashat Miketz,* were able to speak to us. We might find that she, like many of her counterparts today, was a frustrated dreamer. The Torah tells us, "Pharaoh ...gave Joseph Asnat, daughter of Potipherah, priest of On, for a wife" (Gen. 41:45). Asnat, Joseph's wife, mother of Ephraim and Menasseh (Gen. 41:50; 46:20), is a woman whose name appears only three times in the entire text of our Torah. We know very little about her. She is the daughter of a man named Potipherah (who may or may not have been the same Potiphar mentioned earlier in the Joseph story).[2] She is the daughter of a priest, and not just any priest—the high priest of On was known as the "Greatest of Seers."[3] Her name actually means "promised to Nut," the Egyptian goddess of death and rebirth,[4] one of the most prominent deities of ancient Egypt. She is hardly a woman we would expect to be among the matriarchs of Jewish tradition.

The rabbis of the midrash work hard to fill in the details of Asnat's life. They want to make her belong to the Israelite people, to explain why Joseph married a pagan woman. In a discussion of Joseph's new Egyptian name (Gen. 41:45), Rav Ahah suggests, "The name connotes: the one that was hidden here, you have come to reveal her."[5] This appears to refer to another midrash, one that suggests that when Dinah was raped by Shechem (Gen. 34:2), Jacob sent her away. But before doing so, he tied a disc around her neck to indicate that she was a member of his family. The legend indicates that the daughter whom Dinah gave birth to was Asnat.[6] Asnat was then abandoned by Dinah and adopted by the house of Potiphar, where she witnessed and later testified (as an infant!) that it was Potiphar's wife who seduced Joseph and not Joseph who made the sexual advances.[7] We can give the early rabbis credit for trying to give Asnat a personality, but they do not give her what all young women need: ambitions, hope, faith, and, most importantly, dreams. The woman who spends her life in sacred relationship with Joseph, the one who is his *ezer k'negdo,* his helpmate in life, must also be a dreamer. She must be a woman capable of dreaming, and also gifted in remembering her dreams, interpreting them, and then, most importantly, acting on them.

Asnat of the Torah is like many teenage girls today. She is like many women of all ages, women who have dreams but aren't encouraged to be like Joseph, to share those dreams and act on them. Imagine that Asnat was Joseph's wife because she was his true soul mate, his *bashert*. Imagine that she was able to dream and remember the dreams, interpret them for herself and for others, and act on them to bring about blessing, reconciliation, and transformation. Perhaps they were truly partners in the work described in the many chapters of the Joseph saga. Now imagine what it would be like if we could encourage women and men, of all ages, to shape themselves in the image of this Asnat—to be survivors, builders of relationships, protectors of Judaism, dreamers in the full sense of the word.

Phyllis Trible reminds us, "Women can receive divine revelation (like Hagar)....Women can be prophets—Deborah, Miriam and all the rest. Women are also sages. There are the wise women of *Tekoah*.... And women sing songs on various occasions...so women [in the Bible] do a variety of things. But I cannot think of an example of a woman interpreting dreams."[8] I'd like to believe Asnat is that woman. She is the woman who is able to see visions, interpret dreams, and turn them into reality. Asnat is the woman who can inspire teenage girls to move from the back row of the classroom where they are afraid to raise their hands, to the front of the room where they can confidently participate in the learning experience. Asnat is the woman who can motivate the underpaid and exploited office worker to demand better treatment in the corporate environment. Asnat is the woman who can encourage a battered wife to imagine a healthy, nonviolent, loving relationship and leave her abusive husband. Asnat is the woman who can inspire all women to dream.

Dreaming demands that a man or a woman have three basic areas of expertise. First, dreamers remember their dreams. Second, dreamers interpret the dreams and sometimes ask for help. Third, dreamers act on their dreams, often in partnership with other people and with God.

Dreamers remember their dreams. This doesn't mean doing what Pharaoh does, simply waking up with a start and being able to retell the dream (Gen. 41:8). This is not casual remembering. Rather, it is what happened to Joseph when years after his dreams of the sun, moon, and stars and the sheaves of wheat, his brothers stand before him in the Egyptian court, begging for food. "Joseph remembered the dreams he had dreamed about them" (Gen. 42:9). He remembered his youthful dreams, and perhaps he then shared them with Asnat. Perhaps they talked about them, together interpreted what they finally meant, and together devised the plan that would both test the brothers and bring about the reconciliation of the family. It is easy to get sidetracked, to lose sight of a dream or quickly abandon one dream for another. True dreamers, like Joseph and Asnat, are able to remember dreams and see them through to fulfillment.

Dreamers interpret their dreams. We all need help understanding our dreams; we need help to see what the real implications and meanings of our visions can be. The Talmud suggests the following course of action for getting help in interpreting a dream:

> But Rav Chisdah said: An uninterpreted dream is like an unread letter![9] Rather say: Have it made better in the presence of three people. Let the person gather three people and say, "I saw a great dream!" Let them respond by saying, "It is a great dream. May it turn out well. May the Merciful One make it turn out well. Seven times may it be decreed from Heaven that it should turn out well. It will most assuredly turn out well." Then, let them recite three Bad-Things-Turned-Good verses,[10] three Redemption verses,[11] and three Peace verses.[12] Then the person who has had the dream makes a donation to *tzedakah.* Then the three people recite, "Shalom to you, Shalom on us, Shalom for all Israel."[13]

Now this may seem like an ancient, semi-magical ritual to change the meaning of dreams from bad to good. But by sharing a dream with others, and using it as an opportunity to study Torah and do *tzedakah,* we remind ourselves that we are dreamers and that we have the capacity to turn those dreams to good ends.

The verses that are recited serve to remind us of three basic principles of Jewish life. First, we have the ability to do *teshuvah* (repentance).

We can change ourselves and our world. Through our dreams we can turn ourselves and our lives from bad to good. Second, we are all in search of *geulah* (redemption). We are all enslaved in some ways, and our dreams can help us imagine freedom and move toward it. And third, we are all in need of *shalom* (peace). The quest for *shalom,* for true wholeness and peace, for ourselves, our families, our communities, and our world is that goal toward which all our dreams should be directed.

After we study the verses, after we are reminded of our core values, we give *tzedakah*. We share our resources, no matter how abundant or limited they may be. We give to others, lest we become like Joseph in his unadmirable youth, using our dreams only for our own personal advancement. We all need help grounding our dreams in values that are shared by our families, our schools, and our communities. Parents, teachers, rabbis, and friends can be among the three people of Rav Chisdah's plan, who help to shape and interpret the dreams so that they will indeed be great.

Being a dreamer means acting on one's dreams. It is not enough to comprehend and intellectualize dreams. We have to be willing to do something with them. Joseph did not act alone. All the people of Egypt invested in his plan and agreed to participate in both the collection of food and the rationing of food. Joseph was able to act on the dreams because he had faith in God. When Pharaoh asks Joseph to interpret the dreams about the cows and the grain, Joseph responds, "Not I, God will respond to Pharaoh's welfare" (Gen. 41:16).

No one can act on dreams alone. Everyone, and young women in particular, need to be embraced by families and communities that affirm dreaming. Dreamers have to have faith—in themselves, in other people, and in God. Dreamers know that God is in the depths of what sometimes seems like an empty pit, in the confining places that seem like prison cells, in the midst of power and glory and affluence. One midrash suggests that Asnat knew how important God was in the life of a dreamer. She urges Joseph to take their sons to be blessed by their grandfather because, she says, "I have heard that if one receives a blessing from a righteous person it is like receiving it from the *Shechinah*."[14] She wants her children, the dreamers of the future, to have a relationship with their God, to know that they are not alone in the world.

The following talmudic prayer, found in the traditional morning liturgy for the festivals, connects all the dreamers of our tradition and reminds us of the power of dreaming, in partnership with God, to bring *teshuvah, geulah,* and *shalom* to our lives and our world. Imagine it coming from the mouth of Asnat and Joseph. Imagine it coming from teenage girls at the start of each school year. Imagine it coming from the lips of women as they embark upon a new stage on life's journey. Imagine it in your own mouth.

> Sovereign of the Universe, I am Yours and my dreams are Yours. I have dreamt a dream and do not know what it is. Whether I have dreamt a dream about myself, or my friends have dreamt about me, or I have dreamt about others, if they are good dreams, confirm them. Reinforce them, like the dreams of Joseph [and Asnat]. If they require a remedy, heal them, as the waters of Marah were healed by Moses, as Miriam was healed of leprosy, Hezekiah of his sickness, and the waters of Jericho by Elishah. As You turned the curse of the wicked Balaam into a blessing, so turn all my dreams into something good for me....You Who are majestic on high, Who dwells in might, You are peace and Your name is peace. May it be Your will to bestow peace on us.... Amen.[15]

Rabbi Lawrence Kushner is Rabbi-in-Residence at Hebrew Union College–Jewish Institute of Religion. He teaches and lectures widely to audiences of all ages, faiths and backgrounds, and has been a frequent commentator on National Public Radio's *All Things Considered*. In *Honey from the Rock: An Introduction to Jewish Mysticism*, Rabbi Kushner teaches us about recognizing God's messengers.

Malachey Elyon:
Messengers of the Most High

LAWRENCE KUSHNER

The Hebrew word for angel is *malach*. Which also means messenger. One who is sent.

Not cherubic creatures who adorn architecture, valentines, and fantasy. They can be anyone who is sent. Just as anyone who is sent can be an angel. It is required only that there be an errand. One message.

One angel never performs two missions just as two angels never go on one mission. (Genesis Rabba 50:2)

There is one great difference between people chosen to be God's messengers and earthly messengers. While those on errands of this world almost always know that they are sent and where and why, people chosen to be messengers of the Most High rarely even know that they are His messengers. Unsuspecting and unaware. Consumed by their own plans and itineraries. Busy at work on their own schemes. God is already sending them somewhere else.

I do not know how many times in one's life one is also a messenger. But for everyone it is at least once. One to whom it is given to know that their errand is completed is blessed and rare. Not so for most of us.

Remember only that you are not always going where you are going for the reasons you think you are.

...When the angels are sent (as messengers) by His word they are changed into winds, and when they minister before Him they are changed into fire, as it is said, "Who makes His angels into winds; His ministers, a flaming fire."

What is it like to stand into the wind?

Pretty much like talking to anyone.

What is it like to speak to a messenger of the Most High?

Like standing into the wind.

There must have been a time when you entered a room and met someone and after a while you understood that unknown to either of you there was a reason you had met. You had changed the other or he had changed you. By some word or deed or just by your presence the errand had been completed. Then perhaps you were a little bewildered or humbled and grateful. And it was over.

Each lifetime is the pieces of a jigsaw puzzle.
For some there are more pieces.
For others the puzzle is more difficult to assemble.
Some seem to be born with a nearly completed puzzle.
And so it goes.
Souls going this way and that
Trying to assemble the myriad parts.

But know this. No one has within themselves
All the pieces to their puzzle.
Like before the days when they used to seal
jigsaw puzzles in cellophane. Insuring that
All the pieces were there.

Everyone carries with them at least one and
Many pieces to someone else's puzzle.
Sometimes they know it.
Sometimes they don't.

And when you present your piece
Which is worthless to you,
To another, whether you know it or not,
Whether they know it or not,
You are a messenger from the Most High.

Rabbi Elie Kaplan Spitz is spiritual leader of Congregation B'nai Israel in Tustin, California, and is a member of the Rabbinical Assembly Committee of Law and Standards. He also teaches the philosophy of Jewish law at the University of Judaism. In *Does the Soul Survive? A Jewish Journey to Belief in Afterlife, Past Lives & Living with Purpose,* Rabbi Spitz teaches how to live now gratefully and responsibly.

Live Now Gratefully and Responsibly

ELIE KAPLAN SPITZ

My faith in the survival of the soul emerged in stages through first-hand experience and reading. These experiences had a dreamlike quality: elusive, in need of interpretation, and, unless noted quickly, vanishing. Yet my experiences at graveside, my personal paranormal awareness of the death of loved ones, my exposure to past-life regression, and my observation of expert mediums produced a clear pattern. That pattern revealed realms of knowledge that transcended the five senses and pointed to the survival of the soul and its return.

There is no proof for the survival of the soul, only evidence. As in a court of law, the evidence requires analysis and largely hinges on the credibility of the witness. Our openness to the veracity of the accounts rests in significant part on our own experiences with the paranormal. Each piece of paranormal evidence can be interpreted away or minimized. It is only with the accumulation of anecdotes that we may conclude that our soul survives and returns.

Although there is a strong cultural filter at play in all of these accounts, the phenomena do not plausibly stem from wishful thinking or coincidence alone. An examination of the near-death experiences of children with culturally diverse childhoods reveals that there are common elements that cannot simply be products of education or acculturation. Two examples are the failure of children to see a parent greet them in the light unless the parent was already dead (even if the parent had died only seconds prior to the vision) and the ability of patients in near-death experiences to recount events in vivid detail despite having been medically unconscious.

There are transsensory methods of communicating and gathering information. My wife's ability to hold an object and describe to a stranger her childhood dog or the items on her mantel is more than coincidence. James Van Praagh's ability to give my wife details about her grandfather was more than a good guess or our willingness to give meaning to general information. Although I have not observed a person demonstrate xenoglossy, the ability to speak in an "unlearned" language is documented extensively. The spontaneous, corroborated memories of past lives related by children from around the world add weight to the claim that under hypnosis, too, people may access actual past-life memories.

Modernity offers new tools, including hypnosis and electronic communication, that aid in accessing and gathering stories of the paranormal. The accumulating data have engaged influential writers who have begun to make an impact on our mainstream culture. The evidence of paranormal phenomena points to a soul and challenges the ingrained materialistic assumption that reality is limited to what can be tested, seen, or controlled.

Once the topic of the supernatural is opened up for discussion, it is remarkable how many people have a story to tell. For many, these stories were kept private because they were unsure how their friends and family would respond. They often feared that they would be judged as weird or gullible for holding that an encounter they had with a spirit was real. When people tell me their stories, they consistently well up with emotion and vividly remember their encounters precisely because the experience touched a primal part of their inner being. Hence, an additional reason that supernatural accounts are treated as private material is that they are experienced as profoundly personal.

Attention to soul survival is growing rapidly. It is evident in the popular culture, where in recent years such films as *What Dreams May*

Come with Robin Williams, *Ghost* with Whoopi Goldberg, *Dead Again* with Kenneth Branagh and Emma Thompson, and *The Sixth Sense* with Bruce Willis were successful. The closing scene from the film *Titanic* presents the heroine dying and being greeted on the other side by people who have died before her. For many in the younger generation, survival of the soul and reincarnation are plausible.

We see the growth of interest in survival of the soul in our bookstores. James Van Praagh's *Talking to Heaven* (1997) and *Reaching to Heaven* (1999) reached the top of the *New York Times* best-seller list, and Brian Weiss's *Many Lives, Many Masters* (1978) is an international best-seller in more than thirty translations. The focus on the paranormal has also broken into academic circles. In a 1996 book on the influence of culture on mystical accounts, Jess Hollenback of the University of Wisconsin collected tales of mediums, telepathy, and out-of-body experiences to document an underlying core reality that transcends culture, even though it is influenced by culture.[1]

The insights of contemporary researchers parallel the accumulated wisdom of Judaism. Traditional Jewish texts offer nuances of understanding survival of the soul. To realize that new insights are really old is both to gain greater confidence in that which is "new" and to gain motivation to examine anew the guidance that Judaism offers on how to nurture the soul.

Faith in survival of the soul also evokes interest in the Divine. If the soul survives, there is a greater likelihood of an enduring, unseen dimension to reality. If we are destined to return to cultivate our soul, then our lives are purposeful, which indicates an organizing consciousness in the cosmos. Faith in the existence of God is not a product of intellectual proofs (including compelling stories of survival of the soul) but a consequence of living in relationship to God. With a faith in the Divine and in the timeless paradox of free will coexisting with destiny, we see meaning and purpose in what would otherwise be considered a "coincidence."

Faith in survival of the soul changes how we view death. Death is not an end but a door into another realm. Faith offers greater grace in dealing with friends or family who are gravely ill. We may share with those who are terminally ill that they need not be afraid and that their loved ones will greet them on the other side. Such assurance may aid them to die with greater acceptance, comfort, and dignity. Belief in survival of the soul also makes closure on this life even more important. Reconciliation with loved ones, holding hands and expressing love, saying good-byes, and feeling completion offer both an easier transition and the promise of less work to do in the next realm or upon our next return.

A faith in survival of the soul adds greater urgency to living our days meaningfully, which is aided by like-minded friends. Just as our soul needs a body as a vessel of expression, so our body and soul gain from the grounding and reinforcement of a religious community and the tools of a particular, coherent tradition. Adherence to a specific religion is not an end of the religious journey, but a home from which to interact in the larger world. We learn from the wisdom of those who have lived before us, gaining tools for deepening our gratitude to and awareness of the mystery and presence of God. As inheritors of an ancient heritage, Jews are members of an extended family in pursuit of holy living. When we live with a faith in our people's covenant with God, we gain purpose. When we respond to God's call we serve as God's partner in completing creation.

A religious perspective is a product of life experience, but autobiography is shaped as profoundly by our decisions and our goals for the future as by our past. A therapist told me that my wife would shape me in the future as much as my mother had in the past, and he was right. In addition, our aspirations both describe who we are and shape whom we will become.

In that light, I am optimistic about Judaism's future despite the persistence of ignorance and apathy because Judaism offers a richness of values, sacred texts, and tools to transform the mundane into sacred moments. As soul work gains in importance, Jews will look to find tools and community that are offered by Jewish involvement. Judaism's future depends on decisions we make now and on our aspirations.

Although Judaism affirms a world to come and even reincarnation, the emphasis is on how we cultivate our soul in this world through good deeds. In that light, the same Rabbi Yaakov who described this world as only a passageway into the next world also said: "Better is one hour of bliss in the world to come than the whole life of this world; better is one hour of repentance and good works in this world than the whole life of the world to come."[2]

Judaism affirms the lesson of the children that Dr. Melvin Morse studied, who after their near-death experiences all finished school, were drug-free, did not fear death, and said that they were brought back to this world for a purpose. The purpose of one's life may be profound in its simplicity. In the words of the Ba'al Shem Tov, "A soul may wait for a millennium to descend to earth, and then live a whole lifetime for the one moment when he will be able to do another a favor."[3]

We live this life with an opportunity to grow our soul so that we will be ready to respond when needed. We are responsible for how we behave in this world and can use our free will to shape our soul for good. Again, in the words of the Ba'al Shem Tov: "A wise man does not have to wait for his next incarnation; he can begin it [any necessary repairs] in this life."[4]

Our challenge is to live now in simplicity, with gratitude to God, and with a willingness to act generously and responsibly. In the words of Rabbi Menachem Mendel of Kotsk (1787–1859), "Take care of your own soul and of another man's body."[5] We don't live in the sixteenth century, even if we remember it, or in heaven. Our past has meaning and our future has relevance only if we live with awareness and compassion in the present moment. When we are fully focused, that moment is a sacred window through which we may catch a glimpse of our soul's source, the Divine.

Rabbi **Lawrence Kushner** is Rabbi-in-Residence at Hebrew Union College–Jewish Institute of Religion. He teaches and lectures widely to audiences of all ages, faiths and backgrounds, and has been a frequent commentator on National Public Radio's *All Things Considered*. In *The Book of Words: Talking Spiritual Life, Living Spiritual Talk,* Rabbi Kushner teaches us about the primary words we use to describe the spiritual dimension of life and how rethinking what they mean can add power and focus to the lives we live every day.

Yourself

משיח

LAWRENCE KUSHNER

See, days are coming, declares the Lord, when I will fulfill the promise that I made concerning the House of Israel and the House of Judah. In those days and at that time, I will raise up a true branch of David's line, and he shall do what is just and right in the land. In those days Judah shall be delivered and Israel shall dwell secure.

JEREMIAH 33:14–16

The Messiah will only come, goes one legend, when things get so bad we cannot live without him or so good we don't need her. Indeed, we often say that at that time all the contradictions, paradoxes, and antinomies will be resolved.

Love and hate, male and female, even good and evil at last will be in perfect balance. "When the Messiah comes," we will understand how they all fit together and even why it seemed so important that they were once in conflict. But until that time, the syntax written in our brains cannot simultaneously comprehend a thing and its opposite. Because we cannot comprehend everything on one uncontradictory linear plane, we imagine a time when we won't need to. In this way, the notion of a Messiah is a metaphor for the resolution of all contradiction, when paradox will replace linear logic, right brain supersede the left.

| *(mo•shee´ähkh)* | Messiah |

According to Talmud, Rabbi Joshua ben Levi asks Elijah, "When will the Messiah come?" Elijah says, "Go and ask him yourself." Ben Levi finds the "son of David" at the gates of Rome and tells Ben Levi that he will "come today." Ben Levi goes back to Elijah and complains that he has been tricked, for surely the Messiah is not coming today. But Elijah only explains that "Today" refers to Psalm 95:7, which reads, "Today, if you will listen to My voice." In other words, the Messiah will come only when we listen to the voice of God.

"Listening to the voice of God" means attaining a rung of awareness on which hearing God's voice is routine. And once that happens all contradictions are dissolved and you yourself are the Messiah. You already have everything you need and you are where you need to be. Lions will lie down with lambs and then they will eat them because that's what lions and lambs do to and for one another. The way things are just now is messianic. The end of days is now and the Messiah is already here.

MISHNA

In the footsteps of the Messiah presumption will increase and respect disappear. The empire will turn to heresy and there will be no moral reproof. The house of assembly will become a brothel, Galilee will be laid

Zohar

The Messiah will not come until the tears of Esau will be exhausted.

waste, and the people of the frontiers will wander from city to city and none will pity them. The wisdom of the scribes will become odious and those who shun sin will be despised; truth will be nowhere to be found. Boys will shame old men and old men will show deference to boys.

LIVING SPIRITUAL TALK—*KAVANAH*

Tradition wisely warns against "forcing the hand of the Messiah." On the other hand, imagining how much better things could be than they are now only guarantees despair.

Sometimes "the best" is the enemy of "the good." If you allow yourself to measure existence against a perfect standard, life will certainly be miserable. Things, by definition, could always be better than they are now. On the other hand, succumbing to the way things are now is to cease dreaming. The balance, perhaps, is to accept the way things are because, like it or not, for better or for worse, that is literally the only way things are. They, of course, can be different, but only later. To worry about "later" is to miss "now." Remember, one of us may be the Messiah. That possibility shouldn't, but nevertheless does, affect how we treat one another.

On the Spiritual Journey

Fill your heart with desire and
yearning for God. Long to serve
The Holy One properly.
For in practice, considering God's
greatness, no human service is
ever adequate. Just do the
best you can.

* * * *

Make every effort to increase
your longing for God. Of course,
this alone is not enough;
it must be realized in action.
But even if you are not worthy of
achieving your spiritual goals,
the yearning is still very precious
and deserves reward.

— From *The Empty Chair: Finding Hope and Joy—
Timeless Wisdom from a Hasidic Master,
Rebbe Nachman of Breslov*
Adopted by Moshe Mykoff and the Breslov Research Institute

Notes

PP. 9–16
JEWISH DEFINITIONS OF SPIRITUALITY

1. Jeffery J. Weisblatt, "Spirituality," *The American Rabbi* (October 1993): 9.
2. Martin A. Cohen, "What Is Jewish Spirituality?" in *Paths of Faithfulness*, ed. Carol Ochs, Kerry M. Olitzky and Joshua Saltzman (New York: KTAV, 1999), 28.
3. Roland B. Gittelsohn, *Wings of the Morning* (New York: Union of American Hebrew Congregations, 1969), 90.
4. Nancy Fuchs-Kreimer, *Sh'ma* 27/522 (November 29, 1996): 6.
5. Arthur Green, ed. *Jewish Spirituality from the Bible through the Middle Ages* (New York: Crossroad, 1987), xiii ff.
6. Deanne H. Shapiro, Jr. and Johanna Shapiro, "Spirituality in Reform Judaism," *Jewish Spectator* (Winter 1992): 32.
7. Lawrence Kushner, "Facing the Unity of God," *Tikkun* (May/June 1992): 53. Also, "Spirituality Is That Dimension of Living in Which We Are Aware of God's Presence," *Eyes Remade for Wonder: A Lawrence Kushner Reader* (Woodstock, Vt.: Jewish Lights, 1998), 12; "Spirituality Is Personal Immediacy and the Immediacy of God's Presence," ibid., 153.
8. Weisblatt, ibid.
9. Kerry M. Olitzky, "Toward a Personal Definition of Jewish Spirituality," in *Paths of Faithfulness*, 113.
10. David S. Ariel, *Spiritual Judaism* (New York: Hyperion, 1998), 2. See others in the popular *Hadassah Magazine* (November 1996).
11. For further exploration of the idea of the quest for meaning in life, see Viktor Frankl, *Man's Search for Meaning* (New York: Washington Square Press, 1985).
12. All biblical translations are taken from *Tanakh—The Holy Scriptures* (Philadelphia: Jewish Publication Society, 1985).
13. Moses Maimonides, *The Guide of the Perplexed*, trans. S. Pines (Chicago: University of Chicago Press, 1963), 1:40, 90.
14. Gershom Scholem, *Kabbalah* (New York: Meridian, 1978), 155. See also William Blank, *Torah, Tarot and Tantra* (Boston: Coventure, 1991), 37.
15. Blank, ibid.
16. Wayne Dosick, *Soul Judaism: Dancing with God into a New Era* (Woodstock, Vt.: Jewish Lights, 1997), 67–68.
17. Neil Gillman, *Sh'ma* (November 29, 1996), 5.
18. Mindy A. Portnoy argues that there are three complementary aspects of Jewish spirituality: (1) Study, (2) Ritual, and (3) Community. See "Spirituality," *The American Rabbi* 27/4 (February 1995), 17–24.

PP. 34–38
VA-ERA: THE MANY NAMES OF GOD

1. Chaim Stern, ed., *Gates of Forgiveness* (New York: CCAR Press, 1993), 24–27.
2. *Kavvanat Halev* (Jerusalem: Israel Movement for Progressive Judaism, 1989), 72.

PP. 47–51
GOD-LANGUAGE

1. Lynn Gottlieb, *She Who Dwells Within* (San Francisco: HarperCollins, 1995), 7–9.
2. Judith Plaskow, *Standing Again at Sinai* (San Francisco: HarperSanFrancisco, 1990), 123.
3. Ibid., 128.
4. See Marcia Falk, *Book of Blessings* (San Francisco: HarperCollins, 1996). Rabbi Lynn Gottlieb coined this term in her book *She Who Dwells Within*.

PP. 72–77
NITZAVIM: WOMEN AND THE COVENANT

1. Anita Diamant, *The New Jewish Baby Book* (Woodstock, Vt.: Jewish Lights, 1993), 87.
2. Tziporah, however, did circumcise her son with her own hands (Exod. 4:25).
3. See also *Midrash Rabbah* on Deut. 30:11–14, in which the Torah is available to all those who have the initiative to go out and learn, and the sluggard is chided for making excuses and missing the opportunity to learn Torah from a great teacher.
4. J. H. Hertz, *The Pentateuch and Haftorahs* (London: Soncino, 1981), 210.

PP. 78–80
TWO UNIVERSES

1. Deuteronomy 6:4.
2. Job 38 ff.
3. David R. Blumenthal, *God at the Center: Meditations on Jewish Spirituality* (San Francisco: Harper & Row, 1987), 25.
4. Aryeh Kaplan, *The Hasidic Masters and Their Teachings* (New York: Maznaim Publishing, 1984), 21.

PP. 96–99
MIDNIGHT: MYSTICISM, SEXUALITY, AND CREATION

1. Lawrence Kushner, *The Book of Words: Talking Spiritual Life, Living Spiritual Talk* (Woodstock, Vt.: Jewish Lights Publishing, 1993), 115.
2. David Wolpe, *The Healer of Shattered Hearts* (New York: Penguin Books, 1990), 93.

PP. 113–117
A NOTE ON THE HISTORY OF KABBALAH

1. Rabbi Mordecai Miller, *Sabbath Shiurim* [lectures] (Gateshead, England: Gateshead Foundation for Torah, 1969), 86.
2. Rabbi Aryeh Kaplan, *Sefer Yetzirah: The Book of Creation in Theory and Practice,* revised ed. (York Beach, Maine: Samuel Weiser, 1997), 41. The *Sefer Yetzirah* "does not tell us to contemplate the *Sefirot* themselves. Rather, it instructs us to use them in developing an inner sight with which to view the world."
3. Robert Frost, "The Trial by Existence," in *The Poetry of Robert Frost,* ed. Edward Connery (New York: Holt, Rinehart and Winston, 1969), 21.

PP. 121–128
HOW WILDERNESS FORMS A JEW

1. Chaim Potok, *Wanderings* (New York: Fawcett Crest Books, 1980), 81.
2. Samson Raphael Hirsch, *The Hirsch Haggadah* (New York: Feldheim, 1988), 124–128.
3. Bruce Chatwin, *The Songlines* (New York: Viking, 1987), 193.

PP. 129–133
STUDY: OUR RELATIONSHIP WITH COMMUNITY

1. The *minyan* consists of ten people who have reached the age of maturity, traditionally the age of thirteen, though a Torah scroll can sometimes be substituted for the tenth person. Some Jewish traditions still require that only men be counted for a *minyan,* but most Reform and Conservative Jews include women.
2. Abraham Joshua Heschel, quoted in Murray Polner and Naomi Goodman, *The Challenge of Shalom* (Philadelphia, Pa.: New Society Publishers, 1994), 151.

3. Albert Einstein, quoted ibid., p. 204.
4. Abraham Isaac Kook, *Orat ha-Qodesh,* quoted in Daniel C. Matt, *The Essential Kabbalah* (San Francisco: HarperCollins, 1995), 154.
5. Abraham Isaac Kook, quoted in David Ariel, *The Mystic Quest* (New York: Schocken Books, 1998), 184.

PP. 143–147

TERUMAH: COMMUNITY AS SACRED SPACE

1. Pinchas Peli, *Torah Today: A Renewed Encounter with Scripture* (Washington, D.C.: B'nai Brith Books, 1987), 82.
2. Nehama Leibowitz, *Studies in Shemot* (Exodus), part 2 (Jerusalem: World Zionist Organization, Department for Torah Education and Culture in the Diaspora, 1983), 468.
3. Ibid., 472.

PP. 153–156

THE COMMUNITY OF A CONGREGATION:
THE CONGREGATION AS COMMUNITY

1. Bernard Lazerwitz et al., *Jewish Choices: American Jewish Denominationalism* (Albany: SUNY Press, 1998), 125.
2. It is estimated that only 2 percent of American Jews aged 16–19 participated in an "educational trip" to Israel; see Jack Wertheimer, "Jewish Education in the United States" (1999) in *The American Jewish Yearbook* (Philadelphia: Jewish Publication Society), 94. Approximately 40 percent of students enrolled in a Jewish school are enrolled in a day school; see David Shluker, "The Impact of Jewish Day Schools: A Briefing Paper" (JESNA, July 1998). Though estimates of JCC membership vary, it does not exceed 20 percent; see Wertheimer, 84.
3. Data from the 1990 National Jewish Population Study show that although 66 percent claim to have been members of a synagogue at some point, only 45 percent were members at the time the survey was conducted; see Lazerwitz et al., ibid.

PP. 165–166

THE SACRED AND THE EVERYDAY

1. From the daily morning service; originally for a blessing for awakening to the dawn of a new day.

PP. 170–172
THE FEEL OF THE SEASONS AND
BECOMING DEEPLY HUMAN

1. Philip Birnbaum, ed., *The Birnbaum Haggadah* (New York: Hebrew Publishing Company, 1953), 381.

PP. 195–199
THE HISTORY AND OBSERVANCE OF ROSH HODESH

1. Cholent is a meat and bean mixture eaten by Jews of Ashkenazi descent on Saturday. The dish is prepared on Friday afternoon before Shabbat begins and is then placed in a slow oven until lunch on Saturday.
2. *Musaf* is an additional selection of prayers recited on Shabbat, Pesah, Shavuot, Sukkot, Rosh Hashanah, Yom Kippur, and Rosh Hodesh. We recite *Musaf* in remembrance of the additional Temple sacrifice offered on those days.
3. Blu Greenberg, *Foreword to Celebrating the New Moon: A Rosh Chodesh Anthology*, ed. Susan Berrin (Northvale, N.J.: Jason Aronson, 1996), xiv.
4. The Samaritans, who lived to the north of Judea, were descendants of the tribes of Israel mixed with non-Hebrew peoples. Their religion, though based in some ways upon Judaism, was distinct and separate. When the Jews returned from Babylonia in 537 to rebuild the Temple, they barred the Samaritans, whose influence they feared, from assisting them. As a result, the Samaritans became hostile to the Jews and often tried to sabotage Jewish religious observances.
5. See the translation of Exodus 12:2 and Hirsch's comments on this verse in Samson Raphael Hirsch, *The Pentateuch* (New York: Judaica Press, 1986), 250. Cited in Susan Berrin, Introduction to *Celebrating the New Moon*, xxii.
6. Penina Adelman, *Miriam's Well: Rituals for Jewish Women Around the Year*, 2nd ed. (New York: Biblio, 1990), 94.
7. *Zohar Shemot* 2, pages 51b, 125b, 138a, 143a, 144b, 145b.
8. Refer to Gershom G. Scholem, *Major Trends in Jewish Mysticism* (New York: Schocken Books, 1961; originally published 1941), 229–235, for a discussion of sexual dualism in the *Zohar.*
9. Penina Adelman, *Miriam's Well,* 29, 65, and 42.

PP. 203–208
FROM AGE-ING TO SAGE-ING

1. The phrases "From Age-ing to Sage-ing" and "Spiritual Eldering" are registered trademarks of Rabbi Zalman M. Schachter-Shalomi. They are used elsewhere to entitle and describe the contents of his workshops and his writings on this topic.

2. This is built on a base of seven years. Moses' life was based on a model of ten years—and we are approaching this basis more as our life span increases. Moses' life reached 120 years, based on twelve months of ten years. I'm building my model on a shorter life span of approximately seven to ten years per month of life.

PP. 214–217
THE STUDY OF TORAH

1. Torah is referred to by the Rabbis as *mayyim chayim,* living waters.
2. The *Mekhilta d'Rabbi Ishmael, Massekhta d'Vayassa, parashah* 1.
3. See Barry Holtz's poignant comments in this regard in his *Finding Our Way: Jewish Texts and the Lives We Lead Today* (New York: Schocken Books, 1990), 7 (and elsewhere throughout).
4. Stephen Crites, "The Narrative Quality of Experience," *Journal of the American Academy of Religion* 39 (1981), 304.

PP. 218–223
THE IMPORTANCE OF TORAH STUDY

1. See, for example, *M. Megillah* 1:8. The term *Ha-Sefarim* is probably very early, as attested to in Daniel 9:2, where it is used in reference to the prophets.
2. Nahum Sarna, "Bible: Canon," *Encyclopedia Judaica,* vol. 4, col. 816.
3. The term appears in Joshua (8:31–32, 23:6) and Kings (1 Kings 2:3 and 2 Kings 14:6, 23:25), though it may not refer to the whole corpus of the Five Books of Moses in these sources.
4. See, in this regard, B.T. *Hagigah* 14a (and elsewhere throughout).
5. Sarna, *Encyclopedia Judaica,* col. 822.
6. *M. Avot* 1:1.
7. Sarna, *Encyclopedia Judaica,* col. 823.
8. E.g., T. *Sotah* 13:2.
9. T. *Yadayim* 2:13.
10. For descriptions of the Oral Torah, see Norman J. Cohen, *The Way Into Torah* (Woodstock, Vt.: Jewish Lights Publishing, 2000), 57.
11. *Eicha Rabbati Petihta* 2.
12. After describing such duties as honoring one's parents and performing acts of benevolence among the commandments for which there is a reward both in this world and in the world to come, *M. Peah* concludes that the study of Torah is equal to them all.
13. *M. Avot* 6:5. The sixth chapter of *Pirkei Avot* is called *Kinyan Torah,* Acquisition of Torah, and deals at length with the value and characteristics of Torah study. Maimonides, in his *Sefer Mada, Hilkhot Talmud Torah* 3:1, adds that while the crown of the priesthood is given to Aaron and his descendants,

and the crown of royalty belongs to David and his progeny, the crown of Torah is available to all of Israel. Every Jew can come and make it his or her own.

14. Maimonides, *Hilkhot Talmud Torah* 3:2. He is quoting here *M. Horayot* 3:8.
15. *Midrash Tanhuma ha-Nidpas Aharei Mot*. 10.
16. For example, B.T. *Behorot* 35b.
17. Jacob Neusner, "Formative Judaism: What Do We Know and How?" *Judaism* 47 (Summer 1998), 334.

PP. 228–229
MIDRASH: SACRED STORIES

1. Bill Buford, "Comment: The Seduction of Storytelling," *The New Yorker* (June 24, 1996), 12.
2. Stephen Crites, "The Narrative Quality of Experience," *Journal of the American Academy of Religion* 39 (1981): 304.
3. The term *midrash* is based on the verb *darash,* which means "seek," "search," or "demand." The process of *midrash* is to search out contemporary meaning from Scripture.
4. Wolfgang Iser, *The Act of Reading* (Baltimore: Johns Hopkins Press, 1978), 107.
5. Ibid., 157.
6. Aviva Zornberg, *Genesis: The Beginning of Desire* (Philadelphia: The Jewish Publication Society, 1995), xviii.
7. Barry Holtz, *Back to the Sources: Reading the Classic Jewish Texts* (New York: Summit, 1984), 29.

PP. 230–235
HOW TO CREATE A CONTEMPORARY MIDRASH

1. See Peter Pitzele, *Our Fathers' Wells* (San Francisco: HarperCollins, 1995); James P. Carse, "Exploring Your Personal Myth," in *Sacred Stories: A Celebration of the Power of Stories to Heal and Transform the World,* ed. Charles and Anne Simpkinson (San Francisco: HarperCollins, 1993), 223–232.
2. This is a far richer technique than one example can convey. See Esther Netter, "Synectics: Its Application to Jewish Education," Master's Thesis, Jewish Theological Seminary, 1982.
3. "Whether the poets knew it or not, and some of them did, they were writing midrash." David Curzon, *Modern Poems on the Bible: An Anthology* (Philadelphia: Jewish Publication Society, 1994), 3. As Curzon includes biblical texts side-by-side with modern poems, his anthology can be used for studying biblical and modern passages in relation to one another.
4. Barbara Holender, *The Ladies of Genesis* (New York: Jewish Women's Resource Center, 1991); Henny Wenkart, ed., *Sarah's Daughters Sing: A Sampler of Poems by Jewish Women* (Hoboken, N.J.: KTAV, 1990); Alicia Suskin Ostriker,

The Nakedness of the Fathers: Biblical Visions and Revisions (New Brunswick, N.J.: Rutgers University Press, 1994); Judith A. Kates and Gail Twersky Reimer, eds., *Reading Ruth* (New York: Ballantine, 1994).

5. Kenneth Koch, *I Never Told Anybody: Teaching Poetry Writing in a Nursing Home* (New York: Random House, 1977); *Wishes, Lies, and Dreams: Teaching Children to Write Poetry* (New York: Vintage, 1970). Groups or individuals might also write midrashic poems in response to the biblical texts and modern poems presented in Curzon, *Modern Poems.*

6. Jo Milgrom, *Handmade Midrash: Workshops in Visual Theology: A Guide for Teachers, Rabbis, and Lay Leaders* (Philadelphia: Jewish Publication Society, 1992).

7. Thanks to Andrea Hodos and Susan Freeman. See JoAnne Tucker and Susan Freeman, *Torah in Motion: Creating Dance Midrash* (Denver, Colo.: A.R.E. Publishing, 1990).

8. Paul Ricoeur, *Interpretation Theory: Discourse and the Surplus of Meaning* (Fort Worth: Texas Christian University Press, 1976), 23.

9. This is only fitting, since the Rabbis teach that God used Torah as a blueprint when fashioning creation (*Gen. Rabbah* 1:1).

PP. 236–241
THE POWER OF PSALMS

1. Solomon Simon, *More Wise Men of Helm* (New York: Behrman House, 1965), 76.
2. *Jerusalem Report*, Jan. 9, 1997, p. 11.
3. S. Y. Agnon, *Days of Awe* (New York: Schocken Books, 1948), 222.

PP. 249–252
HISTORY TODAY

1. Martin Buber, *At the Turning: Three addresses on Judaism* (New York: Farrar, Strauss and Young, 1952), 39.

PP. 261–263
ALL THE WORLD IS A PLACE FOR PRAYER

1. Ber. 35a.
2. Abraham Joshua Heschel, *God in Search of Man* (New York: Harper and Row, 1955), 43.

PP. 279–281
RECOVERING THE SWEETNESS OF SLEEP

1. See notes to Rabbi Nachman of Breslov's *Likutey Moharan* 35.

2. Yitzhak Buxbaum, *Jewish Spiritual Practices* (Northvale, N.J.: Jason Aronson, 1990), 534–38. His quotations are from Adin Steinsaltz, *The Long Shorter Way,* 240, and Tzadok Hacohen of Lublin, *Tzidkat Hatzaddik #238.* See also Rabbi Nachman of Breslov, *Likutey Moharan Vol. 5, #35,* 103n.

    The Maharal (Rabbi Loew of Prague) stated his firm opinion that we should not stay up at night to do secular work. See his commentary to *Pirkei Avot* (Sayings of the Fathers).

3. *Zohar* I:82b, 274–75. Cf. the following (*Zohar* I:92b, 304):

    Midnight I will rise to give thanks to You because of Your righteous judgments (Psalms 119:62). Since the word "at" is omitted, we may take "Midnight" as an appellation of The Holy-One-Blessed-Be-He, who is addressed thus by David because He is to be found with His retinue at midnight, that being the hour when He enters the Garden of Eden to converse with the righteous.

    Said Rabbi Abba to Rabbi Jacob, "Truly we have now an opportunity to associate with the *Shekhinah.*" So they went and sat by him, and said to him, "Repeat what you just said, for it is excellent. Where did you get it from?"

    He replied, "I learned it from my grandfather." He told me that during the first three hours of the night the accusing angels below are actively going about the world, but at midnight precisely God enters the Garden of Eden and the accusations below cease. These nightly ceremonies above take place only at midnight precisely (cf. Genesis 14:15, Exodus 12:29).... David knew this, because—so the old man told me—his kingship depended on this; and therefore he used to rise at this hour and chant praises, and for this reason he addressed God as "Midnight." He also said, "I rise to give thanks to You for Your righteous judgments," because this is the fount of justice, and the judgments of earthly kings derive from here; therefore David never neglected to rise and sing praises at this hour.

4. Rabbi Yitzhak Isaac of Kamorna, *Ateret Tiferet,* p. 37, #49, quoted in Buxbaum, *Jewish Spiritual Practices,* 535.

5. Buxbaum, *Jewish Spiritual Practices,* 563.

6. *Zohar* II:217b, 306.

7. *Zohar* I:83a, 277. The Talmud speaks of the "watches" of the night as being parallel to those of the day. Talmud *Berachot* 3a: "There are watches in heaven as well as on earth. Rabbi Eliezer says, 'The night has three watches, and at each watch the Holy-One-Blessed-Be-He sits and roars like a lion....' [On earth,] in the first watch the ass brays; in the second, the dogs bark; in the third, the child sucks from the breast of his mother, and the woman talks with her husband." The mystics later expand on this to describe different spiritual potentials that exist at different times of night. The beginning of the night is the time when

shaidim (demons) are up and about; midnight is when the righteous join God in *Gan Eden;* after midnight, the various *sefirot* move about—presumably bringing information down through the worlds.

PP. 327–333
PARTNERS IN REDEMPTION

1. That formula is omnipresent in prayer books that follow the Lurianic rite, but it is far less frequent in other prayer books. The instance noted in the text can be found in Rabbi Nosson Sherman, *The Complete ArtScroll Siddur* (New York: Mesorah Publications, 1984), 4.
2. For an exhaustive study of the Sabbatean movement, see Gershom S. Scholem, *Sabbatai Zevi: The Mystical Messiah* (Princeton, N.J.: Princeton University Press, 1973).
3. Mordecai M. Kaplan, *Questions Jews Ask: Reconstructionist Answers* (New York: Reconstructionist Press, 1956), 83–85.

PP. 368–377
WRITING AN ETHICAL WILL

1. A "living will" is one which provides for those medical measures which one wishes to be taken or not taken in his/her behalf if physicians declare him/her to be in a persistent vegetative state with no likelihood of regaining consciousness.

PP. 380–385
MIKETZ: IN SEARCH OF DREAMERS

1. Peggy Orenstein, *Schoolgirls: Young Women, Self-Esteem, and the Confidence Gap* (New York: Anchor Books/Doubleday, 1995), 280.
2. W. Gunther Plaut, *The Torah: A Modern Commentary* (New York: Union of American Hebrew Congregations, 1981) on Gen. 41:45. Also, *Genesis Rabbah* 89:2.
3. See Nachum M. Sarna, *Genesis,* JPS Torah Commentary (Philadelphia: Jewish Publication Society, 1989) on Gen. 41:25.
4. Judith S. Antonelli, *In the Image of God: A Feminist Commentary on the Torah* (Northvale, N.J.: Jason Aronson, 1995), 118.
5. *Genesis Rabbah* 90:4.
6. *Targun Yonatan, Sofrim* 21.
7. Robert Graves and Raphael Patai, *Hebrew Myths: The Book of Genesis* (New York: Greenwich House, 1983), 237.
8. Bill Moyers, *Genesis: A Living Conversation* (New York: Doubleday, 1996), 346.
9. According to Rav Chisdah, an uninterpreted dream is a bad thing because it

could contain information that is harmful. By knowing the interpretation, one has the opportunity to change or influence the course of events.

10. Psalms 30:12, Jer. 31:13, Deut. 23:6.
11. Psalms 55:29, Isa. 35:10, I Sam. 14:45.
12. Isaiah 57:19, I Chron. 12:19, I Sam. 25:6.
13. My thanks to Danny Siegel for his translation of this passage and for connecting the Talmud passage to *tzedakah* and to the prayer of the traditional siddur.
14. *Midrash Hagadol* 48:1. Cited by Avivah Gottlieb Zornberg, *The Beginning of Desire: Reflections on Genesis.* (New York: Image/Doubleday, 1996), 369.
15. Babylonian Talmud, *Berachot* 55b.

PP. 389–393
LIVE NOW GRATEFULLY AND RESPONSIBLY

1. Jess Byron Hollenback, *Mysticism: Experience, Response, and Empowerment* (University Park, Pa.: The Pennsylvania State University Press, 1996).
2. *Pirkei Avot* 4:17.
3. Quoted by M. M. Schneerson, *HaYom Yom,* 51, cited by Zalman M. Schachter-Shalomi, *Spiritual Intimacy: A Study of Counseling in Hasidism* (Northvale, N.J.: Jason Aronson, 1991), p. 271, fn. 76.
4. Quoted by Schneerson, cited by Schachter-Shalomi, p. 272.
5. Louis I. Newman, *Hasidic Anthology* (Northvale, N.J.: Jason Aronson, 1987), 451.

About the Contributors

Isa Aron, Ph.D., is Professor of Jewish Education at Hebrew Union College–Jewish Institute of Religion's Rhea Hirsch School of Education, where she directs the Experiment in Congregational Education (ECE). Her writing on education and congregational renewal has appeared in such journals as the *American Journal of Education, Tikkun,* and the *Journal of Reform Judaism.* She is author of *Becoming a Congregation of Learners: Learning as a Key to Revitalizing Congregational Life* (Jewish Lights).

Rabbi Miriam Carey Berkowitz (nee Carey M. Knight) was the youngest rabbi to finish the Machon Schechter program and currently is assistant rabbi at the Park Avenue Synagogue in Manhattan. She is a contributor to *The Women's Torah Commentary: New Insights from Women Rabbis on the 54 Weekly Torah Portions* (Jewish Lights).

Ellen Bernstein is the founder of *Shomrei Adamah*—Keepers of the Earth, the first institution dedicated to cultivating the ecological thinking and practices integral to Jewish life. She currently works as Director of Community Building at the Jewish Federation of Greater Philadelphia. She is editor of *Ecology & the Jewish Spirit: Where Nature & the Sacred Meet* (Jewish Lights).

Sylvia Boorstein is recognized as a teacher of Buddhism and mindfulness meditation, and is also an observant Jew. She is a cofounding teacher of Spirit Rock Mediation Center in Woodacre, California, and a senior teacher at the Insight Meditation Society in Barre, Massachusetts. She is a contributor to *Meditation from the Heart of Judaism: Today's Teachers Share Their Practices, Techniques, and Faith* (Jewish Lights), and is the author of *It's Easier Than You Think: The Buddhist Way to Happiness; Don't Just Do Something, Sit There: A Mindfulness Retreat Manual;* and *That's Funny, You Don't Look Buddhist: On Being a Faithful Jew and a Passionate Buddhist* (HarperSanFrancisco). Boorstein's insights are useful to all meditation practitioners, regardless of their religious affiliation. She is concerned with bringing mindfulness to everyday experience.

Dr. Eugene B. Borowitz, rabbi, is the Sigmund L. Falk Distinguished Professor of Education and Jewish Religious Thought at the New York School of Hebrew Union College–Jewish Institute of Religion where he has taught since 1962. He is the only person to have received a national Foundation for Jewish Culture Lifetime Achievement Award in Scholarship for work in the field of Jewish Thought. He is author of *The Jewish Moral Virtues* (with Frances W. Schwartz) and *Judaism After Modernity,* and is a contributor to *Meditation from the Heart of Judaism: Today's Teachers Share Their Practices, Techniques, and Faith* and *Broken Tablets: Restoring the Ten Commandments and Ourselves* (both Jewish Lights).

Anne Brener, L.C.S.W., a psychotherapist and teacher, leads workshops that explore the connection between spirituality and psychology, particularly as they relate to grief, mourning, and healing. These workshops for Jewish and inter-faith audiences give individuals tools to nurture psychological and spiritual growth and promote creativity. She works with individuals and groups in her private psychotherapy practice and teaches and lectures about bereavement, the healing process, Jewish ritual and women's issues. She is author of *Mourning & Mitzvah: A Guided Journal for Walking the Mourner's Path through Grief to Healing* (Jewish Lights).

Dr. Norman J. Cohen, rabbi, is Provost of Hebrew Union College–Jewish Institute of Religion, where he is also Professor of Midrash. Renowned for his expertise in Torah study and midrash, he lectures frequently to audiences of many faiths. He was a participant in Bill Moyers' *Genesis: A Living Conversation* series on PBS. His books include *Self, Struggle & Change: Family Conflict Stories in Genesis and Their Healing Insights for Our Lives; Voices from Genesis: Guiding Us through the Stages of Life;* and *The Way Into Torah* (all Jewish Lights).

Rabbi David A. Cooper has studied meditation and mysticism for over 30 years. His main practice has been spiritual retreats and meditation in a number of tra-ditions. He is the award-winning author of many books, including the best-seller *God Is a Verb* (Riverhead); *The Handbook of Jewish Meditation Practices: A Guide for Enriching the Sabbath and Other Days of Your Life* (Jewish Lights); *A Heart of Stillness: A Complete Guide to Learning the Art of Meditation; Silence, Simplicity & Solitude: A Complete Guide to Spiritual Retreat at Home;* and *Three Gates to Meditation Practice: A Personal Journey into Sufism, Buddhism, and Judaism* (all SkyLight Paths).

Dr. Avram Davis is the founder and co-director of Chochmat HaLev, a center dedicated to Jewish spirituality and meditation. He is the author *The Way of Flame: A Guide to the Forgotten Mystical Tradition of Jewish Mediation;* edi-tor of *Meditation from the Heart of Judaism: Today's Teachers Share Their Practices, Techniques, and Faith* (both Jewish Lights); and co-author of *Judaic Mysticism* (Hyperion).

Dr. Wayne Dosick, rabbi, is a widely recognized teacher, author, and lecturer who has brought ethical guidance and spiritual inspiration for daily living to countless modern readers. He frequently lectures and conducts seminars on ethics in the workplace. Dosick is spiritual guide of the Elijah Minyan in San Diego, California, and an adjunct professor of Jewish studies at the University of San Diego. His books include *The Business Bible: 10 New Commandments for Bringing Spirituality & Ethical Values into the Workplace; Soul Judaism: Dancing with God into a New Era* (both Jewish Lights); *Golden Rules: The Ten Ethical Values Parents Need to Teach Their Children* (HarperCollins); and *Living Judaism* (HarperSanFrancisco).

Rabbi Edward Feld, Jewish Chaplain and Hillel Director at Princeton University for nineteen years, is currently director of the Hillel at Smith College. Active as a teacher of spirituality to university students, scholars and rabbis, he has also worked with Catholic and Protestant spiritual leaders. He was a Senior Fellow at the Shalom Hartman Institute in Jerusalem, and the organizer of its theology seminar. He is author of *The Spirit of Renewal: Finding Faith after the Holocaust* (Jewish Lights), and has lectured at many institutions of learning.

Rabbi Nancy Flam co-founded the Jewish Healing Center in 1991. She is currently director of The Spirituality Institute at Metivta, a retreat-based learning program for Jewish leaders. She is the editor for the Jewish Lights pastoral care booklet series *LifeLights: Help for Wholeness and Healing;* and is a contributor to *Healing of Soul, Healing of Body: Spiritual Leaders Unfold the Strength & Solace in Psalms* and *Jewish Pastoral Care: A Practical Handbook from Traditional & Contemporary Sources* (all Jewish Lights).

Tamar Frankiel, Ph.D. teaches the history of religions at Claremont School of Theology and at the University of California Riverside. She is co-author with Judy Greenfeld of *Entering the Temple of Dreams: Jewish Prayers, Movements, and Meditations for the End of the Day* and *Minding the Temple of the Soul: Balancing Body, Mind, and Spirit through Traditional Jewish Prayer, Movement, and Meditation* (both Jewish Lights), and is the author of *The Gift of Kabbalah: Discovering the Secrets of Heaven, Renewing Your Life on Earth* (Jewish Lights), and *The Voice of Sarah: Feminine Spirituality and Traditional Judaism.* She lectures frequently in the Jewish community and is affiliated with the Jewish Learning Exchange in Los Angeles.

Nan Fink Gefen, Ph.D., is widely recognized as a leading teacher of Jewish meditation. She is co-director of Chochmat HaLev, one of three U.S. centers devoted to teaching Jewish meditation, where she has trained hundreds of students and has led many meditation retreats. Co-founder of *Tikkun* magazine, she is author of *Discovering Jewish Meditation: Instruction & Guidance for Learning an Ancient Spiritual Practice* (Jewish Lights), *Stranger in the Midst: A Memoir of Spiritual Discovery* (Basic Books), and a contributor to *Meditation from the Heart of Judaism: Today's Teachers Share Their Practices, Techniques, and Faith* (Jewish Lights).

Dr. Neil Gillman, rabbi, is Professor of Jewish Philosophy at The Jewish Theological Seminary in New York, where he has also served as Chair of the Department of Jewish Philosophy and Dean of the Rabbinical School. His books include *The Way Into Encountering God in Judaism* (Jewish Lights);

Sacred Fragments: Recovering Theology for the Modern Jew, winner of the National Jewish Book Award; and *The Death of Death: Resurrection and Immortality in Jewish Thought* (Jewish Lights), a finalist for the National Jewish Book Award and a *Publishers Weekly* "Best Book of the Year."

Rabbi Elyse Goldstein is widely recognized as an innovative and thought-provoking teacher of Torah. One of the leading rabbis of a new generation, she is the Director of Kolel, The Adult Center for Liberal Jewish Learning, a full-time progressive adult Jewish learning center. Goldstein lectures frequently throughout North America. Her articles have been widely published in both scholarly and popular journals including *Lilith, Neshama,* the *Journal of Reform Judaism,* and the *Canadian Women's Studies Journal.* She is the author of the award-winning *ReVisions: Seeing Torah through a Feminist Lens* and editor of *The Women's Torah Commentary: New Insights from Women Rabbis on the 54 Weekly Torah Portions* (both Jewish Lights).

Dr. Arthur Green, rabbi, is Lown Professor of Jewish Thought at Brandeis University and former President of the Reconstructionist Rabbinical College in Philadelphia. He is a student of Jewish theology and mysticism who has combined scholarly career and personal commitment. He is the author of *These Are the Words: A Vocabulary of Jewish Spiritual Life* and *Tormented Master: The Life and Spiritual Quest of Rabbi Nahman of Bratslav* and co-editor of *Your Word Is Fire: The Hasidic Masters on Comtemplative Prayer* (all Jewish Lights), along with other books and articles on Judaism, spirituality and spiritual renewal.

Judy Greenfeld is a Certified Fitness Trainer and founder of Homeaerobics, Inc., a personal fitness training company. Incorporating Judaic tradition, mysticism, and Kabbalah, Greenfeld teaches seminars and workshops on movement meditation at temples and universities. She is co-author with Tamar Frankiel of *Entering the Temple of Dreams: Jewish Prayers, Movements, and Meditations for the End of the Day* and *Minding the Temple of the Soul: Balancing Body, Mind, and Spirit through Traditional Jewish Prayer, Movement, and Meditation* (both Jewish Lights). She serves as a cantor at several temples in the Los Angeles area.

Dr. David Hartman, rabbi, philosopher and social activist, is one of the most respected Jewish theologians in the world today. He is the founder and director of the Shalom Hartman Institute in Jerusalem. Named after his late father, the Institute is dedicated to developing a new understanding of classical Judaism that provides moral and spiritual direction for Judaism's confrontation with modernity. Dr. Hartman is presently Professor Emeritus at Hebrew University in Jerusalem. He is the author of several books, including *Love and Terror in the God Encounter: The Theological Legacy of Rabbi Joseph B. Soloveitchik, Vol. 1; A Heart of Many Rooms: Celebrating the Many Voices within Judaism* (both Jewish Lights); and National Jewish Book Award winners *A Living Covenant:*

The Innovative Spirit in Traditional Judaism (Jewish Lights) and *Maimonides: Torah and Philosophic Quest.*

Mark Hass has been one of the staff of the *Detroit News* and the *Miami Herald.* He is co-author with Dannel I. Schwartz of *Finding Joy: A Practical Spiritual Guide to Happiness* (Jewish Lights).

Lee Meyerhoff Hendler is a popular and inspiring lecturer on leadership, Jewish identity, and intergenerational philanthropy. Formerly president of her congregation, she serves on several local and national Jewish organization boards, and is involved in her family's philanthropic activities. She is the author of *The Year Mom Got Religion: One Woman's Midlife Journey into Judaism* (Jewish Lights).

Dr. Lawrence A. Hoffman, rabbi, Professor of Liturgy at Hebrew Union College–Jewish Institute of Religion, is widely recognized as a leader in bringing spiritual innovation into modern Jewish life and worship. He is cofounder of Synagogue 2000, a trans-denominational project designed to envision and implement the ideal synagogue of the spirit for the 21st century. He lectures widely to Jewish audiences and people of many faiths. He is the editor of *My People's Prayer Book: Traditional Prayers, Modern Commentaries,* a momentous 8-volume Jewish Lights Publishing series that opens up the traditional Jewish prayer book as a spiritual resource. He is co-author of *What Is a Jew?* (Collier) and author of *The Way Into Jewish Prayer; Israel—A Spiritual Travel Guide* (both Jewish Lights); and *The Art of Public Prayer, 2nd Edition* (SkyLight Paths), as well as many scholarly works.

Rabbi Karyn D. Kedar was the first woman rabbi to serve in Jerusalem. After living and working in Israel for ten years, she returned to her native America and currently serves as the regional director of the Great Lakes Region of the Union of American Hebrew Congregations. Rabbi Kedar is author of *God Whispers: Stories of the Soul: Lessons of the Heart* and *The Dance of the Dolphin: Finding Prayer, Perspective and Meaning in the Stories of Our Lives* (both Jewish Lights).

Rabbi Lawrence Kushner is a leading teacher of Jewish mysticism and Rabbi-in-Residence at Hebrew Union College–Jewish Institute of Religion. One of the most creative spiritual writers in America, Kushner teaches and lectures widely to audiences of all ages, faiths and backgrounds, and has been a frequent commentator on National Public Radio's *All Things Considered.* Through his teaching, lectures, and many acclaimed books—including *Invisible Lines of Connection: Sacred Stories of the Ordinary; Honey from the Rock: An Introduction to Jewish Mysticism; The River of Light: Jewish Mystical Awareness; The Book of Letters: A Mystical Hebrew Alphabet;* and *The Way Into Jewish Mystical Tradition* (all Jewish Lights)—he has helped shape the Jewish community's focus on personal and institutional spiritual renewal.

Rabbi Jane Rachel Litman is the Rabbi-Educator of Congregation Beth El in Berkeley. She has served Conservative, Reconstructionist, Reform and Gay-Outreach synagogues, and is a consultant on religious education for alternative families for the Metropolitan Community Church and National Council of Churches as well as numerous Jewish congregations and institutions. In addition to her rabbinate, she was a professor of Religion and Women's Studies at California State University at Northridge, and lectured at the University of Judaism and Loyola Marymount College. Widely published in the fields of Jewish women's history and contemporary theology, Rabbi Litman is the coeditor of *Lifecycles, Vol. 2: Jewish Women on Biblical Themes in Contemporary Life*. Rabbi Litman is a regular columnist for Beliefnet.com and "Ask a Rabbi" on AOL. Her writing has won several prestigious academic and community awards.

Dr. Daniel C. Matt is considered one of today's pioneering interpreters of Jewish mysticism, especially in applying it to modern life. He currently lives in Jerusalem where he is composing an annotated English translation of the *Zohar*. He received his Ph.D. from Brandeis University and has taught at Stanford University and Hebrew University in Jerusalem. Formerly a professor of Jewish spirituality at the Graduate Theological Union in Berkeley, California, he is the author of *God & the Big Bang: Discovering Harmony Between Science & Spirituality* (Jewish Lights), *The Essential Kabbalah* (HarperSanFrancisco) and *Zohar: The Book of Enlightenment* (Paulist Press), and has written many articles on Jewish mysticism.

Rabbi Levi Meier, Ph.D. is a clinical psychologist, biblical scholar, and chaplain of Cedars-Sinai Medical Center in Los Angeles. Meier is author of *Moses—The Prince, the Prophet: His Life, Legend & Message for Our Lives* and *Ancient Secrets: Using the Stories of the Bible to Improve Our Everyday Lives* (both Jewish Lights).

Rabbi James L. Mirel has been spiritual leader of Temple B'nai Torah in Bellevue, Washington, for more than a decade. He has served as a religion columnist for the *Seattle Past-Intelligencer* and as a radio talk show host on the award-winning *God Talk*. He is co-author with Karen Bonnell Werth of *Stepping Stones to Jewish Spiritual Living: Walking the Path Morning, Noon, and Night* (Jewish Lights)

Rebbe Nachman of Breslov (1772-1810) was born in the Ukrainian village of Medzeboz. A great-grandson of Rabbi Israel Baal Shem Tov; founder of the Hasidic movement, Rebbe Nachman attained outstanding levels of wisdom. At home in the furthest reaches of Kabbalah mysticism, while at the same time artlessly practical and to-the-point, he taught honesty, simplicity, and faith. Rebbe Nachman attracted a devoted following, simple folk and scholars alike, who looked to him as "the Rebbe," their prime source of spiritual guidance and support. His teachings spread by word of mouth and through his writings; his supreme optimism and down-to-earth wisdom have made him one of the most often-quoted and studied Jewish teachers of all time. His teachings, as excerpted in this volume, were adapted by Moshe Mykoff and the Breslov Research Institute from his original writings.

Dr. Kerry M. Olitzky, rabbi, is well-known for his inspiring books that bring the Jewish wisdom tradition into everyday life, including many books on Jewish spirituality, healing and Jewish religious practice. He is executive director of the Jewish Outreach Institute, and was National Dean of Adult Jewish Learning and Living at Hebrew Union College–Jewish Institute of Religion. His works include *Sacred Intentions: Daily Inspiration to Strengthen the Spirit, Based on Jewish Wisdom; One Hundred Blessings Every Day; Twelve Jewish Steps to Recovery: A Personal Guide to Turning from Alcoholism & Other Addictions;* and *Restful Reflections: Nighttime Inspiration to Calm the Soul, Based on Jewish Wisdom* (all Jewish Lights).

Rabbi Jonathan Omer-Man is the founder and director of Metivta, a school of Jewish wisdom and meditation in Los Angeles. He is a contributor to *Meditation from the Heart of Judaism: Today's Teachers Share Their Practices, Techniques, and Faith* (Jewish Lights).

Rabbi Debra Orenstein, creator of the *Lifecycles* series, is a senior fellow of the Wilstein Institute of Jewish Policy Studies and an instructor at the University of Judaism as well as a spiritual leader of Makom Ohr Shalom Congregation of Tarzana and Westwood, California. A popular speaker and author on Jewish spirituality and gender studies, she is the editor of *Lifecycles, Vol. 1: Jewish Women on Life Passages and Personal Milestones* and co-editor with Rabbi Jane Rachel Litman of *Lifecycles, Vol. 2: Jewish Women on Biblical Themes in Contemporary Life* (both Jewish Lights). Rabbi Orenstein is a frequent guest lecturer and scholar-in-residence across North America. An alumna of the first entering class to include women at The Jewish Theological Seminary, she is a seventh generation rabbi.

Rabbi Daniel F. Polish, Ph.D., is widely recognized for his ability to blend imaginative scholarship with contemporary relevance. He has served as a leader of national Jewish organizations, as a university teacher, and as a congregational rabbi for 30 years. Polish is currently Director of the Social Action Commission at The Union of American Hebrew Congregations. A frequent teacher of both Jewish and Christian audiences, he is author of *Bringing the Psalms to Life: How to Understand and Use the Book of Psalms* (Jewish Lights), as well as the author or editor of three other books dealing with aspects of bringing faith into practical use in our lives.

Rabbi Jack Riemer is a well-known author and speaker. He has conducted many workshops and seminars to help people learn about the inspiring tradition of ethical wills and to prepare their own. He was Rabbi of Congregation Beth Tikvah in Boca Raton, Florida, and the head of the National Rabbinic Network, a support system for rabbis across all denominational lines. He is co-editor with Nathaniel Stampfer of *So That Your Values Live On: Ethical Wills and How to Prepare Them* (Jewish Lights) and editor of *The World of the High Holy Days* (Bernie Books) and *Wrestling with the Angel* (Schocken).

Rabbi Debra Judith Robbins is the associate rabbi at Temple Emanu-El in Dallas, Texas, and is a contributor to *The Women's Torah Commentary: New Insights from Women Rabbis on the 54 Weekly Torah Portions* and *Ecology & the Jewish Spirit: Where Nature & the Sacred Meet* (both Jewish Lights).

Rabbi Jeffrey K. Salkin is spiritual leader of The Community Synagogue in Port Washington, New York. Rabbi Salkin is the author of *Being God's Partner: How to Find the Hidden Link Between Spirituality and Your Work; Putting God on the Guest List: How to Reclaim the Spiritual Meaning of Your Child's Bar or Bat Mitzvah;* and the young person's companion volume, *For Kids—Putting God on Your Guest List.* He is co-author with his wife, Nina Salkin, of *The Bar/Bat Mitzvah Memory Book: An Album for Treasuring the Spiritual Celebration* (all Jewish Lights).

Rabbi Sandy Eisenberg Sasso was the first woman ordained from the Reconstructionist Rabbinical College (in 1974), the first woman to serve a Conservative congregation, and the first rabbi to become a mother. She is rabbi, along with her husband, Rabbi Dennis Sasso, of Congregation Beth-El Zedeck in Indianapolis; they are the first practicing rabbinical couple in world Jewish history. Rabbi Sasso has served as President of the Reconstructionist Rabbinical Association as well as on numerous boards. She has written numerous articles on women and spirituality and lectures nationally on women's spirituality and the religious imagination of children. She is the author of many award-winning children's books, including *God's Paintbrush; In God's Name; A Prayer for the Earth: The Story of Naamah, Noah's Wife; But God Remembered: Stories of Women from Creation to the Promised Land; God in Between; For Heaven's Sake; God Said Amen;* and *Cain and Abel: Finding the Fruits of Peace* (all Jewish Lights).

Zalman M. Schachter-Shalomi, a rabbi and teacher, is professor emeritus at Temple University. His belief in the universality of spiritual truth has led him to study with Sufi masters, Buddhist teachers, Native American elders, Catholic monks, and humanistic and transpersonal psychologists. He is the founder of the Spiritual Eldering Institute in Philadelphia, which sponsors nondenominational workshops to help people grow into elderhood. He is author of *From Age-ing to Sage-ing* and contributor to *A Heart of Wisdom: Making the Jewish Journey from Midlife through the Elder Years* (Jewish Lights).

Rabbi Dannel I. Schwartz is spiritual leader of Temple Shir Shalom in West Bloomfield, Michigan. He is well known for his ability to motivate and inspire. He is the author of *Finding Joy: A Practical Spiritual Guide to Happiness* (Jewish Lights) and *On the Wings of Healing;* his articles on religion and spirituality have been featured in *Moment Magazine, The American Rabbi,* the *Detroit Free Press,* the *Jewish Spectator,* and the *Detroit News.* He frequently is a guest lecturer at universities, synagogues, and community centers on the subjects of spirituality, intermarriage strategies, and modern Jewish philosophy.

Rabbi Sharon L. Sobel currently serves as rabbi of Temple Sinai in Stamford, Connecticut. She is a contributor to *The Women's Torah Commentary: New Insights from Women Rabbis on the 54 Weekly Torah Portions* (Jewish Lights).

Rabbi Rifat Sonsino, Ph.D., is spiritual leader of Temple Beth Shalom in Needham, Massachusetts. He holds a degree in law and a Ph.D. in Bible and ancient Near Eastern studies. He has served as editor of the *Central Conference of American Rabbis Journal,* is the co-author of *Finding God: Ten Jewish Responses* and *What Happens after I Die? Jewish Views of Life after Death,* and is the author of *Six Jewish Spiritual Paths: A Rationalist Looks at Spirituality* (Jewish Lights).

Rabbi Elie Kaplan Spitz approaches the familiar in unfamiliar ways. A spiritual leader and scholar specializing in topics of spirituality and Judaism, he teaches, writes and speaks to a wide range of audiences. He has served as the rabbi of Congregation B'nai Israel in Tustin, California, for more than a decade and is a member of the Rabbinical Assembly Committee of Law and Standards. Rabbi Spitz is the author of *Does the Soul Survive? A Jewish Journey to Belief in Afterlife, Past Lives & Living with Purpose* (Jewish Lights) and many articles dealing with spirituality and Jewish law. He teaches the philosophy of Jewish law at the University of Judaism.

Nathaniel Stampfer is Dean/Vice President Emeritus and Professor of Jewish Studies at Spertus College in Chicago. He is editor of *The Solomon Goldman Lectures: Perspectives in Jewish Learning* (Spertus Press) and co-editor with Jack Riemer of *So That Your Values Live On: Ethical Wills and How to Prepare Them* (Jewish Lights).

Ira F. Stone, Rabbi at Temple Beth Zion-Beth Israel in Philadelphia, began his spiritual odyssey as a para-professional social worker and street worker with drug abusing youth in New York City. A man whose soul finds expression in many forms, he has published poetry and haiku in various journals, as well as essays on Jewish texts and theology. He is author of *Seeking the Path to Life: Theological Meditations on God and the Nature of People, Love, Life and Death* (Jewish Lights) and other books.

Leora Tanenbaum is an editor in Hadassah's national department of Jewish Education. She has co-written *Reflections on Jerusalem: City of David in Classical Texts* and *Zionism: The Sequel—A Leader's Guide* (both Hadassah), and is a contributor to *Moonbeams: A Hadassah Rosh Hodesh Guide* (Jewish

Lights). In her other life she is the author of *Slut! Growing Up Female with a Bad Reputation* (HarperPerennial). Tanenbaum has been featured in the *Washington Post* and *Redbook* and has appeared on *Oprah, Politically Incorrect, CBS News, Oxygen* cable, and National Public Radio.

Rabbi Arthur Waskow is recognized as one of the leading thinkers of the Jewish renewal movement. He has been at the forefront of creating Jewish renewal theory, practice and institutions. Rabbi Waskow founded and directs the Shalom Center, and is a Pathfinder of ALEPH: Alliance for Jewish Renewal, an international network. He is founder and editor of the journal *New Menorah,* and helped found the Fabrangen Cheder and the National Havurah Committee. He is the editor of *Torah of the Earth, Volumes 1 and 2: Exploring 4,000 Years of Ecology in Jewish Thought* and author of *Godwrestling—Round 2: Ancient Wisdom, Future Paths,* which was named "Best Religion Book of the Year" (both Jewish Lights). He is also author of *Seasons of Our Joy* and *Down-to-Earth Judaism.*

Karen Bonnell Werth has been a health-care professional for twenty years. As a psychotherapist and psychiatric nurse, she has worked extensively in the realm of body-mind-spirit with people of all ages and backgrounds. She is co-author with Rabbi James L. Mirel of *Stepping Stones to Jewish Spiritual Living: Walking the Path Morning, Noon, and Night* (Jewish Lights).

Dr. Ron Wolfson is the William and Freda Fingerhut Assistant Professor of Education, the Director of the Whizin Center for the Jewish Future, and Vice President of the University of Judaism in Los Angeles. He is a co-founder of Synagogue 2000, an institute for the synagogue of the 21st century. Wolfson is the author of *The Art of Jewish Living* series, which includes *The Shabbat Seder, The Passover Seder, Hanukkah,* and *A Time to Mourn, A Time to Comfort* (all Jewish Lights).

Rabbi David Zeller is executive director of Yakar Institute, a center of Jewish textual learning and meditation in Jerusalem. A leading teacher of Jewish meditation and mysticism, he works to bring the Divine into ordinary day-to-day practice. Zeller is a contributor to *Meditation from the Heart of Judaism: Today's Teachers Share Their Practices, Techniques, and Faith* (Jewish Lights). Tapes of his teachings are prublishing by Sounds True.

Rabbi Sheldon Zimmerman, Executive Vice President of Birthright Israel U.S.A., Inc., was spiritual leader of Central Synagogue, New York City and Temple Emanu-El in Dallas, Texas, before becoming President of Hebrew Union College–Jewish Institute of Religion. He is a contributor to *Healing of Soul, Healing of Body: Spiritual Leaders Unfold the Strength & Solace in Psalms* (Jewish Lights).

Index of Contributors

About JEWISH LIGHTS Publishing

People of all faiths and backgrounds yearn for books that attract, engage, educate and spiritually inspire.

Our principal goal is to stimulate thought and help all people learn about who the Jewish People are, where they come from, and what the future can be made to hold. While people of our diverse Jewish heritage are the primary audience, our books speak to people in the Christian world as well and will broaden their understanding of Judaism and the roots of their own faith.

We bring to you authors who are at the forefront of spiritual thought and experience. While each has something different to say, they all say it in a voice that you can hear.

Our books are designed to welcome you and then to engage, stimulate and inspire. We judge our success not only by whether or not our books are beautiful and commercially successful, but by whether or not they make a difference in your life.

We at Jewish Lights take great care to produce beautiful books that present meaningful spiritual content in a form that reflects the art of making high quality books. Therefore, we want to acknowledge those who contributed to the production of this book.

Stuart M. Matlins

Stuart M. Matlins, Publisher

PRODUCTION
Tim Holtz, Marian B. Wallace & Bridgett Taylor

EDITORIAL
Sandra Korinchak, Emily Wichland,
Martha McKinney & Amanda Dupuis

COVER DESIGN & ART
Susannah Levin, Burlington, Vermont

INTERIOR TYPESETTING
Doug Porter, Desktop Services & Publishing,
San Antonio, Texas

TEXT DESIGN
Glenn Suokko, Woodstock, Vermont

COVER / TEXT PRINTING & BINDING
Lake Book, Melrose Park, Illinois

Spirituality

Does the Soul Survive?
A Jewish Journey to Belief in Afterlife, Past Lives & Living with Purpose
by *Rabbi Elie Kaplan Spitz;* Foreword by *Brian L. Weiss, M.D.*

Do we have a soul that survives our earthly existence? To know the answer is to find greater understanding, comfort and purpose in our lives. Spitz relates his own experiences and those shared with him by people he has worked with as a rabbi, and shows us that belief in afterlife and past lives, so often approached with reluctance, is in fact true to Jewish tradition.
6 x 9, 288 pp, HC, ISBN 1-58023-094-6 **$21.95**

The Women's Torah Commentary: *New Insights from Women Rabbis on the 54 Weekly Torah Portions* Ed. by *Rabbi Elyse Goldstein*

For the first time, women rabbis provide a commentary on the entire Torah. More than 25 years after the first woman was ordained a rabbi in America, these inspiring teachers bring their rich perspectives to bear on the biblical text. In a week-by-week format; a perfect gift for others, or for yourself. 6 x 9, 496 pp, HC, ISBN 1-58023-076-8 **$34.95**

Bringing the Psalms to Life
How to Understand and Use the Book of Psalms by *Rabbi Daniel F. Polish*

The most beloved—and least understood—part of the Bible comes alive. This simultaneously insightful and practical guide shows how the psalms address a myriad of spiritual issues in our lives: feeling abandoned, overcoming illness, dealing with anger, and more.
6 x 9, 208 pp, HC, ISBN 1-58023-077-6 **$21.95**

The Empty Chair: *Finding Hope and Joy—*
Timeless Wisdom from a Hasidic Master, Rebbe Nachman of Breslov AWARD WINNER!
4 x 6, 128 pp, Deluxe PB, 2-color text, ISBN 1-879045-67-2 **$9.95**

The Gentle Weapon: *Prayers for Everyday and Not-So-Everyday Moments*
Adapted from the Wisdom of Rebbe Nachman of Breslov
4 x 6, 144 pp, Deluxe PB, 2-color text, ISBN 1-58023-022-9 **$9.95**

Ancient Secrets: *Using the Stories of the Bible to Improve Our Everyday Lives*
by Rabbi Levi Meier, Ph.D. 5½ x 8½, 288 pp, Quality PB, ISBN 1-58023-064-4 **$16.95**

Or phone, fax, mail or e-mail to: JEWISH LIGHTS Publishing
Sunset Farm Offices, Route 4 • P.O. Box 237 • Woodstock, Vermont 05091
Tel: (802) 457-4000 • Fax: (802) 457-4004 • www.jewishlights.com
Credit card orders: (800) 962-4544 (9AM–5PM ET Monday–Friday)
Generous discounts on quantity orders. SATISFACTION GUARANTEED. Prices subject to change.

Spirituality & More

The Jewish Lights Spirituality Handbook
A Guide to Understanding, Exploring & Living a Spiritual Life
Ed. by *Stuart M. Matlins, Editor-in-Chief, Jewish Lights Publishing*

Rich, creative material from over 50 spiritual leaders on every aspect of Jewish spirituality today: prayer, meditation, mysticism, study, rituals, special days, the everyday, and more.
6 x 9, 456 pp, Quality PB, ISBN 1-58023-093-8 **$18.95**; HC, ISBN 1-58023-100-4 **$24.95**

Six Jewish Spiritual Paths: *A Rationalist Looks at Spirituality*
by *Rabbi Rifat Sonsino*

The quest for spirituality is universal, but which path to spirituality is right *for you*? A straightforward, objective discussion of the many ways—each valid and authentic—for seekers to gain a richer spiritual life within Judaism. 6 x 9, 208 pp, HC, ISBN 1-58023-095-4 **$21.95**

Restful Reflections: *Nighttime Inspiration to Calm the Soul,*
Based on Jewish Wisdom by *Rabbi Kerry M. Olitzky* and *Rabbi Lori Forman*
Wisdom to "sleep on." For each night of the year, an inspiring quote from a Jewish source and a personal reflection on it from an insightful spiritual leader help you to focus on your spiritual life and the lessons your day has offered. The companion to *Sacred Intentions: Daily Inspiration to Strengthen the Spirit, Based on Jewish Wisdom* (see below).
4½ x 6½, 448 pp, Quality PB, ISBN 1-58023-091-1 **$15.95**

Sacred Intentions: *Daily Inspiration to Strengthen the Spirit, Based on Jewish Wisdom*
by Rabbi Kerry M. Olitzky and Rabbi Lori Forman
4½ x 6½, 448 pp, Quality PB, ISBN 1-58023-061-X **$15.95**

The Enneagram and Kabbalah: *Reading Your Soul*
by Rabbi Howard A. Addison 6 x 9, 176 pp, Quality PB, ISBN 1-58023-001-6 **$15.95**

Embracing the Covenant: *Converts to Judaism Talk About Why & How*
Ed. and with Intros. by Rabbi Allan L. Berkowitz and Patti Moskovitz
6 x 9, 192 pp, Quality PB, ISBN 1-879045-50-8 **$15.95**

Mystery Midrash: *An Anthology of Jewish Mystery & Detective Fiction* AWARD WINNER!
Ed. by Lawrence W. Raphael 6 x 9, 304 pp, Quality PB, ISBN 1-58023-055-5 **$16.95**

Wandering Stars: *An Anthology of Jewish Fantasy & Science Fiction* Ed. by Jack
Dann; Intro. by Isaac Asimov 6 x 9, 272 pp, Quality PB, ISBN 1-58023-005-9 **$16.95**

Israel—A Spiritual Travel Guide AWARD WINNER!
A Companion for the Modern Jewish Pilgrim
by Rabbi Lawrence A. Hoffman 4¾ x 10, 256 pp, Quality PB, ISBN 1-879045-56-7 **$18.95**

Theology/Philosophy

A Heart of Many Rooms: *Celebrating the Many Voices within Judaism*

by *Dr. David Hartman* **AWARD WINNER!**

From the perspective of traditional Judaism, Hartman shows that commitment to both Jewish tradition and to pluralism can create understanding between people of different religious convictions. 6 x 9, 352 pp, HC, ISBN 1-58023-048-2 **$24.95**

These Are the Words: *A Vocabulary of Jewish Spiritual Life*

by *Arthur Green*

What are the most essential ideas, concepts and terms that an educated person needs to know about Judaism? From *Adonai* (My Lord) to *zekhut* (merit), this enlightening and entertaining journey through Judaism teaches us the 149 core Hebrew words that constitute the basic vocabulary of Jewish spiritual life. 6 x 9, 304 pp, Quality PB, ISBN 1-58023-107-1 **$18.95**

Broken Tablets: *Restoring the Ten Commandments and Ourselves*

Ed. by *Rabbi Rachel S. Mikva*; Intro. by *Rabbi Lawrence Kushner* **AWARD WINNER!**

Twelve outstanding spiritual leaders each share profound and personal thoughts about these biblical commands and why they have such a special hold on us.
6 x 9, 192 pp, HC, ISBN 1-58023-066-0 **$21.95**

A Living Covenant: *The Innovative Spirit in Traditional Judaism* **AWARD WINNER!**
by Dr. David Hartman 6 x 9, 368 pp, Quality PB, ISBN 1-58023-011-3 **$18.95**

Evolving Halakhah: *A Progressive Approach to Traditional Jewish Law*
by Rabbi Dr. Moshe Zemer 6 x 9, 480 pp, HC, ISBN 1-58023-002-4 **$40.00**

The Death of Death: *Resurrection and Immortality in Jewish Thought* **AWARD WINNER!**
by Dr. Neil Gillman 6 x 9, 336 pp, Quality PB, ISBN 1-58023-081-4 **$18.95**;
HC, ISBN 1-879045-61-3 **$23.95**

The Last Trial: *On the Legends and Lore of the Command to Abraham to Offer Isaac as a Sacrifice* by Shalom Spiegel; New Preface by Judah Goldin
6 x 9, 208 pp, Quality PB, ISBN 1-879045-29-X **$17.95**

Tormented Master: *The Life and Spiritual Quest of Rabbi Nahman of Bratslav*
by Dr. Arthur Green 6 x 9, 416 pp, Quality PB, ISBN 1-879045-11-7 **$18.95**

The Earth Is the Lord's: *The Inner World of the Jew in Eastern Europe*
by Abraham Joshua Heschel 5½ x 8, 128 pp, Quality PB, ISBN 1-879045-42-7 **$14.95**

A Passion for Truth: *Despair and Hope in Hasidism* by Abraham Joshua Heschel
5½ x 8, 352 pp, Quality PB, ISBN 1-879045-41-9 **$18.95**

Your Word Is Fire: *The Hasidic Masters on Contemplative Prayer*
Ed. and Trans. with a New Introduction by Dr. Arthur Green and Dr. Barry W. Holtz
6 x 9, 160 pp, Quality PB, ISBN 1-879045-25-7 **$14.95**

Life Cycle/Grief

Against the Dying of the Light
A Father's Journey through Loss
by *Leonard Fein*

The sudden death of a child. A personal tragedy beyond description. Rage and despair deeper than sorrow. What can come from it? Raw wisdom and defiant hope. In this unusual exploration of heartbreak and healing, Fein chronicles the sudden death of his 30-year-old daughter and reveals what the progression of grief can teach each one of us.
5½ x 8½, 176 pp, HC, ISBN 1-58023-110-1 **$19.95**

Mourning & Mitzvah: *A Guided Journal for Walking the Mourner's Path through Grief to Healing* with Over 60 Guided Exercises
by *Anne Brener, L.C.S.W.*

For those who mourn a death, for those who would help them, for those who face a loss of any kind, Brener teaches us the power and strength available to us in the fully experienced mourning process. 7½ x 9, 288 pp, Quality PB, ISBN 1-879045-23-0 **$19.95**

Tears of Sorrow, Seeds of Hope
A Jewish Spiritual Companion for Infertility and Pregnancy Loss
by Rabbi Nina Beth Cardin   6 x 9, 192 pp, HC, ISBN 1-58023-017-2 **$19.95**

Grief in Our Seasons: *A Mourner's Kaddish Companion*
by Rabbi Kerry M. Olitzky   4½ x 6½, 448 pp, Quality PB, ISBN 1-879045-55-9 **$15.95**

A Time to Mourn, A Time to Comfort
A Guide to Jewish Bereavement and Comfort
by Dr. Ron Wolfson   7 x 9, 336 pp, Quality PB, ISBN 1-879045-96-6 **$18.95**

When a Grandparent Dies
A Kid's Own Remembering Workbook for Dealing with Shiva and the Year Beyond
by Nechama Liss-Levinson, Ph.D.
8 x 10, 48 pp, HC, Illus., 2-color text, ISBN 1-879045-44-3 **$15.95**

Healing/Wellness/Recovery

Jewish Pastoral Care
A Practical Handbook from Traditional and Contemporary Sources
Ed. by *Rabbi Dayle A. Friedman*

Gives today's Jewish pastoral counselors practical guidelines based in the Jewish tradition.
6 x 9, 464 pp, HC, ISBN 1-58023-078-4 **$35.00**

Healing of Soul, Healing of Body
Spiritual Leaders Unfold the Strength & Solace in Psalms
Ed. by *Rabbi Simkha Y. Weintraub, CSW,* for The National Center for Jewish Healing

A source of solace for those who are facing illness, as well as those who care for them. Provides a wellspring of strength with inspiring introductions and commentaries by eminent spiritual leaders reflecting all Jewish movements.
6 x 9, 128 pp, Quality PB, Illus., 2-color text, ISBN 1-879045-31-1 **$14.95**

Jewish Paths toward Healing and Wholeness
A Personal Guide to Dealing with Suffering
by *Rabbi Kerry M. Olitzky*; Foreword by *Debbie Friedman*

Why me? Why do we suffer? How can we heal? Grounded in personal experience with illness and Jewish spiritual traditions, this book provides healing rituals, psalms and prayers that help readers initiate a dialogue with God, to guide them along the complicated path of healing and wholeness.
6 x 9, 192 pp, Quality PB, ISBN 1-58023-068-7 **$15.95**

Twelve Jewish Steps to Recovery: *A Personal Guide to Turning from Alcoholism & Other Addictions . . . Drugs, Food, Gambling, Sex . . .* by Rabbi Kerry M. Olitzky & Stuart A. Copans, M.D. Preface by Abraham J. Twerski, M.D.; Intro. by Rabbi Sheldon Zimmerman; "Getting Help" by JACS Foundation 6 x 9, 144 pp, Quality PB, ISBN 1-879045-09-5 **$13.95**

One Hundred Blessings Every Day: *Daily Twelve Step Recovery Affirmations, Exercises for Personal Growth & Renewal Reflecting Seasons of the Jewish Year* by Rabbi Kerry M. Olitzky 4½ x 6½, 432 pp, Quality PB, ISBN 1-879045-30-3 **$14.95**

Recovery from Codependence: *A Jewish Twelve Steps Guide to Healing Your Soul* by Rabbi Kerry M. Olitzky 6 x 9, 160 pp, Quality PB, ISBN 1-879045-32-X **$13.95**; HC, ISBN 1-879045-27-3 **$21.95**

Renewed Each Day: *Daily Twelve Step Recovery Meditations Based on the Bible* by Rabbi Kerry M. Olitzky & Aaron Z. *Vol. I: Genesis & Exodus; Vol. II: Leviticus, Numbers and Deuteronomy*
Vol. I: 6 x 9, 224 pp, Quality PB, ISBN 1-879045-12-5 **$14.95**
Vol II: 6 x 9, 280 pp, Quality PB, ISBN 1-879045-13-3 **$14.95**

Life Cycle & Holidays

How to Be a Perfect Stranger, 2nd. Ed. In 2 Volumes
A Guide to Etiquette in Other People's Religious Ceremonies

Ed. by *Stuart M. Matlins* & *Arthur J. Magida* **AWARD WINNER!**

What will happen? What do I do? What do I wear? What do I say? What are their basic beliefs? Should I bring a gift? Explains the rituals and celebrations of North America's major religions/denominations, helping an interested guest to feel comfortable. *Not* presented from the perspective of any particular faith. SKYLIGHT PATHS Books

Vol. 1: *North America's Largest Faiths,* 6 x 9, 432 pp, Quality PB, ISBN 1-893361-01-2 **$19.95**
Vol. 2: *Other Faiths in North America,* 6 x 9, 416 pp, Quality PB, ISBN 1-893361-02-0 **$19.95**

Celebrating Your New Jewish Daughter
Creating Jewish Ways to Welcome Baby Girls into the Covenant— New and Traditional Ceremonies

by *Debra Nussbaum Cohen*; Foreword by *Rabbi Sandy Eisenberg Sasso*

Features everything families need to plan a celebration that reflects Jewish tradition, including a how-to guide to new and traditional ceremonies, and practical guidelines for planning the joyous event. 6 x 9, 272 pp, Quality PB, ISBN 1-58023-090-3 **$18.95**

The New Jewish Baby Book **AWARD WINNER!**
Names, Ceremonies & Customs—A Guide for Today's Families
by Anita Diamant 6 x 9, 336 pp, Quality PB, ISBN 1-879045-28-1 **$18.95**

Parenting As a Spiritual Journey
Deepening Ordinary & Extraordinary Events into Sacred Occasions
by Rabbi Nancy Fuchs-Kreimer 6 x 9, 224 pp, Quality PB, ISBN 1-58023-016-4 **$16.95**

Putting God on the Guest List, 2nd Ed. **AWARD WINNER!**
How to Reclaim the Spiritual Meaning of Your Child's Bar or Bat Mitzvah
by Rabbi Jeffrey K. Salkin 6 x 9, 224 pp, Quality PB, ISBN 1-879045-59-1 **$16.95**

For Kids—Putting God on Your Guest List
How to Claim the Spiritual Meaning of Your Bar or Bat Mitzvah
by Rabbi Jeffrey K. Salkin 6 x 9, 144 pp, Quality PB, ISBN 1-58023-015-6 **$14.95**

Bar/Bat Mitzvah Basics: *A Practical Family Guide to Coming of Age Together*
Ed. by Cantor Helen Leneman 6 x 9, 240 pp, Quality PB, ISBN 1-879045-54-0 **$16.95**

Hanukkah: The Art of Jewish Living
by Dr. Ron Wolfson 7 x 9, 192 pp, Quality PB, Illus., ISBN 1-879045-97-4 **$16.95**

The Shabbat Seder: The Art of Jewish Living
by Dr. Ron Wolfson 7 x 9, 272 pp, Quality PB, Illus., ISBN 1-879045-90-7 **$16.95**

The Passover Seder: The Art of Jewish Living
by Dr. Ron Wolfson 7 x 9, 352 pp, Quality PB, Illus., ISBN 1-879045-93-1 **$16.95**

Children's Spirituality

In Our Image
God's First Creatures
by *Nancy Sohn Swartz*
Full-color illus. by *Melanie Hall*

For ages 4 & up

A playful new twist on the Creation story—from the perspective of the animals. Celebrates the interconnectedness of nature and the harmony of all living things. "The vibrantly colored illustrations nearly leap off the page in this delightful interpretation." —*School Library Journal*

9 x 12, 32 pp, HC, Full-color illus., ISBN 1-879045-99-0 **$16.95**

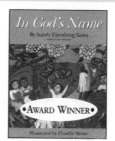

God's Paintbrush

For ages 4 & up

by *Sandy Eisenberg Sasso*; Full-color illus. by *Annette Compton*

Invites children of all faiths and backgrounds to encounter God openly in their own lives. Wonderfully interactive; provides questions adult and child can explore together at the end of each episode.
11 x 8½, 32 pp, HC, Full-color illus., ISBN 1-879045-22-2 **$16.95**

*Also available: **A Teacher's Guide:** A Guide for Jewish & Christian Educators and Parents*
8½ x 11, 32 pp, PB, ISBN 1-879045-57-5 **$8.95**

God's Paintbrush Celebration Kit 9½ x 12, HC, Includes 5 sessions/40 full-color Activity Sheets and Teacher Folder with complete instructions, ISBN 1-58023-050-4 **$21.95**

In God's Name

For ages 4 & up

by *Sandy Eisenberg Sasso*; Full-color illus. by *Phoebe Stone*

Like an ancient myth in its poetic text and vibrant illustrations, this award-winning modern fable about the search for God's name celebrates the diversity and, at the same time, the unity of all the people of the world.
9 x 12, 32 pp, HC, Full-color illus., ISBN 1-879045-26-5 **$16.95**

What Is God's Name? (A Board Book)

For ages 0–4

An abridged board book version of the award-winning *In God's Name*.
5 x 5, 24 pp, Board, Full-color illus., ISBN 1-893361-10-1 **$7.95** A SKYLIGHT PATHS Book

The 11th Commandment: Wisdom from Our Children
by *The Children of America*

For all ages

"If there were an Eleventh Commandment, what would it be?" Children of many religious denominations across America answer this question—in their own drawings and words. "A rare book of spiritual celebration for all people, of all ages, for all time."—*Bookviews*
8 x 10, 48 pp, HC, Full-color illus., ISBN 1-879045-46-X **$16.95**

Children's Spirituality

God Said Amen

For ages
4 & up

by *Sandy Eisenberg Sasso*
Full-color illus. by *Avi Katz*

A warm and inspiring tale of two kingdoms: one overflowing with water but without oil to light its lamps; the other blessed with oil but no water to grow its gardens. The kingdoms' rulers ask God for help but are too stubborn to ask each other. It takes a minstrel, a pair of royal riding-birds and their young keepers, and a simple act of kindness to show that they need only reach out to each other to find God's answer to their prayers.

9 x 12, 32 pp, HC, Full-color illus., ISBN 1-58023-080-6 **$16.95**

For Heaven's Sake

For ages
4 & up

by *Sandy Eisenberg Sasso*; Full-color illus. by *Kathryn Kunz Finney*

Everyone talked about heaven: "Thank heavens." "Heaven forbid." "For heaven's sake, Isaiah." But no one would say what heaven was or how to find it. So Isaiah decides to find out, by seeking answers from many different people.
9 x 12, 32 pp, HC, Full-color illus., ISBN 1-58023-054-7 **$16.95**

But God Remembered

For ages
8 & up

Stories of Women from Creation to the Promised Land

by *Sandy Eisenberg Sasso*; Full-color illus. by *Bethanne Andersen*

A fascinating collection of four different stories of women only briefly mentioned in biblical tradition and religious texts. Vibrantly brings to life courageous and strong women from ancient tradition; all teach important values through their actions and faith.
9 x 12, 32 pp, HC, Full-color illus., ISBN 1-879045-43-5 **$16.95**

God in Between

For ages
4 & up

by *Sandy Eisenberg Sasso*; Full-color illus. by *Sally Sweetland*

If you wanted to find God, where would you look? A magical, mythical tale that teaches that God can be found where we are: within all of us and the relationships between us.
9 x 12, 32 pp, HC, Full-color illus., ISBN 1-879045-86-9 **$16.95**

For ages
4 & up

A Prayer for the Earth: The Story of Naamah, Noah's Wife

by *Sandy Eisenberg Sasso*; Full-color illus. by *Bethanne Andersen*

This new story, based on an ancient text, opens readers' religious imaginations to new ideas about the well-known story of the Flood. When God tells Noah to bring the animals of the world onto the ark, God also calls on Naamah, Noah's wife, to save each plant on Earth.
9 x 12, 32 pp, HC, Full-color illus., ISBN 1-879045-60-5 **$16.95**

Children's Spirituality

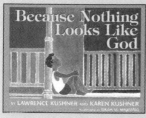

Because Nothing Looks Like God

by *Lawrence and Karen Kushner*
Full-color illus. by *Dawn W. Majewski*

For ages 4 & up

MULTICULTURAL, NONDENOMINATIONAL, NONSECTARIAN

What is God like? The first collaborative work by husband-and-wife team Lawrence and Karen Kushner introduces children to the possibilities of spiritual life. Real-life examples of happiness and sadness—from goodnight stories, to the hope and fear felt the first time at bat, to the closing moments of life—invite us to explore, together with our children, the questions we all have about God, no matter what our age.

11 x 8½, 32 pp, HC, Full-color illus., ISBN 1-58023-092-X **$16.95**

Where Is God? (A Board Book)

by *Lawrence and Karen Kushner*; Full-color illus. by *Dawn W. Majewski*

For ages 0–4

Gently invites children to become aware of God's presence all around them. Abridged from *Because Nothing Looks Like God* by Lawrence and Karen Kushner.
5 x 5, 24 pp, Board, Full color illus., ISBN 1-893361-17-9 **$7.95** A SKYLIGHT PATHS Book

Sharing Blessings

Children's Stories for Exploring the Spirit of the Jewish Holidays
by *Rahel Musleah* and *Rabbi Michael Klayman*
Full-color illus. by *Mary O'Keefe Young*

For ages 6 & up

What is the spiritual message of each of the Jewish holidays? How do we teach it to our children? Many books tell children about the historical significance and customs of the holidays. Through stories about one family's preparation, *Sharing Blessings* explores ways to get into the *spirit* of 13 different holidays.
8½ x 11, 64 pp, HC, Full-color illus., ISBN 1-879045-71-0 **$18.95**

The Book of Miracles

A Young Person's Guide to Jewish Spiritual Awareness
by *Lawrence Kushner*

For ages 9 & up

Introduces kids to a way of everyday spiritual thinking to last a lifetime. Kushner, whose award-winning books have brought spirituality to life for countless adults, now shows young people how to use Judaism as a foundation on which to build their lives.
6 x 9, 96 pp, HC, 2-color illus., ISBN 1-879045-78-8 **$16.95**

Spirituality/Jewish Meditation

Discovering Jewish Meditation
Instruction & Guidance for Learning an Ancient Spiritual Practice
by *Nan Fink Gefen*

Gives readers of any level of understanding the tools to learn the practice of Jewish meditation on your own, starting you on the path to a deep spiritual and personal connection to God and to greater insight about your life. 6 x 9, 208 pp, Quality PB, ISBN 1-58023-067-9 **$16.95**

Entering the Temple of Dreams: *Jewish Prayers, Movements, and Meditations for the End of the Day* by *Tamar Frankiel* and *Judy Greenfeld*

Nighttime spirituality is much more than bedtime prayers! Here, you'll uncover deeper meaning to familiar nighttime prayers—and learn to combine the prayers with movements and meditations to enhance your physical and psychological well-being.
7 x 10, 192 pp, Quality PB, Illus., ISBN 1-58023-079-2 **$16.95**

One God Clapping: *The Spiritual Path of a Zen Rabbi* Award Winner!
by *Alan Lew* with *Sherril Jaffe*

A fascinating personal story of a Jewish meditation expert's roundabout spiritual journey from Zen Buddhist practitioner to rabbi. 5½ x 8½, 336 pp, Quality PB, ISBN 1-58023-115-2 **$16.95**

The Handbook of Jewish Meditation Practices
A Guide for Enriching the Sabbath and Other Days of Your Life
by *Rabbi David A. Cooper*

Gives us ancient and modern Jewish tools—Jewish practices and traditions, easy-to-use meditation exercises, and contemplative study of Jewish sacred texts. 6 x 9, 208 pp, Quality PB, ISBN 1-58023-102-0 **$16.95**

Stepping Stones to Jewish Spiritual Living: *Walking the Path Morning, Noon, and Night*
by Rabbi James L. Mirel & Karen Bonnell Werth
6 x 9, 240 pp, Quality PB, ISBN 1-58023-074-1 **$16.95**

Meditation from the Heart of Judaism
Today's Teachers Share Their Practices, Techniques, and Faith
Ed. by Avram Davis 6 x 9, 256 pp, Quality PB, ISBN 1-58023-049-0 **$16.95**;
HC, ISBN 1-879045-77-X **$21.95**

The Way of Flame: *A Guide to the Forgotten Mystical Tradition of Jewish Meditation*
by Avram Davis 4½ x 8, 176 pp, Quality PB, ISBN 1-58023-060-1 **$15.95**

Minding the Temple of the Soul: *Balancing Body, Mind, and Spirit through Traditional Jewish Prayer, Movement, and Meditation*
by Tamar Frankiel and Judy Greenfeld 7 x 10, 184 pp, Quality PB, Illus.,
ISBN 1-879045-64-8 **$16.95**; Audiotape of the Blessings and Meditations (60-min. cassette), JN01 **$9.95**; Videotape of the Movements and Meditations (46-min.), S507 **$20.00**

Ecology/Women's Spirituality

Torah of the Earth: *Exploring 4,000 Years of Ecology in Jewish Thought*
In 2 Volumes Ed. by *Rabbi Arthur Waskow*

Major new resource offering us an invaluable key to understanding the intersection of ecology and Judaism. Leading scholars provide us with a guided tour of ecological thought from four major Jewish viewpoints.
Vol. 1: *Biblical Israel & Rabbinic Judaism,* 6 x 9, 272 pp, Quality PB, ISBN 1-58023-086-5 **$19.95**
Vol. 2: *Zionism & Eco-Judaism,* 6 x 9, 336 pp, Quality PB, ISBN 1-58023-087-3 **$19.95**

Ecology & the Jewish Spirit: *Where Nature & the Sacred Meet* Ed. and with Intros. by Ellen Bernstein 6 x 9, 288 pp, Quality PB, ISBN 1-58023-082-2 **$16.95**;
HC, ISBN 1-879045-88-5 **$23.95**

The Jewish Gardening Cookbook: *Growing Plants & Cooking for Holidays & Festivals* by Michael Brown 6 x 9, 224 pp, Illus., Quality PB, ISBN 1-58023-116-0 **$16.95**;
HC, ISBN 1-58023-004-0 **$21.95**

Moonbeams: *A Hadassah Rosh Hodesh Guide*
Ed. by *Carol Diament, Ph.D.*

This hands-on "idea book" focuses on *Rosh Hodesh,* the festival of the new moon, as a source of spiritual growth for Jewish women. A complete sourcebook that will initiate or rejuvenate women's study groups, it is also perfect for women preparing for *bat mitzvah,* or for anyone interested in learning more about *Rosh Hodesh* observance and what it has to offer. 8½ x 11, 240 pp, Quality PB, ISBN 1-58023-099-7 **$20.00**

The Women's Torah Commentary: *New Insights from Women Rabbis on the 54 Weekly Torah Portions* Ed. by *Rabbi Elyse Goldstein*

For the first time, women rabbis provide a commentary on the entire Five Books of Moses. More than 25 years after the first woman was ordained a rabbi in America, these inspiring teachers bring their rich perspectives to bear on the biblical text. In a week-by-week format; a perfect gift for others, or for yourself. 6 x 9, 496 pp, HC, ISBN 1-58023-076-8 **$34.95**

Lifecycles, in Two Volumes AWARD WINNERS!
V. 1: *Jewish Women on Life Passages & Personal Milestones*
Ed. and with Intros. by Rabbi Debra Orenstein
V. 2: *Jewish Women on Biblical Themes in Contemporary Life*
Ed. and with Intros. by Rabbi Debra Orenstein and Rabbi Jane Rachel Litman
V. 1: 6 x 9, 480 pp, Quality PB, ISBN 1-58023-018-0 **$19.95**; HC, ISBN 1-879045-14-1 **$24.95**
V. 2: 6 x 9, 464 pp, Quality PB, ISBN 1-58023-019-9 **$19.95**

ReVisions: *Seeing Torah through a Feminist Lens* AWARD WINNER!
by Rabbi Elyse Goldstein 5½ x 8½, 224 pp, Quality PB, ISBN 1-58023-117-9 **$16.95**;
208 pp, HC, ISBN 1-58023-047-4 **$19.95**

The Year Mom Got Religion: *One Woman's Midlife Journey into Judaism*
by Lee Meyerhoff Hendler 6 x 9, 208 pp, Quality PB, ISBN 1-58023-070-9 **$15.95**

Spirituality

My People's Prayer Book: *Traditional Prayers, Modern Commentaries*
Ed. by *Dr. Lawrence A. Hoffman*

Provides a diverse and exciting commentary to the traditional liturgy, helping modern men and women find new wisdom in Jewish prayer, and bring liturgy into their lives. Each book includes Hebrew text, modern translation, and commentaries *from all perspectives* of the Jewish world.

Vol. 1—*The Sh'ma and Its Blessings,* 7 x 10, 168 pp, HC, ISBN 1-879045-79-6 **$23.95**

Vol. 2—*The Amidah,* 7 x 10, 240 pp, HC, ISBN 1-879045-80-X **$23.95**

Vol. 3—*P'sukei D'zimrah* (Morning Psalms), 7 x 10, 240 pp, HC, ISBN 1-879045-81-8 **$24.95**

Vol. 4—*Seder K'riat Hatorah* (The Torah Service), 7 x 10, 264 pp, ISBN 1-879045-82-6 **$23.95**

Vol. 5—*Birkhot Hashachar* (Morning Blessings), 7 x 10, 240 pp (est), ISBN 1-879045-83-4 **$24.95**
(Avail. Fall 2001)

Becoming a Congregation of Learners
Learning as a Key to Revitalizing Congregational Life by Isa Aron, Ph.D.;
Foreword by Rabbi Lawrence A. Hoffman, Co-Developer, Synagogue 2000
6 x 9, 304 pp, Quality PB, ISBN 1-58023-089-X **$19.95**

Self, Struggle & Change
Family Conflict Stories in Genesis and Their Healing Insights for Our Lives
by Dr. Norman J. Cohen 6 x 9, 224 pp, Quality PB, ISBN 1-879045-66-4 **$16.95**;
HC, ISBN 1-879045-19-2 **$21.95**

Voices from Genesis: *Guiding Us through the Stages of Life*
by Dr. Norman J. Cohen 6 x 9, 192 pp, Quality PB, ISBN 1-58023-118-7 **$16.95**;
HC, ISBN 1-879045-75-3 **$21.95**

God Whispers: *Stories of the Soul, Lessons of the Heart*
by Rabbi Karyn D. Kedar 6 x 9, 176 pp, Quality PB, ISBN 1-58023-088-1 **$15.95**

The Business Bible: *10 New Commandments for Bringing Spirituality & Ethical Values into the Workplace*
by Rabbi Wayne Dosick 5½ x 8½, 208 pp, Quality PB, ISBN 1-58023-101-2 **$14.95**

Being God's Partner: *How to Find the Hidden Link Between Spirituality and Your Work*
by Rabbi Jeffrey K. Salkin; Intro. by Norman Lear AWARD WINNER!
6 x 9, 192 pp, Quality PB, ISBN 1-879045-65-6 **$16.95**; HC, ISBN 1-879045-37-0 **$19.95**

God & the Big Bang
Discovering Harmony Between Science & Spirituality AWARD WINNER!
by Daniel C. Matt
6 x 9, 224 pp, Quality PB, ISBN 1-879045-89-3 **$16.95**

Soul Judaism: *Dancing with God into a New Era*
by Rabbi Wayne Dosick 5½ x 8½, 304 pp, Quality PB, ISBN 1-58023-053-9 **$16.95**

Finding Joy: *A Practical Spiritual Guide to Happiness* AWARD WINNER!
by Rabbi Dannel I. Schwartz with Mark Hass
6 x 9, 192 pp, Quality PB, ISBN 1-58023-009-1 **$14.95**; HC, ISBN 1-879045-53-2 **$19.95**

Spirituality—The Kushner Series
Books by Lawrence Kushner

The Way Into Jewish Mystical Tradition

Explains the principles of Jewish mystical thinking, their religious and spiritual significance, and how they relate to our lives. A book that allows us to experience and understand the Jewish mystical approach to our place in the world. 6 x 9, 224 pp, HC, ISBN 1-58023-029-6 **$21.95**

Eyes Remade for Wonder
The Way of Jewish Mysticism and Sacred Living

A Lawrence Kushner Reader Intro. by *Thomas Moore*

Whether you are new to Kushner or a devoted fan, you'll find inspiration here. With samplings from each of Kushner's works, and a generous amount of new material, this book is to be read and reread, each time discovering deeper layers of meaning in our lives.
6 x 9, 240 pp, Quality PB, ISBN 1-58023-042-3 **$16.95**; HC, ISBN 1-58023-014-8 **$23.95**

Because Nothing Looks Like God

by *Lawrence and Karen Kushner*; Full-color illus. by *Dawn W. Majewski*

What is God like? The first collaborative work by husband-and-wife team Lawrence and Karen Kushner introduces children to the possibilities of spiritual life with three poetic spiritual stories. Real-life examples of happiness and sadness—from goodnight stories, to the hope and fear felt the first time at bat, to the closing moments of life—invite us to explore, together with our children, the questions we all have about God, no matter what our age. **For ages 4 & up**
11 x 8½, 32 pp, HC, Full-color illus., ISBN 1-58023-092-X **$16.95**

Invisible Lines of Connection: *Sacred Stories of the Ordinary* AWARD WINNER!
6 x 9, 160 pp, Quality PB, ISBN 1-879045-98-2 **$15.95**; HC, ISBN 1-879045-52-4 **$21.95**

Honey from the Rock SPECIAL ANNIVERSARY EDITION
An Introduction to Jewish Mysticism 6 x 9, 176 pp, Quality PB, ISBN 1-58023-073-3 **$15.95**

The Book of Letters: *A Mystical Hebrew Alphabet* AWARD WINNER!
Popular HC Edition, 6 x 9, 80 pp, 2-color text, ISBN 1-879045-00-1 **$24.95**; *Deluxe Gift Edition,* 9 x 12, 80 pp, HC, 2-color text, ornamentation, slipcase, ISBN 1-879045-01-X **$79.95**; *Collector's Limited Edition,* 9 x 12, 80 pp, HC, gold-embossed pages, hand-assembled slipcase. With silkscreened print. Limited to 500 signed and numbered copies, ISBN 1-879045-04-4 **$349.00**

The Book of Words: *Talking Spiritual Life, Living Spiritual Talk* AWARD WINNER!
6 x 9, 160 pp, Quality PB, 2-color text, ISBN 1-58023-020-2 **$16.95**;
152 pp, HC, ISBN 1-879045-35-4 **$21.95**

God Was in This Place & I, i Did Not Know
Finding Self, Spirituality and Ultimate Meaning
6 x 9, 192 pp, Quality PB, ISBN 1-879045-33-8 **$16.95**

The River of Light: *Jewish Mystical Awareness* SPECIAL ANNIVERSARY EDITION
6 x 9, 192 pp, Quality PB, ISBN 1-58023-096-2 **$16.95**